TUKWILA
Community at the Crossroads

TUKWILA
Community at the Crossroads

Kay Frances Reinartz, Ph.D.

Published by
The City of Tukwila
6200 Southcenter Boulevard
Tukwila, Washington 98188

Cover illustration by Don Paulson

Printed in the United States of America

© 1991 by The City of Tukwila. All rights reserved
ISBN 0-9629652-0-0

Every attempt has been made to verify information presented in this book. No part of this book may be reproduced or transmitted in any form or by any means, electronic or mechanical, including photocopying, without permission in writing from the City of Tukwila.

EDITORIAL STAFF

Author/Project Director/Editor ..Kay F. Reinartz, Ph.D.
Administrative Assistants ....Maxine Anderson
        Darlene Crostick, Gerry Young
Word Processing..................Mary Peters, Tracy Warner
Production Director ....Sharon Dibble
Book Design and Page Layout ....Laura Lewis,
        Sharon Dibble
Illustrations...........................Don Paulson, Patrick Hill
Cartographer ....Patrick Brodin
Proofreader ....Alice Copp Smith
Indexer ....Julie Kawabata

TUKWILA CENTENNIAL HISTORY BOOK COMMITTEE

Maxine Anderson	Ron Lamb
Roger Baker	Wendy Morgan
Ethel Bauch	Louise Strander
Darlene Crostick	Warren Wing
Joan Hernandez	

CHAPTER REVIEWERS

Tukwila Centennial History Book Committee	Tim Parker
Rev. Frank Abbott	Don Paulson
Laura Shomaker Bateham	Charles Payton
Jim Bergsma	Daniel Peterson
Mary Bosshart	Elsie Rinehart
Pat Brodin	Tom Scibor
Ron Cameron	Brian Sheldon
Don Campbell	Dr. Michael Silver
Ross Earnst	Lorraine Stowe
Bill Fouty	Henning Sundby
Daniel Healey	Lona Sweeney
Olive Thompson Hozack	Alma Nelsen Taylor
Walter W. Kassner	Dr. Nile Thompson
Jan Klippert	Harriet Bergquist Tombs
Leslie Martin	Gary VanDusen
Frank McCartney	Mary Ellen Whitehead
Helen Nelsen	Bill Wieland
Fred Nichols	Harvold Wilson

SPECIAL THANKS

South Central School District; Elizabeth Brizzard, Vannetta Dimmit, Helen Jaspers, Marilyn Mettlin, Kathy Trudeau, Kirstine Wistler; Jane Cantu and City Clerk Staff; Ann Claessen, 60 Minute Photo; Ernie Dornfield, King County Archives; Ross Earnst, Director of Public Works; Dr. Cheryl Hansen; Allen Jones of the State SPI; Julie's One Hour Photo; King County Assessor's Office; King County Public Works Department; Joe Koch, White River Historical Museum; Carolyn Marr, Museum of History and Industry; Northwest Collection, Suzzallo Library, University of Washington; Charles Payton, King County Historic Preservation Program; Renton Historical Museum; Mike Saunders and Philippia Stair, Washington State Archives, Puget Sound Branch; Tukwila Community Center; Tukwila Fire Department; Tukwila Historical Society; Tukwila Library; Foster Library; Duwamish Improvement Club; Museum of Flight; Dr. Paul Spitzer, the Boeing Co.; Tukwila Chamber of Commerce; Southcenter Corp.

COMMUNITY VOLUNTEER SUPPORT

Great efforts require special people. Everyone who worked on this book falls into that category. Hundreds have contributed bits and pieces of information, but due to space limitations are not listed here. If we did not mention your name please accept our apologies as well as our thanks for your assistance. The greatness is still yours to share.

KEY

AR	=	Artist	PH	=	Photography
CON	=	Consultant	RA	=	Research Assistant
GO	=	General Office	TY	=	Typist
GR	=	Graphics	WP	=	Word Processing
OH	=	Oral History	WR	=	Writer

LOVERS OF HISTORY

Volunteers who made major commitments of time and talent to the community history book:

Maxine Anderson, GO, OH, RA, WR	Ron Lamb, WR, RA, PH, OH, CON
Betty Baker, RA, OH, GO	Freda Leahy, RA, WR
Roger Baker, RA, OH, GO, PH, GR	Wendy Morgan, RA, OH, WP, WR, CON
Mary Bosshart, WR, RA, OH, TY, WP	Peri Muhich, PH, RA
Patrick Brodin, AR, RA, GR, PH	Curtis & Margaret Nesheim, WR, RA, PH
Darlene Crostick, RA, GO, OH, PH, TY, WR	Stacia Norris, WP, GR
Carol deRose, RA, TY, WP	Don Paulson, AR, RA, OH, WR
Sharon Dibble, AR, RA, GR, CON	Elsie Rinehart, OH, WR, RA, PH, GR
Angeline Frese, GO	Evelyn Santora, RA, GO
Richard S. Frith, RA, WR, GO, WP, CON	Tom Scibor, RA, OH, GR, PH
Mabel Gylden, RA, WR, GO, PH	Celia Square, GO, RA
Alice Hanson Gustafson, WR, RA, OH, PH	Louise Strander, RA, WR
Joan Hernandez, OH, WR, RA	Mary Ellen Whitehead, RA, OH, TY, GO, PH, GR
Patrick Hill, AR, RA, GR	Warren Wing, OH, WR, RA, PH
Sue King, RA, GO	Gerry Young, RA, GO, OH, TY, PH

VOLUNTEERS

JoAnn Albertson, RA	Karen Livermore, RA, WR
Ethel Bauch, RA	Sandi Mills, TY, WP
Jim Bergsma, RA, CON	Jerry Newton, RA
Carroll Bigelow, OH, RA	Christy O'Flaherty, WP
Terry Bitzig, RA, WP	Kelcie Peterson, GO, TY, WP
Esther Brodin, RA	Nadalene Pritchett, GO, RA
Hubert Crowley, RA	Mary Story, RA
Jim Graves, RA, WR	Jim Santora, RA
Stanley Gustafson, RA, PH	John Strander, Jr., WR, RA
Jerry & Lois Hamilton, OH	Lona Sweeney, OH, RA
Gail Hepker, RA	Nancy Taylor, PH
Frank Hunter, GO	Meg & Ray Torghele, PH, RA
Sarah Jensen, RA, OH	Karen VanDusen, OH, RA, TY, WP
Ralph & Thelma Kissinger, RA, OH	Virginia Whitney, RA
Nancy Sandine Lamb, RA, TY, WP	
Dorothy Lindberg, RA	

Table of Contents

Dedication vii
Preface x
Introduction xi
Prelude xii
  by David Buerge

Part I
Pioneering in the Duwamish River Valley

1 The First Settlers in King County 2
2 Life on the Duwamish in the 1850s 18
3 The 1860s—Building Homesteads, Families and Community 31
4 Establishing Farms and Communities—1870-1899 52
5 Immigrants Find the Valley—1880-1900 66

Part II
Twentieth Century Communities

6 The Meadows on the Duwamish River 78
7 Opening the Valley 89
8 Foster—Joseph Foster's Legacy 109
9 Riverton on the Duwamish—Seattle's Most
   Picturesque Suburb 128
10 Communities Flower on the River Banks—
   Duwamish-Allentown and Quarry-North Riverton 153
11 Ticket to Tukwila, Town on the Hill—1909-1928 180
12 Tukwila, Crossroads of Commerce—1928-1990 198
13 Dairy Farms, Nurseries and Market-Garden Farms
   Flourish in the Duwamish Valley 215
   by Kris Freeman and Kay Reinartz
14 The South Central School District 224
   by Ron Lamb
15 Districts and Neighborhoods—Renton Junction,
   Riverton Heights and McMicken Heights 240
16 Neighboring Communities Join the City at the Crossroads 256
Appendix A—Tukwila City Government and its Leaders 269
Appendix B—Historic Houses 1990 275
References 276
Index 281

DEDICATION

*This History of Tukwila, Washington
Written on the Occasion of the
Washington State Centennial
Is Dedicated to
Honorable Joseph Foster
Pioneer Settler, Legislator and Foremost Citizen of Foster,
King County and Washington Territory
1828-1911*

Photograph courtesy Museum of History and Industry

When Joseph Foster first came as a pioneer to King County, Washington Territory, in 1853, it was still an almost unbroken wilderness with only a few tiny settlements. He lived to see a great commonwealth built in that wilderness, and played a conspicuous part in its formation through his active leadership in the Washington Territorial Legislature for three decades. Joseph Foster was an exceptional man who not only established the first community encompassed by today's Tukwila, but also worked tirelessly in public service, thereby shaping the future of Washington and King County. In his day he was well known throughout the Northwest.

Joseph Foster was born in Hamilton, Ontario, Canada, April 10, 1828, son of English immigrants Thomas Foster and Rosetta Laska Foster. When Foster was still a young child the family moved to Geauga County, Ohio. His father was a Methodist minister, and the children were reared in a home where they learned early to accept and fulfill the responsibilities of life. Rev. Foster's approach to life was marked by piety and austerity. For example, as a young man Joseph loved music, and traded his rifle for a violin. Convinced that the violin was an instrument of the devil, his father insisted that he get rid of it, which Joseph did, and never learned to play.

When Joseph was about 14, he was apprenticed to learn a trade. His parents chose tailoring rather than plastering, which had been the choice for his three older brothers, because he seemed to have frail health, and tailoring was deemed less physically taxing. In due time he became a journeyman and worked as a tailor for about eight years. Leaving tailoring, he found work on steamboats on the Great Lakes and amused himself running a Punch and Judy show as a sideline. Interested in seeing the country, he next went to Pennsylvania to work and then on to Wisconsin. While in Wisconsin Joseph, 24, and his brother Stephen, two years his junior, decided to "go west."

The adventurous brothers traveled west on the overland trail in the summer of 1852, going first to the California gold fields. In April 1853 they arrived at Elliott Bay, where they staked land grant claims on the Duwamish River near the confluence of the Black and White (Green) rivers. Joseph Foster obtained 160 acres under donation claim legislation. For the next 12 years Foster spent his time in a variety of activities including improving his claim, logging and clearing land for others, and managing his own logging business. Over the years, he purchased land adjacent to his as the opportunity arose.

Washington Territory was established the year Foster arrived, 1853, and he soon became interested in territorial government and politics. In 1858, at age 31, Joseph Foster was elected the representative from King County to the territorial legislature, a step which marks the beginning of his outstanding career in public service that extended to 1886. He was elected to the legislature for 11 terms, serving in both the upper and lower houses a total of 22 years. Although he was an ardent Democrat, his outstanding ability and objective nonpartisan public spirit won him votes from many Republicans, and he was often the only Democrat to be elected from staunchly Republican King County.

Among his successful bills, the results of which are still enjoyed at the end of the twentieth century, are the Seattle to Fort Colville via Snoqualmie Pass road and the University of Washington location bill. It was on Foster's initiative that the Washington Territorial University was established in Seattle rather than Olympia. Foster sponsored this bill because he was convinced that the presence of the University would be a great benefit for the people of King County. Committed to the American principle of equality for all–including women– Foster sponsored the successful Washington Territory Woman Suffrage Bill in 1883.

On June 11, 1865, Joseph Foster married Martha Jane Steele, Duwamish Valley pioneer, who drove her family's wagon over the Oregon Trail from Missouri in 1864. Those who knew them report that it was a very compatible marriage of kindred souls, who remained lovingly devoted to and supportive of one another for the 46 years of their marriage. The couple's children were Charles, 1866, Rosetta, 1869, and Emily, 1873, all of whom died in a single week in 1877, during a diphtheria epidemic. Two more children were born, Joseph Thomas in 1879 and Hillory Adams in 1880. Hillory's wife Flora Fleming reported that the Fosters and their surviving sons shared the same interests and ideals, and were a close-knit family held together with strong ties of affection and understanding.

Joseph Foster was astute in business matters and made numerous wise investments after coming to the Duwamish Valley. By the mid-1880s he had accumulated 440 acres of land and his many successful enterprises supported the family. The farm land was rented out and Foster divided his time between managing his business interests and civic service.

Joseph Foster loved rural life and was devoted to maintaining the homestead, which remained the main family home. Whenever Foster was home he worked regularly in the fields and garden. As the years passed, he was frequently urged to move to Seattle, where he would be closer to the hub of political and business activity; however, he never seriously considered leaving the Duwamish Valley.

Foster was well known throughout Washington Territory and universally respected. His ability and his sterling reputation for honesty and wise decisions led to his being offered the governorship of Washington Territory in 1887. He declined this highest honor in favor of dedicating his energies to King County, and his local community and family.

His greatest long-term tangible influence in the Duwamish Valley can be seen in education and parks. Although he did not have an opportunity for a high degree of formal education, he was a learned man who was well read. He energetically promoted education and learning. In 1892 he helped establish the original public school district in the Tukwila community, Foster School District, and helped build the first school on land that he donated. The South Central School District evolved from the Foster District. Named for Joseph Foster, Foster High School continues to provide the young people of the community with a good education a century later. With the relocation of the Foster School from its original site, the site has become a community park, as Joseph Foster no doubt would have wanted.

Throughout their lives the Fosters maintained a warm and hospitable home that was the focal point of the community of Foster—indeed, of the entire upper Duwamish Valley—for almost half a century. An intangible but important legacy Joseph Foster left his home community was a model of public service and community spirit which has been an inspiration to many community leaders. As he gained in years he came to be affectionately known to friends and neighbors as "Uncle Joe." He was a man who was equally ready to discuss the crops, the local school curriculum, or the larger political issues of the day. Tom Clark, who knew Foster well, said of him, "He was a wonderful man; no better character lived on earth, Uncle Joe."

Joseph Foster died on January 17, 1911, at age 82. Foster's estate was estimated at more than $500,000 and included 300 acres in his homestead, business and residence lands in Seattle, Georgetown and Foster. There was widespread mourning and a flood of tributes to this foremost citizen of Washington from across the Northwest, commending his ethical character and accomplishments for the public good.

The day of Foster's funeral and burial in the family plot at Lakeview Cemetery, Seattle, a special Interurban funeral train stopped at Foster Station, where Joseph Foster's casket was put aboard a car draped in black crape and American and Washington State flags. The train had many cars and at every stop mourners boarded the train. As the train slowly made its way down Foster's beloved Duwamish River Valley, through Seattle and up Capitol Hill, thousands paused to gaze at the solemnly draped car. Tears welled up in the eyes of many, while others sadly shook their heads in unspoken grief. It was the passing of a great citizen and a great man. Martha, Joe and Hillory, silently seated by Foster's casket, understood that their Joseph Foster also belonged to the people of Washington. From the station to Lakeview cemetery hundreds—county and state leaders, and valley neighbors—silently walked behind the casket in honor of Joseph Foster and his life's work. Martha Steele Foster died in 1926, Joseph T. in 1905 and Hillory in 1950. There are no direct descendants.

Contemporary biographers said of Foster:

His talents and integrity profoundly impressed his associates in the Legislature, and throughout his tenure of office his opinions were always received with the greatest respect. He declined to grant any favors for which a consideration was offered to him, and so great was his sense of honor that he declined to use even the passes commonly provided by railroads for legislative members.

In a tribute to Joseph Foster written 50 years after his death, C. T. Conover wrote, "Foster was a typical pioneer, who knew his way around." Foster was all that and more. He was a man who could fell a tree with a ten-foot circumference single-handedly in one hour. Those same hands made his children's clothes. He was a home-loving man who spent much time away from home working for the common good. He was adventurous and he was stable. He was a visionary who took time and energy away from his personal interests and profit and gave them freely and generously to benefit the common good. The fruit of his work done in the nineteenth century will continue on into the twenty-first century.

Preface

Lying at the junction of three ancient river valleys, looking out over a meandering river and a stately mountain, Tukwila has been a crossroads forever. The area has always been a meeting place, a stopping point for those journeying through the valleys, and a trading, shipping and transport center.

The history of Tukwila is the story of those who stopped beside the river, who built homes, farmed the land and worked to build a supportive community. It is the story of how the early leaders envisioned the prosperous commercial center we enjoy today, and began laying the groundwork for our place in the region. It is the chronology of Tukwila's willingness to grow and to change with the times, while stubbornly keeping those strong community values that make the city a real hometown. The history book covers the history of Old Tukwila and all of the areas annexed in 1989-90.

The challenge of telling Tukwila's story was a community effort begun in 1989 with enthusiastic support from Mayor Gary VanDusen and the Tukwila City Council. Within the archives of the City and the Tukwila Historical Society there were some pictures, a few papers written over the years, newspaper clippings and official documents. However, there were no real archives of information for those who wished to know more. The City of Tukwila selected Dr. Kay F. Reinartz, consulting historian and author of other King County community history books, to direct the research work and write the book. Dr. Reinartz was selected because of her unique "community participation" approach to community history.

A history book community advisory committee was created with whom the historian worked closely in planning and executing the project. Through this committee the community participated in decisions regarding the scope of the history as well as technical and content aspects of the book. But this is only a small part of the way in which the community participated in creating its own history book.

A research plan was made, and the community was invited to participate in gathering and interpreting their own history and that of their predecessors in the Duwamish and lower Green river valleys. People came from all of the communities and districts to help with research, to share stories, and to provide leads to the "historical puzzles" that abounded. Volunteers traveled with Dr. Reinartz to county, regional and state archives, combing dusty files for information on the area. Old fragile Foster High School records were found and copied for preservation. Humorous stories were collected and thousands of telephone calls made. Over 60 people wrote memoirs. Three people trained to be skilled oral history interviewers collected over two dozen oral histories. Several volunteer artists and a cartographer joined the excitement of charting the history, producing beautiful and accurate illustrations including an original painting for the book's cover. Over 150 photographs were gathered from regional archives and family albums to graphically tell Tukwila's story.

Thousands of hours were donated by the community volunteers supporting the history research. As the book project sponsor, the City of Tukwila provided assistance throughout the project, providing photocopying, word processing and technical support by the staff. Many other City employees supported the book as volunteers.

Like the Tukwila community, the history book volunteers dedicated their time and energy to build a lasting legacy. Tomorrow's community is built on yesterday and today. Our neighbors and friends—those who have made the greater Tukwila community their lifelong home, those who have moved in, and those who have left—will find in these pages the warmth of the past, the comfort of the present and the challenge of the future.

The Tukwila History Book Committee

Introduction

Tukwila—*Community at the Crossroads* is the story of the pioneers who settled along the Duwamish and lower Green (formerly White) rivers. It is also the story of the generations that followed and nurtured the work of the pioneer stalwarts, leaving their own imprint on the communities that sprang up on the hills, as well as in the valleys. It is the story of the emergence of the City of Tukwila as a major economic, political and social force in South King County, Washington.

In the early days the pioneers who settled along the course of the Duwamish River composed a single community, and the history chronicles this community. In the first decade of the twentieth century the population in the Duwamish Valley grew sufficiently to support a number of separate, identifiable communities. From this period forward the history book focuses exclusively on the area that is today the City of Tukwila.

The term "historic study area" is used in discussing the history. This area encompasses the land that is within the borders of the City of Tukwila in 1990, including Old Tukwila, Foster, Riverton, Duwamish, Allentown, Thorndyke, McMicken and Cascade View. This area is bordered on the north by Seattle city limits in the area of Boeing Plant II. The southern boundary meets the city limits of Kent, and to the east the city limits of Renton. Tukwila's western border is complex, sharing a common boundary with the City of Sea-Tac on the south half and unincorporated King County on the north. The northern portion of the western city limits follows natural geographic features, streets and roads, and property lines.

A word about historic names—the contemporary Green River runs down the natural channel of the White River, which changed its course in 1906. The names White River and White River Valley are used in the history book up to 1906, after which time the new name Green is applied to the river and valley. The names of most of the streets in the study area were changed from the original plat names to a King County system using numbers around 1938. Throughout the history the names in use at the time of the historical discussions are used.

A detailed map is included for each community showing the street layout, locations of businesses, churches and schools, as well as special places ranging from 1890-1930. Both the original street names and the current names are provided. A map of the Duwamish and lower White river valleys, showing historic locations and landmarks from 1851 through 1905, is found in the back of the book and should be referred to while reading Chapters 1-7.

The community history of Tukwila is firmly interwoven with the development of "Puget Sound Country," King County and Seattle. All of the annexed communities, districts and neighborhoods included in this history book, with the exception of Old Tukwila, were under the jurisdiction of King County until recently.

Certain themes run through the history, the most significant of which is a deep love of community, nature and the land. This is most often expressed as devotion to rural life and the richness of country village values. The theme of the river flows through the history, just as it flows through the valley. The river was a major factor in bringing settlers to the valley. Changes in transportation, economics and society have diminished the community focus on the river. However, one of Tukwila's proudest hours was when it saved the venerable Duwamish and Green rivers from destruction in the 1950s. As the twentieth century ends, once again people are looking to the Duwamish River—now to clean and preserve it as a place of beauty and refreshment for the civilization-weary heart and soul and as a renewed home for native plants and animals.

For every reader *Tukwila—Community at the Crossroads* is a journey into greater Tukwila's collective community past. It is the story of the dreams, adventures, experiments, courage, conviction, vision, love, commitment and fulfillment of those who have made their homes here for over 140 years. Come then to the banks of the Duwamish, and let us begin our journey through history.

Kay F. Reinartz, June 1991

PRELUDE
by David Buerge

THE GEOLOGY OF THE TUKWILA AREA

The geologic history of Tukwila can be read in three chapters: the hard rock that forms the hills guarding the valley; the steep valley walls whose layered strata describe the world of the Ice Age; and the flat valley floor whose pages are the layers of sediment brought down by the river.

The oldest rocks, named the Tukwila Formation, are 40 to 50 million years old. These rocks may be seen in the northern part of Tukwila where roads, railroads and quarries have cut into several low rounded hills. Deposits found in this part of the city, especially the Poverty Hill area, contain fossilized shells, fish teeth and crab claws, indicating that the rock in which they are found originated as deposits in salt water of moderate depth. Farther south, oyster fossils and the remains of driftwood honeycombed with shelly tubes left by boring worms are evidence of a brackish shoreline environment. The coarse nature of the rock grains and their mineral content indicate volcanic origins, possibly spewing forth from a volcano in the vicinity of Issaquah. The Tukwila Formation was created by conditions similar to those in contemporary times, a seacoast flanking a volcanic highland.

The Tukwila Formation is overlaid by the Renton Formation, which includes thick seams of coal. The coal is the remains of the lush vegetation that flourished in extensive coastal swamps. The exertion of great pressure on sediment overlaying the decaying vegetation transformed it into coal. The presence of coral and fossils characteristically found in subtropical and tropical zones indicates a warmer climate.

A recent theory proposes that the rocks of the Tukwila and Renton formations may have been deposited on the shore of a large island located far out in the Pacific Ocean called the North Cascade microcontinent. About 40 million years ago, this microcontinent, carried atop a moving oceanic plate, collided with the North American continent moving westward on its plate. The pressure of the collision, which lasted millions of years, buckled the apron of sediments into a pattern of northwest-southeast trending folds. One of these ancient folds cradles the Duwamish River.

THE ICE AGE

About three million years ago prolonged periods of cold in the Northern Hemisphere ushered in the Ice Age and chapter two of our history. Out of the coastal mountains of British Columbia, a vast tongue of ice flowed south into the Puget Sound lowland. On its journey it collected tremendous amounts of rock debris gouged from the mountains and scraped up along the way. Called drift, this was ground up by the internal motion of the ice into gravel, sand and silt. The period of this first glaciation was followed by a long interglacial period lasting at least 50,000 years. The climate then was probably much as it is today.

The layers exposed on the valley walls tell of four different glaciations. Each new advance obliterated the interglacial world that preceded it and left behind new layers of sediment and new landscapes in its retreat. The last advance began 25,000 years ago, when another huge ice lobe slowly ground its way into the Puget lowland, halting 15 miles south of Olympia, about 14,000 years ago.

Above Tukwila the ice may have been as much as 28,800 feet thick, and the tremendous pressure its mass exerted upon the land surface below was sufficient to gouge out three long troughs. Today, Hood Canal and Admiralty Inlet fill two of these. The third has become the Green and Duwamish River valleys, as well as that filled by Lake Washington.

With the end of the Ice Age the third chapter of the area's geologic history began. By this time, looking south from the site of 1990 City Hall there would be many recognizable landmarks. The valley is a giant trough dug by the ice. As a part of the ancient Puget Sound, the trough was filled with seawater. Tukwila Hill and Brummer's Hill are two of many ancient rocky hills re-excavated from the glacial drift. Appearing as hills in recent time, originally they were part of a large island separated from the mainland by a long arm of the sea which reached far up into the Lake Washington basin. At the end of the last Ice Age Mount Rainier was about 2,000 feet higher. The land was bare and gray, but soon grasses and brush took hold, and as the climate warmed trees were reestablished. Soon the Cedar River built a delta in the eastern channel separating the Lake Washington basin from the rest of the salt water. Streams poured fresh water from the mountains into the basin, flushing out the remaining salt water, and Lake Washington was created. The lake grew deeper as the delta rose, and its outflow combined with the Cedar River to produce the Black River.

About 3,000 years ago the summit of Mount Rainier collapsed during a major eruption. A tremendous avalanche of mud and shattered rock swept down the northern slope of the mountain and was funneled by the canyons of the White River and its west fork out onto the lowland, where it spread out over at least 125 square miles of land, creating the White River Valley. The cataclysmic mudslide filled the eastern portion of the ancient Puget Sound channel as far north as the present city of Kent.

The avalanche deposit, known as the Osceola Mudflow, diverted the White River toward its outlet at Auburn. As the river cut a new channel through the mudflow and underlying glacial material, it built a delta fan atop the rubble already in the channel. Over time the sediments brought down by the river pushed out the sea and created a flat valley floor, giving it its present character.

That closes the third chapter. The volcanic highland of the microcontinent and its folded margin, the Ice Age sediments exposed in the unstable valley walls, and the river floodplain shape the world we live in.

THE FIRST PEOPLE

In early historic times, the main village of the Duwamish stood in what is now Renton, but other villages lined the river banks from Elliott Bay all the way to Maple Valley. To the Duwamish people, the watercourse made up of the Duwamish, Black and Cedar rivers was one river that they called the *t-hw-duw*, which meant something like "going inside," which is where it took people who paddled their canoes upstream from the bay. The people living beside it were known as the *duw-AHBSH*, "inside people," a name since anglicized to Duwamish. Other groups living along adjacent rivers were closely related.

The Duwamish made their home in a very favorable natural environment. Near their confluence, the Black and White rivers flowed between natural levees built up from heavier riverborne sediments deposited during floods. Between these levees and the valley walls, the floodplain was swampy and covered with a dense growth of hardhack and willow thickets and bordered by gallery forests of alder, maple, cottonwood, and occasional groves of cedar, fir and yew. During floods, the marshy floodplain vegetation held water like a sponge, releasing it slowly through a maze of intersecting drainage channels. The highlands were mantled with towering coniferous forests broken here and there by swamps and luxurious, parklike meadows.

It is estimated that about 300 people lived in the Tukwila area in the eighteenth century; probably no more than 2,000 lived along the length of the three river system, and not many more than double that throughout the entire Duwamish River watershed.

VILLAGES IN THE VALLEYS

In Tukwila, longhouses clustered at two locations: at *sko-AHL-ko*, meaning "confluence," where the Black and White rivers met, and further up the White River near the southern margin of a swamp west of the river called *bis-HOO-kid*, "where there are swans." Longhouses consisted of a frame of uprights and rafters sheathed by split, adze-hewn cedar planks. If it were not burned accidentally or destroyed in some other way, a longhouse might last a generation, but by then rot and the buildup of vermin that normally accompanied prolonged human habitation generally drove the residents to build a new one a short distance away.

Although the longhouse site might shift, evidence indicates that people settled in general areas for long periods of time. In 1981 archaeologists excavated the floor of a longhouse on the Black River that had been occupied in the fourth century A.D. Artifacts recovered indicate the area near the confluence was rich enough to make its residents relatively wealthy and influential over 1,000 years ago.

It is believed that a village was located at the confluence on the point of land between the rivers. An 1862 land survey map shows a lake, named White Lake by the settlers, at this point, separated from the rivers by the levees. This was an intermittent feature produced by flood waters, and the village's two longhouses, each said to have measured 60 by 120 feet, probably stood on the levees or on high ground back from the lake somewhere within the present confines of Fort Dent Park. On the north side of the Black River, on a flat called *t-ah-WEH-deech*, "river duck," there were houses of undetermined size. West of the confluence, beneath the bluff presently rising above Interurban Ave., there were four medium-sized longhouses measuring 50 by 100 feet. The name of this house site is the anglicized version of the place name *skah-LEELS*, "bad looking," which referred to the muddy rocks in the river here. It is probable that not all of these house sites were inhabited at the same time, and the four longhouses at *Skal-alius* may represent the maximum number of longhouses that stood at the confluence site.

South on the White River, two more longhouses measuring 60 by 120 feet stood beside the river at the head of the swamp that extended from S. 180th St. to Southcenter. Another longhouse may have stood on the river's west bank at what is now Bicentennial Park.

Each longhouse commonly sheltered several related families. Together they made a house group, a self-sufficient economic unit whose members shared food and other goods and who spent the winter months under a single roof. One or more house groups were united by kinship, residence and exogamy (marriage to partners from other house groups). This constituted a winter village group. Exogamy broadened a group's economic base since the right to gather food at certain places was passed down through family lines and distributed through marital ties. A member of one winter village group who married into another retained the identification with his or her birth village, and when he or she died, the body was often transported back to the home winter village burial ground. The fact that an Indian burial ground is remembered to have been located on the hillside west of the confluence suggests that the house groups there made up a winter village group, but the lack of a burial site for the house groups at *bis-HOO-kid* suggests that they were affiliated with the major *stuk-AHBSH* winter village.

THE YEAR BEGINS WITH SPRING

For the people living at these locations, the year began in late February, when a chorus of frogs heralded the onset of a new season of life. Storytellers elaborated upon the lascivious adventures of Mink, who came ashore from his raft of snags and impregnated virtually anything that moved. As the fertile earth grew green, families prepared to leave the longhouses to harvest the product of his virility. In late winter a man who had the Father of Smelt for a supernatural ally would sing the fish upstream, where the people caught them in tube weirs woven from cedar. Steelhead trout also appeared in the rivers and were caught with spears and nets. Hunters left for the swamps to capture elk that came to browse on the brilliant blooming skunk cabbage, and parties of women went out to gather greens and to cultivate the village gardens and dig up nutritious bulbs with their digging sticks.

If there were gardens at the confluence, the location has been forgotten, but a place on the west bank of the White River near the *bis-HOO-kid* longhouses called *KWELH-kwelh,* "lots of edible roots," surely was one, and another just south of it called *tsk-AHL-bahts,* "gooseberries," was probably another. Women kept the gardens free of unwanted vegetation by weeding out invaders and by burning the plots over every few years. A small oxbow lake in Orillia called *bs-tsol-ahl-ahts,* "where there are cattails," between the river and Longview Ave. S., since filled in, was a place where women harvested cattails for their starchy roots and their thick, pithy stalks that were sewn into springy sleeping mats.

In April, groups traveled down the river to the bay. There fishermen trolled for salmon congregating in the estuary. When dogwood trees were in bloom was said to be the time when clams were fattest, and when people hiked to the beaches to set up camps, dig up the clams and dry them over smoky fires. After the floods subsided in late spring, the Chinook salmon began moving up the rivers, giving the name to the salmonberries that ripened on the banks at the same time.

The first salmon caught on the river was honored as a great chief, sprinkled with eagle down and carried to the village in a joyous procession. There it was ritually prepared and cooked, and pieces of it were distributed to all the people, who consumed it in a kind of sacramental meal. Afterwards, its remains were reverently buried or returned to the river, head facing downstream, so its spirit would return to its people and call them to honor their ancient covenant with the Changer to ascend the rivers and surrender their robes of flesh.

At the confluence, the people of *sko-AHL-ko* could fish the runs on two rivers. To do this, they erected large log tripods in the channels and set fencelike screens against them that blocked the fishes' upstream progress. Thus blocked, the milling fish were scooped out of the water with dipnets by fishermen standing on the tripods and dumped into canoes that took them ashore, where they were cleaned and dried. The weir screens were constructed to let smaller fish through and they were left in the water only long enough to catch the number of fish the people needed. The rest, the greater part of the run, was allowed through to spawn, and the integrity of the fishery was preserved. Smaller fence weirs were also constructed across streams such as Springbrook Creek.

SUMMER AND AUTUMN ACTIVITIES

High summer was a time for social gatherings and the celebration of the potlatch, known locally as a *SGWEY-gwey*. The host of this celebration gave away gifts to invited guests and gained a name for himself as a man whose generous giving manifested his power to amass wealth. A *SGWEY-gwey* might serve as an occasion to announce the assumption of a noble title, to celebrate one's child's coming of age or to announce a marriage. It might also be accompanied by athletic contests, horse races, gambling matches and trade with groups from distant regions.

With the onset of fall, berry-picking season ended, the runs of several species of salmon crowded the rivers, and fishing was carried out in earnest, often at night by moonlight or the flare of sputtering pitchwood torches. Fall was also the time of waterfowl migrations. Down near the bay, huge nets were hoisted into the night air across flyways to snare the birds startled up and driven into them. On the rivers bird hunting was done at night from canoes on which fires were kindled on earthen beds to attract the curious animals out of their marshy hiding places, where they could be snagged with birding spears. Hunters also lay in wait for them in blinds erected along the bank. Two spots on the river in northern Tukwila, *kwee-LAH-us,* "duck blind," where I-5 crosses the river, and *ku-LUH-hu,* "a hole in the bank where a creek cuts under," opposite the Foster Golf Links, appear to have been used for this purpose. The latter spot highlights a phenomenon still to be observed on the river. Where the current undercuts the bank, the earth is commonly carried away, but where the brush is thick, a root mat remains and curls down forming an arch. Even today, these can be long and roomy and serve as excellent duck blinds.

By late October and early November, the weather began to turn and families began to return to the longhouses. The ingathering was the signal for the *SPEEG-pee-gwud*, the "power sing," when the people's supernatural allies returned to them. Those beings whose powers manifested themselves in ceremonial activity required their hosts to put on "power sings" to which kin were invited to help the host sing his power song and witness his demonstration of power. This might involve the handling of fire, the miraculous healing of self-inflicted wounds or the supernatural animation of ceremonial objects capable of dragging their holders around the longhouse where spectators assembled and quickened the air with their powerful, rhythmic singing.

The arrival of winter's cold inspired the recitation of the North Wind-Storm Wind myths and the performance of rain-calling rituals. It was also the occasion for the most dramatic of all Duwamish ceremonials, the Spirit Canoe, during which teams of shamans undertook a perilous journey to the land of the dead. The dance-drama was enacted over the course of several successive nights in a specially built house before an audience who helped the shamans sing their songs by pounding poles against roof planks in a rhythmic, thundering beat. It was believed that "little earths" who inhabited the hill east of Fort Dent Park were the supernatural beings that enabled shamans to make their mystic journey.

MYTHIC SITES IN THE DUWAMISH VALLEY

hile Tukwila is not the site of the largest or most important Duwamish village, or any of the archaeological digs that have expanded our understanding of the past, its boundaries encompass something far more significant—most of the sites celebrated in Duwamish mythology.

The myths describe the exploits of the "Ancients," the First People, the supernatural beings who inhabited the world in the myth-time before human beings were given dominion over the earth. The First People were brought into being by the shadowy figure called the Old Creator. They go by the names of Muskrat, Land Otter, Beaver, Blue Jay, Skate, Killer Whale, Wolf, Mountain Lion, Ant, Towhee and a host of others that identify their characteristic traits that manifest themselves in the animals whose forms they assumed at the end of the myth-time. Others like North Wind, Storm Wind, Sun, Moon, Willow, Boulder and Flint were transformed into natural forces or objects. The myth-time is described as a time when "animals were people": when, in spite of their fabulous powers, the First People spoke, lived and acted very much as people do today.

Most of the myth sites are the rocky hills excavated out of the glacial drift during the last glacial advance. The myths associated with these landmarks tell about the battles between titans, monsters and heroes of a mythic age, and of a great transformation that brought the mythic world to a close in spectacular fashion and ushered in the human era. In few other parts of Washington are myth sites so concentrated as they are in the Tukwila area, and the fact that native groups throughout the Puget Sound region recited myths about them attests to their regional importance.

Most intriguing in terms of Tukwila's history is the possibility that the first bit of earth Muskrat brought up from "below" may have formed a little hill the Duwamish called *SBAH-bah-teel*, "little mountain," or "old mountain," where it was said the Ancients lived to make the four divisions of the world. It is identified today as the little promontory rising just west of Tukwila, crowned by the River Vista Apartments near the intersection of Highway 99 and 116th Way.

The most important group of myths associated with landmarks in Tukwila tell about the battle between North Wind and Chinook Wind. North Wind overcame Chinook Wind and established himself on the Duwamish River.

Sacred Boulder. The little hill upon which North Wind settles is none other than *SBAH-bah-teel*, where the Ancients lived to make the four divisions of the world. North Wind's name in the story is *STO-blah*. The diminutive form of the name, *STO-blah-ah*, "little North Wind," was given to a boulder in the river at the foot of the little mountain that could only be seen during periods of low water. It has since either been destroyed or buried under Highway 99.

In other versions of the myth, the *ku-LAH-hahd*, "the barrier," is described as a fish weir North Wind built of ice to keep salmon and other fish from migrating upstream. At the end of the myth, half of it is swept away in the flood and what remains is turned into stone in the great transformation. These remains, outcrops on the east bank of the river, are still visible at low water at the foot of S. 112 St.

Quarry Hill. The only survivor of Chinook Wind's people is his wife, the grandmother of Mountain Beaver Woman's son. She took refuge on Quarry Hill on the west bank south of North Wind's village. To torment her, North Wind sent ravens to defecate on her face, and that is the source of her name *skwu-LAHTS*, "the face is marked," or "dirty-face." Before the hill was quarried away, its eastern face formed a prominent bluff whose stony surface was streaked with dark mineral stains just as the grandmother's face was streaked with the ravens' excrement.

According to Ann Jack, a Green River shaman born about 1840, rain would come after the myth about North Wind and Chinook Wind was recited, at least before whites came into the country and broke the spell. The power of the spoken myth brought the mythic powers to life. In an action designed to enable the grandmother to bring the rain, Duwamish women took baskets of water to the streaked eastern face of her hill and washed it, purifying her so she could manifest her power. People passing by in canoes would also splash water toward the hill with their paddles.

Poverty Hill. The place of safety to which Mountain Beaver Woman retired to bear her son was the house of her father, Mountain Beaver. In one version she travels on an underground road—in fact, a burrow such as that made by mountain beavers. She surfaced north of Poverty Hill, on the east bank, at a small, truncated hill that is currently traversed by the South Boeing Access Road. The hill looks much like a larger version of the mounds mountain beavers commonly push up in pastures and golf courses, and it was called *sh-HEE-yah-du*, "mountain beaver." John Peabody Harrington, an ethnolinguist who collected information in the Duwamish Valley near the turn of the century, was told by the Indians that the hill was North Wind's sister and a mean woman. A smaller hill east of it, also traversed by the South Boeing Access Road, appears to have been another of her brothers, but his name was not recorded.

CHIEF SEATTLE

Enmity between the interior peoples and the groups further down near salt water led to a pitched battle in Tukwila. Leading the force of Puget Sound fighters was Chief Seattle, whose mother, *she-LAH-tsa*, was said to have been a slave from a low-class village called "fleas' house" that stood a short distance upstream from the noble *stuk-AHBSH* longhouses at the foot of the logjam. Seattle's father, *tshwee-YEH-hub*, was a Suquamish headman. By his own account, Seattle was born on Blake Island and as a child witnessed Vancouver's arrival off Bainbridge Island.

A man of great leadership ability, Seattle became a respected leader. According to historian Cornelius Hanford, Seattle and his cohorts ambushed a raiding party made up of "mountain people," as they came down the White River in canoes. These were probably Klickitat men whose families wintered on the upper Green and White rivers. Seattle had his people fell a large tree across a swift-moving section of the river very near where the bridge now crosses to Fort Dent Park and position it so that it rested just above the water. When the raiders' canoes rounded the bend, the paddlers were unable to stop before the canoes hit the log and were swamped. The raiders fell into the water, and as they struggled ashore, Seattle and his men came out of hiding and killed them. This success catapulted Seattle to a position of prominence among the central Puget Sound peoples in spite of the taint of his low birth.

THE DUWAMISH PEOPLE

The Duwamish appear very early in the Hudson's Bay Company fur trading post "Journal of Occurrences." On July 17, 1833, there is mention of beaver and excellent leather being traded by the "Nuamish tribe." On February 17, 1834, an interpreter at the fort, Jean Baptiste Ouvrie, was sent north to trade in the vicinity of Ouvrie's River, the first historical mention of the Duwamish River. The Duwamish continued to trade, however, and on September 24, 30 beaver skins were brought to the fort by the "Toughnewamish," the clerk's version of *t-hw-duw-AHBSH*.

It is possible to reconstruct only a shadowy history of the native community at the confluence during the latter half of the nineteenth century. The introduction of western diseases and firearms to Northwest Coast Indians by early explorers may have been responsible for a marked decrease in population and a rising tide of violence as groups sought to rebuild their numbers by undertaking raids to capture women and children. This often provoked retaliation, and the Klallam Indians preserve the memory of a raid they carried out against the *stuk-AHBSH* on the lower White River to recover a stolen child. Raiders from the Snoqualmie Valley often lurked along the lower White River, and Indians from east of the mountains rode horses over the passes into the upper Green and White river valleys, where they married into local families. The construction of a sawmill on the Black River and the creation of a millpond that greatly improved the fishing appear to have lured some native families away from the confluence.

CONFLICT BETWEEN THE SETTLERS AND NATIVE PEOPLES, 1855-1856

Brought on by growing hostility between Americans and Indians, by intense dissatisfaction with the treaties which turned most of the Indian lands over to the settlers, and the cavalier attitude of many Americans toward the Indians' rights, the war began east of the mountains with the Yakima people and quickly spread west. It exploded with particular violence in the White River Valley in October 1855, when native warriors murdered several pioneer families.

Because of its strategic character, the confluence of the Black and White rivers was the focus of considerable activity. Toward the end of 1855 a fort was built there by territorial volunteers to shelter scouting parties sent out from Fort Duwamish several miles downstream. On January 26, 1856, a hostile native force attacked the Seattle village and burned the settlers' buildings, the sawmill on the Black River, and the forts. Afterwards, the hostile force itself fortified the confluence.

In October 1856, after hostilities had ended, the native people returned to their village sites to fish. Most appear to have congregated at the main Duwamish village in Renton for protection and to await action on their plea for a separate reservation in the area. When it became obvious to them that this would not be forthcoming, the group split up and the people returned wherever possible to their original house sites.

Period of Coexistence

After the treaties were ratified the Indians had one year to remove themselves to the reservations. Since the Duwamish were sent to Auburn, far from their home on the river, many chose to stay where they had always lived, even if they could not obtain title to the land. The settlers often staked their claims at native village sites because the Indian women's gardens provided ready-made farm plots and the native population was a convenient source of cheap labor. Many settlers found it to their benefit to permit native people to continue living at or near their old village sites, where they could be hired to clear the land and perform the work that farmsteads required to become profitable.

Soon the unremitting pressure of the development characterizing EuroAmerican civilization broke up the old house groups. One of the last residents of such a group on Henry Adams' land was Ben Solomon, a Duwamish man whose father had lived on the Cedar River. In the mid-1890s Ben moved to *bis-HOO-kid*, married a Yakima woman, Mary Selah, and together they began a family in a longhouse on the riverbank. To help support them Solomon fished the river and hunted ducks in the marshes near Georgetown, which he traded to Chinese immigrants for sacks of flour. His child Lottie, born in 1902, was one of the last Duwamish people born on the river, and sometime afterwards the Solomon family moved to the Suquamish reservation.

Although census records do not provide such a detailed record of the community at the confluence, we know it survived as a cohesive unit until 1910. The 1880 census of the Duwamish District identifies 42 Indians living along the river, some of whom doubtless lived at the confluence. An Indian identified as "Jack, age 50" may have been Jack Foster, the headman of the group identifying themselves as the Black River People. The last manifestation of the old settlement patterns were the tent villages that appeared up to 1918 in the summer and fall near *bis-HOO-kid*, where people from on and off the reservations gathered before heading up the river to harvest berries and vegetables in the valley farms. Although some Duwamish moved to neighboring reservations, most assimilated into the urban society. A 1919 report on off-reservation Indians sponsored by the Commissioner of Indian Affairs counted some 143 individuals under the heading "Duwamish Tribe." An 1897 U.S. Army Corps of Engineers map of the Duwamish River locates an Indian village on the west bank of the Duwamish River at what is now the southern end of the Foster Golf Links. A 1910 map shows the same village still in place, but after that it disappears.

Struggle for Identity and Official Recognition

In 1925 the Duwamish ratified a constitution with which to govern themselves, and in 1927 they joined several other tribes from western Washington in an unsuccessful suit against the federal government in the U. S. Court of Claims, *Duwamish et al. v. the United States*, in which they claimed the government had failed in its treaty obligation to provide them with a reservation. The Duwamish people are not officially recognized as a tribe.

In the twentieth century, the tribe has labored to maintain its identity and maintain amicable relations with the greater society. Because the Supreme Court ruling that "treaty Indians" were entitled to 50 percent of the fish that could be caught without endangering the stocks applied only to recognized tribes, the Duwamish were excluded. As a result of this ruling many tribal members, who were also members of other recognized tribes, withdrew from the tribe, greatly reducing its numbers. In 1990 about 300 people retained their membership in the tribe, and it continued to press the government for official recognition.

PART I
PIONEERING IN THE DUWAMISH RIVER VALLEY

INTRODUCTION

Long before the first settler arrived in the Duwamish River valley, Spanish and English explorers reached the northern Pacific Coast. Later, fur trappers for the Hudson's Bay Company ventured into the rivers and forests of Puget Sound. Neither the Spanish nor English presence was lasting. American exploration of the area came much later, but it became permanent; primarily because the exploration was soon followed by settlement and cultivation of the land. The early explorations did, however, help fuel interest in the untamed West. Economics and a sense of "destiny" also spurred the desire for to settle in the Pacific Northwest.

Descriptions of those early explorations must have sounded as inviting to nineteenth-century Americans living on the Eastern seaboard as they do to twentieth-century Americans looking back on a landscape now lost. Isaac Ebey's description of the Duwamish in the early 1830s sounds a responsive chord with us today, though the river scene he described is no more: "…here and there a beautiful plain of unrivaled fertility, peeping out through a fringe of vine-maple, alder or ash…"

Portraits such as Ebey's rendered well in the popular publications of the day. Tales of the frontier West held a deep fascination for many. The autobiography of Davy Crockett was a bestseller, as were the stories of James Fenimore Cooper. But more than a romantic notion of the frontier, the West offered an opportunity—a chance to stake a claim and become a property owner through hard work.

And the settlers came: The Collins party, the Foster brothers, the Steele family, Emmett Robbins, C. C. Lewis, William Gilliam—hardy souls seeking a new start in a new land, some leaving their names as a mark on a country that was wilderness when they arrived. They struggled west by oxen or on foot. The more fortunate boarded sailing ships that offered days of boredom, punctuated by fearsome storms.

Getting to the wilderness was only the beginning of the struggle, however. Once on the land, they had to "prove up"—improve their claims—under the terms of the Donation Land Act of 1850 and subsequent land-grant legislation. Most decided to, in the words of the old hymn, "gather at the river." They had to clear the land of virgin forest and stumps before they could till the rich soil and plant their first crops. A few, like the Robbins family, chose the less fertile hillsides to avoid the periodic flooding in the valley. Their task was no less daunting, however, as they contended with thin soil and the multitude of glacially deposited rocks.

The new immigrants displaced those who had previously hunted, fished and gathered nature's harvest freely. Native people quickly found themselves strangers in their own land. Conflict arose, but the outcome in favor of the more numerous and technologically advanced newcomers was never in doubt.

Extremes in weather, fire, separation from family members and hostility from the native people were typical of the many rigors the settlers faced. The back-breaking work of turning a wilderness to farmland also had to be overcome.

During this period, the river continued to be the crossroads of commerce, with riverboats and ferries serving as transportation. As numbers of pioneers grouped together, settlements were formed. Mox la Push, the name applied to a large area of the Duwamish and White river valleys for political purposes, eventually was divided into settlements, such as Foster. To connect the settlements with Seattle, pioneers helped build bridges and roads like Military Road. The railroad further improved travel. Settlements grew and multiplied, creating the foundation for the next stage of development of the area—the formation of the twentieth-century communities.

The Collins party, first settlers in King County, approaching the mouth of the Duwamish River with the scow About Half-Way Up, July 1851. On June 21, 1851, the Collins scouting party reached the northern district of 1990 Tukwila. Artist's conception by Patrick Hill.

CHAPTER 1
THE FIRST SETTLERS IN KING COUNTY

Why Did Americans Emigrate to the West?
Some were prompted by mere love of change, many more by a spirit of enterprise and adventure; and a few, I believe, knew not exactly why they were thus upon the road. With these reasons were more or less mixed up as a very important element—a desire to occupy the country as a basis of title in the dispute between the government of the United States and that of Great Britain.

    Jesse Quinn Thornton
    Oregon Trail Emigrant 1846

EARLY EXPLORATION OF THE NORTHWEST

s explorers and settlers found their way into Puget Sound, they soon concluded that Elliott Bay offered the best harbor on the sound. Into the bay flowed a serene river that was well protected by a headland. This river came to be known as the *Duwamish*—Puget Sound Salish meaning "Inside People." The name was that of the Native Americans who lived in large numbers around the meandering river. This river was selected by the first Euro-American settlers in King County for their homes. To fully understand the story of the first settlers, it is useful to briefly look at the history of the region and the series of events that preceded the establishment of the first community in King County—the community that is the focus of this history book.

The first white man to sail across the 42nd parallel north was the Spaniard Bartolome Ferrelo in 1543. Next, these Pacific shores were viewed by Sir Francis Drake. Other adventurous explorers from Spain and England followed, but none ventured ashore until 1775, when Bruno Heceta landed near the present Point Grenville. Just the year before, Juan Perez had discovered Nootka Harbor, on the west coast of Vancouver Island. This place became the headquarters for

THE FIRST SETTLERS IN KING COUNTY

all of the explorers and fur hunters for the next two decades. It was at Nootka Harbor that a clash occurred between Spain and England that threatened to result in war, and each side sought to embroil the United States. After years of disagreement, the dispute was finally settled with the Nootka Convention in October 1792.

The same year a momentous event occurred when the American Robert Gray discovered and named the Columbia River for his ship, *Columbia Rediviva*. Gray's exploration became a key factor in the American claim to the vast area that was called Oregon Country. The American claim was strengthened by the Lewis and Clark Expedition in 1804-06. The first permanent American settlement in the Northwest was Astoria, Oregon, a fur trading center established by John Jacob Astor in 1811.

Among the first Europeans to see the magnificent beauty of the Oregon Country was David Thompson, who explored the Columbia River system in 1809-11 searching for furs. In the 1820s the Hudson's Bay Company came into the region seeking beaver pelts, which were in high demand in Europe and elsewhere. By the 1830s American trappers were actively competing with the Hudson's Bay Company in the Willamette Valley. By 1834 American Methodist missionaries Jason and Daniel Lee were working with the Native Americans in the valley, and their presence attracted more Americans. Around 1838 the first American settlers arrived in what was destined to become Washington. However, north of the Columbia the American influence was minimal. Until the early 1840s the Hudson's Bay Company maintained local control without challenge over the Oregon Country wilderness, which extended from the 42nd parallel north to about the 54th parallel.

Through these events and activities, and others to follow, between 1840 and 1860, the region destined to be known as the Pacific Northwest finally went to the Americans through their fulfilling three fundamental requisites for national title—discovery, exploration and occupation. This history book charts these phases for the Duwamish River Valley and for the northern three miles of the Green (White) River Valley in King County, Washington.

The steady increase in tension over occupation rights in the 1830s prompted the Americans to take dynamic action to solidify their interests and control over the area, and in 1843, the year the Oregon Trail opened, a provisional Oregon government was set up that was actually a republic within a republic, since the status of the region had not been determined at this time. In 1844 the Oregon territorial legislature met at Oregon City, drafted a code of laws, elected officers to govern and enacted a law defining boundaries. After several years of negotiating, in 1846 the 49th parallel north was agreed upon by the United States and England as the compromise boundary between 42° north latitude and 54° 40' north latitude. Thus, control of the vast region passed from the Hudson's Bay Company to the Americans.

THE DUWAMISH RIVER IS EXPLORED BY EURO-AMERICANS, 1820-1840

In June 1827 a Hudson's Bay party exploring Puget Sound under James McMillan entered Elliott Bay. Party member John Work recorded his observations of the Duwamish River. This is the first known written record of the river. The party was experiencing typical cold, rainy June weather:

> Wednesday, 8th [1827], some rain in the afternoon, wind Easterly. We were on the water at 7 o'clock and made, according to estimation, a distance of 36 miles....We were 7¾ hours on the water....We, this day proceeded through a fine channel formed, as the other, by the mainland and an island. Passed an opening on the E. side in the morning and on the same side a bay [Elliott Bay] into which the Sinanimis River [Duwamish River] flows.

The next recorded observation of the Duwamish River by white explorers was made in the 1830s by Dr. William F. Tolmie, Hudson's Bay Company District Manager, who went up the river with Jean Baptiste Ouvrie, company agent. Referring to the river first as the "Charles River" and then as "Ouvrie's River," the undated diary entry states the object of the trip as "looking for a spot favorable for an establishment." Since Pigeon Point had already been selected by Ouvrie as the site for a trading post/fort, a support station site was probably the goal.

The party started out on a summer evening in a large canoe paddled by six Indians. Tolmie notes that while approaching the mouth of the river they saw several parties of *Tuamish* [Duwamish] people along the coast in the vicinity of the river. They also saw a substantial village on the banks of a second river (the Black) that flowed from a large lake (Washington) to Ouvrie's River. (In 1980 the native Duwamish village, *Sba'badid*, was discovered by archaeologists on the banks of the Black River. Over 500 Hudson's Bay trade beads were found, together with other trade goods and traditional native artifacts at the site.)

Col. Isaac Neff Ebey made the third written report of the river. In 1847 Ebey traveled from Missouri to Oregon Country with a wagon train over the Oregon Trail. Traveling by Indian canoe in the summer of 1850, he explored the shores of Puget Sound seeking a homestead site. While on Elliott Bay he had his native guides paddle him up the Duwamish River to the Black River. At the confluence of the rivers he continued up the Black to the large lake from which it flowed, which he named Lake Geneva (Lake Washington).

Col. Ebey wrote to Michael T. Simmons, editor of the *Oregon Spectator*, Oregon City, about his Puget Sound explorations. On October 17, 1850, Ebey's following account of his trip up the Duwamish appeared in the newspaper:

> The next river north, is the Dewams [Duwamish]. This river falls into a bay [Elliott] of the same name, below Vashon's Island, and immediately opposite Port Orchard. This bay forms a beautiful little harbor of about four miles in width and some six miles in length. This bay, like the Powalp [Puyallup], is surrounded by woodland. The river, for the distance of about twenty miles, has an average width of about forty yards, with a deep channel and placid current.
>
> The river meanders along through rich bottom land, not heavily timbered, with here and there a beautiful plain of unrivaled fertility, peeping out through a fringe of vine-maple, alder or ash, or boldly presenting a full view of their native richness and undying verdure. Other plains of more extensive character are represented (from the report of someone else) as being near at hand, and sufficient fertility to satisfy the most fastidious taste.
>
> At a distance of about twenty miles from the bay, the river forks—the left fork bears the name of the Dewams [Black River]. It has its source about ten miles to the north in a large clear lake [Lake Washington]. This stream has an average width of about twenty yards. The country along its banks partakes of the same character as that lower down the river. A few miles of this stream will be found quite rapid, offering very fine opportunities for mill privileges. Sandstone, of a good quality for building materials, make their [sic] appearance along this stream.
>
> Where the wagon road [Hudson's Bay Company trail across Naches Pass] crosses this river, plains of unrivaled fertility are found, covered with the most luxuriant growth of grass I have ever met with, a great deal of it being from three to four feet high, in which the red and white clover are found sprinkled with a liberal hand.…The tide flows up this river a distance of more than twenty miles.

While Col. Ebey frequently overestimates the distances involved, the natural environment he describes is a wonder. He holds a special

THE FIRST SETTLERS IN KING COUNTY

place in Duwamish Valley history for the first recorded impression of the river and valley.

THE FIRST SETTLERS IN KING COUNTY

John Holgate

The attractiveness of the Duwamish Valley as a homestead site resulted in its being chosen by King County's first settlers. Nineteen-year-old John Holgate is distinguished as the first pioneer to make a commitment to settling in King County. The son of a couple from the eastern seaboard who had pioneered first in Ohio, and then in Iowa, where John grew up, Holgate traveled from Iowa to Oregon with a Quaker wagon train in 1847. After a number of adventures, including involvement in the Indian wars with the Cayuse, in which he assisted Capt. Gilliam's forces in avenging the murder of the missionaries Marcus and Narcissa Whitman, Holgate landed in Olympia. He heard of a wonderful bay to the north on Puget Sound and in August 1849 he hired Indian guides to paddle him from Tumwater to the bay, where he explored for a homestead site. He found a place he liked on the lower Duwamish River.

Upon returning to Portland for his belongings, Holgate enthusiastically reported how attractive the area was for settlement. Historic documents reveal a direct link between John Holgate's early exploration of Elliott Bay and the Arthur Denny party's migration to Elliott Bay in the winter of 1851. According to John Holgate's sister Abbie Holgate Hanford's account of the period, "On his [John's] return to the Willamette he gave such glowing descriptions of the country he had visited that a number of persons from that section were induced to visit the Sound and see for themselves." She specifically mentions David Denny, Lee Terry and John Low.

Unfortunately, John Holgate was not able to return immediately to his claim or file on the land. Instead he returned to Iowa because of the death of his father. When he came back to the Duwamish Valley in 1852, Luther M. Collins had filed a claim on the same site and was living on the land. Holgate subsequently filed a claim closer to Seattle. Holgate Street is named for this young pioneer. His sister Abbie and her husband, Edward Hanford, filed a claim on adjacent land. John died in 1868 while prospecting for gold during the Boise, Idaho, Gold Rush.

The Collins Party

In June 1851 the first settlers in King County made their way to the banks of the Duwamish River. The party of seven was led by Luther M. Collins, 34, who was accompanied by his wife, Diana Borst Collins, about 30, and their children, Lucinda, 13, and Stephen Collins, 7. The others were Jacob Maple, 58, his son Samuel Maple, 22, and Henry Van Asselt, 31. As is so often the case in life, a series of coincidences led to these people meeting, settling together, becoming lifelong friends and relatives by marriage, in the case of the Maples and Van Asselt.

By 1851 Diana and Luther Collins had already lived four years in the Northwest. Before coming to Puget Sound country, the adventurous pair had first settled in Illinois and then in Iowa. In the summer of 1847 they joined a wagon train bound for Oregon Territory on the overland trail, very rough at that time, with their two children, then nine and three. The Collinses brought a small herd of livestock with them over the long Oregon Trail. Luther's plan was to breed and sell livestock to the settlers in Oregon Territory. The couple staked a claim on the Nisqually River on Puget Sound and began the hard work of creating a homestead in the wilderness. They had brought a variety of fruit tree cuttings with the intent of selling nursery stock as well as livestock, and had soon produced an extensive stock of seedlings. Collins had a restless, highly adventurous nature, and when word of the discovery of gold in northern California reached Puget Sound, he took off for the gold fields, leaving Diana on the Nisqually claim with the children to fend for themselves.

Most of the early settlers in the Duwamish and White river valleys traveled overland on the Oregon Trail, which opened in 1843. In the first two decades most people reached Portland via the Oregon Trail and completed the journey by traveling from Portland to Elliott Bay by steamer. After 1853 the difficult Naches Pass was used by some wagon trains until Snoqualmie Pass was opened in 1865. Courtesy Seattle Historical Society.

Short with a wiry, powerful build and remarkable broad muscular hands, Van Asselt arrived in America with no assets but his hands and head. In the next three years he worked his way to Iowa, where he banded together with seven other men to travel west on the Oregon Trail in 1850. The men walked much of the way hauling their gear in two oxen-drawn wagons. After spending the winter working in a shingle mill in the Willamette Valley, the group went to the California gold fields. They were among the lucky ones, and after five and a half weeks of panning for gold they divided their accumulated gold dust and found that each man had about $1,000—a small fortune, indeed.

Interested in investing their gold in land, five of the men, including Van Asselt, traveled north to Oregon Country. On the journey they met Luther Collins, who was going home with his own pouch of gold. Jacob and Samuel Maple and Hill Harmon were with Collins.

Luther Collins was tall, with a fair complexion and handsome features. He was an intelligent and dynamic person. He was described by contemporaries as "a rough, boistering sort of a fellow; bold and venturesome; impatient of legal, moral or social restraint; strong, determined and willful; a leader among men with whom he usually cast his lot." In spite of his occasionally abrasive manner he had a good deal of natural charisma.

Collins was also an intrepid entrepreneur. Around the campfire he nightly told stories of the great Puget Sound country, painting pictures of the blue waters and blue skies; mountains

While in California Collins met Jacob and Samuel Maple, most recently from Iowa. The elder Maple, a widower of 58, was already an old man by the standards of the day, when life expectancy was around 60. Short of stature, Maple was a man of remarkable vitality, stamina, strength and wilderness lore. He was a seasoned frontiersman with a real sense of adventure who had literally grown up on the frontier. Born in 1793, as a child of seven he moved with his parents from the Monongahela in Pennsylvania to the Ohio frontier. In 1840 he had moved his own family to Iowa Territory to homestead. His son Samuel was young, tall, strong and farm bred, with a good deal of common sense and his father's daring spirit. (The Maple family has no connection with the Maple Valley community.)

Unlike his companions, who were American born, Henry Van Asselt was an immigrant. He came to the United States from Armela, Gelderland, Holland, in 1847 at the age of 23.

cloaked with forest; and valleys lush with ferns, salal and holly trees. The region had a delightfully mild climate, and the salty waves of Puget Sound lapped over acres of clam and oyster beds. Collins told the men that the rivers were alive with silvery salmon and trout, and the woods bright with red, blue and black berries, and all manner of game. And, he assured them, the soil was black, rich and deep. His voice singing the song of Puget Sound, he convinced the men to accompany him back to the Nisqually.

Years later, descendants of some of these men related that the group had made their way from the Columbia River to the Duwamish River by the following means: Leaving Portland by boat, they traveled up the Cowlitz River as far as possible, then overland to Olympia (about 65 miles) and thence to the Nisqually by schooner. Carefully looking the area over, Van Asselt was not satisfied. He felt that the sandy soil would not support the kind of community that he wanted to be a part of, with schools, churches and the refinements of civilization. By this time the serious-minded but congenial Dutchman had achieved a position of great respect in the group, and the consensus was that they did not want to stay on the Nisqually.

Diana and Luther Collins were determined to form a community with their companions, and agreed that they would move if the group could find a place everyone liked. Collins told the men that 40 miles down Puget Sound, on a river that flowed into Elliott Bay, there was good country that would support a large community. The main drawback, in Collins' opinion, was the large number of Indians living in the area. Always business-minded, Collins consented to lead the group if they would cover the expenses of the trip. The men agreed to hire Indian guides to paddle them to investigate the river system that came to be known as the Duwamish, Black and White rivers.

It is unclear in the historical record exactly who went with Collins on the initial exploration trip. Some accounts claim it was the two Maples and Van Asselt. Eli Maple, another son of Jacob Maple, later reported that the Maples and a man named Thompson went with Collins and the Maples on the initial scouting trip. (The man referred to is probably John Thornton, who was a member of Van Asselt's group that left California with Collins and eventually settled near Port Townsend.) It is most likely that Van Asselt did not go on the scouting party, since he was sick as a result of accidentally shooting himself in the shoulder and arm while cleaning his gun on the steamer trip up from California. Weakened by the wound, he remained behind with Diana and the children on the Nisqually.

The scouting party left the Nisqually around mid-June and reached the Duwamish River on June 21, 1851. They explored as far as the Meadows—the area of King County International Airport, within the 1990 Tukwila city limits.

The party was impressed with the fine tidal stream and extensive areas of open meadow with rich fertile bottom soil, which they called "little prairies." These prairies were free of large trees and lacked the dense vegetation that grew almost everywhere. They had been created by the combination of ancient beaver dams and silt brought down by periodic floods. Not having to spend long precious days clearing the land before a crop could be put in had much appeal, since it meant they could realize a harvest that very season. What they had been told about the large Indian population was quite evident, and they reported observing about 700 Indians living at Duwamish Head and 300 along the riverbank.

THE HISTORICAL DEBATE: THE COLLINS PARTY VS. THE DENNY PARTY

For over a century there has been disagreement among King County historians over when the first settlers arrived in the county. It has been widely believed that the Arthur Denny party's arrival at Alki Point in November 1851 constitutes the first settling party. Others have believed that the record is too vague to clearly establish when the first settlers arrived. Careful study of historical records indicates that the Luther Collins party arrived first and, in fact, had established a viable community on the Duwamish River by the time the Arthur Denny party arrived. Examination of Arthur Denny's writing suggests that he wanted to establish his group, represented by his brother David Denny, Charles Terry and John Low, as arriving in Elliott Bay within a few days of the Luther Collins party. However, the weight of the historical evidence verifying the earlier arrival date for the Collins party on the Duwamish proves beyond a doubt not only that the Duwamish Valley was the location of the first settlement in King County but that the Duwamish settlers came three full months before the David Denny scouting party reached Elliott Bay. The Duwamish settlement was established nearly a half year before Arthur Denny's Alki settlement.

It is significant that with the passage of time the tendency to accept Denny's version of the settlement dates over conflicting evidence has diminished. Perhaps objectivity toward the historical facts has replaced earlier historians' commitment to aggrandize those who achieved prominence and position in Seattle in the nineteenth century and, coincidentally, were personal friends of the historians. There is a variety of evidence verifying the Collins exploration party's arrival on June 21, 1851, and immediate establishment of their settlement on the Duwamish River, including personal testimony, newspaper reports and proof of an 1851 season harvest. Consideration of the logical actions of experienced frontiersmen in their circumstances adds credibility.

In 1888 Arthur A. Denny published his short history, *Pioneers on Puget Sound*. According to Denny's account, the Collins party first arrived on Elliott Bay on September 15, 1851. David Denny's scouting party, going up the Duwamish on September 25, 1851, met them along the riverbank. David Denny also reported seeing the Collins party moving their possessions onto their claims on September 27—twelve days after they supposedly arrived.

Significantly, David Denny is credited with establishing his settlement at Alki Point by the end of September, thereby making the Alki—i.e. Denny—settlement date essentially the same as the Duwamish settlement.

It appears that once Arthur Denny put this version of the order of events into writing, King County historians as a whole accepted the story as conclusive. Examination of a number of King County histories published over the past 90 years shows the Collins party's arrival date varying from September 12 to September 21, 1851. Some historians acknowledge that the September arrival is suspect.

THE DUWAMISH SETTLERS' PERSONAL TESTIMONY

Personal testimony by the original Duwamish settlers and their direct descendants support June 21, 1851, as the arrival date. Denny's date was openly challenged in 1937 by Professor Hillman F. Jones, a lawyer and curator for the Washington Historical Society Museum, and Judge August Toellner, both specialists in the history of the Duwamish Valley. Prof. Jones came to the Duwamish Valley in 1875 and taught at the Duwamish School. He later became a lawyer and maintained a practice in Seattle for a number of years. He was personally acquainted with the surviving original settlers — the Maples, Henry Van Asselt, and Lucinda and Stephen Collins. Luther Collins died in 1862. Jones reports that the members of the original Collins pioneer party told him that they had traveled by canoe to Pigeon Point at the mouth of the Duwamish River on June 21, 1851. They made their way up the river to the Meadows area the same day, camping that night in the vicinity of what later became King County Airport in northern Tukwila.

In his *History of King County*, 1919, Clarence Bagley is ambivalent about the first settlers in King County. While he quotes Arthur

Denny's version in a context suggesting this is the correct story, in other places his somewhat disorganized historical narrative reports that Eli Maple testified the original party arrived on June 21, 1851. Careful reading of Bagley suggests that the author questioned the reliability of Arthur Denny's dates, but was unwilling to openly state this. Bagley reports Denny's dates as "those commonly accepted." He also includes Maple's contradictory testimonial and newspaper accounts supporting the June 1851 arrival date. Daniel Bagley, Clarence Bagley and Arthur Denny shared a lifetime friendship that began when they traveled west to Oregon Territory in the same wagon train.

Experienced Frontiersmen and Frontierswomen

Considering that the Collins party was made up of highly experienced frontiersmen and farmers, it is unlikely that they would have been seriously exploring for homestead sites in September when the lateness of the season would have eliminated the possibility of putting in a harvestable crop to tide them over the winter. Moreover, having been in the Northwest for several years, the Collinses were very aware of the onset of the autumn rainy season and the necessity for good shelter. In addition to themselves, they had two young children and over two dozen head of livestock that they needed to protect from the weather and feed through the winter.

Luther Collins reported that on their third day on the Duwamish they planted a crop of potatoes in the Meadows area before returning to the Nisqually. This means that they had brought seed potatoes with them on the exploration trip—not an unlikely move by a man who had taken the trouble to bring a breeding herd 2,000 miles. The Collins party enjoyed the harvest of this crop, the first planted in King County by settlers, and shared it with the Denny party. This is corroborated by Arthur Denny, who reports that the Duwamish settlers' provision of potatoes for the Alki settlers, arriving in the dead of winter, saved the small, weak, ill-prepared group from scurvy. Some records report that turnips were planted as well as potatoes.

The summer of their arrival the Collinses also planted fruit trees on the Duwamish. In October 1855, the editor of the *Puget Sound Courier* of Steilacoom reported that L. M. Collins had brought in samples of his harvest of over 300 bushels of "fine, luscious peaches raised on his farm….The second year's bearing." The editor further reports that "Collins has a large nursery and orchard with over 1,000 trees… The trees were planted the fall of 1851."

It is worthwhile to consider the activities of the Duwamish settlers their first season on the river: finding and repairing a scow, moving their belongings from the Nisqually, clearing land, building cabins, planting and harvesting potatoes, planting 1,000 fruit trees, cutting firewood for the winter, gathering and preserving food for the winter. There simply would not have been enough time to get it all done after September 27 and before the winter rains.

The Collins party members often told the story of their moving to the Duwamish. Having staked their claims, the men returned to the Nisqually to bring back Diana, Lucinda, Stephen and Van Asselt, plus everyone's gear and the Collinses' livestock. Before the move Collins searched up and down the Sound until he located and bought a scow, and "sided it up" to confine the animals. This activity could have taken several weeks. Once the scow was ready, the party's goods were loaded along with the animals and people, and they set off down the Sound. The boat proved to be unseaworthy and sank soon after they set out, but not before the animals were brought ashore.

The repaired scow was loaded with the group's worldly goods and navigated by Jacob Maple, who kept it close to shore. It was a slow trip, with everyone else, including the children, driving the animals along the tide flats. There were many stops to pull bellowing cows and squealing pigs out of the gullies and washways that they fell into on the rough beach. Thus did the party make its way to Alki Point. There the scow was reloaded with men, women, children and animals, and the awkward Ark-like vessel was maneuvered over to the mouth of the Duwamish with utmost caution and rode the inflowing tide up to the claim sites.

Arthur Denny's account of the Duwamish group initially arriving in September was undoubtedly based on his young brother David's report of the Collins party passing Alki Point with the scow. According to the account of the Duwamish settlers themselves, around September 26 they took the scow back to the Collinses' Nisqually place to pick up additional belongings and a load of tree cuttings from the orchard Diana had been cultivating on their land. Collins had sold the land to a man named Ballard, a friend of the group who had come west with Van Asselt in 1847. David Denny's inaccurate reporting of the Duwamish settlers' activities was undoubtedly augmented by the fact that at the time, according to several sources, the 19-year-old youth was physically ill, in addition to being psychologically traumatized by a bad scare during his group's exploration of the upper Duwamish. He had spent the entire night of September 25 alone with their Indian guides, filled with fear and anxiety over the failure of Terry and Low to return from a land exploration jaunt undertaken that day in the company of local Indians.

On November 13, 1851, five months after the Collins party settled on the Duwamish, the Arthur Denny party arrived at Alki Point traveling on the schooner *Exact* from Portland. This group established the second settlement in King County.

Getting Started

How the Collins party decided on the location of the individual claims is unknown; however, when the claims were filed, the Collinses had the 640 acres nearest the mouth of the river (later Georgetown), Samuel Maple's 164-acre claim lay next to Collins', and Van Asselt's 320-acre claim was just south of Maple's. Jacob Maple took up residency on a parcel of land next to Samuel's, but the claim was proved up in the name of another son, Eli, who took up residency in 1852.

Everyone set to work planting crops, cutting trees and clearing land. Jacob Maple hired out, clearing land for the Alki settlement in the spring of 1852. Sam Maple and Henry Van Asselt worked together as partners felling trees and hewing timber. Van Asselt had a good hand with oxen, and as more settlers came in the pair were in high demand, since most land required extensive clearing of the natural vegetation before crops could be put in. The work brought each man four to five dollars a day. After about three years of working together they totaled their assets and found that they had $3,600 to their credit, in addition to over $2,000 in improvements on their claims. The latter were lost in the conflict with the Indians in 1855-56.

Several brigs sailed into Elliott Bay in 1852. On one of them were John and Eva Buckley. Having crossed the plains with an early wagon train, the Buckleys had been in Oregon Territory since October of 1846. The Buckleys arrived on the Duwamish around February 10, 1852, to stake their claim to 639 acres on the west side of the river, directly across from Van Asselt's land. A remarkably adventurous, mature couple, John, originally from Connecticut, was 54, and Eva Burger Buckley, a few years younger than her husband, was from Calloway City, Missouri. They had been married 25 years when they settled on the Duwamish and had no children with them. For many years the Buckleys, together with Jacob Maple, held the honored position of elders of the Duwamish pioneer community. (They have no connection with the founders of Buckley, Washington.)

The next addition to the Duwamish community was Eli Maple, 20, who came out to join his father and brother on the frontier. He left the family farm in Iowa in April of 1852, traveling overland with a wagon train as far as Portland, where he took a steamer to Elliott Bay.

THE FIRST SETTLERS IN KING COUNTY

THE FIRST PIONEER WOMEN IN KING COUNTY

Diana Borst Collins and her daughter Lucinda Collins hold the place in regional history as the first white women in King County. About 17 when she married Luther Collins, 20, Diana Borst was a suitable counterpart for the daring Luther Collins—adventurous, but more steady and stable. Diana is a classic pioneer woman. She drove the family's covered wagon the 2,000 miles to Oregon Territory in 1846, while her husband drove a small herd alongside. After they staked their first claim on the Nisqually River, she remained consistently on the land looking after the growing livestock herd, delivering the new calves and colts, and cultivating the crops which included extensive propagation of nursery fruit tree stock.

While Luther worked on the homestead when he was home, Diana often worked alone or with the help of Indians and her children, since the restless Luther was frequently gone for weeks or months prospecting for gold or pursuing other adventures. Diana and Lucinda learned the Indian language and the ways of the native people, which proved invaluable in the successful establishment of the Duwamish community, was located in an area already heavily populated by Native Americans. David Denny reports being impressed with Diana's and Lucinda's fluency in the native language. There are many stories of Diana and Lucinda doing the talking for the Duwamish settlers in dealing with the Indians.

Eventually Diana's brother, G. M. "Jerry" Borst, came to Puget Sound and opened up the Snoqualmie Valley to settlement. Joining her uncle in the Snoqualmie Valley with her second husband John Fares, Lucinda once again held the distinction of being the first pioneer woman in the region.

There appear to be no descendants of these two women. Lucinda adopted a boy from a wagon train passing through Snoqualmie Pass whose parents had died during the journey, but there is no further record of this adopted son and his activities. Diana's son Stephen married an Indian woman and had a child, but there is no known record of the line of descent. The commonly held assumption is that there are no survivors. Diana died in 1874 and Lucinda in 1884. They were both buried in the old Pioneer Cemetery in Seattle, later the site of Denny Park.

The entire journey took almost six months and he arrived on October 12, 1852. He inquired as to the whereabouts of his father and brother, and Doc Maynard directed him to the Duwamish and helped him hire an Indian and canoe to paddle him up to Collins' place, where Jacob was staying helping with the nursery stock. Needing another hand with the autumn nursery work, Collins immediately hired Eli.

Next Eli and his father went to work felling timber for processing at Henry Yesler's brand-new sawmill, built in the winter of 1852. Eli Maple recalls:

> My father and I took a contract for getting out 7,000 telegraph poles and 5,000 boat poles; these we packed out of the woods to the water on our shoulders. We rafted them by hand alongside of the ship as there were no steamers to do our towing. This supplied us with money enough to go to the Columbia River and buy two yoke of oxen which cost us $600. We drove them to Olympia and shipped them down on a scow to the Duwamish River. Then we went to farming as well as lumbering.

The scowload of apple, peach, plum and cherry tree seedlings and cuttings that the Collinses had brought from the Nisqually orchard in 1851 flourished in the loamy river-bottom soil. The enterprising pair sold the good-quality growing stock to other settlers, all of whom desired orchards. Their crops, including the fruits, grew to enormous size, and they shipped some of the largest from the harvest of 1852 to Olympia. Luther and Diana Collins apparently were highly skilled at propagating trees, and in 1853 they advertised in the *Olympian* that they had on hand 200,000 apple, peach, plum and cherry cuttings for sale at the rate of $12.50 per hundred trees. The Collinses' crop for 1853 was valued at $5,000.

Collins soon began running his trusty scow, named *About Half-Way Up*, around the Sound delivering nursery stock and livestock to their customers, and hauling cargo and passengers as space permitted. In December 25, 1852, he advertised in the Olympia *Columbian*:

> Ho for Seattle! The Dewamish [sic] Bay clipper scow *About Half-Way Up*, L.M. Collins, master, will have immediate dispatch for Dewamish Bay, touching at all points and town sites between Olympia and Seattle. Accommodations unsurpassed in Northern Oregon. Passengers will be allowed the privilege of boarding with the captain provided they find their own provisions.

Thus not only did Collins offer travel on a first class scow, but passengers who brought their own lunch along could eat with the captain.

Collins was interested in keeping the scow busy while home on the Duwamish. Among the first requests put before the King County Commissioners in 1853 was his application for a license to operate a ferry on the Duwamish River. It is unlikely that the ferry ever operated because there were no roads, hence insufficient traffic to support a ferry, and almost no one had draft animals and wagons to ferry. People easily crossed the river in canoes. However, if the ferry had been operated, it would have been located approximately where the West Seattle Bridge is in 1990. The fee registered by Collins, $1.50 for a wagon and team, was triple the fare actually charged by C. C. Lewis, who began operating a ferry across the Duwamish River in 1855. For several years the only settlers in the county having teams, except Thomas Mercer in Seattle, were the Duwamish settlers who got their draft animals from the Collinses.

LIFE ON THE EDGE OF THE PUGET SOUND WILDERNESS, 1852-53

The California Gold Rush of 1849 substantially influenced the early settlement of Puget Sound. Many of the young men who became Puget Sound pioneers originally came west to try their luck panning for gold, including Van Asselt, the Maples and the Fosters. Luther Collins and John Buckley, already in the Northwest, joined the Gold Rush.

In addition to bringing men west, the California Gold Rush was also responsible for inflating the price of goods needed by Puget Sound settlers. The influx of tens of thousands of fortune seekers, with only a minority engaging in food production or even shipping, made food and supplies scarce and expensive all over the west coast of North America. For example, in 1850 wheat sold for $6/bushel; eggs, $1-2/dozen; and flour, $75/ barrel (50 lb.).

The high prices were somewhat balanced by the high price paid for another scarce commodity—labor. A strong man could earn $5/day clearing land. Those skilled in a needed trade, such as carpentry, made a hefty $12/day. By 1852 prices were dropping a little and beef sold for 15-20 cents/lb.; flour, $40/barrel; potatoes, $1/bushel; onions $4/bushel; butter, $1/lb.; and cheese, 40 cents/lb. Building materials were in high demand, and sawed fir lumber sold for $25/1000 board feet; cedar lumber, $30/1,000 b.f.; cedar shingles, $5/1,000; pilings, 3 cents/foot; squared lumber, 16 cents/b.f. Most settlers tried to do without buying more than the bare essentials, since it depleted their meager cash supply.

In autumn of 1852 the Duwamish pioneer community consisted of two married couples, a widower, three bachelors and two children. The Duwamish Valley was not the only place people were settling. By the summer of 1853, in addition to Seattle, there were several little clusters of settlers in the vicinity. On the west side of Lake Duwamish (Washington) there were four claims. On the south side of Elliott Bay there were four claims, and one in Rainier Valley. There were several others on the Black River.

During the severe winter of 1852-53 rough seas prevented ships from entering Puget Sound for several months, causing the settlers much hardship. While the Duwamish pioneers were more comfortably settled in their homes than most around the area, they, like the others, lived on a basic diet of potatoes, fish, clams, venison, sugar, syrup, tea and coffee, and whatever berries or other fruits they had collected and dried. Their flour came from Chile, and sugar, mostly in the form of mats, came from China. Seattleites ate salt pork and rancid butter shipped around the Horn from the Atlantic states, while the Duwamish pioneers enjoyed fresh milk and sweet butter thanks to the cows the Collinses had brought west.

THE FOSTER BROTHERS JOURNEY TO THE DUWAMISH VALLEY

The overland journey of two 1853 Duwamish pioneers—Joseph and Stephen Foster—is recorded by Flora Fleming Foster, Joseph Foster's daughter-in-law. Their story provides insight into the decision making, activities and experiences of those making this historic, difficult and dangerous journey halfway across the North American continent.

Joseph and Stephen Foster, single and in good health, were spending the winter of 1851 working in Wisconsin when they decided to go west. They spent the winter saving their money, dreaming of the exciting adventures to come and making plans. Early in the spring of 1852 they quit their farm jobs and travelled to St. Charles, Illinois, where they bought a team of oxen and a small two-wheeled cart. They outfitted themselves with blankets, a cook kit, an axe, tools, two rifles, ammunition and provisions, which they loaded onto the cart until it was piled high and had to be lashed tightly with crisscrossed ropes. For clothing, they decided they could get along with "the shirts on their backs" and took only an extra pair of boots, knowing they would wear out at least one pair. They took only a limited amount of food, planning on hunting and replenishing their supply along the trail. Cart packed and oxen harnessed up, the adventurous brothers turned their faces west and began walking. They walked every step of the 2,000 miles to Oregon Country.

THE ABUNDANCE OF NATURE

Rev. David Blaine recorded his impressions of the natural abundance of Puget Sound in his first letter back home to New York, dated December 6, 1853:

"As for fruit we can live very well without it as the superabundance of berries here will serve as a substitute. These abound during nine or ten months in the twelve. We have strawberries, raspberries, dew berries, salal berries, salmon berries, cranberries, whortleberries and wild grapes of a superior kind. These ripen successively and are picked by the Indians and brought in by the barrel. Cranberries and whortleberries are still hanging on the bushes in abundance. They are larger and more solid than our berries at home in the states.

There is an abundance of game in the woods, consisting of deer, wild cattle (these belong to the Hudson Bay Company, but have run wild), bears, wolves, panthers, squirrels, skunks and rats. Pheasants, grouse, gulls and ducks and crows are as tame here as the hens at home. They are very numerous. There are also a great many eagles, ravens and cranes. Our Sound, or inland sea, besides its many other excellent qualities, abounds in fish of almost every variety. Salmon are very abundant, cod fish, herring, sardines, oysters and clams. Whales come spouting along now and then. Halibut are caught at certain seasons of the year. The Indians do most of the fishing. The oysters here are of an inferior quality and small size."

At the Platte River, Nebraska, they found a caravan of 28 wagons, which welcomed the friendly, strong young men. This was a small wagon train compared to a few years later, when caravans of 100 to 200 were common over the Oregon Trail. The group was blessed with an exceptionally trouble-free journey. They passed what were to become famous pioneer landmarks that were used to chart the journey's progress: Loop Fork, Nebraska; Sweetwater, Wyoming; Bear River, Utah; Fort Boise, Idaho; and The Dalles, Oregon. They reached Fort Vancouver late in July. In less than four months they had covered the Great Plains, crossed the Rockies and the Cascades, forded countless creeks and rivers, and made friendships that would last a lifetime.

Joseph and Stephen Foster were young and curious. Flora Fleming Foster relates the brothers' early adventures after arriving on the West Coast:

> Arriv[ing] at last in the far west, the brothers were ready to earn a little money. Uncertain as yet as to their final home or occupations, they meant to see the country, view the opportunities, and work at whatever looked most promising. Stephen found his services in demand as a brick layer and plasterer. Portland, Oregon, across the Columbia from Vancouver, had been chartered as a city the year before their arrival and had then a population of perhaps a little less than three thousand, but was growing rapidly.
>
> Joseph was soon hard at work running small flatboats or scows, loaded with freight, from the mouth of the Columbia River, up river as far as the Cascades, now Cascade Locks, near Bonneville. These flatboats were propelled by means of paddles and a pole following close to the river bank, and it was sometimes necessary to get off the boat and wade in order to push the craft off of the sand bars.
>
> As both [brothers] felt themselves financially able to go on, they went to Oregon City for a few weeks and from there to the Rogue River in southwestern Oregon, working in gold mines. Mining did not prove very profitable for them, but they went on into California and tried their luck for a time in the mining area near Eureka and Shasta City.
>
> When they heard of a possible opportunity to go on a farm and work for wages and meals that they did not have to cook for themselves, they welcomed it, though neither up to that time had done any farm work. The farmer, named Sutter, needed men to plow and do other early spring work and to cut wood. He told the boys when they applied that other men had come looking for work, but he had not kept them because they were not regular farmers. They assured him that he had better try them, as they could do any work that he would put them at.
>
> So he said he wanted a certain field plowed and would send his "steady" man to help them get started. This man harnessed the two teams, a team of horses and a pair of mules. Joseph, ever watchful to give Stephen the easier part, said, "You take the horses and I'll manage the mules; and don't miss a move the fellow makes. We'll have to do it next time."
>
> They overcame all difficulties and did the work, plowing and cutting wood, and everything else Mr. Sutter asked of them. Their work was appreciated and praised, as well as paid for, and it was not until Joseph offered to cut and fit a dress for a teacher boarding at the farm, when the season was nearly over, that the truth of their former very slight acquaintance with farming operations was disclosed.
>
> The school teacher was bemoaning the rain, saying that she had been wanting for a long time to go to Sacramento to get a silk dress cut and fitted. Joseph spoke up and offered to perform this service. The lady was amazed. "You!" she said and was on her way to saying much more when Steve broke in, "He's the very man that can do it. Why he's a tailor by trade!"
>
> After some explanations and confessions, accompanied by much merriment at that dinner table, the teacher had her dress made to her entire satisfaction.

Having saved a goodly nest egg, the brothers finally left the happy situation with the Sutter family for a look at San Francisco. In the city everyone was talking about Australia as the land of real opportunity. The Fosters were filled with enthusiasm for foreign adventures and one morning bought tickets on a ship sailing that very evening. By midday Stephen had changed his mind and, wanting to stick together, the

THE FIRST SETTLERS IN KING COUNTY

brothers sold their tickets and booked passage on the brig *Carib* headed for Puget Sound. They reached Alki Point at 4 a.m., April 4, 1853. Charles Terry took them off the ship two hours later in a hand-carved cedar canoe paddled by Indians.

The brothers were impressed with Puget Sound and decided to find some good land and take government claims. Wanting to explore around the sound for claim sites, they followed the custom of hiring two Indians with a canoe to take them up the Duwamish River. They reported that while traveling upstream they met the Collins family, Van Asselt, Timothy Grow and Dr. Sam Grow, Sam Maple, and an old couple named Buckley.

At the junction of the rivers they continued on the Black River to Lake Duwamish (Washington). They camped for the night at the mouth of the Cedar River. Returning to the confluence of the rivers the next day, they talked over everything that had looked favorable. Joseph Foster decided to stake his claim right at the confluence of the rivers, the place the Indians called Mox la Push, predicting that a great city would one day arise at this point. Stephen chose land a little ways farther down the Duwamish, where the river made a long narrow loop. This came to be known as Foster Point.

The pair set to work immediately building a cabin of shakes from a large cedar tree close by. Once their shelter and immediate homestead was established, they went off to cut trees at Graham's Point. They sold their first logs to Yesler's Mill, and for the next 12 years they continued to supply Yesler and other sawmills with logs when they were not otherwise occupied.

DONATION LAND GRANTS

Settlers were drawn to Puget Sound in the 1850s by the U. S. government's offer of land to be had free or at very nominal cost. The government was interested in bringing in American settlers for several reasons, the most pressing being to win the ongoing controversy with the English over ownership of the San Juan Islands. The United States based its claim to the Northwest on discovery and exploration. Now it would cement the claim by populating the area with thousands of American settlers.

In the 1830s and 1840s settlers took land by "squatters' rights"—a method which did not always lead to clear title. A series of land acts passed by Congress, beginning in 1850, provided the means for making a claim and receiving clear title. Most of the land in the Puget Sound area and the Duwamish Valley in the 1850s was acquired under the Donation Land Act of 1850, which was extended to 1855, or under the Pre-Emption Land Act of 1841. The Donation Land Act, the first law in American history to give land free to homesteaders, was limited to Oregon Territory.

The Donation Land Act of 1850 offered those who had come to Oregon Territory with intent to settle by December 1, 1850, up to 640 acres for a married couple, and 320 acres for a single man over the age of 18. Land was not available to single women. Only two couples in King County qualified for this, the most generous of all the land grants. Luther and Diana Collins and John and Eva Buckley each received one square mile of land. The renewed Donation Land Act of 1851 offered free to settlers coming in by December 1, 1855, 320 acres for married couples and 160 acres for single men over 21.

The third and longest-lasting land grant legislation was the Pre-Emption Act of 1841, which was in effect in Washington from 1854 to 1891. Under the Pre-Emption Act anyone who was the head of a household, including widows or single men (but not single women) over 21, who had not already received 320 acres by other land grant was granted a preferred or pre-emptory right to buy 160 acres for $1.25 per acre. The cost typically ran from $200 to $400 and could be paid for over a number of years. Land preempted within the Railroad Grant limits—40 miles on either side of the tracks—was $2.50 per acre from 1870 to 1889. Under the Pre-Emption Act a number of the valley's donation claimants increased their land hold-

Joseph Foster's original Donation Claim homestead at Mox la Push, confluence of the White, Black (right fork) and Duwamish (left fork) rivers, ca. 1853, looking north. The hill behind Foster's cabin is Sbah-bah-teel (little mountain or old mountain). Fort Dent was built in the vicinity of Foster's cabin in 1856. Artist's conception by Don Paulson.

ings in the valley, some doubling their acreages. Many of these claims lay on the hillsides and in the White River Valley.

WILLIAM H. GILLIAM PROVES UP HIS DONATION CLAIM — FROM FILING TO CLEAR TITLE

Following William Gilliam's activities in acquiring his land grant illuminates this important focus of the lives of the Duwamish settlers for the first years in the Valley. Gilliam's claim lay between Foster's and Abraham F. Bryant's. Born and raised in York Town, Virginia, Gilliam, 23, came to Washington Territory October 12, 1852. He spent the winter looking over the area and by June 1, 1853, he had settled on the land lying along the White River with the northern boundary meeting Joseph Foster's.

The following chronology illustrates the basic process that all the Duwamish land-grant recipients went through to receive clear title to their land:

June 1, 1853, Gilliam moves onto the land he is claiming.

April 6, 1855, *Certificate of Occupancy* filed at King County seat, Seattle.
Joseph Foster and Abraham Bryant each file on adjacent land and sign affidavits at the cabin of Duwamish Justice of the Peace, C. C. Lewis, that they are:
> in no way interested in the tract of land claimed as a DONATION RIGHT by William H. Gilliam … ; that he is personally acquainted with the said William H. Gilliam and knows that he personally resided upon and cultivated the tract of Land continuously since the first day of June, 1853, to the sixth day of April, 1855.

June 1, 1857, Foster and Gilliam appear before David "Doc" Maynard, King County

The First Settlers in King County

A heritage of stumps from the enormous trees that were logged during the early days of clearing the land remained throughout the nineteenth century and into this century in some cases. The great red cedar, naturally resistant to rotting, was the longest lasting. This photo was taken in the 1920s. Farming, buildings and roads were planned around the great stumps, which were playhouses for generations of children. Courtesy University of Washington Special Collections.

Steps For Acquiring Land Under Pre-Emption Law

1) File a Declaratory Statement (D.S.) identifying the land that the claimant had made settlement on and intended to use his/her preemption right on.
2) Live on and improve the land for the legally specified length of time commonly—called "proving up."
3) Provide proof of residency and improvement and provide payment.
4) Receive patent issued under the signature of the President of the United States, which transferred legal title of public land from the federal government to private or state ownership.

Commissioner. Foster swears that William Gilliam has been living on his stated claim continuously from June 1, 1853, to June 1, 1857, "excepting when driven off by hostile Indians."

March 24, 1863, Gilliam and Foster appear at the Territorial Land Office, Olympia. Foster swears again verifying Gilliam's continuous occupation of his claim; Gilliam pays filing fees. William H. Gilliam receives clear title—a patent—to 160 acres of prime White River bottom land.

CHAPTER 2
LIFE ON THE DUWAMISH IN THE 1850S

The rivers are our brothers....They quench our thirst, they carry our canoes and feed our children....You must give the rivers the kindness you would give your brothers.
　　Chief Seattle

Black River with homestead on bank. Courtesy Renton Historical Museum.

The 1850 U.S. census for Oregon Territory showed a total population of 13,294, with 457 in the Puget Sound District. By the end of 1852 there were approximately 20,000 settlers in the territory and a growing interest in dividing the huge territory for administrative purposes. Clarence Bagley announced in his massive 1919 *History of King County* that the Duwamish settlers, being farmers, occupied themselves with farm work and took "but a small part in the political activities of King County." However, careful study of the King County Commissioners' record and other governmental documents beginning in 1852 shows that Bagley's quick dismissal of the Duwamish pioneers from early county history is erroneous. Undoubtedly, Bagley, faced with an overwhelming amount of historical information on the founders and developers of Seattle, most of whom he knew personally, chose to simply not look into the active role of the Duwamish pioneers. The records show that members of this group were consistently involved in King County and Washington territorial politics and government. Luther Collins and Joseph Foster stand out as regional leaders in this historic period.

On December 22, 1852, Thurston County, which encompassed all of Oregon Territory north of the Columbia River to the Canadian border, was divided into Thurston, King, Pierce, Island and Jefferson Counties. King County, named for Rufus King of Alabama, Vice President under President Franklin Pierce, was thus established while the land was still a part of Oregon Territory. Luther M. Collins was appointed to represent King County in the Oregon Territorial Legislature in 1853, along with John N. Low and Arthur A. Denny.

Everyone agreed that the distance between

LIFE ON THE DUWAMISH IN THE 1850S

Formation of King County, Oregon Territory
First Resolution: A New County, 1853

Be it remembered that on this 5th day of March, A.D. 1853, the County Commissioners Court of King County was convened in the house of D. S. Maynard in the Town of Seattle, and duly organized in accordance with an act of the Legislative Assembly of Oregon.

Present: L. M. Collins* and A. A. Denny, Commissioners and H. L. Yesler, Clerk, the following business was transacted:

Ordered that the following named persons be summoned to serve as grand jurors-to-wit: George Holt,* Jacob Maple,* Samuel Maple,* Henry Price, Henry Smith, Edward A. Clark, and James Wilson.

And as petit jurors: David F. Denny, Wm. N. Bell, John Sampson, John Moss, Wm. Carr, David Maurer, John Strobel, and Henry Van Asselt.*

Ordered that the court adjourn to meet on the first Monday.

Signed,

L. M. Collins*
A. A. Denny
Commissioners

* *Duwamish Valley Settlers*

the counties north of the Columbia River and the Oregon Territory capital in Salem was too great to allow for good communication between the capital and the far-flung county seats. Thus, after the creation of the new counties agitation began for a separate territorial government to be created for the region north of the Columbia River. A convention was held at Monticello, near the mouth of the Cowlitz River on the Columbia, to petition Congress for the creation of a new territory to be called "Columbia." The seven delegates from King County were Luther M. Collins, Charles C. Terry, George N. McConahan, William Bell, John Low, Arthur Denny and Dr. David Maynard. The memorial was adopted on March 2, 1853, with the name changed from "Columbia," to "Washington."

Of the 17 men making up the initial King County government, almost one-third were from the Duwamish. In addition to commissioner and juror posts, others appointed to political office from the Duwamish were Bennett L. Johns, Constable, and John Holgate, Assessor.

In the years following the foundation of King County, those pioneering the Duwamish Valley filled a number of county offices. Appointed in 1853, in 1854 Luther Collins was elected King County Commissioner. Jacob Maple, John Buckley, Henry Van Asselt, Louis V. Wyckoff, Timothy Grow, Joseph and Stephen Foster, Charles Brownell and William Gilliam served on the county grand and petit juries. The same year Collins was appointed the first King County Road District Supervisor, and Stephen Foster served as Deputy Sheriff for Sheriff Carson Boren.

From 1855 through 1857 men from the Duwamish Valley were frequently elected to the prestigious county commissioner post, the top office in the county: Cyrus Lewis, 1855-1856, Francis McNatt, 1857, and Henry Adams, 1860. In the 1850s county commissioners were paid at a rate of $6/day while serving at session. Fifteen cents a mile travel expenses were paid to elected county officials to attend sessions at the county seat.

MOX LA PUSH PRECINCT

The year King County was established the entire county was a single precinct and all official activity took place in Seattle, the county seat. In 1854 additional precincts were established at Stuck, Auburn and Mox la Push (Fort Dent Park area). The precinct name was the Chinook jargon name for the confluence of the Black and White rivers, Mox la Push ("two mouths"). The name arose from a natural phenomenon of the area. In the nineteenth century the Black River floodplain was sufficiently flat that during spring flood the pressure of the White River's waters reversed the current of the Black River, forcing it to empty into Lake Washington. Hence, the river had two mouths.

Initially, the Mox la Push precinct did not have well-defined boundaries but included all the voters living on the Duwamish, Black and White rivers and environs. In May 7, 1860, the boundaries of Mox la Push were simply defined as the area lying between Luther Collins' northline and the northline of G. P. Bissel's land in the White River Valley, south of what became Orillia. In the records, the precinct name Mox la Push is variously spelled Moxlapush, Moxt La Busch, Mox lapuch, Mox le Push, and Mox lapush.

For the first ten years the Mox la Push precinct polling place moved from cabin to cabin. Being situated at the confluence of the rivers, Joseph Foster's cabin was a convenient location and served as the official polling place for a number of years. Cyrus C. Lewis, Abraham Bryant and John Thomas, from the White River, served as the first election judges. Cyrus Lewis was appointed Justice of the Peace, a position he held for many years, and Abe Bryant was constable for the entire precinct district. The next year election judges were Henry Adams, Sam Grow, C. C. Lewis, and Abe Bryant. Voting again took place at Joseph Foster's, while neighbor Charles Brownell served as election clerk. In 1859 Mox la Push precinct was reconfirmed by the county commissioners and the polling place moved across the river from Foster's to L. V. Wyckoff's cabin.

In May of 1860 voting took place at Ben Johns' house near the Lewis ferry landing. On May 8, 1865, the Mox la Push polling place was moved to the ferry landing which had recently been taken over by Joseph Steele. The Duwamish River Road crossed the river at the ferry landing, making it the crossroads of the valley and as such the most accessible location. Settlers typically traveled by water to the polling place.

The main issues placed before the voters at this time were selection of officials and taxes. For example, in the election held on June 6, 1857, the following taxes were approved: 2 mill school tax, 3 mill county tax, 1 mill territorial tax. Road tax was 25 cents for each $100 of income, and $9 road tax on each person defined as "liable" to pay road tax. A taxpayer could perform road construction labor in lieu of paying cash.

TRAVEL IN THE EARLY 1850S

Until the construction of the local railroad line in the 1870s, travel in the Duwamish and White river valleys was by water, Indian trail or the rugged roads built by the settlers. The rivers were the highway for traveling, shipping produce, and receiving mail and supplies. Almost all of the early exploration and travel was done via canoes paddled by hired Indian guides. The river valley settlers quickly adopted a special Indian type of canoe for their river travel, and everyone had at least one canoe which was very satisfactory for light loads or a few passengers.

The rich river-bottom soil produced bumper crops that provided enough surplus to sell in the village of Seattle. To haul heavy loads a simple barge was improvised by firmly lashing poles laid across the hulls of two large canoes placed side by side. The cargo of potatoes, hay, butter, fruit or animal skins was secured to this platform. Hogs or other small livestock were not put on the platform but tied in the bottom of the canoe, and the slow careful trip down the river began. If a sudden storm blew in, the boatman had a hazardous time of it. Depending upon the starting point, the journey could take a few hours or more than a day. The trip had to be timed with the outgoing tide, since the mouth of the Duwamish was a muddy delta at low tide. In the late 1850s, enterprising Indians started a canoe ferry service for the settlers, charging $1 a two-canoe barge load.

Traveling around Puget Sound from Olympia to Victoria was possible on one of several small steamboats in operation from the early 1850s. The best known was the *Eliza Anderson*.

LIFE ON THE DUWAMISH IN THE 1850S

From 1853 to 1870 the stern-wheeler made a weekly round of the little settlements scattered along the shore, carrying human and animal passengers, delivering supplies and handling the mail. Most important of all, the *Anderson*'s genial skipper always came ashore and shared the news from San Francisco, Portland, Olympia and the pioneer toeholds up and down the Sound.

The *Eliza Anderson*'s home port was at the territorial capital, Olympia. The regular passenger fares from Olympia were Seattle, $6.50; Port Townsend, $12.50; and Victoria, $20. Horses and cattle were charged on a flat-fee basis at the rate of $15 per head; sheep and hogs, $2.50; and freight $5 to $10 per ton, determined by measurement. Because it was the only boat that made regularly scheduled runs, the *Eliza Anderson* always had a lot of business.

The rough terrain characteristic of the Puget Sound basin, combined with heavy vegetation, did not lend itself to the easy carving of roadways. However, the settlers wanted the convenience of established roads. The first roads built in King County were routed through the Duwamish Valley. In 1854 the Territorial Legislature passed resolutions calling for the construction of three roads.

One of the roads was Military Road, which some sources report Ulysses S. Grant and Fredrick Dent helped lay out in 1855, when they visited Washington Territory. Beginning at Fort Vancouver, it ran to Fort Steilacoom and thence into King County, where it followed the ridge on the west side of the White River Valley. A connecting road led to C. C. Lewis's ferry, where the Duwamish River was crossed, and the road continued to central Washington and Walla Walla. The entire route was not completed until 1860, at which time Joseph Foster served as the King County Road Commissioner overseeing the work. King County Road No. 1, technically a territorial road, linked Seattle to the Military Road. Henry Van Asselt served as a county "citizen road viewer" during the construction of this road.

While the Military Road was often called a county road, in fact, the first real county road was the Duwamish River Road. This road was built as a result of the initiative and labor of the Duwamish Valley pioneers. In 1854 a petition was drawn up and signed by all of the settlers on the Duwamish River. Receiving the petition, the county commissioners approved the road, and it was recorded as King County Road No. 2. The road connected with the Fort Steilacoom-to-Seattle territorial road at Van Asselt's claim, thence led up the Duwamish Valley to the C. C. Lewis ferry crossing finally reached Seattle by way of Beacon Hill. The early county roads were built by the settlers themselves with little or no technical support from the county. The formalities of petition and official county designation were not always observed. Undoubtedly the "road viewers" were busier building than viewing.

For decades the roads were little more than glorified trails carved out of the wilderness, just wide enough for a single wagon. Indeed, many, such as the Duwamish River Road, followed established Indian and game trails. They followed the natural contours of the land, hugging the ridges whenever possible to get away from the eternal mud characteristic of the low-lying areas. Laid out by laymen, the roads often had very steep grades. The density of the forest posed a formidable problem and often the road simply skirted around big trees that stood in the way. For many years there were no bridges; and except for an occasional ferry landing at major river crossings, rivers had to be forded.

On April 4, 1853, the county commissioners divided King County into road districts with the Duwamish River serving as the dividing line. District No. 1 lay north of the river and was overseen by William N. Bell of Seattle; District 2 lay south of the river and was under George Holt, settler on the lower Duwamish. The next year, the commissioners decided to regard the entire county as a single district for the time being and appointed Luther Collins as King County Road Supervisor. Throughout the rest of the century, the county commissioners created and abolished road districts as they felt appropriate, with the area south of the Duwamish being known at various times by the district as numbers 2, 3 and 6.

The Duwamish Valley Community Grows

A census taken in the summer of 1853 reported 3,965 settlers for the newly created Washington Territory, with 170 in King County. Population numbers for the other counties existing at that time were Clark, 1,134; Island, 195; Jefferson, 189; Lewis, 616; Pacific, 152; Pierce, 513; and Thurston, 996. In the Duwamish Valley there were 13 settlers. This was almost eight percent of the population of King County at that time. By December 31, 1855, 20 settlers had filed donation claims in the Duwamish Valley and most of the land bordering the river was taken. In the next decade, the remaining valley bottom land was claimed, including most of the future Duwamish-Allentown area, the area east of the river at Foster Point, and the Southcenter district. The historical map found in the back of this book shows the location of the land claims.

By 1856 a definite community had formed in the Duwamish Valley, in spite of the distance between homesteads resulting from the large claim acreages. The Collinses and Buckleys had one square mile each, and many others had one-half square mile. Their location along the river allowed the settlers to see each other frequently, fostering a close-knit, strongly supportive community. Including those on the northern section of the White River, the community consisted of 25 adults, five married couples and 15 single men, three of whom were widowers. There were only five adult women, all married to other pioneers. Fourteen children, seven of which were Bennett Johns', made the total community 39 people. Johns, 44, had lost his wife Elizabeth on the trip out when she drowned as they were crossing the headwaters of the Snake River. The wagon train was 90 days out of St. Louis when the tragedy happened. Johns' eldest daughter Elizabeth had assumed her mother's responsibilities in looking after her six siblings. A few months after arriving she married Timothy Grow. The community had many related adults, including the three Maples, the Grow brothers, the Foster brothers, and Henry Meader and Sarah Meader Brownell—father and daughter.

As in all frontier communities, in 1856 single young men predominated, although the community had a notably larger proportion of older people than was typical. The average age of the 11 single (never married) men was 25, while the married men ranged from 29 to 54, with an average age of 38. Figuring in the three widowers, Jacob Maple, 58, Ben Johns, 44, and Henry Meader, 59, as married men, the average age of this group is 53—more than double the age of the bachelors. Almost half of the men were over 34.

Not all the first-comers were from farm backgrounds. There were, in fact, a number of trades and professions in the community: Joseph Foster, tailor; Stephen Foster, plaster/mason; William Gilliam and Henry Meader, coopers (barrel makers); Charles Brownell and Henry Adams, carpenters; Van Asselt, furniture maker; Louis Wyckoff, blacksmith; Cyrus C. Lewis, lawyer; Dr. Samuel Grow, physician; and August Hograve, engineer.

Like other pioneers in Puget Sound country in the mid-1800s, the Duwamish settlers were largely American born and from the eastern part of the United States. Some were the children of immigrants. Ohio and Iowa were the only states which figured in the background of a number of people. There were three European immigrants: Henry Van Asselt, Holland; August Hograve, Germany; and George Holt, England. To qualify for a donation claim, immigrants had to become naturalized American citizens—a process that took a number of years. Fulfilling this requirement on February 13, 1854, Henry Van Asselt took the citizenship oath in Yesler's cookhouse in Seattle, with a goodly collection of settlers and Indians looking on. Van Asselt was the first naturalized American citizen in King County.

Life on the Duwamish in the 1850s

Because of the way records have traditionally been kept in the United States, there is only scattered information on the women pioneers. It is estimated that the women—all of whom were married—were within five years of their husband's age. Undoubtedly, some of the women, like their husbands, were not from farm backgrounds and initially lacked the skills needed for making homes in the wilderness. These skills covered a wide range including cooking and baking over an open fire, butchering, all types of food processing and preserving, constructing and repairing clothing by hand, health care, and dealing with injuries and sickness in people and animals. Undoubtedly, the older, experienced women, such as Eva Buckley and Diana Collins, helped the other women learn new pioneer skills. As the bachelors gradually married and set up households, the older women functioned as midwives assisting at the birth of the children. In addition, the presence of women created a real sense of a permanent community. The importance of this cannot be underestimated as a factor in conteracting the tension implicit in living in an unfamiliar wilderness.

Like the older women, the older men brought a wealth of skills including farming, caring for animals, carpentry, and making and maintaining tools. They were a great help to the young men who, in many cases, had only a slight knowledge of these important skills. In addition to practical skills, the mature married settlers provided social and spiritual support, and guidance for the entire community. It was at their cabins that the bachelors congregated, and there was undoubtedly many an hour of quiet conversation during which advice and counsel were given.

Making homes in the wilderness took energy, stamina and good health. The level of success was directly related to the pioneer's life experience, range of skills, wisdom and self-confidence. It took courage. It took faith. While the former are the hallmark of youth, the latter qualities are more fully developed in the mature person who has lived many years. Without a doubt, the presence of a higher than average number of mature people in the Duwamish community accounted for the speed with which the community and its leadership were established in the formation of King County.

Isolation and Loneliness

Once settled on their claims, the pioneers had many things to deal with, not the least of which were isolation and loneliness. The claims were too far apart for quick casual visits, and the clearing work had to be done on one's own place. The men often worked together clearing land for the sake of camaraderie, as well as tackling jobs that were too strenuous for one man alone. In the good weather things went fairly well, but the climate was cooler in the nineteenth century, and the rivers—the Columbia, Willamette, Cowlitz and Duwamish—often froze over, preventing canoe travel, and weeks or even months passed without communication between homesteads.

Letters written at this time show that not having news from home was one of the most serious deprivations the pioneers felt they were enduring. Almost every settler had quite recently left behind a home, and in some cases a spouse or sweetheart. Mail service was very slow, with four to six months often elapsing before a reply was received to a letter sent "back east." In the winter of 1853-54 there was no mail delivery into Salem, the central mail distribution point for Oregon Territory, for over two months, and in 1855 no service for nine weeks. The poor mail service was a constant topic of conversation. When they arrived, letters were often shared with everyone along the river for the sake of political and other news.

Pioneer Livelihoods

In general, the settlers were too busy to malinger over their loneliness. While the land was gratis under federal land-grant

TUKWILA—COMMUNITY AT THE CROSSROADS

> **PIONEER LETTERS**
>
> In 1852, a letter mailed in St. Louis or Chicago for Washington Territory first went east to New York. There it was put on a steamship and taken to the Isthmus of Panama, whence it was carried by muleback to Panama City. Then it was put on a ship headed for San Francisco. It eventually arrived in Salem and then Portland. From Portland, King County's mail was brought by river steamboat to Monticello, near the mouth of the Cowlitz, then taken overland to Olympia. Next it was brought to Elliott Bay by canoe, sloop or schooner. The mail route between Olympia and Seattle was contracted out to anyone willing to take it on. In 1852-53 Robert Moxlie carried the mail from Olympia to the Seattle Post Office weekly by Indian "canoe express." Moxlie's last Indian-canoe mail run was on August 15, 1853, and brought 22 letters and 14 newspapers to the Elliott Bay settlers. Throughout the rest of the 1850s and 1860s, the *Eliza Anderson* carried the mail to the pioneer settlements. Letters and newspapers cost 25 cents postage. The rate dropped to 10 cents by the end of the 1850s.

legislation, proving up the claim in order to receive clear title required hard manual labor and money. Cash was in short supply for most pioneers, and opportunities to earn cash even more scarce. Clearing land, logging and mill work were the main types of paid work available. Most of the men spent part of their year logging and clearing land for hire—the same work they did the rest of the year on their own claims. Joseph and Stephen Foster turned to logging shortly after establishing their homesteads. The brothers, together with neighbor Abe Bryant, were among the half dozen men who carried the first log into Yesler's mill in Seattle on hand spikes. This was a historic moment, for it marked the beginning of one of greatest periods of lumbering in American history.

Yesler's mill was an important place to the men on the Duwamish because it was where most of them made their money—either selling logs to Yesler or working for Yesler as mill hands. Louis Wyckoff served as Yesler's mill engineer for a time. Ships visiting Elliott Bay left their cargoes of food, tools and supplies on Yesler's wharf, and picked up lumber and local products for export. Settlers all around Elliott Bay, including those up the Duwamish, set their clocks by the Yesler's mill whistle.

The limited job situation rapidly changed as sawmills proliferated. Tobin's sawmill on the Black River offered the valley men work. Joseph Foster and William Gilliam formed their own logging company around 1856 and hired others to cut and haul logs to the sawmill. In addition to selling logs, the company produced squared timbers, shingles and pilings, all hand-hewn with a broadax.

While most of the settlers were engaging in simple farming in the small cleared areas, the Collinses nursery stock venture was thriving. The rich river-bottom soil of the Duwamish was astonishingly fertile. In 1859 the papers reported that L. M. Collins had cabbages weighing close to 50 pounds each, turnips weighing in at 30 pounds each and beets 12 pounds each. Another grower produced a 29-pound beet. Perhaps the Collinses took up application of chopped kelp as fertilizer, an agricultural method introduced by Doc Maynard that greatly increased production.

Most of the pioneers brought with them tools and supplies to get started with, but it was not practical to bring much either by wagon or by ship. Thus, all of the settlers sooner or later bought supplies, tools and animals. The first mercantile enterprise in King County was John Low's and Charles Terry's store, the New York Markook [Trading] House, located at Alki. Purchases were paid for by barter or one of the various types of international currency that served as legal tender in the territory. Charles Prosch reports that he observed in common usage in the 1850s fifty-dollar octagonal gold slugs, Spanish doubloons, Oregon-made Beaver Money, U.S. silver dollars, and almost everything else that was of large denominations and circulated in other parts of the world. The first recorded account for the New York mercantile is with the Collinses. It appears that as soon as the doors were open Diana sent Luther over to pick

LIFE ON THE DUWAMISH IN THE 1850S

FOOD AND SUPPLIES, 1857 PRICES	
Pork, per lb.	20¢
Flour, per 100 lbs.	$10.00
Potatoes, per bushel	$3.00
Butter, per lb.	$1.00
Onions, per bushel	$4.00
Eggs, per dozen	$1.00
Beets, per bushel	$3.50
Sugar, per lb.	12½¢
Coffee, per lb.	18¢
Tea, per lb.	75¢ and 1.00
Molasses, per gallon	50¢ and 75¢
Salmon, per lb.	10¢
Whiskey, per gallon	$1.00
Sawed lumber, fir, per M	$20.00
Shingles, per M	$4.25 to 5.00
Pilings, per foot	5¢ to 8¢
Square timber, per foot	12¢ to 15¢

Published in the *Olympian*, October 3, 1857

up six pans, one large and two small water pails, six pint basins, two frying pans, a coffee pot, a pair of candlesticks and a dipper.

WEDDINGS AND OUTINGS

Among the settlers who came to the valley after 1852 were a few single women, who were quickly courted by the numerous bachelors. Five of the bachelors married within ten years of arrival: Timothy Grow married Elizabeth Johns, February 9, 1854; Dr. Samuel L. Grow (Tim's brother) married Eveline M. Avery (daughter of neighbor John Avery), February 7, 1855; Henry Van Asselt married Catherine Maple, December 25, 1862; Joseph Foster married Martha Steele, June 23, 1865; and William Gilliam married Mary Jane Russell Murphy, May 1, 1873. Tim and Elizabeth Grow's son, Louis Kossuth Grow, born in 1855, was the first child born of the union of two Duwamish pioneers who met, courted and married on the banks of the river.

The same month Tim and Elizabeth were married by C. C. Lewis, Justice of the Peace, White River Valley settlers John Thomas and Mary Ann Russell were married. The groom's wedding suit was made by Joseph Foster at his neighbor Louis Wyckoff's blacksmith shop on First Avenue, Seattle. Foster improvised a table of planks on sawhorses and heated the goose, or tailor's iron, on the forge. In spite of the conditions, Foster managed to turn out a fine outfit which was distinguished as the first suit of clothes made in King County.

The first decade on the Duwamish was marked by more work than play. However, the long months of unremitting work and isolation were occasionally broken by joyous social gatherings, all the more intense because of their rarity. The winter weddings were a delight, and summer picnics soon became a tradition.

One of the earliest large regional gatherings was the King County Fourth of July celebration held at Alki in 1853. It was a grand day, with the Duwamish settlers starting out early in the morning by canoes for Alki. The day officially began with a 21-gun salute. Much excited visiting took place as old friendships were renewed and new acquaintances made. A picnic dinner was shared in a grove, followed by a reading of the Declaration of Independence and remarks by several speakers. As the summer twilight faded into night, the pioneers forgot their days of hard work and remembered happy gatherings of other places and other times. They danced until late into the night on an improvised dance floor of split logs, to the strains of fiddles and guitars that had somehow survived the rough trip to Puget Sound. Most of the settlers living up and down the Sound, including those from the Duwamish, spent the night at Alki, preferring to make the trip back home in daylight with a favorable tide to help them up the river.

CHURCH AND SCHOOL

The Duwamish community had children from the very beginning. Lucinda and Stephen Collins were the first pioneer children in King County. Cyrus and Polly Lewis had been married eight years when they came to Washington Territory from Miami County, Ohio. They started west with two sons—Ira, five, and Joseph, three. Caroline was born during the journey west. After they settled on their claim, Joseph died, but four more sons and another daughter were born. Widower Ben Johns had seven children left at home after his eldest daughter Elizabeth married. In 1856 there were 11 school-age children, with at least six more who would be ready for school within three to five years. However, more years were to pass before there would be a regular school. Meanwhile, throughout the 1850s, mothers continued to teach their children the "Three Rs" at home.

Along with a desire for a school was the desire for religion. The settlers as a group shared a strong religious conviction and supported the pioneer ministers and priests who came west along with the land seekers. As throughout most of the American western frontier, Methodism was the church of the Duwamish pioneers. The first recorded religious worship service on Elliott Bay was on Sunday, December 4, 1853, in Seattle, with Jacob Maple, Diana Collins and Henry Van Asselt attending. In January 1854 the Church Society was organized, with Jacob Maple, Diana and Luther Collins and Henry Van Asselt providing support. In May of 1855 Rev. David and Catherine Blaine, Seattle's first teacher, paddled up the Duwamish to the White River to evaluate the area as site for a mission. They concluded that there were too few settlers living on the rivers to justify coming out from Seattle to hold regular services. Five years later Rev. D. L. Spaulding regularly paddled up the river from Seattle and held Sunday worship services, complete with sermons, in the largest pioneer cabins.

Indian Relations

While the Duwamish settlers were pleased with their convenient location on the waterways and found the land rich and productive, the large native population living close by proved to be both a help and an ongoing problem. The Indian men were most helpful in providing transportation by canoe and hauling the settlers, produce and goods for a modest fee. The Indian women were friendly with the pioneer women establishing their homes on the river, and the two groups of women learned much from each other in gathering and preserving food and in the treatment of illness.

However, each year there were incidents reflecting tension between the native residents and the newcomers. The settlers were quite alarmed and disturbed by an incident that took place at the mouth of the Duwamish during 1852. G. W. Loomis was driven off of his homestead by an Indian named Grizzly who seized and held his house. A little later, the Pearce brothers' house, close to the Duwamish on

Chief Seattle, Friend of the Settlers

Chief Seattle grew up in the area of Mox la Push. He gained a position of prominence with his people as a result of his success in vanquishing a raiding party of "mountain people" in the vicinity of Fort Dent Park. Chief Seattle was very well acquainted with the settlers in the Duwamish and White river valleys, and was a welcome guest at their gatherings from the 1850s to the 1870s. Legend tells that in honor of the marriage of Henry Van Asselt and Catherine Maple, Jacob Maple's daughter, Chief Seattle and his people celebrated one of the grandest potlatches ever witnessed by the settlers.

Joseph Foster and Chief Seattle formed a close friendship that lasted throughout their lifetime. Seattle's high regard for Foster is demonstrated by his daughter Angeline naming her son Joe Foster, as a namesake for Foster. It was a practice among some of the Indians to name children after prominent white men. Chief Seattle and his grandson lie not far from one another in Squamish, in the local churchyard. Seattle's tombstone is marked Chief Noah Sealth, his baptismal name.

Plummer's Hall, Seattle. When word of the Indian attack on the settlers in the White River Valley reached the Duwamish pioneers, they retreated to Plummer's Hall in Seattle until a sturdy log fort was built. Courtesy Seattle Historical Society.

Elliott Bay, was robbed by an Indian named Tom Peppar and his companions. Next, Samuel Maple's house was plundered. Collins, Van Asselt, the Maples, Joseph and Stephen Foster, George Holt and August Hograve went after the thieves each time Indians stole from the river settlers, and in each case were successful in retrieving their goods without trouble.

As the settlers learned the native people's culture, they were able to deal with problems in less confrontational ways. The women and children were often more successful at this strategy than the men, and took the lead in many cases. Lacking white children for playmates, Lucinda and Stephen Collins had spent a great deal of time with the Indians living on the Nisqually and the Duwamish. The native people were generally fond of children, and often very affectionate toward white children.

It was because of her familiarity with the Indian culture that Lucinda Collins was able to save Henry Van Asselt's life. The trouble began when a certain Indian's dog took up regularly harassing Van Asselt's calf that he kept staked near his cabin. A little short-tempered one day, the Dutchman decided he had enough barking and bawling from the animals, and shot the dog. When 14-year-old Lucinda heard of this she told Van Asselt that there would be great trouble because "You might as well kill the Indian as his dog."

Soon a group of irate Indians arrived looking for Van Asselt. Telling Van Asselt and the other white men, who had gathered, to stay in the cabin, Lucinda went out to talk with the natives. Lucinda knew that the Indians believed that the presence of lead in a person's body imparted supernatural powers. Thus, she told them that Van Asselt had a bullet lodged in his body and that made him invulnerable. She continued, "He is sure with his gun; daylight or dark, sunlight or moonlight, he can shoot and kill." Calling Van Asselt out of the cabin, Lucinda directed him to demonstrate his marksmanship. Throwing his rifle to his shoulder, Van Asselt took aim at a crow passing overhead. His rifle cracked and the bird fell at their feet. From that day on the Indians treated Van Asselt with great respect and honored him as a chief.

WAR BETWEEN THE SETTLERS AND THE NATIVE AMERICANS

From 1855 to 1865 the discovery of gold in various locations throughout the Northwest created a series of little "gold rushes" that drew the men away from their claims for a few months or longer. Farmers from Elliott Bay, who would be erstwhile miners, dropped everything to join the excitement at Colville, Rock Creek, Stehekin, Lillooet, Wenatchee, Florence, Boise, the Fraser and Thompson rivers, and elsewhere. In these locations the streams yielded enough placer gold to bring in thousands of men overnight. These Northwest gold rushes were a factor in precipitating the outbreak of the 1855-56 hostilities between the settlers and Indians. In addition, the appearance of ever-increasing numbers of independent prospectors in eastern Washington, coming from Washington, Oregon and California, was understood by the Indians as an omen of the invasion of white people to come.

In the fall of 1857 the editor of the *Olympian*, who had recently returned from a tour of Puget Sound, observed that King County had suffered more severely in the recent conflict between the settlers and Indians than any other area on the Sound. The settlers in the White River Valley were hit the hardest. The uprising began suddenly in the fall of 1855, taking the settlers by surprise. Hostile Indians went through the White River Valley killing the adults, burning buildings, fences and crops, and driving off the livestock. The lives of children were spared in many cases. News of the White River Massacre, as the settlers called it, was hastily carried to the Duwamish homesteaders by a friendly Indian who warned them of the impending danger. They ran to their canoes and fled to Seattle, where they joined others at Plummer's Hall, which served as the village stronghold. A fort was quickly built, and the women and children lived there throughout the winter of 1855-56.

Meanwhile, the men served in the volunteer defense troops. There were two groups: C. C. Hewitt's Company H, organized and active from October 25, 1855, to January 25, 1856; and Lander's Company A, active from February 9, 1856, to July 29, 1856. Many of the men, like William Gilliam, first served in Hewitt's Company H until it disbanded in January, and then signed up with Lander. Luther Collins served as a volunteer, and in his usual rough, highly independent and unorthodox personal style engaged in taking of "Siwash tufts of hair," i.e., Indian scalps, as trophies of those he had killed. This practice was not condoned by the military officers or the other settlers. Late in 1855 the *Traveler* steamed up the Duwamish to the junction of the rivers, transporting the men of Company H and towing six large canoes loaded with provisions. This is the first recorded riverboat trip up the Duwamish.

Joseph Foster immediately joined the volunteers and served throughout the entire war as a packer and scout. At the outbreak of the hostilities he went to Fort Steilacoom and served under Lieut. Nugent and also Lieut. Slaughter (for whom present-day Auburn, Washington, was originally named). He was with the forces of Capt. Malloy at Connell's Prairie, near Auburn, where several men were killed in a skirmish with the Indians. Foster was returning from a military pack trip over the rough Naches Pass trail when the conflict on Elliott Bay came to a close.

Although the hostilities between the settlers and Indians ended on Puget Sound in the summer of 1856, in August of 1857 the early Duwamish River explorer Col. Ebey was killed by Indians at his homestead on Whidbey Island to avenge the cold-blooded murder of a prominent Indian chief near Olympia by settlers. The conflict did not end in eastern Washington Territory until the fall of 1858. The settlers did not rest easy for many years after this trouble.

AFTERMATH OF THE HOSTILITIES

It was estimated by contemporaries that between 1850 and 1862 more than 2,000 white people—settlers, miners, trappers and others—were killed in conflicts with the native population in the Northwest. The number of Indians killed is unknown. The hostilities with the Indians drove a good number of settlers away. By the end of 1860, four years after the official end of the hostilities on Puget Sound, King County had neither regained its population nor recovered from its losses. Thus, the population in 1860 was not substantially larger than it had been in 1854.

The war was very costly to the Duwamish pioneers. The trouble had broken out in October, and most of the harvest was lost through burning or plundering. The Collinses had just harvested their peaches. After the outbreak of the hostilities, the three Maples and Henry Van Asselt hid by day and tended their crops by night, in order to be able to realize a harvest in spite of the war conditions. Many people went two years without a harvest, since by the time the government decided that the conflict had been resolved and discharged the volunteers from Lander's Company A in late July 1856, it was too late to plant a crop. They managed to get through the winter of 1856 foraging from the land, river and sea.

By the winter of 1856 most of the settlers had returned to their claims. The Collins family

LIFE ON THE DUWAMISH IN THE 1850S

Fort Dent. In March of 1856 simple forts were constructed along the Duwamish River, with Fort Duwamish being near the mouth of the Duwamish, and Fort Dent at Mox la Push, the confluence of the rivers. The forts were built to provide a place of refuge for the settlers if hostilities flared up again. The river forts were never used for defense, and by the 1950s all vestiges of the forts were gone. Artist's conception by Don Paulson.

had been the last to leave at the outbreak and were the first to return to their claim. Some people did not return to the valley, preferring to live in Seattle, where they felt it was safer. Others left the Puget Sound area. All of the married couples with families returned to the valley. Damage claim records filed with the territorial government record that the following Duwamish settlers had their homesteads burned by the Indians: the Brownells, the Collinses, the Lewises, Ben Johns, the Maples, the Grow brothers, William Gilliam, Joseph Foster, Henry Adams, and Henry Meader. The record includes details of the damage claims. For example, Luther and Diana Collins' reported loss was $2,873 for house, furniture, outbuildings, livestock and miscellaneous. Almost everyone filed claims for the loss of house and furnishings.

Regardless of the loss of the improvements, the land remained and the young orchards were bravely growing. The settlers lost their buildings and livestock, but they still had their hands and hopes for the future. For the most part they were filled with energy and optimism, and set to work once again to create a Euro-American civilization in the wilderness they were taking from the native people. Now men and women alike carried their rifles with them when they went to the fields to plow and sow, tend their orchards, or draw water from the river. The land responded as before, and the newspapers reported bumper crops harvested in the autumn of 1860.

Fraser River Stampede

In 1858 rich gold fields were discovered on the Fraser River in Canada. This gold rush drew more men from King County in 1858-59 than the other regional gold rushes. Arthur Denny and Henry Yesler organized a King County party of 82 men, which was unsuccessful in getting farther than the Wenatchee country because of trouble with the Indians. Joseph Foster and his friend Tom Prather fared better. They chose to travel all the way to the gold fields by steamer. Enjoying good luck, the pair of adventurers spent a few profitable months in the placer country and returned to Puget Sound in the autumn in time for Foster to take up his duties as a freshman member of the Territorial Legislature in Olympia. Two Duwamish pioneers lost their lives in the 1860s while searching for gold in Idaho: Luther Collins died in 1862 on the Snake River during the Boise gold rush, and John Holgate died in 1868.

Fredrick Dent, for whom Fort Dent was named, was in the Northwest only briefly, during the spring of 1856. Dent was closely associated with General U.S. Grant throughout his life, serving as Grant's aide-de-camp during the Civil War and personal secretary at the White House. Being married to Julia Grant, Dent was also Grant's brother-in-law. Courtesy Library of Congress.

Duwamish Pioneers 1850-1862— Historically Significant Events

June 21, 1851 — Collins scouting party reaches the Meadows on the Duwamish River. Collins party plants potatoes—first settlers' crop in King County.

First settlers arrive in King County: Diana Borst Collins and Luther M. Collins with children Lucinda and Stephen; Jacob Maple, and Samuel Maple and Henry Van Asselt.

Summer 1851 — First livestock brought into King County by Collins pioneer party.

March 1853 — Monticello Convention establishes Washington Territory. Luther M. Collins appointed representative from King County, Oregon Territory.

Luther Collins appointed one of two first King County Commissioners.

April 1853 — Joseph & Stephen Foster homestead in the Duwamish Valley.

Feb. 9, 1854 — Elizabeth Johns and Timothy Grow married—first marriage in the Duwamish Valley.

1855 — First road in King County, the Duwamish River Road, built by the Duwamish pioneers.

1855 — Louis Kossuth Grow born—first child born in the Duwamish Valley.

1858 — Joseph Foster, Democrat, representative from King County, begins first term in Washington Territorial Legislature.

1858 — First discovery of coal in King County, by Dr. M. Bigelow and Luther Collins, on the Black River.

1862 — Van Asselt School opens—first public school in King County.

CHAPTER 3
THE 1860S—BUILDING HOMESTEADS, FAMILIES AND COMMUNITY

Susannah and Milton Robbins' homestead located in the area of S. 131 St. and Military Road was unique for its position high on the hillside, later known as Riverton Heights. After being flooded out of their riverside cabin in 1866, Susannah concluded it was hazardous living in the valley bottom. L to R: unknown man, Milton Robbins, Susannah Steele Robbins and youngest son Clement, ca. 1870. The Robbinses' large log house survived into the early twentieth century. From C. Bagley, History of King County.

The Fraser River gold rush of 1858 brought energy and activity back to King County. Since the people streaming to Seattle from the gold fields were almost all men, the scarcity of women was more pronounced than ever. The 1860 census reported 310 settlers in King County, 180 of whom lived in Seattle. In the entire county there were 37 married couples and 71 children. Single men numbered 137 compared to 14 single women—almost ten single men for every unmarried woman. Most were American born; only one settler out of ten was an immigrant, with Ireland, Germany and England being the predominant countries of origin.

THE DECADE BEGINS WITH THANKSGIVING

On November 9, 1860, Territorial Governor Henry M. McGill proclaimed November 29th "as the day of Thanksgiving and praise to Almighty God." As the rain fell outside, the settlers from the Duwamish Valley and lower White River Valley gathered together to sit down to their Thanksgiving Day celebration. In solemn yet joyous terms, they gave thanks for their health, prosperity, and preservation through earthquakes, cold winters, conflicts with the native people, and many other trials. There was much to be thankful for. Most of the pioneers had been in the Duwamish Valley at least five years, and some nearly ten. Houses, barns and fences had been built and rebuilt after the 1855 war. The crops, herds and orchards were growing, and children had been born. The settlers believed in their future and that of the Northwest.

While the settlers found the bounty of nature in the Northwest to be astonishingly rich, they were perplexed by the climate, so temperate, yet at times harsh. The winter of 1861 was one to remember. The normally mild winter weather disappeared just before the Christmas holidays, when snow began falling. When it stopped snowing the mercury dropped to four degrees below zero, where it stayed for days. The shallow lake located on Louis Wyckoff's claim at Mox la Push, named White Lake by the settlers, froze solid for half a foot, and was enjoyed by ice skaters until two more feet of snow fell. Travel on the river naturally stopped, and the settlers were cabinbound until the river thawed enough to navigate. The pioneers always recalled this season as the "Big Winter."

Joseph Foster's Legislative Work in the 1860s

The severe winter weather, however, did not keep Joseph Foster from getting to Olympia to take his seat in the legislature as the representative from King County. Now in his second term, Foster had confidence and experience, and demonstrated the progressive vision and effective leadership that were to mark his long political career. In 1860 Foster sponsored H.M. No. 1, which provided for the construction of the Military Road from Seattle via Snoqualmie Pass to Fort Colville. Through Foster's personal efforts the bill passed both houses that session.

Another piece of legislation sponsored by Foster in the 1860 session that significantly shaped Washington history was a bill to locate the Territorial University in Seattle. Foster initially had concluded that it was better for the future of King County to have the Territorial capitol located in Seattle rather than the University. But after a conversation about the long-term implications with Rev. Daniel Bagley in the winter of 1860, Foster changed his mind and saw to the passage of a bill locating the University in Seattle.

In the 1890s, as the original pioneers looked back over the years since the beginning of settlement, a debate raged over who was "the father of the University of Washington." Arthur Denny said he was, and others gave Joseph Foster the credit. Foster made the following public statement, which reflects his characteristically confident yet modest approach to issues of his day:

> I think I should be in a position to know all about the question as to who has the best right to be called the "Father of the University of Washington." I introduced the bill in the Legislature locating the university at Seattle. I got the bill passed and signed. Who, then, knows more about it than I do? Before the Legislature adjourned I came home on a visit and talked with everybody interested. I remember two men out of the lot. I met Arthur A. Denny and he and I agreed that my bill was a good thing, because we could trade that university off in one or two years and thereby get the territorial capitol for Seattle.
>
> When I met Daniel Bagley, I told him of the nice little plan that Mr. Denny and I had in view—Bagley knocked that plan into a cocked hat in about two minutes. He said to me, 'Nonsense, Joe, don't do anything of the kind. You've got something far better than a capitol. You go back to Olympia and get John Webster, Edmund Carr and me appointed regents or commissioners and I will show you that a university is better than a capitol.'
>
> He talked to me more on that line and got me convinced, so I went to Olympia and did what he asked me to. Bagley worked like a Turk on that job and built the University of Washington in a year. He handled the whole business, and if the University has got a father, his name is Daniel Bagley.

Postal Service and County Political Activity

In 1863 there were four voting precincts in King County. Mox la Push precinct was divided in two, with the lower

THE 1860s—BUILDING HOMESTEADS, FAMILIES AND COMMUNITY

Duwamish Valley becoming Duwamish precinct, which was also the name of the postal substation established under the Black River Post Office, one of four post offices in the county. The upper Duwamish Valley and lower White River area, as well as the Black River, continued to be Mox la Push. By 1869 there were seven precincts in the county, with Mox la Push precinct ranking third in number of cast votes, following Seattle and White River.

Throughout the 1860s the river settlers continued to actively participate in King County government. In 1860 Henry Adams served on the county grand jury. Following in the footsteps of Luther Collins, who first filled the office, in 1866 C. C. Lewis was appointed King County Road Inspector and Joseph Foster served as county election judge. In the 1860s Duwamish Valley residents assumed major county offices with Louis Wyckoff, keeping order as King County Sheriff. As King County Commissioner, William H. Gilliam used a two-story warehouse built by Yesler on the south side of his wharf for the commission house. The next year Gilliam was appointed Seattle Postmaster and located the post office in the same building. Both of these men continued to be residents of the valley as they worked in Seattle. They were, in fact, the first Duwamish Valley commuters. Undoubtedly, their trips between Seattle and their valley homes were not daily. Eventually Wyckoff sold his land, but Gilliam kept his homestead until his death.

Local communication made major strides when the first local newspaper started up, with the premier issue of the *Seattle Gazette* (later the *Seattle Intelligencer*) appearing just before Christmas 1863. King County residents were truly connected to the rest of the United States when telegraph lines were run up the coast from California by the Union Telegraph Company. In the Puget Sound region, the lines followed the Military Road and then cut across the Duwamish Valley on Joseph Steele's and Joseph Foster's land. The first telegram was sent from Seattle on October 26, 1864.

PIONEER ROAD BUILDING

When the settlers returned to their farms after the open conflict with the Indians ended in 1856, they were determined to build roads connecting the settlements along the Sound to assure safety and progress. The Duwamish River Road, little more than a widened trail at first, linked the Duwamish Valley with Seattle around 1855. Overland travel to Seattle further improved with the building of County Road No. 14, popularly known as the "Beach Road." Proposed by Doc Maynard, the road ran from Main Street in Seattle, south along the base of Beacon Hill, which was the beach at that time, to meet the Alki Road near the mouth of the Duwamish. For years this was the route taken by east- and south-bound travelers leaving Seattle. The section of the Military Road linking Seattle—and the Duwamish Valley—to Fort Steilacoom was completed in 1860.

Throughout the 1860s the Duwamish pioneers backed a series of road petitions, including one for Road No. 8, to connect territorial roads located between the White and Black rivers; Road No. 13, to connect the Seattle-Black River Road with the Duwamish River Road; Road No. 19, to connect the Seattle-Martins Ferry Road with the Seattle-Steilacoom Territorial Road; Road No. 20, petitioned for by C. C. Lewis, to connect his and Lemuel and John Holgate's claims with the Black River Bridge.

Building roads using animal and manpower in the rugged terrain of the Puget Sound basin was slow and laborious. The first roads followed ancient Indian paths, which were also game trails for the abundant animal population. After much work by the settlers these trails were transformed into dirt roads about eight feet wide—wide enough for a single wagon—with passing turnouts at intervals. The first Rule of the Road passed in King County in 1869 required vehicles meeting on a road to turn out to the right. Roads built where drainage was poor,

TUKWILA—COMMUNITY AT THE CROSSROADS

From 1860 to 1916 Military Road was the only road linking Seattle with Fort Steilacoom, Tacoma and Vancouver. This important route passed through the Duwamish Valley. Note the turnout on the left. If two wagons met on the narrow road, one had to back up to such a turnout to allow the other to pass. Photo by Asahel Curtis, courtesy Washington State Historical Society.

e.g., low-lying areas including river bottomland, were constructed as puncheon or "corduroy" roads. The prepared road bed was "corduroyed" with split logs placed across stringers laid down on the soft and often muddy earth. Such roads were expensive to build and maintain. The uneven surface was hard on draft animals, wagons and drivers alike. As parts of the puncheon rotted out, holes developed where a horse or ox could easily break a leg or suddenly throw a wagon off balance, turning it over. For all their shortcomings, corduroy roads in the timber-rich Puget Sound country were the most practical solution for the seriously muddy roads. However, hand-built roads required many hands.

Road construction crews were created by legislation requiring all able-bodied males between the ages of 18 and 50, excepting ministers, to work on the roads three days a year. The King County Road Supervisor accepted road construction labor in lieu of cash for property taxes. One day of labor was exacted for each $1,000 property valuation. Taxpayers worked on road construction wherever the county needed them until 1867, when they were required to serve only in their own districts. In addition to roads, labor was needed for bridge construction and maintenance.

Dozens of small and large streams flowed down the hillsides into the Duwamish and

The 1860s—Building Homesteads, Families and Community

White rivers. People crossed streams on logs or people waded through the cold water. As time permitted, simple corduroy bridges were built across the more treacherous streams. These bridges were not of a solid construction and quickly developed holes, which led to accidents. In 1871, as a result of too many accidents caused by galloping horses, the King County Commissioners prohibited travelers from moving faster than a walk over county bridges. This was the second road ordinance in King County.

Dozens of cedar log bridges were built by the valley pioneers. First, long cedar logs were laid across the stream. Next, short slabs of cedar were laid like ties across the logs. In the early bridges the entire structure was somewhat makeshift, with the base poles placed on the ground and cross-ties simply laid unsecured on top. Sometimes soil was thrown over this in an attempt to make the road smoother. In rainy weather the surface of a corduroy bridge was dangerous. In all kinds of weather the driver had to watch carefully when crossing such a bridge so that an animal's foot or a wagon wheel did not sink into a hole, or that the bridge poles did not fly up under the weight of the wagon. Being more sure-footed, oxen were less nervous on these roads than horses. Courtesy King County Public Works Dept.

The Black River Bridge

The first substantial bridge across a major river flowing into Puget Sound in King County was the Black River Bridge, which allowed the Military Road to cross the river on Joseph Foster's land at Mox la Push via a connecting road. The $60 appropriated for this project in 1863 were the first funds on record designated for bridge construction in the county. The historic bridge was built in the summer of 1867 by Shorey and Russell, contractors. The Black River Bridge was built high above the water's surface to permit the passage of boats. The 20-foot-high abutments were of cedar logs, and the stringers spanning the river were 75 feet long. The entire structure was very strong and was a credit to the engineering and construction skill of the contractors. The *Seattle Intelligencer* glowingly reported, "King County may now boast of a good, if not the best, bridge in the Territory." The Black River Bridge was the sole bridge over the upper Duwamish for 36 years. Until the construction of a series of bridges in the opening years of the twentieth century, other river crossings were by ferry.

Duwamish River Ferries

The first verified ferry service on the Duwamish River was begun by Cyrus C. Lewis in 1855, in support of the Duwamish River Road. The next year Lewis applied for a ferry license together with neighbor Bennett Johns, whose claim lay directly across the river from Lewis's. Johns soon lost interest in the enterprise and Lewis carried on alone. When the Military Road was completed from Fort Steilacoom to Seattle in 1860, it linked with the Duwamish River Road near Orillia and crossed at the C. C. Lewis ferry. Lewis's Landing was a focal point of valley activity, being the only crossroads where travelers could shift from water to road travel if they so desired. Around 1864 Lewis sold 120 acres of his river bottom to Joseph Foster, and the tract with the ferry to Joseph Steele. From this time on, Lewis's ferry and riverboat landing were known as the Steele Landing. The Steele ferry was generally operated by sons James and John; however, whenever the boys were not around to run the ferry, daughters Martha and Emily handily operated the ferryboat and regularly carried travelers across the river.

Eventually there were other ferries on the Duwamish and White rivers. As riverboat travel increased, ferry landings became public boat landings. At the height of riverboat activity there were about a dozen established landings on

Martha Steele Foster's brothers James and John Steele were in their early teens when they came to the valley with their parents. They grew up on the Steele Landing homestead at Foster Point. One of their responsibilities as growing boys was operating the ferry that had been established by C. C. Lewis in 1855. After establishing a farm in the Sunnydale area, near his niece Jane Fenton Kelly, James Steele came back to the family homestead after the elder Steeles passed away and was farming there when Tom Clark came in 1897. Courtesy the Robbins family.

the Duwamish and White rivers. Verified landings in the historic study area are Orillia, Black River Junction, the C. C. Lewis/J. Steele Landing (changed hands in 1864), the Meadows Landing, and a lower Duwamish landing near Myrtle Street in Georgetown (historic name unknown). There are references in the written record to ferries under the names Keller and Martin. However, at the time of writing the location of these ferries was not known. Some believe that there was a landing in the vicinity of the James Nelsen farm. This has not been verified.

Clarence Bagley, who observed the Duwamish-White River ferryboats firsthand while delivering mail in the valley in the 1860s and 1870s, described them as follows:

> Wooden scows, large enough to carry a farm wagon and a team of horses were used, with the river currents as sole power. A cable was stretched across the stream, and to this cable was attached a trolley, usually with two pulleys. A rope tied to each end of the ferry was led around a wheel in the center of the scow. By turning this wheel and quartering to the current, the ferryman was able to get his heavy scow across the river. This method was common to the entire western United States, wherever the stream was sufficiently narrow to admit stretching a rope from bank to bank.

The county charged a $2 fee for the first ferry operator's license in 1855. Five years later a license cost $6. In 1861 C. C. Lewis paid $12.50 for a license. It appears that most of the ferry operators charged essentially the same fares, although there is evidence of occasional attempts to attract trade by fare cutting. For example, in 1873 the Black River Ferry fares were half the going rates for teams and wagons and for extra horses. It is possible that because of their relatively greater volume of passengers, arising from their location at the river junction, they could afford to charge less.

RIVER FERRY FARE SCHEDULE, 1875

Pair of horses, wagon and driver .... 50¢
Each additional pair of horses .... 50¢
One horse, wagon (or buggy),
    and driver .... 37½¢
Horse and rider .... 25¢
Foot passenger or
    wagon passengers .... 12½¢
Loose cattle or horses .... 6½¢
Loose sheep, hogs, goats .... 2½¢

THE 1860s—BUILDING HOMESTEADS, FAMILIES AND COMMUNITY

In service 1868-80, the Comet *was part of Captain Sam Randolph's fleet of boats and the most successful of the riverboats because of her flat-bottom design. Catherine Randolph, the skipper's wife, served as superintendent of construction in their boat company and oversaw the design and construction of the* Comet *and named it, possibly inspired by the historic visit of Halley's Comet. Artist's conception by Don Paulson.*

THE HEYDAY OF THE RIVERBOATS

By the late 1860s there were enough people living in the river valleys to encourage enterprising boat owners to provide regular riverboat service to Elliott Bay. The river steamer immediately became the main form of transportation. During the heyday of the steamboats there were at least five or six boats regularly navigating the rivers including the *Lily*, the *Gem*, the *Black Diamond* and the *Winette*. Probably the best known of the old-time riverboats were the steamers *Comet* and *Lily*. The riverboat was normally a flat-bottomed boat, from 65 to 75 feet long, that was navigable in as little as 18 inches of water. Basically a scow, it was awkward to maneuver. Since the river was too narrow upstream for the boats to turn around, the trip downstream was made stern first, with the boat being carried along by the current.

Riverboat service tended to follow the seasons. The heaviest loads were shipped during winter high water. As the river became shallower in early summer, the boats were towed by horses along the treeless banks. It was commonplace for a riverboat to run aground in a shallow area. The boat would be freed with ropes pulled by men on shore. Every boat was equipped with long poles to push the boat free when it was

TUKWILA—COMMUNITY AT THE CROSSROADS

grounded. In the dry summer months traffic halted completely.

The round trip from Seattle to Black River Junction took about two days, including tying up at night. Night travel on the winding, shallow course, marked by mud bars and log snags, was an invitation for trouble. Schedules were very approximate, since every trip was susceptible to unpredictable problems such as running aground, or hitting deadheads and snags. Skippers adopted the custom of dragging their anchors going downstream as a dredging technique to help deepen the channel and keep it clear.

No one was very much concerned with exact schedules at that time, and the riverboats made their trips according to when the skipper and crew were ready to go. A riverboat would tie up at any farm where it was flagged down to pick up or deliver mail, take aboard potatoes, hops or other farm produce, and board passengers. Each trip was hazardous. A sunken log might put a hole in the hull that could result in the loss of an entire load of coal or farm produce. In the early 1870s a scow carrying a good number of hogs had a hole ripped in its hull when the boat hit a log. As the cargo deck sank, the squealing cargo "jumped ship" and scrambled up the muddy banks. It is reported that wild pig hunting became a popular pastime thereabouts in the next few years.

The riverboat skippers and valley farmers had a friendly, personal, informal relationship. Capt. C. G. True was a skipper with a good sense of humor who enjoyed his work. The story goes that one time, around 1874, Captain True was on his way down the river when a woman on the bank called out for him to hold up because she had produce she wanted to send to market in Seattle, including fresh eggs. Alas, she was short a few eggs to make an even dozen and wanted the skipper to wait while her hens laid the needed eggs. "All right," Capt. True cheerily called back, as he cut his engines, "but tell them hens to hurry!" And thus did he hold up his boat in the middle of the river for three quarters of an hour while the hens did their work. The congenial skippers often took on special errands for the river homemakers, such as picking up thread or matching a piece of broadcloth at the stores in Seattle.

In addition to business benefits, the riverboats allowed for easy travel and communication between settlers previously isolated, and river valley dwellers became more involved with each other's interests and cares. The story goes that a boatload of people from the upper White River asked Capt. Sam Jackson to stop his steamer at the Maples' place so that they could all see Eliza Jane and John Wesley Maple's new twin girls they had heard so much about.

Because the riverboats were large and could be anchored almost anywhere, they were rented for meetings, church services and wedding parties. The flat bottom of the boat made a perfect, if occasionally splintery, dance floor, and the fiddlers would position themselves at the side of the boat while the dancers whirled around the deck in reels and polkas. Being on the water did pose hazards, however. According to one account, at a riverboat wedding held in the vicinity of Tukwila Hill around 1880, a drunken guest fell overboard and drowned before he could be rescued.

The narrow-gauge Seattle-Walla Walla Railroad, connecting Renton and Seattle, drew traffic away from the river in the late 1870s, and by the time the Northern Pacific came through the valley into Seattle in 1887 the steamers had ceased running regular schedules, although the river continued to be used for shipping.

THE MAPLE-VAN ASSELT WEDDING

The Duwamish Valley community received a major addition at the end of 1862 when Jacob Maple, 68, returned from eight years in Iowa with his extended family, daughter Mary Ann, her husband Martin Cavanaugh and two-year-old daughter, Tabitha, single daughters Catherine and Lucinda, and son John Wesley. The group arrived in late November, after more than seven months on

The 1860s—Building Homesteads, Families and Community

the trail. The new land-grant legislation, the Homestead Act of 1862, had motivated people to go west in spite of the conflict of the Civil War. The Maple-Cavanaugh party traveled with a wagon train that included nearly 400 people. Martin Cavanaugh had been elected wagon master.

After a late June start, the wagon train had been beset with troubles all the way including Indian attacks, illness and food shortages. Crossing the Cascades in early winter was just one additional agony for the group. An example of their problems was the death of one of the oxen, necessitating pressing a gentle milk cow into draft-animal service. Although it might seem like a small problem, in fact pairing the two animals made for difficult, slow travel. The ox, seasoned to pull a heavy wagon under all variety of conditions, was bred for large bones and big muscles, while the cow was a much lighter built dairy animal with no experience pulling. At long last the party arrived at Eli Maple's doorstep, their clothes in rags and with only $1.75 to their names. Moreover, Mary Ann was in an advanced stage of pregnancy; she gave birth on New Year's Day, six weeks after their arrival.

It was commonplace for women to undertake the strenuous pioneer overland trip either while pregnant or with a new babe at the breast. Ezra Meeker, who set out on the Oregon Trail in the late 1840s, when the trail was still very rough, with his 17-year-old wife and 5-week-old infant, commented: "The birth of children was not an infrequent incident on the plains, the almost universal report following, 'mother and babe doing as well as could be expected,' the trip being resumed with but very short interruption, the little one soon being exhibited with the usual motherly pride."

Exhausted and emaciated as the Maple-Cavanaugh newcomers were, 45-year-old Henry Van Asselt saw Catherine Jane Maple as the woman of his dreams, who would end his 20 years of bachelor solitude, and promptly fell in love with her. They were married five weeks later on Christmas Day, 1862. Judge Thomas Mercer performed the ceremony, and Mary Ann and Martin Cavanaugh stood up for the couple. The couple had three daughters and one son. Van Asselt lived to be 85, and Catherine lived to 95.

The uniting of the families of these two original Duwamish Valley pioneers was marked by a grand celebration. Almost everyone living in the area of the Duwamish, Black and White rivers attended, and many came out from Seattle. Chief Seattle came, accompanied by 700 of his people, all in festive attire and bearing many wonderful gifts, as was the Duwamish people's tradition when they attended such a party. The Indians were very interested in this wedding, which they viewed as bonding the families of two "chiefs." In acknowledgment of their early friendship with Chief Seattle, Jacob Maple stood formally with daughter Catherine and his old friend Henry Van Asselt in front of the fireplace, where they all shook hands with and received the blessings and gifts of Chief Seattle. They remained in the receiving line many hours as hundreds of Indians filed through the room and "look[ed] with awe at the white squaw, or *klootchman*, who had become the wife of their friend Henry Van Asselt."

The lavish wedding dinner included venison, turkey, duck, fish, clams, potatoes and corn. The generous Indians had brought large amounts of food to add to the feast. The dinner was followed by a wedding dance with squares, the Virginia Reel, Threading the Needle, the Opera Reel, Weaving the Wheat and other popular dances of the day. Around 2:00 a.m. Van Asselt gave out and fainted on the dance floor but undeterred, the merrymakers continued dancing to past three o'clock.

It was often said that those living on the Duwamish from the middle 1860s, Jacob Maple had close to the controlling interest in Duwamish Valley land through his sons and daughters and their husbands: Samuel Maple, Eli Maple, John Wesley Maple, Catherine and Henry Van Asselt, Mary Ann and Martin

Cavanaugh, and Lucinda, married to Daniel Schneider. As soon as Jacob Maple arrived with his extended family of ten adults and three children, the Maple clan became a focal point of community activity. Their main farmstead was in the area of what has become Boeing Field.

THE CIVIL WAR

When the Civil War broke out in 1861 on the other side of the continent, it did not seem possible that the small group of Americans living in the wilderness bordering Puget Sound's salty waters could be affected. This was not the case. Instead of going to the frontier to homestead, young unmarried males were conscripted to fight the War between the States, and the steady influx of newcomers slowed to a trickle. The Duwamish Valley settlers numbered at least as many as in 1855; however, Seattle was noticeably quieter.

As news of the Civil War came to King County via letters and months-old newspapers, some concerned citizens felt that "a military organization among themselves was a matter of importance in these stirring times." A self-armed, self-governed, private company called the King County Rifles was organized at Seattle on November 19, 1861. The group consisted of 60 men and eight officers. Henry Van Asselt served as Sergeant and several valley pioneers joined him. In fact, the group was meant to be a warning to possible local Rebel sympathizers, and focused on promoting and strengthening pro-Union sentiment.

The Civil War became a key issue in King County politics at this time, with Joseph Foster at the center of the controversy because of his pacifist stance. When Foster was elected King County's representative to the Legislature in December 1863, he was noted to be "a good Union man." Not everyone in the territory supported the Union point of view. Many of the pioneers originated from the Deep South or near border states such as Indiana or Ohio.

In June of 1864, a controversy raged in Washington over what should be the Territorial Legislature's official stand on the Civil War. A series of resolutions were proposed endorsing Mr. Lincoln's wartime actions, including "honesty and patriotism, the suspension of the writ of habeas corpus, and the emancipation proclamation," as well as Lincoln's war measures. Joseph Foster criticized the resolutions for their promotion of the war, suggesting that the legislature refrain from taking a stand on the war and let everyone be guided by his conscience. The territorial newspaper the *Standard* reported that "Mr. Foster, by way of showing his contempt for the Administration [Lincoln's] and its war measures, did move to strike out all the resolutions and insert the Ten Commandments." The vote was 13 for adoption of the resolutions and 10 against.

That year Foster was the sole candidate put forth by the Democratic Party in King County. The editor of the *Seattle Gazette* believed Foster's reelection would signify that the majority of King County's citizens were opposed to the prosecution of the war, and in sympathy with the rebellion. He wrote on June 4, 1864, "We have hitherto regarded King County as loyal to the Government, notwithstanding the election of a 'Peace Democrat' to the Legislature; consequently, we shall await the result of the pending election with no ordinary solicitude." Foster handily carried King County, which was staunchly Republican at that time, as he would again and again in the coming years.

In the autumn of 1864, concern with the Civil War was suddenly replaced by fear of trouble with the local Indians, as the news spread like wildfire of the shooting death of three homesteaders, two men and a woman, in Squak (Issaquah) Valley. The deed was done by Indians avenging the murder of a Snohomish chief and two Indians by white men the previous year. No further violence occurred, but the incident refreshed memories of the terror of the Indian War of less than a decade earlier.

THE 1860s—BUILDING HOMESTEADS, FAMILIES AND COMMUNITY

THE STEELE FAMILY COMES TO THE VALLEY

While the Civil War curtailed the migration of adventurous young men, it provided the impetus to bring the Steeles to Puget Sound. The story of the Steele family's pioneer experience illustrates how the political and economic events of the period shaped the lives of ordinary Americans. The Steeles' story is important to Duwamish history because several members of the family played key roles in the settling of the valley and building a foundation for the twentieth-century communities of Foster, Duwamish, Allentown and Riverton. The account of the Steele family's experience is told from the perspective of Jane Fenton Kelly, Joseph and Jean Steele's granddaughter. Jane was Susannah C. Steele Robbins' child by her first marriage to James Fenton. Jane was nine in 1864 when the family migrated to the Duwamish Valley. She wrote her account in 1931 at age 64.

Joseph Steele, 60, and Jean Wilson Campbell Steele, 56, had been married 38 years when they migrated to Puget Sound. Descendants of Scottish and Irish immigrants who had come to America before the American Revolution, the couple had met and married in Kentucky, where they lived for a few years. As the U.S. government opened land for settlement in the following decades, the Steeles followed the "moving frontier." They moved to Iowa Territory in the 1840s and, seeking a warmer climate, they traded their prosperous farm in Van Buren County, Iowa, for a place in Missouri in 1860. Unfortunately, the Missouri farm soon became the theater for fierce fighting between the Union and Confederate forces. Jane recalls lying in bed with her sister Ella at her grandparents'

Steele-Robbins-Foster family tree. Joseph and Jean Steele brought with them an entourage of adult children and grandchildren. All of them eventually married locally and established their own homes. Because of their relation to such a large number of valley households, Joseph and Jean Steele were jokingly called the "Father and Mother-in-Law of the Duwamish."

```
Joseph Steele (1804-    )
m. Jean Wilson Campbell (1808-    )
    — Hugh N. Steele
    — Marianne Steele
    — Martha J. Steele (1837-1924)
        m. Joseph Foster (1828-1911)
            — Charles Foster (1865-1877)
            — Rosetta J. Foster (1864-1877)
            — Emily A. Foster (1873-1877)
            — Joseph T. Foster (1878-1905)
            — Hillory Foster (1880-1950)
                m. Flora Fleming (1881-    )
    — Sarah Emily Steele
    — John Franklin Steele
    — James Thomas Steele
    — Joseph William Steele
    — Susanna Steele (1830-1916)
        m. James C. Fenton
            — Jane Fenton
                m. Mike Kelly
                    — Ebon Kelly
            — Ella Fenton
                m. Henry Burton
                    — Harry Burton (1877-1958)
        m. Milton N. Robbins (1825-1899)
            — Evelyn Robbins (??)
            — Edith Robbins
            — Emmet Robbins (1860-1925)
                m. Margaret Seese (1867-1957)
                    — Kearney Robbins
                    — Abbey Robbins
                    — Chester Robbins (1890-1922)
                        m. May Chambers (1893-1974)
                            — Cecile Robbins
                            — Melvin Robbins
                    Elmer L. Robbins (1891-1980)
            — Clement Robbins (1868-1938)
                m. Agnes McDonald (1878-1959)
                    — Milton N. Robbins (1898-1974)
                        m. Thyra A. Hilden (1899-1982)
                    — Marvin N. Robbins (1921-    )
                    — Evelyn R. Robbins (1927-    )
                        m. Adolph Sevruk (1921-1975)
                            — Noreen
                            — William
                            — Steven
                            — Laurie
                            — Paul
            — Neville Robbins (1909-1979)
                m. Margaret M. Bass (1909-1979)
                    — Chester M. Robbins (1928-    )
                        m. Connie Koener
                            — Michael
                        m. Katie McLaughlin (1930-    )
                            — John
                            — Patrick Robbins (1963-    )
                    — Helen Robbins (1931-    )
                        m. Carl Hove (1928-    )
                            — Carlyn
                            — Robyn
                            — David
```

When Joseph and Jean Campbell Steele came to the Duwamish Valley they were accompanied by six of their children, whose ages ranged from 13 to 30. A bachelor when he arrived, son Joseph William married and built his house near the Steele Landing on Foster Point. This photograph of Joseph's children (names unknown) was taken about 1880 on the front porch, which is unusual in this period because most family portraits were taken in a studio. Courtesy Museum of History & Industry.

farm and hearing the Civil War battle guns booming in the fields nearby.

Wanting to get away from the dangers of the war, the elder Steeles proposed "going out west" to their adult children, including their daughter Susannah and her second husband Milton Robbins, who were still living in Iowa. Susannah and Milton were easily persuaded, Jane recalls, "as times were getting harder and harder [as a result of the war] and it was encouraging to think of going out west, where we could take land and make new homes far from the war."

The party set out on May 14, 1864, traveling in three wagons. The Robbins family had its own wagon, and the Joseph Steele family had two wagons—a spring wagon driven by Martha Steele, 28, in which her mother and sister Emily, 22, rode, and a heavy lumber wagon, which Joseph drove himself with his adolescent sons Joe, Jim and John. An older daughter, Mary Ann, stayed behind in Indiana with her husband. The eldest son, Hugh, was living in Victoria, B.C. Hugh had made his way to Puget Sound at age 19, working his way across the Great Plains by driving a flock of sheep for the Mormons to Salt Lake City, Utah.

The exciting story of the Steeles' journey to the Duwamish Valley is well told in Jane Fenton Kelly's own words:

> It took a few weeks to prepare for such a trip. They must have a good team of horses and a lumber wagon, the bed of which had to be filled with provisions to last about six months. Flour, sugar, bacon, coffee, molasses and dried fruit were packed in solid and then a light pine floor [built] on top. Our beds and clothing were on top of that. Then a new white cover over the wagon with "BOUND FOR CALIFORNIA" on it. There were many other slogans used, such as "OREGON OR BUST." Nearly all the emigrants had horses that year, while before oxen had been used....

The 1860s—Building Homesteads, Families and Community

Jane Fenton Kelly, author of Duwamish Valley pioneer memoir, who came to the valley in 1864. In the spring of 1872 Jane and Michael Kelly fell in love. She wrote, "After dinner Mike and I wandered out in the orchard. It was knee deep in clover and the trees were in bloom in the orchard. The birds never sang so beautifully. There never had been a day so perfect for either of us. When we came to go home, never was there a happier couple in the whole wide world." In the 1880s she, with Michael, established the Sunnydale community (Burien). Courtesy the Robbins family.

Mr. Kennedy drove his milk cows and milked them every night and morning. When we made out camp in the evening Mrs. Kennedy would call out, "Whoever wants to churn can have the buttermilk!" There was always someone who wanted it.

About the saddest thing was leaving our dolls and books, as we could only take the barest necessities.... We started our long, perilous journey, following the Old Oregon Trail, until we turned south for California.

This was the second trip across the plains for my stepfather [Milton Robbins]. He had crossed in 1851, two years after gold was discovered in California. He was taken very sick in California with typhoid fever, and after recovering returned to Vermont.

One evening we came to a nice clear brook. The horses were hungry so we stopped, thinking to camp for the night. Mother had kept her "salt rising" bread dough warm in the wagon, put the dough into loaves in the Dutch oven at once. The fire was almost ready when hostile Indians rode up, saying "How! How!" pretending to be friendly. We knew they meant mischief. They did not stop, but rode on toward the horses. The boys and men went to the horses lest they might stampede them. Then the two rode back in the direction from which they had come. We thought they were going to get help. Someone said that we had better move on to where the main train was camped, about two miles farther on. Grandmother said, "Why Susie, what are you going to do about your bread?" At the same time taking the bread out of the oven and putting it back into the pan. We all began to pack while the men put the horses to the wagons. When we caught up to the train, they had driven in a big circle and the women and children were all inside while the men were all outside with their guns standing guard. One white man lay there, dead, having been shot by the Indians that afternoon. They dug a grave before daylight and drove the wagons over it so the Indians would not disturb the remains. This man was one of three that were traveling alone, and this was their third trip.

We saw another buried that same way. A woman who had been driving her own wagon across the plains had been killed crossing a creek. The bank was very steep and her wagon turned over. Her gun hung on the inside of the cover and struck her head as the wagon went over....

When we got to Nevada, our provisions were getting low. Our flour was all gone. We reached a town named Austin, where we got flour. We had been out of bread for twenty-four hours, and Mother and Aunt Martha lost no time until they had satisfied us with hot cakes. It was not long now until we came to the California line.

The first houses we saw were three neat log houses.... One house was close to the road. We could see through the open door. The table was set for the evening meal with nice china dishes. It looked so good to us, so homelike to us, as we had been out for so long a time. The woman was out by the fence with a fieldglass, looking anxiously in the distance. She told us she was looking for Indians. The report had reached them that the Indians were going to make a raid on them that night. This was a beautiful summer evening. It was near camping time, but we went on a far as we could, and camped by a little creek with no wood. Mother cooked supper with greasewood switches. The next day a man riding hoseback overtook us and told us that the three houses had been burned and the people killed.

After two months in California, where the men did farm work and the adult women cooked for their employers, the entire group set sail for Victoria, B.C., to visit Jane's uncle Hugh Steele.

We stayed two months with Uncle Hugh, then took the *Eliza Anderson* for Seattle. We stayed for one week at the Occidental Hotel in Seattle.... Uncle Hugh came to Seattle with us to buy Grandfather a farm. He went about ten miles out and bought a place which afterward Grandfather found the man had no title to. It still belonged to the Government, so he went and filed a homestead on it, and lived to prove up on it. At this time all land lying along the river bank was filed on and no one thought the hill land would ever be settled, as the timber was so thick and tall and the ground so gravelly. Grandfather's place was on the Military Road which led to Fort Steilacoom.

Martha Jane Steele Foster, ca. 1885. A comely, dark-haired, serious-eyed woman with great mental and physical abilities and a strong resolute character, Martha shared intellectual and political interests with her husband, Joseph Foster. Martha accompanied Foster to Olympia when the Territorial Legislature was in session, where together they enjoyed the intellectual and social life of the capital. Courtesy Museum of History & Industry.

FOSTER'S COURTSHIP

By 1864 Joseph Foster had been in the Duwamish Valley 11 years and had done very well. In addition to his original 160-acre donation claim at Mox la Push, he had bought his brother Stephen's claim at Foster Point. Tired of the monotonous work of clearing land, Stephen sold his claim to Joseph for the price of a team of horses and $300. That gave Joseph a total of 320 acres. Foster moved onto Stephen's claim and made his home there, while improving both claims according to the requirements of the land-grant

THE 1860S—BUILDING HOMESTEADS, FAMILIES AND COMMUNITY

agreement. In addition to proving up two claims, he operated his logging business with partner William Gilliam. He did not farm very much of his land or keep a herd.

The Steeles' homestead was across the river and a little north of Joseph Foster's cabin. From his doorstep Foster, now 36, could see Joseph Steele's older daughter, Martha Jane, flitting in and out of the Steele house going about her work. She, in turn, noticed the tall, handsome, black-bearded man going about his work, caring for his animals and seeing to his garden and hay field. Soon Foster began crossing the Duwamish in his canoe to visit for a little while. Joseph would visit with the entire family and then he and Martha would go for a walk. One of their favorite walks was along the river to Martha's sister Susannah Robbins' place.

As time went on, Joe Foster's trips to the Steele place became more frequent and he was more interested in simply seeing Martha. In order to dispense with the family visit, he developed the habit of entering the house through the gate on the river side of the house, which opened directly into the room where Martha usually worked. In this way Joseph Steele did not always see when Foster came. Steele was not pleased with this change and nailed the river-side gate shut as a hint to Foster that he was to use the other gate that led into the dining room where the family sat. Steele's motivation is not known; however, there is a good chance that he greatly enjoyed his conversations with the knowledgeable Hon. Joseph Foster, who was always very well informed on the issues of the day. Perhaps Steele was reluctant to lose his Martha, who was a great help to the family, and wanted to prevent the couple's private tete-a-tetes. Martha's niece Jane Fenton Kelly reports that the next Sunday, when the courting couple took their customary walk to her parents' place up the river, Foster told them with amusement: "Old Stockin' nailed up the front gate so I can't slip in that way any more!" Joseph and Martha were married at the Steele home on June 23, 1865.

THE FOSTER AND ROBBINS HOMESTEADS

In the busy years of establishing homesteads, records of the activities are rarely kept, except in the memory. Sketches of Martha and Joseph Foster's lives while establishing their homestead have survived, as has one for Susannah and Milton Robbins.

After his marriage to Martha Steele, Joseph Foster no longer left his homestead to work. Instead, he threw himself into clearing extensive tracts and adding barns and buildings. The couple acquired a dairy herd, and twice a day Martha milked 10 cows and Joseph milked 12 or 14. In those first years after their marriage, the Fosters' lives were filled with planting, cultivating and harvesting potatoes, hay and beans, as well as kitchen and flower gardens. Their days were busy with the milking, caring for horses, pigs and chickens, making butter, keeping house and caring for their children—Charles, Rosetta and Emily. They generated cash by selling livestock, logs and Martha's butter.

Martha told her daughter-in-law, Flora, years later, that many a day passed when she and Joseph did not have enough time to visit during the day, and so they often sat up late at night reading and conversing. Eventually the Fosters bought an additional 120 acres from neighbor Cyrus Lewis to make a total of 440 acres. Their 200 acres of rich river bottom land stretched from the confluence of the rivers to what became Allentown.

The Robbinses' early years were intertwined with the Fosters'. Susannah Steele Robbins and her husband, Milton Robbins, established their homestead in the area that would become known as Riverton. The couple filed a claim on 153 acres on the hillside on the west side of the Duwamish River in the vicinity of S. 131 St. and Military Road. The land was good and there was plenty of pure spring water, but the dense vegetation and swampy areas made clearing especially difficult. Susannah was eager to get established and was ready to move onto the claim immediately in 1864. Milton, however, felt they should rent for a while and develop at least a small parcel suitable for farming before they actually moved onto the homestead.

Joseph Foster gave his brother-in-law Milton Robbins a helping hand in getting established by offering him a job and a place to live while Robbins was clearing his hillside land. Robbins helped Foster clear river bottom land, and the two families then cultivated the acreage on shares. Robbins built his young family a temporary cabin on the same side of the river as the Fosters' place (west side, vicinity of the Foster Golf Course). The rented farmland lay directly across the river. Every morning Milton paddled a canoe across the river to work. Their first crops were potatoes and hay.

Soon they bought a few hogs and cows and began developing a dairy herd. Susannah sold butter in Seattle, sending it to market via Duwamish Indians who had established a canoe transport business carrying produce to the Seattle market for the valley settlers. With the money he earned working for Foster, Robbins hired local Duwamish natives to help him clear his claim. Six years later, in 1870, the Robbinses had built a house and barns on their claim and moved onto the land. In another 10 years, the Robbinses had a thriving dairy farm and were prospering raising hops. The Robbinses had five children after they came to the Duwamish Valley—Ida, Emmett, Evelyn, Edith and Clement.

THE FIRST GREAT FLOOD

The spring of 1866 was a particularly wet one. Early in June the rain suddenly stopped, and the pioneers sweltered under temperatures reaching 114 degrees in the shade in wooden buildings. The high water that year was only a prelude to the winter of 1867, which brought the worst flood on record. The Duwamish and White river valleys were covered with water that was reported up to seven feet deep at Kent. Fences, the winter cordwood supply, and houses were washed away. Some people lost their livestock, while others almost lost their lives. One family, trapped in their house by flood waters, escaped by chopping a hole in the roof and paddling to high ground on a hastily improvised raft. The Cedar River Bridge was washed into Lake Washington.

The flood hit while Martha and Joseph Foster and family were away in Olympia for the legislative session. Sue and Milt Robbins felt secure in their nearby cabin because they had been assured that the river never rose to the level of their house. However, on December 10, at about four o'clock in the afternoon, Sue's brother Jim came by in his canoe to warn them that the river was flooding badly in the low areas and rising rapidly. Looking toward the river they saw big logs and much debris tearing down the channel. The Robbinses did not want to leave; however, Jim insisted and they finally gave in and left with him in the canoe, not bothering to secure their belongings against flooding.

By morning the water was pouring in over the windowsills. Everything left on the floor and on low shelves was soaked with muddy river water. Susannah's personal trunk of mementos and photographs that she had safeguarded on the journey from Indiana to the Iowa farm, and then on the long overland trek, were destroyed. This was a heartbreaking loss. Of immediate practical consequence was the loss of the winter's food staple—potatoes. The Robbinses' bumper crop of potatoes were stored in a rack that Milt had built. The vegetables were covered with split cedar boards and then earth to protect them from freezing. The floodwaters washed away the cedar boards and scattered the potatoes everywhere. Before the water went down, there was a heavy frost and the potatoes were ruined. It was a lean winter, but the neighbors shared their potatoes with the Robbinses. This flooding experience convinced Susannah that she wanted her permanent house, which they had not yet built, high up on the hillside safe from the highest floodwaters.

It is reported that Joseph and Martha Foster and Timothy and Elizabeth Grow were the

The 1860s—Building Homesteads, Families and Community

hardest hit of the Duwamish settlers; however, there are no details of their experiences.

The following summer, 1868, King County experienced a terrible drought. No rain from the first of July to the last of October, coupled with high temperatures, damaged the crops. The tinder, dry conditions resulted in the outbreak of terrible forest fires that shocked and frightened the people. For two months the air was hazy with smoke.

Farming in the 1860s and the First County Fair

The 1860 King County census reported for the county 287 milk cows, 55 horses, 47 oxen and 230 swine. Agricultural production for the same year was 1,395 bushels wheat, 920 of oats, 773 of pears, 14,282 of potatoes, 2,655 pounds of butter and 99 tons of hay. In the early 1860s, cash crops for the settlers were potatoes, onions and hay. The women often sold butter and eggs. In Seattle potatoes went for 30 to 50 cents a bushel.

The Duwamish farmers were progressive and scientific in their approach to agriculture, and in June 1863 many of them participated in forming the King County Agricultural Society. On October 21, 1863, the society put on the first King County Agricultural Fair at Yesler's Hall in Seattle. The Duwamish homesteaders were well represented. Ann Kelly McNatt won a prize for her famous butter, and she and husband Francis McNatt exhibited the best vegetables they could find in their large garden. Sam Maple brought in fruit from his orchard planted in 1852 with stock from the Collinses' nursery. Jacob Maple won a prize for the largest apples with fruit that measured seventeen inches around and weighed about two pounds each.

Henry Van Asselt and Francis McNatt decided to take their horses, and early the day of the fair met with Sam Maple, who was taking a pair of his prime oxen. The three neighbors guided their animals along the Duwamish River

Joseph Foster and the Dexter Horton Bank

In the 1860s Dexter Horton ran a store in Seattle. There were no banks in the territory at this time, since money was scarce and there was very little need for a bank. Dexter had a reputation for integrity and honesty that prompted loggers and miners who came to town from time to time to bring him their pay for safekeeping. Horton would hide the man's pouch in the store—in the depths of a barrel of coffee was his favorite place. In 1870 Horton concluded that he should start a bank and asked Joseph Foster to go in with him in founding the bank. Convinced that he was already busy enough with his own enterprises, plus his regular work in the Washington Territorial Legislature, Foster said, "No, but I'll lend you the money to help you start your bank," and he did. Thus did Joseph Foster help found the first bank in Washington Territory.

Road, followed Beacon Hill ridge and arrived in good order in Seattle with just enough time to rub down the animals, brush out their tails—and manes in the case of the horses—and find a good spot near the exhibit hall. Four other settlers also brought teams and two brought cattle. It was a grand day for everyone in King County, and gave the settlers a sense of pride in what they had achieved in their eight years of grinding hard work.

Religion Comes to the Valley

The settlers' desire for religion and education began to be met in the 1860s. Religion came to the pioneers through circuit preachers, summer camp meetings, and the establishment of a small community church in the Duwamish Valley. From 1860 to 1875 Methodist and Presbyterian ministers based in Seattle saw that someone went out to preach. Catholics were under the Diocese of Steilacoom until 1864, when they became the religious charges of Father Prefontaine of Seattle, who came out to say Mass in private homes until the White River church was completed in 1876. A Catholic church was also established at Renton.

Sometime in the 1870s a little Methodist church was built by the community at Van Asselt's. There was no resident preacher, but circuit preachers led community worship about once a month, with community lay ministers taking the pulpit other Sundays. Martin Cavanaugh was a leader in the lay ministry and was reportedly good at exhorting a congregation "to mind their step." Jane Fenton Kelly relates that singing and religion were a part of the daily school routine in the 1860s: "Our teachers… had us read a chapter in the New Testament and sing every morning as opening exercises."

Having regular Sunday services definitely led to more socializing and building of community spirit among the settlers. Jane remembered that "After we got to going to church we would all gather [afterwards] at some neighbor's house for dinner and visit and sing all afternoon." As new people moved into the area, there were more places to go to on Sunday afternoon and social life became more diverse. Jane recalls that in 1869

> The people farther up the river began having social dances. About two thirds of these people were Irish Catholics and had no church to go to. They were fond of dancing and were jolly good people…. How we did enjoy those dances! The young men at that time put on their very best manners and took a partner if they could get one. There were more men than women at that time. They would have the first and last dances with their partner and the rest of the evening they danced with the others. They never allowed a woman to be a wallflower, even if she was older and married.

While the social delights of song and dance were drawing in the young people, frontier evangelical preachers made their way to Puget Sound to see that the pioneers, often cut off from formal religious guidance for years, did not lose touch with God.

The first notice of a camp meeting appears in a June 1868 issue of the *Seattle Intelligencer*. The gathering was held on the banks of the White River near Brannan's schoolhouse. Four different preachers were on hand for the three-day meeting. "Friends of the Meeting" offered free transportation on the steamboat *Gem* for those living along the Duwamish, Black and White rivers who "might go up the river on Friday, June 26th, and remain until the close of the meeting." Duwamish settlers traveling up to the camp meeting also enjoyed the unprecedented convenience of being able to pick up a few needed supplies at L. Smith's General Store, at Alvord's Landing. This was the first store to be opened outside of Seattle in the river valley region.

Along with religion, education and learning were strong values of the pioneers. This is reflected in the founding of a county library organization in January 1860, named the Seattle Library Association. One-fifth of the charter members were from the Duwamish, including Joseph Foster, William Gilliam, George Holt, and Henry Van Asselt. The Library Association gathered books—largely from members' personal collections—and loaned them to others.

THE FIRST SCHOOLS

The need for a school became more pressing as the number of children increased. Jane Fenton Kelly reports that there were summer schools held in 1866, 1867 and 1868 at Black River Junction because it was easier and safer for the young people to make their way to school than in the winter. She and her sister Ella walked one and one-half miles to school. Some of the older students paddled canoes many miles to school.

Later the girls attended the Black River School, located near the future site of Renton—a three-and-one-half-mile walk for the Fenton girls. Jane reports that the schoolhouse was a little shack built on the order of an Indian house. It had a sand box in the middle of the

THE 1860s—BUILDING HOMESTEADS, FAMILIES AND COMMUNITY

room where a wood fire was kept burning all day for warmth and light. Smoke escaped through an opening in the roof. A young man from Black River named Howard Weston was the teacher. It was a small group of children attending the school and they all played ball together during recess.

Jane recalls that it rained all winter. Now 13, she and Ella, 11, walked seven miles a day traveling to and from school all that winter on a trail that was ankle-deep in mud almost continuously. Since the school day ended around 3 p.m., the children reached home just around dark in the short winter days. Jane relates one adventure:

> One night we were about half way home when we came to a low snag in the road. The trees were so tall and the days were short then, and it looked a little dusky. A wildcat, or lynx, had crossed the road not 20 feet ahead of us. We stopped and held our breath a moment, knowing we could not go back, but must go on. Ella was the youngest, but was the first to speak. She offered up this simple little prayer, "God protect us," and taking hold of hands we walked on through the dusk very fast. We saw no more of the lynx.

In every home the children had daily chores to perform, in addition to going to school. The Fenton girls arose very early, around 5 o'clock a.m., started the fire, heated water, washed up, and combed and braided their long hair which they put into four braids that they wrapped across the back of their heads. They made their own breakfasts and lunches, and restoked the stove and refilled the kettle so that there would be hot water for the rest of the family, who were just getting up as the girls were preparing to leave for school. Their stepfather paddled them across the river, where they set off down the trail. When they arrived back that evening they called out and their father came over to fetch them home.

Being a parent on the frontier of the wilderness had its worries. Because there was a great deal of work to be done, parents had little spare time to accompany their children in their often very long travels to school. Indeed, checking when something was amiss was very difficult. One day when school was over for the day it was raining in torrents, and the teacher and Charlie Tobin from Black River, who was "sweet on" the pretty Jane, insisted that the Fenton girls should not walk home in the downpour, but stay with the Smitherses, who lived close to the school. Jane and Ella agreed, but felt guilty because they were sure their folks would worry. Sure enough, at 7:30, pitch-dark outside and still pouring down rain, a knock on the Smithers' door announced the arrival of Milton Robbins looking for his beloved stepdaughters. Finding them safe and content, he ate supper with the family, and after a hot cup of coffee set off alone for home, leaving the girls to stay the night.

SPELL DOWNS, SINGING CLUBS AND PARTIES

Just as the stuff of a courtship consisted of long walks along the banks of the river, all social activities were created by the people themselves. Quilting bees for the women, and friendly log-rolling competitions among the men, were occasions for relaxing and socializing. Being able to speak well and spell correctly was much esteemed in this era, and "spell downs"—a contest in which the best speller won—were popular. People of all ages joined in this favorite recreation.

One of the most popular pastimes was singing together. Jane Fenton Kelly recalls that her uncles Jim and John Steele, young men in their early twenties, used to take her and Ella in their lumber wagon to the Van Asselt church for services on Sunday and during the week for "singing school." Another family living close to the Steeles' homestead had two girls and a boy who were picked up and taken along. She wrote "We had lots of enjoyment in our own way. There were no musical instruments and no

A Grand Pioneer Party—January 1866

Mary Ann Maple Cavanaugh

In the fall of 1865 all the Maple household had planned to have a party.... We started to get out invitations in the latter part of October, and sent some by post, some by personal invitation, and some by Indian messengers who took them up and down the river in canoes. This much out of the way we next began to think what was to be eaten:

Bill-of-Fare

Soups
Chicken Soup, Clam Chowder, Stewed Clams

Fish
*Smoked, Boiled and Fried Salmon
Salmon Trout Sour*

Fowl
Grouse, Duck, Quail, Snipe

Roasts
Venison, Smoked Bear, Ham

Vegetables
Mashed Potatoes, Roasted Squash

Condiments
*Honey-in-Comb, Preserved Wild Blackberries,
Oregon Grape Jam*

Beverages
Milk and Coffee

The day of the party finally came along, and we were all heartily glad when we should have the family and the old time neighbors and friends in my father's hospitable home. Some of the people came on horseback, and Henry L. Yesler, M.B. Maddock and Bailey Gatzert came out from the city in the only wagon that was available. Mr. and Mrs. [Lucinda Maple] John Snyder walked three miles through the woods along a trail to get here. Robert Maple was in Oregon at the time and came up by way of the Columbia River as far as Kalama, and then by way of the Chehalis River and Tumwater, Olympia, Steilacoom, and along the old Military Road from that place.... [Martha] and Joseph Foster and [Jane Fenton] Kelly came down in a rowboat from Black River Junction. The rest of the party included Jacob Maple, Samuel Maple, Eli Maple and John Wesley Maple.... [Catherine and] Henry Van Asselt and family and others. And last but not least was our old friend Chief Seattle (Sealth).

The greatest of all our greetings came when Chief Seattle, with his skin and fur bedecked war canoe, with its fifty paddlers came around the bend and sang one of their songs of friendship upon landing in front of the house on the bank of the Duwamish River. He stepped out as became the sire and marshall of a tribe of savages, and with all the salaam that he could muster wished us happiness and joy at the festivity. Then he had his braves bring to us the skins of cougar and mink, some moccasins and some fish and salmon eggs, and with them offered us his good will and hearty cheer.

The day was a perfect one, and by evening all the guests had arrived and were in the midst of the jollification we had planned. Soon the dinner was cooked, and all sat down under the shed made of cedar shakes and commenced to eat the vittles we had, and to tell tales of the many days since they had been at an occasion of like nature....Stories were told of crossing the plains, of the gold fields in California, of the strides made in Idaho, of those along the Frazer river, of trips of the great and infrequent steamers that came along once in two months from San Francisco. Each had a tale of hardship in the forest to tell, of how many stumps they had dug, and of when they would get another acre of ground cleared, of some fortune they had been blessed with, such as having an apple seed, which they had planted in the ground grow and become a tree.... Joseph Foster made mention of the fact that he had brought the University to Seattle with the assistance of Daniel Bagley.

Then there was talk of all the people who lived on the Sound in those early days, and it must be related here that the whole company was thrashed over.... Just think of it! Why, we don't even try to keep track of the people who live within a mile of our place here now, they come and go out so fast.

Soon the shades of evening waned and the darkness of night came on, and later the moon rose and arranged one of those dreamy effects which puts one into a reverie and weaves a romantic halo around the whole. Some of us younger ones leaned out the windows and looked at the moon as it shone through the evergreen forest with its virgin growth, and in places reflected its light on the ever moving river.

Large parties of Indian canoes were moving up the river, and the slow plaintive song which they sang as they kept time with their beating oars added to the romantic situation, until the sound finally grew dimmer in the distance and ended in a soft zephyr.

The 1860s—Building Homesteads, Families and Community

critics, so we would sing all the way there and all the way back." Soon the Duwamish Singing Society was organized by Mary Ann Maple and Martin Cavanaugh. The group met regularly, with Martin often leading the singing with his rich tenor voice. People sometimes traveled more than an hour each way on foot or horseback to spend the evening singing with others. Arriving home close to midnight, they would be up at dawn for their day of hard labor.

The Duwamish Valley social event of the decade, second only to the Maple-Van Asselt Wedding, was the Maple clan's party of January 1866, held at Jacob Maple's. Mary Ann left a vivid account of the grand party written 50 years later, in 1906.

In the 1860s the Fourth of July was the great summer event on Puget Sound, with settlers scattered about the shores on isolated claims traveling great distances to attend. In the early decades only one Fourth of July celebration was held in the region so that everyone could attend the same gathering, renew old acquaintances, meet newcomers and, in the case of the single people, start up or carry on a courtship.

In November 1867 the circus came to town. The Great Western Circus put on its show in Yesler's Mill, and almost everyone up the Duwamish, Black and White rivers turned out to see it. The trapeze and ropes for the tightrope walker were strung from the great shed ceiling. Logs and moveable machinery were cleared out and a circus ring built—already conveniently filled with sawdust—for the juggling acts, performing dogs and bears, and other marvelous feats. Freshly sawn lumber was fashioned into benches for the women, while the men stood around in back. The children sat in the sawdust down front and watched the show, their eyes sparkling with delight. Many, born in the territory, had never seen such wonders in their short lives. When the bareback rider appeared astride her steeds, clothed only in a camisole, pink tights and a ruffle for a skirt, some of the bachelors' eyes were glistening.

It was a real holiday for everyone after the hard work of the summer and harvest season. Enterprising people had brought produce with them to sell—fresh butter, potatoes, onions, turnips, eggs and even pigs. Most people stayed in Seattle for a few days buying supplies—flour, sugar, coffee, tea, and candies—and simple gifts for Christmas. Women bought wool yarn and yards of cotton, linen and wool fabric for the winter's sewing to clothe the family. The men searched through the hardware for replacement parts for tools broken that summer, they would repair before the cabin fire that winter. People visited with old friends, made new friends, and saw the sights of the flourishing village. All in all, it was a grand time.

While at this time the population remained small, with people only slowly coming to the area, this was to be short-lived. In 1869 the Union Pacific Railroad completed the first transcontinental line connecting San Francisco with the rest of the country. Now settlers bound for Puget Sound could take the train across the Great Plains and mountains to California, and then travel by steamer to Seattle.

CHAPTER 4
ESTABLISHING FARMS AND COMMUNITIES—1870-1899

Duwamish River oxbow, looking south toward Mox la Push, ca. 1880. The Black River Junction Bridge can be seen in the background on left. The Seattle-Walla Walla narrow-gauge railroad station is just in front of the bridge. The hill to the left is Sbah-bah-teel. Courtesy Paul Dorpat.

Farming Lands

The inducements offered to settlers in this Territory [Puget Sound] are far greater than in any section of the United States. Here everything is in its infancy; numerous tracts of land are being cultivated and yielding enormous profits, but, these owing to the great extent of the country and difficulty of access, from the scarcity of roads, are few and far between.... A trip on the railroad to Renton and Newcastle will take but one day, yet the farming districts between the city of Seattle and these places are both extensive and productive, with plenty of cheap land to be had along [the] White, Duwamish and Black rivers as well as Squak creek and Cedar river.... The only class of settlers that this young country requires is the man with a family who has the persevering, energetic and industrious habits of a pioneer.

    Directory of the City of Seattle, 1887

The Duwamish Valley area grew slowly in the 1870s and 1880s. The 1870 King County census reported 277 settlers in the Duwamish, Black and White river valleys. The population growth allowed the formation of communities that relieved the extreme isolation of the first decades of settlement, and brought the benefits and joys of communal life.

This was also a period of hard times. In the winter of 1871 tension developed between the settlers and the Indians once again, and several pioneer families left the valley including the Maples, who returned in 1874 and rented Henry Van Asselt's farm. One unusual growing season resulted in the total loss of the potato harvest. The tubers rotted in the ground. There were several years of serious spring flooding with the high water carrying away fences, buildings, animals and stored crops. However, the soil was rich, and generally good harvests were gathered. Major setbacks during this period were experienced by most peoples as a result of a number of economic recessions and the dependence on a single cash crop, hops, in the 1880s.

A counterbalance to the hard times of the 1870s came when the Timber Culture Act

ESTABLISHING FARMS AND COMMUNITIES—1870-1899

offered homesteaders and pre-emptors a chance to obtain additional free government land. A settler was granted up to 160 acres under the condition that he or she plant and maintain a minimum number of trees on part of the land for eight years. The settler had 13 years to prove up a timber claim, and since there were no residency requirements, a timber culture claim and a homestead or preemption land claim could be had simultaneously. The objective of the Timber Culture Act was to encourage settlers to plant trees, and supply firewood and timber for themselves. A number of Duwamish pioneers acquired an additional 160 acres of land under this legislation.

FARMING IN THE DUWAMISH AND LOWER WHITE RIVER VALLEYS

The process of proving up a land grant required clearing the land for agriculture as a condition of ownership. The work was slow and went on for years. Records illustrate the small acreages cleared after many years of work. Henry Adams, whose claim lay near William Gilliam's along the White River near Orillia (later Southcenter), had filed a claim for 320 acres in 1855. Fifteen years later, he had 60 acres cleared and under cultivation, while 260 remained unimproved. That year he raised 80 bushels of wheat and 150 of oats. Adams had established a notable dairy by the 1880s. He had actually cleared a substantial acreage compared to many others. For example, after 15 years, John Thomas had cleared only 20 of his 137 acres. Most settlers were able to clear only two or three acres in the best years.

The Duwamish Valley was blessed with black loamy soil containing large amounts of vegetable mold on top of clay subsoil that was effective in retaining moisture through the dry season—a great asset in crop production. In the bottom lands near the river, the soil consisted of rich deposits of alluvium. The combined work of floodwaters that carried soil down into the valley, and centuries of beaver dams that left broad, flat, silt-filled ponds, made the valley floor ideal for farming. The soil under cultivation was described by a contemporary observer as "quick, light and friable, yielding astonishing crops of hay, hops, grain, fruits and vegetables for a series of years without manure and with only indifferent plowing."

WOMEN'S WORK

Women played an important part in the team effort of proving up a claim. When their husbands were working out for cash, the women remained on the land managing the farm—fields, orchards and animals—singlehandedly with what help was available from the older children and occasionally from hired Indians. Women often generated cash by selling butter, vegetables and fruit from their gardens and orchards. Diana Collins, Eva Buckley, Martha Foster, Polly Lewis, Elizabeth Grow, Jean Steele, Susannah Robbins and the other pioneer women on the Duwamish had a wide range of skills, including cooking, food preservation, clothing construction, knitting, farming and animal husbandry. Important among their numerous skills was medical knowledge of caring for sick humans or animals. The unidentified pioneer woman in this

Courtesy University of Washington Special Collections.

photograph is busy with spring airing of the family bedding with the help of her son. The abundance of complex pieced quilts shows this woman's artistic interests, which she put to use while making needed bedcoverings.

TUKWILA—COMMUNITY AT THE CROSSROADS

DUWAMISH FARMERS—WORKING ON THE HOMESTEAD AND WORKING OUT

roving up a claim required money, as well as hard manual labor. Settlers needed to buy materials, seed, draft animals, tools and machinery. Most of the Duwamish pioneers divided their first years between working on their homesteads and generating cash needed for proving-up expenses. By the middle 1870s there were cash-work opportunities beyond the logging camps and lumber mills. For example, salmon packers were hired by Levy & Wilson on Carkeek's wharf. Salmon packing created numerous jobs, for the fish had to be cleaned, scraped, washed and salted down in large vats. After eight days in a brine, they were packed in barrels and sent to market. Salmon packing was an autumn job, which put it into competition with the fall harvest. However, it paid good money, and school-age boys and girls skipped school to work in the packing sheds. Women also did this work.

SCHOOLS

Children were an integral part of their parent's activities and assisted with the work as much as they could for their age. The school year was adjusted according to the need of the young people's help on the family homestead in late September-October. Thus the fall term started early, i.e., August, with a harvest break of several weeks, or it started late, after harvesting. By 1870 there were schools at Van Asselt, Black River and Orillia. Children attended whichever school was the closest.

A description of the Maple School built in 1878 provides a picture of a typical school of the period in the valley. The building was about 25 by 55 feet. Entering the schoolhouse door, students stepped into the cloakroom—an anteroom where coats, hats and lunches were left. The drinking water pail was also kept here.

ELLA FENTON BURTON'S TEACHER'S DAYBOOK, 1886

Notes from Ella's Teacher's Daybook provide a glimpse into the lessons of the pupils and concerns of the teacher.

Second Reader Course
Reading: Short lessons, word method, natural manner of speaking. Marks of punctuation. After each recitation pupils write lessons on slates. Teacher writes portions on board to be copied.
Spelling: Words from the reading lesson and names of common objects, both oral and written.
Writing: Long pencils, ruled slates, or paper. Small and capital letters to be copied from charts or board; simple words to be copied from board.
Drawing: Straight lines continued.
Numbers: Count, read, write numbers to 100. Add and subtract tables through the 10s. Multiplication through 5s. Practical exercises in adding and subtracting numbers not to exceed 20. Count by 2s, 5s and 10s to 200. Signs + and -. Roman numerals to XX.
Geography: Continue map of Names of counties in Territory. Mountain ranges, peaks, local rivers, largest cities and towns in Territory.
Language: Compose short sentences about familiar objects. Short sentences from dictation.

June 15, 1886
My Dear Mrs. Dolan,
    Your children have been tardy 9 times during the 23 days they have attended school. This is a great inconvenience in the school, as well as a loss of time to the tardy pupils. Hoping that, in the future you will see that they are prompt in attendance I am
    Respectfully,
    Ella Burton

June 22: Truly, these are our longest days…. As usual had an inspector [school inspector].
June 25, 8:45 am: Wildcat seen by boys. Shall hear nothing but bear, cougar and wildcat stories now. Thundershower this morning. My lunch pail disaster. I did not repair it though. Cloudy and cool this morning.
June 26: "All the way my Saviour leads me. What have I to ask besides. Though my weary steps may falter, and my soul athirst may be, gushing from the rocks before me, lo, a stream of joy I see."
June 28, 8:10 pm: "Poor miners! Poor miners! Hungry and cold!" — I cannot pity them. They never taught school.

Establishing Farms and Communities—1870-1899

The rest of the building was a single room filled with hand-made desks each large enough to seat two students. There was an outhouse behind the schoolhouse, and the school was heated with a pot-bellied stove which the older boys had to tend in the cold months. Books and other learning materials were put on shelves built along the walls. Pupils had to buy their own textbooks. A *First Grade Reader* cost 37½ cents; a *Third Grade Reader*, 87½ cents; geography 62½ cents; and speller, 37½ cents.

Duwamish River School, Miss Emma Huff and class, 1887. On August 10, 1878, King County formally established school districts throughout the county. Three districts served the Duwamish Valley at this time: Maple District No. 2; Orillia, District No. 5; and Black River, District No. 6. In 1892 the Foster School was established as District No. 104. The photograph is of one of the Duwamish River schools; however, the specific school is not identified. Courtesy Seattle Historical Society.

The Railroads, Coal and Valley Growth

In 1870 the Northern Pacific Railroad began construction of a transcontinental railroad to run from Duluth, Minnesota, to Kalama on the Columbia River, Washington Territory. There was an immediate upswing of interest in the Northwest and a vigorous flow of population into the region. This halted in 1873 when Jay Cooke & Co., the financiers backing the construction of the railroad, failed. This failure triggered a national financial collapse and the Northwest experienced a "panic"—the term used in the nineteenth century for economic depression that set back regional development. But the discovery of coal deposits helped restimulate the local economy and create jobs for cash-poor homesteaders.

In 1873 E. M. Smithers discovered a good-quality vein of coal in the Renton area, and with two partners started mining operations as the Renton Coal Co. The coal was transported via a horse-powered tramway from the mines to the Duwamish River, where it was barged down to Yesler's Wharf in Seattle. Hauling the coal was fraught with troubles. Coal-laden barges "turned turtle" in the river, dumping the entire load, or the steamboats towing the barges snagged and the coal sank into the water. These problems were eliminated when a specially designed small steamer, the *Addie*, was built to tow the coal barges.

The communities along the eastern side of Puget Sound had long dreamed of being connected with the rest of the country by the railroad. In 1873 it looked as if the Northern Pacific Railroad was running its tracks to Seattle. That hope was dashed when word came on July 14, 1873, that the final decision had been made to locate the railroad terminus on Commencement Bay, Tacoma. King County was devastated, but refused to give up. Those living in the area of Seattle were determined to build their own railroad link to the main line.

On May Day, 1874, a red-letter day in local history, the people living on the Black and Duwamish rivers climbed aboard a riverboat that, beginning at dawn, made its way down the

55

river picking up almost everyone, who brought with them tools and baskets of food. Neighbors and friends visited and enjoyed the journey to Seattle. Then the work began. The valley dwellers joined the people from Seattle and the environs at a point about 100 feet east of the intersection of Spokane St. and Grant St., where they set to work building a railroad. That day they graded a stretch of roadbed up the Duwamish Valley to about the Meadows. A spur of the N.P.R.R. used that grade well into the twentieth century. A hearty picnic dinner was laid out in an abandoned sawmill by the women. The goal was to have 15 miles graded by winter—12 were completed by October.

The narrow-gauge tracks were laid as far as Steele's Landing, where they dead-ended until 1875, when the last five miles to the Renton coal mines were completed. The grand opening celebration for the Seattle-Walla Walla Railroad, held in the spring, found every settler for 20 miles around present. Ribbons were cut and speeches were made about the bright future for the area. Best of all, everyone got to ride the train from Renton through the verdant Duwamish Valley to Seattle and back home. It was a happy day for everyone. Many of the children born in Washington had never seen a train before this day. It was 1875 and they had the train! That night Duwamish homesteaders sighed as they dropped off to sleep thinking "civilization was indeed coming to this wild outpost."

A regular schedule was established, with cars leaving Seattle for Renton and Newcastle every day, except Sunday, at 6:30 a.m. and 1 o'clock p.m. People caught the train at Black River Junction, leaving their teams at Joseph Foster's place. Those living in the Duwamish Valley and near the river junction were indeed lucky, for among all the communities in King County they had both riverboats and railroad for public transportation to Seattle and market.

Without a doubt, life was getting a bit easier for the pioneers. However, the local weather continued to offer surprises. On November 16, 1875, the most severe windstorm on record hit Puget Sound. Three warehouses were blown apart in Seattle, a house was turned upside down, a ship in the harbor was blown ashore. The chimneys of the Territorial University were carried off and the large pillars on the front of the building threatened to collapse. In the Duwamish Valley sheds, fences and trees were thrown every which way, and roads were obstructed with fallen trees. Fortunately, the fall harvest was mostly in, but the orchards were littered with broken trees. There were no injuries to people.

Converting the dense Puget Sound forest to farmland occupied the settlers for decades. This stump puller, relying on pulleys and oxen power, was one way of clearing the fields. For decades building sites and roads all were determined by the location of tree stumps. Courtesy The Old Seattle Paperworks.

ESTABLISHING FARMS AND COMMUNITIES—1870-1899

Big snow, King County, January 1875. In January 1875 and again in 1880, the area experienced a severe cold snap that froze over little lakes like Angle Lake and White Lake for several weeks. All of the rivers flowing into Puget Sound were frozen. When the Duwamish River ice broke up, it floated out into Elliott Bay as three-to-six-inch thick ice cakes which a strong southwest wind drove up against Seattle's wharves, preventing the movement of any ships for many hours. The house of Louis Wyckoff is on the upper right. Wyckoff was a Mox la Push area donation claim settler, Seattle blacksmith, and King County Sheriff in the 1860s-1870s. Courtesy Seattle Historical Society.

COMMUNITY LIFE AND ORGANIZATIONS

In the 1870s there were sufficient people and leisure time to form community organizations. Among the most significant of these organizations was the Grange. In the twenty-some years since the Collins party set foot on the river's bank, the farmers in the Duwamish Valley had gained a reputation not only for excellence in the quality and quantity of crops and animal husbandry, but also for their progressive approach to agriculture. Nowhere is this more evident than in their leadership in agricultural organizations. In 1876 Francis and Ann McNatt were key instigators of the King County Farmers Club. A short time later they dissolved this organization in favor of a new national farm organization called simply "the Grange." The National Grange was an offshoot of the Patrons of Husbandry, which was organized by eastern farmers in protest against the wrongs suffered by farmers at the hands of the railroads, manufacturers and financiers.

On January 27, 1878, a charter was granted to petitioners in the White River, who formed White River Grange No. 9. The same day Duwamish Grange No. 11 was granted its charter. The 24 valley farmers signing the Duwamish application as founding members included Ann and Francis McNatt, Sam Maple, Mrs. Eli Maple, Julius Horton, Mrs. A. E. Horton, Stephen Collins, Milton Robbins and Susannah Robbins. These Grange chapters were short-lived and both disbanded in 1880 for unexplained reasons. However, the Grange reorganized in the valley after the turn of the century.

In addition to organizations supporting agriculture, the people formed cultural and social groups. In 1872 the Washington Territory Pioneers Association was formed with William Gilliam and Henry Van Asselt as central organizers. Since membership was restricted to people who had come into Washington before 1856, all of the Duwamish Valley donation claims settlers qualified. In the spring of 1877, marksmen in King County and Victoria, B.C., agreed to have a rifle marksmanship contest on the Fourth of July. The U.S. marksmen organized under the name Seattle Rifle Team, with the famous local sharpshooter Henry Van Asselt participating. Everyone enjoyed the match with the Canadian neighbors so well that the club continued with the Card farm on the lower Duwamish being the favored target practice site.

In September 1877 the Duwamish farmers heard the boom of cannon floating over from Elliott Bay. The cannon announced not renewed hostilities with the Indians but the arrival of the *Constitution*. At 3,600 tons it was the largest steamship ever to enter Puget Sound; in fact, it was the largest on the Pacific to that date. Many from the Duwamish and White rivers made excuses to go into Seattle in the following days to see the grand ship. One observer's reaction was that she looked "as big as Mount Rainier."

In spite of the many changes in the region, as the wilderness was "cleared" in favor of the serene landscape of tidy farms, the area continued to be somewhat wild. In an effort to rid the community of wild animals, in August 1886 the King County Commissioners announced that the county would pay bounties on wild animals that were killed and brought in, according to the following schedule: cougar and panther, $5; bear, $4; wildcats, $2.

STAYING HEALTHY

Emigrant handbooks were frank about the rugged demands of pioneering the wilderness. One such book states:

> The first requisite for a person proposing to emigrate to a new country, with a view to improving his condition, is *good health*.... For nowhere more than in a strange land, among strangers, is there a need of the buoyancy of spirit enabling one to bear up under disappointments and hardships.... For on the frontier the struggles are severe and labor oppressive.

When the Collins party arrived in 1851 the life expectancy at birth in the United States was about 40 years. If an infant survived the first year, its life expectancy increased by at least a decade. In the nineteenth century people frequently dealt with a variety of potentially fatal health problems, the most common of which were infections and complications from injuries, and communicable diseases. Smallpox, typhoid fever, diphtheria, scarlet fever and tuberculosis were familiar to everyone.

With few exceptions, women gave birth at home with the aid of women neighbors and, ideally, a qualified midwife. Husbands were normally not called in to assist with the birth. In fact, they were generally advised to "find something to do in the barn." In 1874, 20-year-old Eliza Jane Snyder Maple, wife of John Wesley Maple, gave birth to premature twins. The combined weight of the infant girls, named Cora Ellen and Dora Helen, was seven pounds. The smallest, Cora, was only two pounds three ounces. Young Dr. Henry A. Smith came to oversee the care of the newborns. Dr. Smith had come to Puget Sound from Pennsylvania after completing medical school at age 24. His donation claim was on Salmon Bay, in the area later known as Smith's Cove. Dr. Smith recommended the tiny Maple babes be kept wrapped in cotton batting for the first six weeks. The Indians were very excited about the birth of the twins, and the women brought Eliza Jane fish oil to rub on the tiny infants for nourishment. Both girls lived to be more than 60 years old.

The personal history of William Gilliam's wife Mary Jane Russell illustrates both how close to death the pioneers lived and how women were pressured to marry in the frontier society heavily populated with single men. Mary Jane Russell was the daughter of the White River pioneer Samuel Russell, originally from Auburn, Illinois, and sister of Mary Ann Russell, the first bride in King County. It was said that Mary Jane was a very beautiful woman. In 1856, at age 19, she married Charles C. Terry at Port Madison. The wedding took place in an Indian war canoe off the Suquamish Indian Reservation, and Chief Seattle was their honored guest. Terry died of tuberculosis 11 years later in 1867, and the day after Terry's death Mary Jane delivered a baby girl. In 1871 Mary Jane, now 34, married Charles S. Murphy. Murphy died two years later of unknown causes.

In 1873 Mary Jane married 43-year-old William Gilliam, now a somewhat prominent and wealthy man, who was the Seattle Postmaster. Described in his youth as a handsome man five feet ten inches tall, with grey eyes and rich brown hair, Gilliam had waited 20 years to marry. On August 24, 1875, after only two years of marriage, Mary Jane suddenly died of unknown causes. There was a large funeral procession and she was buried in the Masonic Cemetery in Seattle. Gilliam lived on into old age a single man and was buried by the Indians on the Black River. Gilliam Creek is named for this pioneer.

It is quite likely that at least one of the deaths in Mary Jane Russell's marital history was from a communicable disease. The year 1877 was a terrible one for disease in King County. In the spring a smallpox epidemic broke out that spread from Seattle as far as Tacoma. As the incidence of smallpox cases diminished in the autumn, another dread disease appeared—diphtheria. During that winter over half of the children in King County died of the disease. Joseph and Martha Foster lost all of their children in a single week—Charles, ten, Rosetta, seven, and Emily, four. Called back from Olympia, where he had gone for the biennial legislative session, Foster arrived after all the children had died. With the help of neighbors, he bathed and dressed the children's bodies in clothing which he had made himself and buried them on the farm. Martha herself was stricken with the disease, and Joseph sat sleepless by her bedside for days, ministering to her physically and spiritually as she fought for her life.

Back in Olympia, Foster's colleagues in the legislature mourned with him and passed an official resolution expressing their deep concern and sorrow for his loss. The text of their sentiments is a part of the permanent record of the House Proceedings. A similar resolution was passed by the Territorial Council (Senate). It is partially quoted here as testimony to the affection of Joseph Foster's colleagues, as well as evidence of the close and personal nature of relationships in those days:

> Resolved, that having heard with profound grief that the household of our fellow member, Hon. Joseph Foster of King County, has since our brief session commenced been deprived by death of an only son and two daughters....His household is broken up, and we learn with sorrow that the grief stricken mother lies at death's door. Surely we have evidence that when sorrows come they "come not single spies but in battalions." The vacant seat of our brother reminds us of his afflictions. We are for the time deprived of the counsel and experience of one who at previous sessions in either branch of legislature has been prompt and vigilant in the performance of duty. While entering this excuse for our brother's continued absence we assure him, in this hour of his gloom, our most heartfelt feelings of sadness....

The epidemics frightened everyone, and made civic leaders realize it was time to establish some kind of public health care center. The King County Farm had been established on a 160-acre tract that was left by John Thompson, who had died intestate in March 1865, leaving no heirs. Originally part of Diana and Luther Collins' donation claim, the land lay near the mouth of the Duwamish River.

Looking for a group to take charge of the activities of the county farm, the county commissioners asked the local Catholic Church representatives to take on the job. Mother Joseph and the Sisters of Providence of Vancouver, Washington, were asked to take over, which they did on May 11, 1877. They established what came to be known as the first King County Hospital at the Duwamish Valley county farm. In 1893, a new three-story brick county hospital, designed by Mother Joseph, a skilled architect, was built on the site. This was one of 27 hospitals she built in the Northwest.

During the 1880s and 1890s, the prevailing disease in King County was typhoid fever. The typhoid bacillus had not been discovered, hence explanations for its spread were pure speculation. In fact, typhoid is a waterborne bacillus, which propagates rapidly under favorable conditions. The valley residents' water supply came from home wells, streams and the river. No sewer system existed and most people had an outhouse cesspool in their backyard. During the rainy season these often overflowed, spilling their contents into the drinking water wells. During severe flooding, home cesspool sewage was swept into the main flow of the river, polluting the water, including the drinking wells and reservoirs for humans and animals.

These conditions were bad for everyone, but particularly serious for the many dairying operations located in the valley. At different times local typhoid epidemics in Seattle were directly traced by the King County Public Health Officer to specific milk distributors, including at least one in the Duwamish-lower White River area. Investigation showed that typhoid-polluted stream water was being used for washing the milk cans.

In the early days there was little known about how disease spread. Immunizations, when they were done, were inadequate, and there was little in the way of therapeutic measures for communicable diseases. Isolation and quarantine were the main techniques observed to control these dreaded diseases. A smallpox epidemic broke out in 1892 in the outlying communities. Spread of the disease was traced to railroad workers. County health officials spent their time meeting ferries, boats and trains as they searched for smallpox cases. During the 1894 scarlet fever epidemic, every school in the county was closed and public gatherings forbidden. All schoolbooks in the Duwamish Valley schools were collected and burned in an effort to stop the spread of the disease. It was not until the twentieth century that these dreaded killing diseases were controlled.

POLITICS—1870-1890

hrough the 1870s the Duwamish and Black River was divided into two precincts—Mox la Push and Duwamish. In 1884 the Mox la Push precinct was dissolved. The precincts now were Duwamish and White River. The Duwamish precinct polling place was the Maple School in 1884, and the Duwamish School in 1887. In the 1870s the weekly mail delivery continued to come to the Duwamish postal station, under the jurisdiction of the Black River Post Office. In the 1880s mail delivery increased to twice weekly.

County taxes focused on schools and transportation. For every dollar of assessed property value the citizen was taxed at the following rates: school, six mills; roads and bridges, two mills; county roads, four mills; and territorial roads, two and one-half mills.

WASHINGTON WOMEN VOTE—1886-1888

aving served regularly in the Territorial Legislature since 1858, by 1880 Joseph Foster was an institution in that governing body. The dominant issue at the 1884 session was Woman Suffrage. American women had been struggling for many years to achieve

ESTABLISHING FARMS AND COMMUNITIES—1870-1899

> ### WINNING A HUSBAND TO WOMAN SUFFRAGE
>
> When Washington women received the right to vote in 1886, many husbands were disgruntled with what they saw as loss of male privilege. Jane Fenton Kelly had such a husband in Mike Kelly. Mike told her that if she went to the polls to vote he would leave her. Jane recalls: "Now this was getting serious, as my mind was fully made up to go. I did not argue, but I said to myself, 'No boy is coming over here from Ireland to dictate to me what I shall do politically.'" Knowing that her hotheaded Irish husband had a poetical and imaginative nature, Jane sat down and wrote a poem to him which won him over. She confides that she sensed that he was, in fact, proud of her.
>
> **A Woman's Sentiments on Woman Suffrage**
> *Jane Fenton Kelly, 1886*
>
> *Oh! Man! Why dost thou dread*
> *To let woman with thee walk*
> *In public as in private*
> *And of our country's welfare talk?*
> *Is it not she to whom*
> *Your children come for knowledge*
> *Long before they seek it*
> *In public school or college?*
> *Then if she should wish to step*
> *Upon the round of fame*
> *Give her then a helping hand*
> *And tarnish not her name!*
> *Does she not bless your home,*
> *And purify your life*
> *Whenever she is with you*
> *In pleasure, or in strife?*

their legal rights as American citizens to vote in all elections. The western territories and new states were the most willing to give women the vote, and did in all locally controlled elections. However, this did not allow women to vote in national elections.

In 1884, in its eleventh biennial session, Council Bill No. 44, extending voting rights to women, was brought before the Washington Territorial Legislature by Joseph Foster, who also led the forces in the Washington Legislature championing Woman Suffrage. He worked tirelessly to sway the legislative ballot to the "pro." In his many talks and writings on the issue, he reminded men that the women of the territory were crucial to the success of the work of settling the area. He emphasized that, in addition to looking after the health and welfare of their families, the women were the instigators of many of the activities and institutions that were creating the communities across Washington Territory including school systems, libraries, public health care and orphanages for the care of the many children left alone through the untimely death of their parents.

The men of the territory listened to Foster and his colleagues, who energetically supported the women's right to vote. The bill was passed and signed into law by Governor Eugene Semple. Home again on the Duwamish, Joseph received enthusiastic thanks from his own Women's Rights activist, his wife Martha, and all of the women up and down the river, who threw a party to thank "Uncle Joe" and to generally celebrate this great victory for American women.

Joseph Foster and the other men on the Woman Suffrage Committee received hundreds of letters of appreciation. However, not everyone was pleased, and Foster and each committee member also received a starched white petticoat from their disgruntled antagonists. Foster accepted the garment with characteristic good humor and gave it to a neighbor's daughter.

Washington women proudly voted in the next election; however, the Territorial Court soon overturned the law, only to have the legislators vote it through again the next session. In 1887, on the eve of statehood, Foster was offered the governorship of Washington Territory. Though appreciative of the great honor this invitation represented, Foster declined the high office and followed his plan to retire from public service.

THE GREAT HOPS CRAZE

In 1880 there were 6,529 farms in Washington, about half in western and half in eastern Washington. King County,

Milton Robbins' hops dryer and storage barn, Riverton Heights area. Flat boxes filled with hops by field pickers were hauled by wagon to the hop dryer, where moisture was removed with hot dry air to retard spoilage. Once dried, the hops were baled. An average bale weighed 200 pounds. From 1910 to 11 Robbins' dryer served as temple for the Masonic Delta Lodge 172. Courtesy Museum of History & Industry.

in the mid-1880s, reported substantial harvests of potatoes, hay, oats and fruits. In 1884, 8,200 tons of hay were harvested in the county. Hay sold for $12/ton, with an acre yielding three tons or $36 per acre. The typical yield of potatoes was 300 to 500 bushels per acre, which sold at 50 cents a bushel or $250 per acre. The land yielded 50 bushels of oats an acre, and sold for 50 cents a bushel or $25 per acre. Apples sold for $1 a bushel and plums for $2 a bushel.

In the late 1870s a new crop, hops, was introduced that, for a decade, was to overshadow all other crops and provide a good supply of cash in support of the pioneers' homesteading efforts—and end in financial disaster for some. In 1875 a White River farmer, living two miles south of Orillia, planted a crop of hops. The plant grew extremely well, produced an abundant harvest and brought a good market price. Cash-needy farmers were quick to recognize the great value of the plant, and from 1878 to 1892 hops were a major focus of agriculture in the Duwamish, White and Puyallup river valleys. By the end of the 1870s Milton Robbins, Joseph Foster, the Steeles, Francis McNatt, the Shinn brothers, Henry Adams, the Tituses, Henry Miller and others were heavily into hops growing.

Hops had a high yield per acre and sold high. Assuming that Robbins, who developed a large hop farm, averaged 100,000 pounds of hops a year, in 1879, when the hops sold for 25 cents a pound, Robbins made $25,000. In the coming decade, prices ranged from 18 cents to $1.08 a pound. The average cost of production in 1882 was 10 cents a pound. At the beginning, the average yield was 1,600 pounds per acre cultivated, which netted $144 to $1,440 per acre. This was much more than potatoes, oats or hay.

Soon the "hops craze" affected every farm in King County. By 1882 over 200 acres of farmland was planted with hops yielding 300,000 pounds. The 1882 harvest brought in $180,000, of which $150,000 was over and above expenses. The productivity of many farmers was outstanding. Improved cultivation methods had boosted the average yield to 2,250 pounds per acre. By 1884 there were 90 farmers cultivating hops in the county, with a total of 870 acres under cultivation. The yield: 979 tons, worth $489,000, market value.

INDIAN HOP PICKERS

From planting through harvesting, hop culture was complex and labor intensive. Hops grow from bulblike roots (rhizomes) that produce vigorous vines. Farmers erected tall climbing poles for the mature vines, which often reached 15 feet. In June the hop vines produced cone-shaped catkins that were allowed to ripen until the beginning of September, when they were harvested by careful hand picking.

Hop pickers in the White River Valley. Hops were harvested by careful hand picking and placed in a basket or flat box which was loaded into field wagons. The youth in the center is holding a hop rake used to reach the top of the tall vines. Picking was piecework and a picker received $1 per basket. During the 1880s the entire population of King County turned out to help harvest the hops. Many city people, such as the fashionably dressed women in this photo, regarded hop harvesting as a holiday. Courtesy White River Historical Museum.

As more acres were planted to hops, it was quickly apparent that a much larger work force was necessary than was available locally. By 1882, hop growers were relying on Indian workers to harvest the huge crop. The Indians came from British Columbia, Neah Bay and the Yakima Valley. They came on foot; they came on horseback; and they came in horse-drawn wagons. Old-timers told of how they could hear the Yakima people coming from Snoqualmie Pass. First there was the low thunder of hundreds of hooves pounding the earth, then the dust cloud to the east, and then the earth underfoot began to vibrate as they drew closer. They were noisy and they were fierce, and the coastal Indians, who also came to work the harvest, retained their old fear of the plateau people. Ella Fenton Burton, Jane Fenton's sister, recorded in her Teacher's Daybook for September 3, 1886, "Hops-pickers are passing and repassing. Sleek, well dressed, good looking Indians." The size of the needed work force was astonishing. It is recorded in 1884 a full 3,000 Indians arrived to work in the Puyallup Valley alone.

The majority of the Indians came by the river, paddling their canoes from Vancouver Island and even Alaska. During hop-picking time there were as many as 1,000 canoes along the banks of the upper Duwamish River. The stretch of White River near the James Nelsen farm was a favorite camping place.

James Cameron, Orillia pioneer settler, recorded that "the Coast Indians would come up the river in their big dug-out canoes in which they carried their dogs and cats, as well as their families and all their household possessions. These Indians would make their camp along the river and in the hops fields. Where Briscoe School now stands, there was an Indian camp of which an Indian named Dr. Jim James was chief." The Indians were deemed excellent hop harvesters, going to the fields with the first light of dawn, taking their lunches with them and remaining at the work until pitch dark. Experts made as much as $3 a day, but the average picker made $1.25. The Indians never accepted paper money, which they called *cultus chickament*, meaning "no-good money." They insisted on being paid in silver dollars.

The valley was lively during the harvest season and an exciting festive atmosphere prevailed. When they came the Indians brought goods to trade, including beautiful art and craft work. The Orillia stores boomed. When unscrupulous white men sold liquor to the Indians, there would often be trouble and fighting. After the excitement of the harvest was over, it was very quiet, and the valley farmers hurried to finish preparing for winter.

The market peaked in 1882, with prices never again matching that year. No matter, the "hops rage" was on, and each year farmers added more acreage to hops up to 1890, when the market broke as a result of a little insect—the hop louse. The hop louse was first detected in King County in 1889, and had a moderate impact on the crop that year. In 1890 the hop louse infested the vines everywhere and ruined the industry almost overnight. Prices dropped to eight cents a pound and then four cents a pound, and by 1892 hops were a thing of the past.

Hard Times for the Valley Farmers

Almost from the very beginning of the pioneer period many Duwamish Valley farmers, short on money, had signed notes secured by their land for supplies and equipment. The objective was to pay off the debt with income from the harvest. As a result of this practice, over the years many families lost parcels of land bit by bit to Seattle merchants. The strong market value of hops enticed many farmers to borrow, in some cases heavily, against the harvest using their land as security. With the crop failure of 1890, almost overnight some

There could never be too many hop pickers, for the picking had to be done quickly while the plant was prime. By 1882 the hop harvest was too large for the local labor supply, and Indian pickers, who came from throughout the Northwest and Alaska, were relied upon. Here Indian workers fill hop crates with the ripe hop flowers. Courtesy Museum of History & Industry.

of the wealthiest farmers were reduced to poverty and many lost substantial amounts of their land. The impact of the hops failure on the economy of many a farm family was doubly serious, since often hops were being raised to the almost total exclusion of any other marketable crop. In addition to losing land, in 1890 a substantial portion of the population suffered from no income for a year.

This was just the beginning of the financial difficulties of the 1890s. The national Great Panic of 1893 was delayed in hitting King County by the wave of dynamic growth the region was experiencing. The depression's full impact hit in 1896, when banks failed, businesses closed and local development slowed to a crawl. Traveling up the Duwamish and White river valleys in 1890, one would have noticed considerable economic depression.

THE GREAT PANIC

Unemployment problems had begun in 1891, when mechanics and laborers from all over the United States, who had been attracted to Seattle by the building boom following the Great Fire of 1889, found there was no work.

In 1893 the most significant economic recession of the century developed—called the Great Panic. It evolved from widespread extreme speculation in real estate and railroad securities, as well as other commodities. States, counties, municipalities, companies and individuals had contracted high levels of indebtedness. Banks were very willing to loan seemingly anyone money for any purpose. Many agencies, as well as individuals, assumed debts far beyond their means.

The disaster devastated King County. Seven of the railroads operating in the county failed and went into the hands of receivers. Of the 23 banks in the county, all failed but nine. People living in the valley who banked in Kent lost their funds as the bank failed. The Renton Bank, however, managed to pull through.

The farmers directly felt the effects of the Panic as farm produce brought the lowest prices on record. Jobs became scarce and wages were greatly reduced. Clothing and groceries also cost less. Valley farmers who rented out their land lost the land in some cases as rents dropped below cost. Land values in the south part of the county depreciated from 40 to 80 percent. For several years during the 1890s, the only land sold was by the county sheriff for debt, by the county treasurer for back taxes, and by arrangement between debtors and creditors.

In 1896 the county was making a very slow comeback from the Panic and no one expected any significant improvement for several years. This changed in a single day. On July 17, 1897, the following message was telegraphed across the United States: "The steamship *Portland* has just arrived in Seattle with a ton of gold on board." The Alaska-Klondike Gold Rush was on. All kinds of foodstuffs were immediately in high demand for the Alaskan market. Ways of processing food into compact form that would resist frost and decay were hastily developed—with varying degrees of success—and the demand for farm products continued to rise. The Duwamish Valley farmers, like their neighbors in the White River and Puyallup valleys, experienced a refreshingly quick increase in farm produce prices, and prosperity returned as the century drew a close.

Chapter 5
Immigrants Find the Valley—1880-1900

Passenger train coming through the Northern Cascades. In the 1880s the railroads launched a vigorous campaign to bring settlers to the Northwest. Special "emigrant trains" were set up. The trip from St. Paul, Minnesota, to Portland, Oregon, was 1900 miles, took 7 days and cost $45 a full ticket on the Northern Pacific. Courtesy Seattle Historical Society.

Who should go to Washington Territory:

The class of immigrants needed are those ordinary and mechanical laborers, "horny-handed sons of toil" who combine frugal habits with unflinching industry; the idle, the lazy, the lethargic and the riff-raff are positively not wanted. Health, courage and earnest toil are required here as elsewhere, and the immigrant must not look for a bed of roses, but must be prepared to endure all of the privation of life incident to a new country, yet always have ahead of him the bright lode-star of success, bringing with it peace and plenty.

   Immigrant Handbook for Washington Territory, 1887

By 1880 there had been settlers living in the Duwamish Valley for 29 years. The firstcomers, affectionately known to their neighbors as the "Old Timers," were passing away. In the summer of 1880 two of the four surviving members of the Collins party died: Samuel Maple in July, at age 53, and his father Jacob Maple in September at age 83. This left only Stephen and Lucinda Collins and Henry Van Asselt of the original seven who made up the first settlement in King County. The deaths of the Maples were symbolic of the end of the era of pioneering in the true wilderness. Quickly moving toward statehood, Washington was on the verge of a major population influx that, once begun, would continue until World War I.

The Population

Between 1880 and 1889 three censuses were taken in King County as a part of the push for statehood. In 1880 the

Immigrants Find the Valley — 1880-1900

population for the Duwamish district, which included the entire valley, was reported as 199 settlers. In 1885 there were 475 inhabitants, a 250 percent increase. The 1889 count registered 906 white inhabitants—an increase of 450 percent from nine years earlier and almost 200 percent from four years earlier. The next census, 1892, revealed that the population had doubled in three years, with 2062 inhabitants reported.

In 1880, adult males accounted for 38 percent of the total population, adult women 25 percent and children 37 percent. The Duwamish Valley continued to be a single woman's paradise, with three bachelors for every unmarried woman. After decades of single males predominating, married couples became the majority, with six out of ten adults being married. There were a total of 52 families living in the valley at this date. Because the couples had come west early in their marriages, or married after arriving, six out of ten of the children were born in Washington Territory.

After Washington, the states of origin with noteworthy representation were New York, Missouri, Iowa, Ohio, Illinois, Massachusetts, Indiana, Kentucky and Pennsylvania. The most frequently given occupations were laborer and farmer. There were four carpenters and one blacksmith reported; other occupations present were dentist, shipbuilder, fisherman, manufacturer and postmaster. Women generally listed their occupations as housewife, housekeeper and cook. Few of the settlers were immigrants; only one out of ten was foreign born, with Germany and Canada leading as countries of origin.

The proportion of the population that was foreign born was to change dramatically almost overnight. Thus, in 1885 one out of five people were immigrants, and by 1889 one out of three. More than 50 percent of the foreign-born were from northern Europe, with Germany, Sweden, Norway and Denmark most represented.

This abrupt increase in immigrants coming into the area in the 1880s was a part of a national trend. It was unique in the history of American immigration up to that time because of the large proportion of non-English-speaking immigrants. This trend was to swell to a full-scale flood by 1900 and continue until 1918, with southern and eastern Europeans dominating in the later years. Historically this phenomenon is known as the "Great Migration," and a large proportion of Americans living in the country at the end of the twentieth century trace their families' entrance into the United States to this period.

Settlers Coming by Rail

In the 1880s the newcomers who poured into Puget Sound and the valley—Americans and foreign born—came on every train arriving from the eastern states. In 1883 King County's population was 10,424. By 1885 it had grown to 16,160.

In the 1880s a vigorous campaign was launched to bring people into the Northwest. The railroads themselves were behind the majority of this activity, since they had only benefits to receive from settlers coming west on the train, including passenger fares, shipping revenue, and sale of railroad land to settlers.

Special "emigrant trains" traveled from the Midwest to the Northwest. The fare included a space in the emigrant sleeping car—basically Spartan bunk car where travelers provided their own bedding. This was a service that only the Northern Pacific offered and it made the rail line popular. Travelers either brought their own food for the trip, which they ate on the train, or bought meals at regular eating stations along the route. Shipping costs were high, with $4.55 charged per 100 pounds of extra baggage.

An organized party of 30 could reserve an entire railroad car for their exclusive use for $370. Groups of friends and relatives from the Midwest or East Coast moving to Puget Sound often booked an entire car. And did they have fun! Visiting, reading, playing games, telling stories and spinning dreams of their future occupied the time. The children roamed the length of the train making friends with young people from all over the U.S. and Europe—even if they did not speak the same language. For the hard-working people from farming and working-class stock, who were willing to take on the Herculean task of building farms in the Northwest, the train trip was the closest thing to a vacation that many of them had ever experienced. Lifetime friendships were established, and more than one courtship began on the "trip out."

As in the 1850s and 1860s, for those starting out from the Atlantic Coast or Europe, traveling by water was a logical alternative to the train. The Pacific Mail Company's steamship line was the most common conveyance, while English and German steamers made the most regular direct voyages to the Isthmus of Panama. Portland was the principal point of entry and settlers traveled by train to their Puget Sound destinations.

Immigrant handbooks were printed in many languages to guide the migrant in making her or his decision to move, how to prepare, and what to expect in the Northwest. A popular handbook declares that "the laborer, the mechanic, the real farmer, dairyman, fruit-grower or stock-grower, and large and small capitalists are among the Territory's most urgent requirements at the present time. Every man, especially those who are fitted to farm work, can find, in time, some kind of employment." Doctors, lawyers and all those professionals who are "unaccustomed to labor with their hands" are advised "not to come," as there is insufficient work to support them at the level to which they are accustomed.

While women are much desired and the "thrifty common-sense wife" is lauded as the greatest blessing that the pioneering man can have, women per se are not encouraged to come. One handbook warns, "Women generally above the grade of domestic servants; in fact, any 'lone' woman had better refrain from emigrating for the same hardships, with severer, ulterior consequences than as the man's await them." Immigrants are admonished to bring with them at least $500, above and beyond travel expenses, with which to establish themselves—to build a house and to buy livestock, seed, farming tools and provisions.

Thanks to the railroad's promotion program, the region attracted a phenomenal number of people, which skyrocketed the combined population of Seattle and Tacoma from 4,631 in 1880 to 78,843 in 1890. Farms in the vicinity of these burgeoning cities had rapidly expanding markets for their products. Dairying, poultry and vegetable farming paid good returns, and after the hop failure farmers in the Duwamish and White river valleys began focusing on supplying the local city markets. At the time of statehood, King County led the state in potato production, market-garden produce and milk production.

IMMIGRANT FARMERS BUILD FARMS IN THE VALLEY—THE NELSENS

This shift to dairying and market-garden produce around 1890 coincided with the historic lead that the Scandinavians took in the Great Migration to America. As a result of overpopulation and the poor future outlook in Scandinavia, young single women and men began coming to America in large numbers in the 1880s—preceding the mass migration of the turn of the century from southern and eastern Europe. Between 1880 and 1920 about 40 percent of the population of Scandinavian countries immigrated to the United States. Coming from farm backgrounds, these people sought farms, and were attracted to the Northwest by its good soil and general similarity to the Nordic lands. A part of this great demographic move were the Danish Nelsens of the Duwamish and lower White River valley, now known as the Green River Valley.

The story of the Nelsen brothers—James, Herman, and Fred—who emigrated from Denmark in the 1880s and settled in the area provides insights into the life decisions and hard work put into realizing their objectives that characterized the people populating the valley

Immigrants Find the Valley — 1880-1900

The Nelsen brothers of the White River Valley, vicinity of Renton Junction and Orillia. L to R, back to front: Fred, James, Ole, Herman. All of the Nelsens distinguished themselves in community service. One project they accomplished together was the building of the Lutheran Church at Orillia with the help of James O. Cameron, Orillia storekeeper. Courtesy Alma Nelsen Taylor.

in this period. Their efforts to establish themselves, their formation of families, and their contributions to their community and region demonstrate the dreams, goals, determination and effort that they, and others like them, made during their lifetimes. Two sisters, Sophia and Mary, and another brother, Ole, also immigrated and settled in the Northwest. However, since they did not live in the valley their stories are not recorded here. The Nelsen brothers lived in the vicinity of Renton Junction and Orillia, i.e., Fort Dent Park and the Southcenter district.

Other immigrants came to the Duwamish and White river valleys between 1890 and 1910, who, working in a manner similar to the Nelsens, also established themselves and were a credit to the valley. Among the most prominent of these are Peter Cerini, Swiss dairyman, the Meadows; Joseph LaFranchi, Swiss dairyman, Duwamish; Archie Codiga, Swiss dairyman, Allentown; Jacob Nielsen, Danish dairyman, Riverton; and John Strander, Swedish nurseryman, Foster. These and others in the area each have a unique story of their personal experience building a life in the valley. However, the Nelsens have been selected because of their civic spirit demonstrated by outstanding community and regional leadership and service.

The Nelsens demonstrate how the cultural background of foreign-born immigrants shaped the economy of the area. The Nelsens came from a region in Denmark where dairy farming was the main focus and as children they worked on dairy farms as hired hands. Because of the high standards they were exposed to in the dairy industry in Denmark, they distinguished themselves in King County with the excellence of their dairying operations.

Nels and Maren Olsen of Karebaek, Denmark, had ten children, six of whom emigrated to America. In Denmark it was not the custom to use a family surname; however, at the time of entry into the United States the Nelsens took the name Nelsen, i.e., "son of Nels," as their surname. For each of the Nelsens, formal education ended between the fourth and ninth grade. James withdrew from school at age 9 and went to work as a farm hand. Herman left home to support himself at age 12.

JAMES NELSEN

Entering the U.S. in 1881, James Nelsen made his way to Washington by way of Illinois after two years working near his sister Sophia's farm. In 1883 Sophia, with her husband Fred Ditlivesen and family, and James Nelsen caught an immigrant train to Puget Sound. After a short stay in Seattle doing odd jobs, James went to work on the farms of Danish immigrants Chris Jorgensen and Martin Nelsen in the Black River Junction area. With three years' savings Nelsen bought his first tract of

Known as Indian Joe or Black Joe, this Duwamish Native American worked for James and Fred Nelsen and other farmers. From the first days the settlers relied on Indian workers' help with the tough work of clearing land. The 1880 census lists large numbers of native people as employed laborers. Indian laborers enumerated with the Henry Adams household are Jimmy, 30, Ilacu, 23, and Johnny, 25; Caroline, 20, a housekeeper; and Mary, 25, laborer. Courtesy Alma Nelsen Taylor.

land—about 25 acres of woods and marsh. Nelsen suffered from the same problem as the earlier donation claim pioneers—land but no money with which to improve it. He returned to Seattle and became a coachman for the prominent Seattle banker Bailey Gatzert, who was closely associated with Jacob Furth.

While working in the Gatzert household Nelsen became friends with Mary Dobler, a German immigrant who was Babette Gatzert's maid. Like James Nelsen, Mary Dobler was raised in a rural area, and was an adventurous and self-sufficient person. She has come alone to the United States in 1882 at age 19. In 1885 James and Mary were married and returned to his land to develop a farm. Their land was heavily covered with trees and dense brush, and part of it was swampy, which made immediate cultivation impossible. However, James's older brother Ole, who had recently come from Denmark and married another Danish immigrant, joined James and Mary, and the four young people pooled their money and rented a nearby piece of cleared land which they farmed together. With the gain from that year, James and Mary turned to industriously clearing and draining their own land.

The couple had settled on Henry Meader's donation claim and were among the first to extensively clear and develop for agriculture the rich White River bottom land in the vicinity of the confluence of the rivers. Long days of hard manual labor, combined with wise business decisions, allowed them to prosper, and they soon bought the Ringsdorfs' 210-acre hop farm nearby, which had seven cleared acres. It was a small parcel but enough to increase their income sufficiently to allow them to save money for more land. The rest of the Ringsdorf land was still in its natural state. They raised potatoes and hops. To raise cash Jim worked out as a hop foreman in the valley, while Mary ran the farm in Jim's absence and looked after the children, Harry born 1888, Frank, 1890, and Sidonia, 1895.

Nelsen built a small house for his family at what later became 16010 W. Valley Rd. Eventually they acquired 280 acres of additional land. They began their dairy milking a few cows and selling the milk in Seattle, sending it first by boat down the river and after 1902 on the Interurban. Gradually they increased their dairy herd to 70 good-grade cows and shifted from selling milk retail to selling it on a wholesale basis.

By the 1920s the Nelsens had a modern dairy operation that met the highest standards of the day. On their large acreage they grew corn, hay and grain. They raised all the feed for their animals, storing it in a pair of tall silos. The Nelsens' herd consisted of quality Holstein and Guernsey cows, and registered Holstein sires. Eventually, the problem of the soggy land was resolved by laying tile to drain the land. Fully developed, the Nelsens' farm had substantial modern outbuildings and a large handsome Victorian home, built in 1905 by Mr. Olsen, a local Danish carpenter. Their last child, Helen, was born in the house in 1906.

In the 1910s Nelsen bought a fine piece of Vermont granite from the Catholic Ladies Aid,

IMMIGRANTS FIND THE VALLEY — 1880-1900

In the Victorian classic box style, the James Nelsen House is on the Washington State Register of Historic Places. The house was moved 60 feet west in 1964 to make room for the West Valley Highway. The historic house is basically unchanged from the original construction. James Nelsen is on the left, Mary is holding Helen, Sidonia is on the right, and Frank and Mr. Goode, a neighbor, are on the porch. Courtesy Helen Nelsen.

remained in the family home throughout her life seeing to its maintenance and preservation.

In addition to farming, James Nelsen was involved with a number of significant community-building activities. With three others he founded and maintained the Independent Water Company, a private water supply system which served parts of the Tukwila community for 50 years. In addition, he was the County Road Supervisor for the South King County District for 15 years. Nelsen was one of the original organizers of the Renton Citizens Bank later known as the First National and then, as Peoples Bank. Nelsen also supported the area schools by serving on the Renton School Board for many years.

who had acquired it with the intent of commissioning a statue of the pioneer priest Father Prefontaine. That project fell through, and Nelsen got the stone. Barging it up from Tacoma, he commissioned Sam Barrett, a stone carver and painter living in Riverton, to transform the stone into the pair of substantial lions that have guarded the front of the house for over 70 years.

The Nelsens' dairy barn, built in 1903 south of the house, was a large frame structure crowned by a pair of seven-foot gable-roofed cupolas. In 1969 the barn was moved across the West Valley Highway near the entrance to Longacres Racetrack, where it served as the Renton Auction Barn until demolished in 1990. However, the original homestead barn, built in 1887, remains.

The Nelsens' son Harry became an electrician, Frank became a steamboat engineer, and Sidonia (Kettering) managed the Nelsen family water company. Helen joined the First National Bank of Renton (later Peoples Bank), and

Nelsen was a strong advocate of cooperation among the farmers, and was a founder and director of the King County Dairymen's Association. Both Mary and James Nelsen were active for decades in the White River Grange, based in Orillia. Mary and James maintained a strong sense of Danish ethnic identity through affiliation with the Danish Brotherhood and Sisterhood and the Danish Lutheran Church. A prominent Democrat, Nelsen was also a member of the King County Pioneer Association and the Pioneers of Washington. Most of James and Mary's children graduated from college.

James Nelsen lived in the Renton Junction area for 66 years. After his death, the following tribute was made to Nelsen and his life: "King County remembers him among its most progressive and successful farmers and the rules which

Herman and Margaret Andersen Nelsen's Merrymount Dairy Farm, Inc. on the 1916 Pacific Highway, near Orillia. With an outstanding dairy herd of 75 cows—Holsteins, Guernseys and Jerseys—the dairy received widespread recognition as one of the best dairy plants in western Washington, in the era before federal regulation. Courtesy Tukwila Historical Society.

govern his life are such as constituted the basis of all honorable and desirable prosperity, while his personality is one that inspires esteem and friendship."

HERMAN NELSEN

Herman Nelsen immigrated in 1889, coming directly to James Nelsen's farm. After helping his brother for a year, Herman went to work for a neighboring farmer, Neils Andersen, another Danish immigrant. After Andersen died, Herman Nelsen managed the farm for Margaret Andersen, and later they were married. Together they owned 60 acres on the White River (the Henry Adams donation claim) and leased an additional 120 acres.

Herman and Margaret Andersen Nelsen maintained a very efficient and immaculate dairy farm operation. They used modern equipment, including an ice plant with a daily capacity of two tons of ice, a bottle washer and a bottle filling machine, all electrically operated—a very modern innovation for the day.

Herman Nelsen was a lifetime member of the White River Grange and a member of the State Board of Directors from 1915 until his death in 1936. In addition, Nelsen was a director of the Orillia Water Supply Co. and the Seattle Milk Shippers Association. He was also the secretary-treasurer of the Renton-Kent National Farm Loan Association. Margaret Andersen Nelsen had six children by her first marriage, and she and Herman had one son, Marcus, a graduate of Eastern Washington State University, who was the Kent postmaster for many years.

The eldest Nelsen brother, Ole, settled in the lower Cedar River area in the 1890s, where he developed a large successful dairy farm opposite the Veenhuizen farm. Ole's son Herman later owned and operated the farm.

FRED NELSEN

Fred Nelsen, the second-youngest of the Nelsen brothers to emigrate from Denmark, was born in 1871 and came to the United States in 1889. He traveled directly to his brother James in the White River Valley. Fred worked for a number of farmers in the following years, including Chris Jorgensen, who had settled at Black River Junction around 1870. In 1898 he married Jorgensen's daughter Dora. The couple bought 100 acres of land from James that lay at the confluence of the rivers. Like his brothers, Fred went into dairying and developed a large, prosperous modern dairy in the area known as Renton Junction after the building of the Interurban. The Nelsens had six daughters, Rose, Elsie, Hilda, Alma, Eleanor and Dorothy, and one son Evan. Most of the Nelsen children graduated from college.

Fred Nelsen's hired man and a Duwamish native plowing at Renton Junction, looking east. The Nelsen farmstead is in the background, left of the Interurban trestle. The hill in background later became the Black River Quarry. Courtesy Alma Nelsen Taylor.

Fred and Dora are distinguished for their civic spirit and community leadership in local organizations and the Grange, where they served on local, regional and state levels. They were charter members of the White River Grange No. 238 in 1908. In 1919-21 Dora served as state Pomona. Active for over a half a century, Fred served the Grange in many capacities including State Grange Overseer and Master, 1919-25, and State Grange Executive Committee Emeritus, 1953-63. He was the State Grange Treasurer for 24 years. In 1958 he received the Grange Leadership Award. He organized 15 Granges across Washington and in 1958 received the high honor of Gold Sheaf Member status, for 50 years of service.

Fred Nelsen greatly supported cooperatives, an idea that was first successfully realized in Denmark in the 1880s. Nelsen provided able leadership with the Western Washington Cooperative Movement and served as President of the Grange Cooperative Wholesale for 30 years. He was a founder and charter member of the Board of Directors of Group Health Cooperative of Puget Sound.

Fred Nelsen's civic interest extended beyond the concerns of farming. In 1934 he was named by Governor Martin to the newly created State Planning Council. A Democrat throughout his life, Nelsen also served as the District Representative in the State Legislature from 1917 to 1919.

On the local level, for many years he and Dora actively served on the Renton School Board, where their children attended high school. In 1964 the Fred Nelsen Junior High

Fred and Dora Jorgensen Nelsen dairy farm, Renton Junction. The large Victorian house, designed by the owners and the carpenter, Mr. Olsen, was a busy, happy place, with six daughters and one son who helped with the farm work. The Fred Nelsen house and barn remain standing in 1990, the prancing horse weathervane atop the big barn overlooking the nearby crossroads. Courtesy Alma Nelsen Taylor.

DANISH-AMERICAN CHRISTMAS TRADITIONS

Alma Nelsen Taylor

Great preparation went into the celebration of Christmas. At least one whole day was set aside for cooky making—spritz, kleiner, and Danish coffee cake.

When Christmas Eve came, in the morning several of us would go with Dad and his axe across the river to the woods, now Tukwila Park, and find a tree tall enough to "reach the ceiling." We hauled it back on our homemade horse-drawn wagon and Dad would take it into the living room and put it into a homemade frame. There was always much talk about where to cut it so it would be sure to almost "touch the ceiling." The wonderful fresh fir smell is memorable.

Then came the excitement of Christmas Eve. After the evening chores were done, milk bottled, etc., we would all march behind Dad to the barn to give the animals a present of extra grain for Christmas. I remember taking handfuls of "cow salt" and scattering it on top of the extra hay so it would taste good.

Our Christmas Eve supper was always chicken soup and Danish dumplings, and mother's famous Parker House rolls. The kids were then relegated to the kitchen, where the dishes were done. Then the popcorn popping began and we strung the popcorn. As each string was finished, Mother would come and take it back to the living room and hang it on the tree. Mother and Dad did all the decorating, and we were not allowed in the living room until Dad rang a loud bell and slammed the hall door shut, calling "Santa, have a good trip." When he opened the living room door to us there stood the wonderful sight of 100 candles burning on the tree and presents stacked under it. Each one of us would get one present we had hoped for.

The hired man, who lived in a small one-room house beside the big house and boarded with us, was always invited to "come in for the tree." Christmas carols were sung and all was merry. We children almost always got a pair of new red boots to wear while doing our chores. The hired man always got a pair of bedroom slippers.

School, Renton, was dedicated to the memory of Fred Nelsen and his community service. Both Fred and Dora Nelsen were proud of their Danish heritage and remained active in the Danish Brotherhood and Sisterhood throughout their lives, as well as the Danish Lutheran Church.

An energetic, generous, caring and idealistic person, Fred Nelsen expressed his vision of community service in the following words delivered to the 55th National Grange Conference in Portland, Oregon, in 1921:

> [The Grange] has never been commercialized or subsidized, but of, by and for the farmer and actuated by the highest motives, it holds a record individually and collectively of unselfish service and accomplishment, which places it in a place all its own and richly entitles it to the esteem and confidence it enjoys.

Dora Nelsen died in 1938. In 1940 Fred married Meta Jonientz. She died in 1962, and Fred died in 1963 at the age of 92.

The Nelsens have been described as belonging to "that desirable class of foreign-born American citizens whose inherited tendencies of industry and perseverance have constituted important factors in the upbuilding of the Pacific Northwest." Through conscientiously operated businesses, as well as regional leadership of the caliber of the Nelsens, the valley gained recognition and respect throughout the region for agricultural progressiveness in the period from 1890 to 1940.

Fred and Dora Nelsen family in the 1909 Alaskan-Yukon Exposition parade, Seattle. The large Nelsen family was highly involved in community and regional activities, and regularly mixed fun with their civic service. Courtesy Eleanor Nelsen Robinson.

Part II
Twentieth-Century Communities

Introduction

At the beginning of the twentieth century, the Duwamish and White river valleys still lay a tranquil, pastoral area of wooded hills and lush river bottom dotted with tidy prosperous farms. This was to change rapidly in the next two decades as an unprecedented flood of people found the Northwest. In the period following statehood in 1889, Washington experienced its own version of the great American Westward Movement. For three decades Americans from the older parts of the country and foreign-born immigrants poured into Washington.

Several factors caused this flood of newcomers. This period was the height of the great population migration to the U.S. As the supply of cheap land and timber available under land-grant legislation diminished, people frantically rushed to the Northwest—the last frontier—to make their fortunes. In addition, Seattle's massive public works projects of the 1890s-1910s, such as leveling Denny Hill and digging the Lake Washington Ship Canal, focused national attention on Seattle and attracted thousands of laborers who had lost their jobs as a result of the 1890s depression. By the 1890s the railroads, anxious to build a market for their shipping business, worked with real estate developers in conducting national marketing campaigns designed to pull people to the Northwest.

Efforts to bring people to Washington were successful, and between 1890 and 1920 the number of people living in the state increased more than fifteenfold. In 1890, state residents numbered 518,013, compared to 1,141,990 in 1910—a 120 percent increase, six times the national rate for this period. In all of Washington, King County grew the fastest, with Seattle being the hub. The population of Seattle essentially doubled every seven years between 1880 and 1920. The 1880 census reported for Seattle 3,533 residents; in 1890 it reported 42,390, a twelvefold increase. By 1910 Seattle's population had grown to 237,194—an impressive figure that was over half the population of the entire state only 20 years earlier.

The setback of the Panic of 1893 was only a pause in the region's dynamic growth. The Alaska Gold Rush of 1897 helped pull King County out of its economic slump. Recognizing the coming demand for homesites, in 1893 Julius Horton, Dexter Horton's older brother, subdivided the farmland near the mouth of the Duwamish, naming it Georgetown for his son George, who was back east in medical school. Residential and commercial lots sold and other developers took note.

For the first half century after the Collins party opened up King County to settlement, the majority of the people moving to Puget Sound were seeking farms. After 1900 the newcomers were more likely to settle into jobs found in the factories, shops and service businesses around Seattle. The people choosing to live in the Seattle area wanted small acreages or simply homesites. As the cost of real estate rose in Seattle, new suburbs developed in the environs offering affordable home sites. The Interurban electric rail service, beginning in late September 1902, linked outlying areas previously deemed too far from Seattle for city workers' homes. The years immediately following the startup of the Interurban also witnessed the building of improved roads and a series of bridges across the Duwamish and greatly improved travel in the valley.

With the exception of Foster, which has its roots in the nineteenth century, all of the communities in Tukwila formed as a result of these historical factors. At the end of the twentieth century the northernmost section of Tukwila is not a residential community, but basically an industrial/commercial district. This district, lying geographically the closest to Seattle, was the first portion of Tukwila to be developed. Historically known as the Meadows, it has a rich history.

CHAPTER 6

THE MEADOWS ON THE DUWAMISH RIVER

Opening in 1902, the Meadows Racetrack briefly enjoyed great success with crowds of 10,000 to 20,000. Admission was $1; many people brought lunch baskets and picnicked on the banks of the Duwamish River. During its heyday the best horses and jockeys in the country raced at the Meadows. Courtesy Donald Campbell, Longacres Racecourse, Inc.

The Duwamish River, in the shape of a horseshoe, encloses the grounds on three sides. Its banks are lined with soft-wood trees, whose beautiful verdure gives the grounds a rare charm and contributes greatly to the beauty of the landscape. It looks...like a natural park, and one who has spent a day on the grounds cannot but feel the incongruity of the new buildings with their bare yellow exteriors. Looking at the track, the feeling is inevitable that the grandstand, paddock, clubhouse and stables ought to be old moss-grown structures in keeping with the natural location of the race course. All this adds infinite charm to the place....

"A Magnificent Race Track,"
Seattle Times, *July 27, 1902.*

The return of prosperity after the Panic of 1893, combined with rapid population growth, created an interest in recreation and leisurely pastimes that would have been unthinkable even a decade earlier. One of the most remarkable expressions of the newly achieved sophistication of the Seattle area at the turn of the century was the development of the racetrack and amusement center called the Meadows. In its second season the racetrack adopted the name the Meadows, the name the area had been known by since pioneer times.

In its natural state the Meadows was a large flat grassy area on the east side of the Duwamish River, partially enclosed by an oxbow. In 1990 the area forms the northernmost section of the City of Tukwila and is the site of varied operations, the largest of which are the Boeing Airplane Company, the King County Airport, and the Museum of Flight. The picturesque oxbow was eliminated when the lower Duwamish River watercourse was straightened in 1916-17; however, Boeing continues to call its employee parking lots the Oxbow lots. After it served as a racetrack, and before it was taken over by commercial interests, the Meadows played a role in King County's public health for a number of years, when it was the site of The Meadows Tuberculosis Sanitarium.

Lying in Henry Van Asselt's and Francis McNatt's donation claims, the land changed hands a number of times as Van Asselt and McNatt sold off their land in the 1880s. Charles Terry acquired the land and sold it to C. C. and H. A. Davis in 1891, who platted part of the land as Davis's Meadow Tracts and advertised 5-acre tracts. Because of the economic drag of the Panic, lots did not sell and the land remained undivided.

KING COUNTY FAIR ASSOCIATION

In 1901 a private venture called the King County Fair Association organized with the objective of establishing a fashionable, first-class racetrack close to Seattle on a par with those of the eastern states. At that time horse racing was the most popular spectator sport in the Northwest. An established western Washington racing circuit already included tracks in Vancouver, Centralia, Olympia, Lacey, Tacoma, Kent, Everett, Mount Vernon, Whatcom and Lynden. The Fair Association was determined to make Seattle a major racing city. The Fair Association's master plan was to develop the Meadows area into a general recreational center with a permanent amusement park where, in addition to racing, a variety of events could be staged, including the King County Fair. The immediate objective was to build a first-rate racing park including a one-mile track, 6,000-seat grandstand, fashionable clubhouse, stalls for 400 horses and streetcar service to the entrance. The course was nationally sanctioned, with professional officials, good prize money and well-maintained facilities.

The regional uniqueness of the flat Meadows terrain had given rise to horse racing before 1900. There are reports that the Indians raced in the area. The pioneers had held races at a site to the north on Luther Collins' claim. After 1870, when the first of several Seattle jockey clubs began organizing local racing, there had been at least one track on the Duwamish River, where mixed meets of thoroughbred and trotting, i.e., harness, racing were staged annually. Since 1891 the closest racetrack had been in Kent, and there was strong support in Seattle for a good track close to home.

THE MEADOWS OPENING SEASON

In the summer of 1902 the air at the Meadows was filled with the steady purring of saws and smart snap of hammers hitting their targets as first the paddock, then the grandstand, and finally the clubhouse took shape. Positioned between the grandstand and the paddock, the elegant Meadows Clubhouse symbolized the ambitious goals of the Fair Association. On racing days the spacious lawn between the Meadows Clubhouse and the track was dotted with rose, blue, green and yellow Japanese umbrellas to provide the ladies with an appropriate setting for showing off their fashionable summer gowns.

The opening of the Meadows track augmented local interest in harness horses, since it offered good conditions for both training and driving. At this time there were a number of very well bred harness horses owned by private parties around King County. Recognizing the popular appeal of seeing locally known people race, the Fair Association scheduled a series of Saturday matinee amateur races for merchants and professional men who drove their own fast horses. The stakes were silver cups, fancy blankets and harnesses.

On August 18, 1902, the Meadows Racetrack and grounds formally opened. The Interurban service had not yet started, people traveled to the track via railway cars, or via Seattle's inadequate streetcar service, which required numerous transfers and much waiting for connecting cars. The newspapers report that on opening day 3,000 people made their way to the new track, many arriving before the gates swung open at 1 p.m. They found the Meadows grounds to be smartly laid out, with every detail carefully planned to create the atmosphere of a well-established track. The sun shone brightly all day, and a fresh breeze blowing off the Duwamish kept the American flags that topped each post surrounding the track dancing gaily throughout the afternoon.

Top: Meadows Racetrack 1904—infield and judge's stand—looking northeast past Beacon Hill in background. Bottom: The Meadows Clubhouse had balconies on each floor, offering a splendid view of the race course, and no trouble was spared to make the clubhouse tastefully comfortable. Club members enjoyed a stylish ladies' parlor, a plush gentlemen's smoking room and bar, a library, and a dark-paneled dining room with fresh white-linen-covered tables where a late breakfast, coffee, or winner's celebration dinner could be enjoyed. Separate and distinct from the Fair Association proper, the Meadows Club was an important feature of the enterprise. Courtesy Seattle Historical Society.

The first Meadows racing season concluded with an auto race billed as a "novel and exciting sport." Three automobiles showed up for the race, the first ever in King County. It was not much of a race, since the gasoline-powered entry was too slow to compete with the two steam-powered machines. While a race between only two machines was deemed by the crowd to be considerably less exciting than a race between thoroughbreds, it was novel enough to cause a craning of necks. The automobile time was 2 minutes 45 seconds. Later in the day one of the winning horses was pitted against the winning

The Meadows on the Duwamish River

Opening day of the Meadows Racetrack, August 18, 1902. To help transport thousands of racing enthusiasts to the Meadows, the Northern Pacific Railroad ran cattle cars from the King Street Station to the Meadows siding. Six weeks later the Interurban began service with the Meadows Station being served by both the Interurban and Seattle electric trolley. Courtesy of the Museum of History and Industry.

car; the horse easily bested the machine in a mile dash.

The event following the auto race was advertised as the "Siwash Derby." Native Yakima women raced their ponies, riding bareback. This event was followed by an Indian "War Dance" put on by colorfully costumed dancers.

Although the opening racing season at the Meadows was a great success, the Fair Association encountered difficulties during the winter and, in spite of early publicity announcing there would be a 1903 racing season, nothing materialized. The next season, 1904, fulfilled the promise of 1902. The track was popular with Seattle's best society, and crowds of 10,000 to 20,000 jammed the grounds. Four hundred more stalls for horses were constructed and several national racing records were broken.

At this time racing was expanding dramatically throughout the western United States and Canada, fueled by mining booms and easy money, and by recent anti-gambling legislation aimed at curtailing racing on the East Coast. A flood of expensive eastern horses hit the Meadows in 1904, along with an army of trainers, grooms, wealthy owners, legitimate bookmakers and gamblers. Unfortunately, a fringe element of race-fixers and con men also came to Northwest racing. The track flourished, as both thoroughbred racing and trotting were popular. Patrons gambled either by parimutuel wagering or with bookmakers licensed by the track management.

On Sundays, when national rules forbade professional racing, popular special programs combined amateur harness racing and races featuring women jockeys or Native American jockeys on native-bred ponies. Pursuing its goal of a diversified recreational center, the Fair Association staged balloon ascensions and baseball in the infield. The Meadows' 1905-08 racing seasons were among the largest and most ably managed in the country, and the racing season expanded from 14 days to 73 days.

POPULIST REFORM MOVEMENT CLOSES THE MEADOWS

Just as the Meadows appeared to be successfully established, larger national currents were to put a damper on its seemingly bright future. In reaction to the excesses that characterized the "Gay '90s"—crass materialism and widespread alcohol and narcotic drug addiction being the most noticeable—the Populists instigated a reform movement committed to eliminating these evils. Locally, the prohibition and suffrage groups joined forces in a vigorous anti-racing movement, and the reputation of the Meadows deteriorated rapidly after 1908. Some analysts believe that justification for the attacks on the racetrack is dubious. Reports of race-fixing were isolated, and officiating appears to have been conscientious.

The reform movement sweeping the nation emphasized self-improvement and healthful recreation. The Meadows was associated by reform activists with "Georgetown low life." There were reputed to be at least six saloons and gaming houses that ran after-hours operations, and heroin and cocaine were rumored to be widely available. In addition, newspaper editorials critical of racing sometimes included vicious anti-Semitic attacks on the Georgetown brewers and distillers who supported the Meadows racetrack.

The public began to see racing as a liability, and early in 1909 Washington's legislature passed stringent legislation against racetrack gambling. Other western states soon followed.

Being situated on an oxbow of the Duwamish, the Meadows area was regularly inundated with floodwaters, as in November 1906. However, the racing season was held during the dry months. Courtesy Washington State Historical Society.

Sunday boating on the Duwamish near the Meadows. The natural beauty of the Meadows area was enjoyed by boaters who would often pack a picnic basket and after a pleasant hour on the river pull ashore to dine and watch the lazy river. Courtesy University of Washington Special Collections.

Deprived of its major source of income, the Meadows racetrack could no longer sponsor high-quality racing. In Seattle, small-scale and poorly patronized nongambling race meets were held for a few years at a half-mile track in Madison Park, built for the Alaska-Yukon Pacific Exposition and located just off McGilvra Boulevard.

THE FIRST KING COUNTY FAIR AT THE MEADOWS, 1912

A decade passed with racing and special events being held at the Meadows, but no county fair, in spite of widespread interest in establishing an annual agricultural, educational and manufacturer's fair. In the winter of 1912 the Pomona Grange provided the necessary initiative. The King County Fair was set for September 9-14, 1912. The Meadows site was leased, and the funds to pay for the event were raised from private sources, since it was too late to get public funding for that year.

The fair trustees announced that the objective of staging the fair was to "assist in the upbuilding of the agricultural, educational and manufacturing interests of King County and the Northwest." The Duwamish Commercial Club, with members in Tukwila, Riverton, Foster and Renton Junction, was heavily involved from the very beginning, since the fairgrounds lay in their territory and the Fair Association invited the local communities to actively participate in planning the County Fair.

The Duwamish Commercial Club designated September 12 as Duwamish Day at the County Fair. Community planning meetings, open to all valley residents, were held, with separate meetings for men and women. The Commercial Club was determined to make Duwamish Day a great success and start a new tradition of a "Get Together Day" for valley residents at the county fair. Reflecting knowledge of their local history, and justifiable pride, a spokesman told newspaper reporters: "When it comes to history, old Uncle Henry Van Asselt and Sam Maple were the first pioneers of King County in 1851, so why not let all the Old Timers come out to the original place of settlement in this county, at the King County Fair!"

Community leaders encouraged "everyone [to] get together and talk this thing up and finally meet in good fellowship September 12th." The Duwamish Day idea really "caught hold" and, in the words of Duwamish historian August Toellner, "awakened a spirit of local pride in [the] valley that has seldom been excelled in the community." Toellner enthusiastically reports:

> Van Asselt has a crackerjack baseball club that is looking for the gore of some other

TUKWILA—COMMUNITY AT THE CROSSROADS

Duwamish Valley aggregation; Duwamish is having her young folks from the school fix up prize pumpkins raised by the kids; Riverton is always ready with beautiful floral displays; Foster comes in on some prize hens and fruit; Tuckwila [sic] will be in line; Allentown and Black River will have their quota....

Although they were invited in late, once the valley women became involved with preparing for Duwamish Day enthusiastic support came from every quarter. The valley newspapers report that the women made a strong commitment to making the fair "a real people's fair." In some of the communities, such as Duwamish-Allentown, the women canvassed door to door to recruit interest, exhibitors and workers. After holding their own planning meetings, the Women's Committee met with the men at the Duwamish Commercial Club. The male habit of smoking cigars at such gatherings was not appreciated by the women, who remarked to the journalist covering the story that the ladies "hoped they wouldn't be smoked out as at some previous meetings."

While the fair highlighted crops and agricultural interests, the exhibits were diversified. The schools put on exhibits showing the pupils' skills. In the agricultural area, after vegetables, animals received the highest premiums. The Agricultural College of Pullman offered a scholarship to the young man who showed himself to be the most skilled judge of dairy cows. A women's exhibit area was set aside for the display of women's needlework, artwork, baking and home canning. A special class existed for the work of women over age 60. The Women's Committee saw that a nursery and playground were available for children, with trained nurses and playground supervisors on hand at all times so that mothers could leave their children while they tended their exhibits and enjoyed the fair.

Duwamish Valley Day was a great success and brought the communities up and down the river together sharing their produce, flowers and livestock. Each community built an exhibit, and the Grange went all out. The old feelings of unity among the entire Duwamish Valley that characterized the first 50 years came back. In spite of such a brave beginning, the County Fair was held only one more year at the Meadows.

THE MEADOWS BECOMES A SPORTING RESORT

In 1914 the Northwest Speedway Company took over the Meadows, announcing its intention to maintain the Meadows as a permanent sporting resort where various types of events could be held including automobile racing, round-ups, polo games, football and horse racing. The plan received enthusiastic endorsement from leading civic organizations, and an ambitious first season of activities began. The reopening of the Meadows

Daredevil pioneer flyer Charles K. Hamilton flying his biplane over the Meadows racetrack infield, Beacon Hill in background, March 1910. On his publicity posters Hamilton promised to thrill his audience with his "patented" dive—which on first try ended with him nose-down in the duck pond. Having given a money-back guarantee to the audience, the next day he successfully completed the stunt, and thrilled the audience by taking a local beauty for a ride in his plane. Courtesy Museum of History & Industry.

84

THE MEADOWS ON THE DUWAMISH RIVER

Auto racing at the Meadows, 1909. In 1904 the first automobile racing "season" in King County was held, with two meets at the Meadows. The October meet featured famous auto racers including Barney Oldfield. The Duwamish Valley communities turned out a few days before the October race to see Oldfield driving down the Duwamish River Road through their towns on his way to Seattle. Courtesy Museum of History & Industry.

as an amusement center was seen as positive for the Duwamish Valley, since it would put more money into circulation in the area. Unfortunately, the developers ran out of money and the Meadows closed.

In 1917 the great grandstand burned. That same year the Duwamish waterway was completed and the oxbow surrounding the track was filled in. Less than 15 years after its grand opening, the Meadows racetrack on the banks of the Duwamish was already only a memory. In the next few years the Meadows area had a variety of uses, including a dairy for a short time, and a depot for goods going to Russia before the Bolshevik Revolution. The nearby Bayview Brewery, the original site of Rainier Beer, used it as a feed mill during Prohibition. Van de Vanter's elegant home at the eastern edge of the racetrack property became a popular roadhouse until it lost all respectability. It was eventually remodeled and used as a part of the Meadows Sanitarium on Airport Way. In the early 1930s the land was sold. One more chapter was yet to be written for the Meadows.

COMMUNITY HEALTH

At the beginning of the twentieth century, epidemics continued to take their toll. It was not unusual for schools to be closed or delayed in opening, as in the autumn of 1902, when the County Board of Education announced that schools would open two weeks late that year, September 15, because of the prevalence of diphtheria.

TUKWILA—COMMUNITY AT THE CROSSROADS

The state of medical knowledge and health care at the beginning of the twentieth century was definitely improving, but often only symptoms could be treated. People frequently had to tolerate a great deal of stress and pain from simple injuries, such as was the case when Peter Cerini suffered from a simple scratch. Cerini was a prominent Swiss-Italian farmer whose beautiful dairy farm was located between the Meadows and Duwamish from 1900 to 1920. Cerini's children attended the Duwamish School, where he served on the school board. He also was a leader in the Duwamish Commercial Club. Cerini scratched his hand on peeling paint while working on his dairy the morning of May 15, 1912. He caught the Interurban for Monroe, where he was going to look at some cattle. On the train his arm began to throb, and by the time he reached a drug store in Monroe it was swollen. He telegraphed a physician in Seattle and took the train back to town, going directly to Minor Hospital on First Hill. His arm was continuing to swell and had turned black. He received intensive treatment and on the third day was released, still in poor condition. It was a long time before the arm was back to normal. While infections such as Cerini's were serious problems, the greatest health concern by 1900 was tuberculosis (TB).

TENT TB SANITARIUM ON THE DUWAMISH

"You have tuberculosis!" For several generations of Americans, these words were among the most frightening and disheartening a person could hear, and many people heard them in the era 1880-1940. In the early decades of the twentieth century, TB killed more people in the United States than any other communicable disease and was the leading cause of death, for any reason, in the 15 to 35 age group. In an attempt to control the spread of the killing disease that was reaching epidemic proportions in some places, in 1903 and 1907 Washington passed laws authorizing county health officers to "quarantine and isolate" people diagnosed as having the disease. There was no vaccination or medication treatment for TB at that time. Total rest and "living a healthy life" was the prescribed treatment.

The Anti-Tuberculosis League of King County, organized in 1909 with Mrs. Bessie Davis as director, identified over 1,000 people in the county needing immediate treatment for TB. The League wanted to remove the infected people from their communities immediately, and attempted to establish a temporary tent TB sanitarium on the west side of Queen Anne Hill. This effort was routed by an army of angry homeowners, who blocked the hospital wagons loaded with tents and equipment with loud protests and a brigade of brooms and mops. The League next attempted to set up its tent sanitarium in the Tukwila area of the Duwamish Valley, only to meet with another outcry. Finally it managed to unload the wagons and set up the tents in the Meadows area. The TB treatment center remained on the spot for several years, during which time a few buildings were added, although most of the patients continued to live in tents.

The attitude toward those stricken with TB in this period was not unlike Medieval attitudes toward lepers or the late-twentieth-century attitude toward victims of the deadly disease AIDS. In 1912 a successful citizen's petition, heartily endorsed by the Duwamish Commercial Club and signed by hundreds of valley residents, demanded that the county remove the tent camp. The following public statement was issued justifying removing the TB sanitarium:

> The present location is congested. Three sewers empty into the Duwamish within a few feet of the tents, the odor permeating the air for blocks around. The rental value of the property in the vicinity of the tents has greatly depreciated by reason of the proximity of the tuberculosis tents; families do not care to live where they can hear the coughing and groaning of the patients.

In the coming years a number of public and private sanitariums opened. In 1928 the King County Tuberculosis Hospital, Morningside, with 165 beds, opened in Georgetown. In 1943 an additional 45-bed building called the Meadows Annex was opened at the Meadows.

King County Airport and the Boeing Plant

By 1917 the dredging, filling and straightening of the lower Duwamish was completed under the auspices of Commercial Waterway District No. 1. For a few years truck farming flourished on the reclaimed floodplain. Filling and grading in the Duwamish Valley continued during the 1920s. In places up to 18 feet of fill was used to level the floodplain. A large tract of Duwamish Waterway fill land owned by Giuseppe Desimone in the early 1930s was bought by the Boeing Co. and became the site of Boeing Plant II. As airplanes became more common, a simple airfield was laid out running southwest to northeast. The landing-strip surface consisted of a layer of cinders placed over landfill.

In 1928 King County acquired the property and further developed the airport, named Boeing Field in honor of William Boeing, founder of the local aeronautical industry. The official dedication ceremonies took place on July 26, 1928, with 50,000 people in attendance. Following the ceremonies the ground was broken for construction of the first county-owned hangars. During the 1930s Boeing Field was the only passenger terminal in the Seattle area. Purcell Ave., which originally led to the Meadows racetrack gate, was eliminated by the airfield.

During World War II the airfield was enlarged as air traffic greatly increased. As a civil defense measure, 50-by-20-foot barrage balloons were flown over the field and the nearby Boeing plant. In addition, the airfield was painted with suburban scenes to camouflage it from the air.

The balloons over Boeing Field also hovered over Quarry Hill, where there was an anti-aircraft installation and a prisoner of war (POW) camp. The camp was highly secret, with even the nearby King County residents being unaware of its existence. A few local residents of the Quarry District and Duwamish community knew of the camp, but kept the secret in the interest of national security. At the time of this writing, long-term residents felt free to discuss the camp. Some living on Poverty Hill recalled often seeing the POWs in the health treatment center for the prisoners located at the base of Poverty Hill. A former camp guard related that the camp was guarded 24 hours a day, but there was low security and the POWs often walked freely around Quarry

For a few years after the completion of the Duwamish Waterway, before industrial development took over, truck farmers grew bumper crops in the fertile reclaimed floodplain. Looking north on East Marginal Way, approximately the location of Boeing Plant II in 1990, the small "c" marks the Seattle city limits sign. In 1989 the boundaries of modern Tukwila met those of the City of Seattle at this point. Photograph taken August 20, 1927. Courtesy Warren Wing.

Hill and its environs. There were no incidents of trouble when they made contact with the local residents.

The Watson family became acquainted with the prisoners, who were mostly young Italians and Germans between 17 and 20 years old, when a couple of Italian youths walked into their yard one evening in 1944. The family made friends with a number of "the boys," as they called them, often having them over for dinner. The young Italian POWs developed great affection for the Watsons, and many years later several made trips back to Seattle to attend the funerals of Mr. and Mrs. Watson—Duwamish Valley residents who had the courage and love to show kindness to those lonely boys. When the Watsons' son returned after the war—after spending many months in a POW camp in Germany—he reported that he had been treated with great kindness by the civilians.

The Museum of Flight

The Museum of Flight is an independent, nonprofit cultural foundation dedicated to the preservation of aircraft and related artifacts, as well as the knowledge, enjoyment and self-discovery of flight. Founded in 1964 as the Pacific Northwest Aviation Historical Foundation, the Museum is located in Tukwila at the southwest corner of Boeing Field at 9404 East Marginal Way S.

The Museum of Flight opened its first wing at its Tukwila location in 1983 in the historic "Red Barn," the Boeing Company's original manufacturing plant. Built in 1909, the Red Barn was donated to the Museum of Flight by the Port of Seattle in 1975 and moved to its present location that year. Restoration of the Red Barn was completed in 1983 and marked the first phase in an extensive program to build a substantial air and space museum in the Pacific Northwest. The Great Gallery opened to the public in July 1987. Exhibits in the Red Barn trace aviation history from its early beginnings through 1938. Exhibits in the Great Gallery chronicle the story of flight, from mythology through the early days of wood aircraft to the latest accomplishments in air and space technology.

The 185,075-square-foot museum complex includes a 268-seat theater and auditorium, meeting rooms, extensive educational facilities, a library, and the largest aviation archives on the West Coast. The Museum of Flight was financed with over $26.4 million in private contributions from individuals and companies around the world. This major museum in Tukwila is recognized regionally, nationally, and internationally. The Museum of Flight also manages and maintains an extensive Restoration and Interpretive Center at Paine Field in Everett.

With the opening of the Museum of Flight, the Meadows area has, in fact, returned to an earlier use of the area for recreational and leisure pursuits. The museum grounds, with its trees and landscaping, are a welcome relief from the stark cement, brick, metal and plastic environment that characterizes the heavily developed industrial district. The beautiful oxbow of the lower Duwamish is gone forever, but environmentally conscious industrialists, regulated by legislation, no longer pour pollutants into the ancient river. On sunny days workers walk along the riverbank during their lunch hour, treading the land that in times gone by brought forth food for the Native Americans and then the Duwamish pioneers. The use of the land changes, but the land remains.

Chapter 7
Opening the Valley

Spring flood, 1910. Floodwaters subsiding, the Interurban is once again making its regular runs up the valley. Serious floods occurred regularly until the Howard Hanson Dam was built in 1962. The view is from Foster looking north from near the later route of Interurban Ave. Quarry Hill is in center background. Courtesy Warren Wing.

Many people remember the melodious sound of the steam engine whistles, and some may recall the cheerful whistles which the Milwaukee Road used on their electric trains, but no doubt, few remember the high chiming whistle announcing the arrival of the Interurban.

    Warren Wing
    Interurban Historian, Duwamish Community

The rolling river provided the Duwamish and White river valley settlers the means to travel conveniently, receive mail and ship produce. It made close contact with Seattle possible from the beginning, and several donation-claim settlers appear to have done a fair amount of commuting in the 1850s and 1860s. Gradually roads improved, making the wagon route to Seattle faster—as fast as a horse could travel. Water travel continued to be the most convenient way for transporting heavy goods and produce. The coming of the railroads—first the Seattle-Walla Walla narrow-gauge railway and then the Northern Pacific—cut into the riverboat's shipping, and regular service slacked off in the late 1880s.

From 1887 the Northern Pacific ran down the White and Duwamish river valleys. There was a station at Orillia where freight and passengers were taken aboard several times a day. In spite of the railroad, in many ways the valley farmers were more cut off than they had been 10 years earlier because the train was not as accessible as the riverboats, which stopped almost any place to take on passengers and freight. In addition, hauling produce to the railway station required reliable roads and bridges.

The twentieth century has been marked by a series of major public works in King County that have radically altered the Duwamish and lower White river valleys. In the opening years of the twentieth century the major public works projects undertaken in the valley itself involved transportation and had the effect of opening the valley as never before. These works included the construction of numerous bridges and roads. The ongoing problem of severe flooding was diminished by the construction of the Duwamish Waterway early in the century and then totally resolved with the construction of the Howard Hanson Dam in 1962. Also of historic impact was the construction of the Lake Washington to Puget Sound Ship Canal. The innovation that had the most dynamic immediate impact on the region was the starting of the Interurban rail service.

TUKWILA—COMMUNITY AT THE CROSSROADS

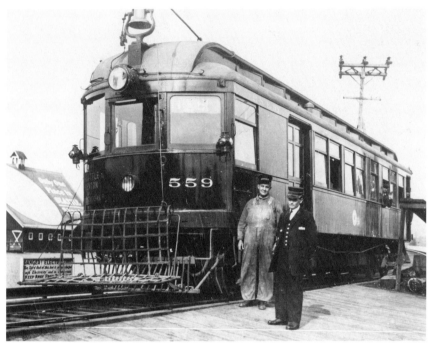

Puget Sound Electric's 559 at the Renton Junction Station alongside Fred Nelsen's barn, ca. 1915. On the left is Howard Wellman, motorman, with Horace Rumery, conductor. Long-term Interurban motormen and conductors from the early Tukwila communities were Frank Baker, Roy Henderson and Joe Bow. Note the third-rail warning sign to the left of the train baggage carrier. Courtesy Warren Wing.

THE INTERURBAN SPURS THE SUBDIVIDING OF THE VALLEY

The Interurban was a major factor in the initial formation of the Duwamish River Valley communities. It is questionable whether some of the communities, including Old Tukwila, would have formed as early as they did—or at all—without the presence of the Interurban. The Interurban opened the valley to suburban growth and development.

In the decade before the Interurban, the valley farms began to disintegrate. If a date were to be set marking the beginning of the breakup of the farms, it would be May 3, 1890, when I. H. and Carrie E. Vails, who had a farm on Timothy and Elizabeth Grow's donation claim, subdivided a portion of their farm, calling their plat Pottery Works Addition, for a nearby factory. Their subdivision was a favorable location for homeseekers desiring country living close to Seattle. The old (1855) Duwamish Road, now called Beacon Avenue, ran along the east side of the subdivision. In the next 10 years, parcels of land were sold here and there to business interests and speculators.

The pace of development changed from a gradual trend to a veritable race overnight with the startup of the Interurban. Forward-looking people like Joseph Foster initiated subdividing in 1901. As the Interurban startup date of September 28, 1902, drew closer more plats were filed. Seeing the trains regularly speeding down the valley provided the needed impetus for the "wait and see" developers, and between late 1902 and 1912, 44 plats were filed for the

HISTORY OF THE INTERURBAN, 1902-1928

Warren Wing and Kay Reinartz

The Interurban operated between September 25, 1902, and December 30, 1928, and changed the course of history of the Duwamish Valley. It was fast, frequent and economical, and provided excellent service. The Interurban made it possible to run down valley into Seattle or up valley to Renton, Kent, Auburn and on to Tacoma, in less than an hour, several times a day. It was like returning to the convenience of the riverboat days—only the travel was much faster and the routes longer. People and goods could be transported between Everett and Tacoma on the Interurban at speeds up to 60 and 70 miles an hour, in contrast to travel via team and wagon that jogged along on dusty, bumpy roads in the summer and through axle-deep mud in the winter.

Warren Wing's lifelong fascination with trains began as a lad when he would urge his mother to go to Seattle from their West Seattle home so they could ride on the Interurban. Beginning in the the 1980s, Wing has written a series of books on the history of the Interurban in King County, with more volumes planned for Pierce County and elsewhere. Wing writes his books from his home facing the river in Duwamish. For 30 years he delivered the mail to Riverton residents. Courtesy Robert Johnson.

historic study area covered by this book. The subdividing of the farm land intensified each year, reaching a peak in 1907, after which it slowed. By 1912 virtually all the land that was destined to be a part of the municipality of Tukwila in 1990 had been subdivided.

The Interurban's growth and the initial formation of the Duwamish Valley communities happened simultaneously almost in every case (Foster existed long before the electric railway). The community names were definitely cemented by their adoption as names for the Interurban stations. Except Tukwila, the communities all formed without the benefit of municipal status, and the Interuban station name somehow made the community's name official.

The electric rail system was backed by the large Boston-based investment firm Stone and Webster, whose plan was to build a system that would eventually run from Vancouver, B.C., to Portland, Oregon. The Puget Sound Electric Railway was one of several dozen early twentieth-century investment schemes of this national company. Originally named the Seattle-Tacoma Interurban Railway, it was renamed the Puget Sound Electric Railway after a financial shake-up. The parent local company was known as the Seattle Electric Company.

The Interurban operated on 600 volts furnished by the parent company and fed to the cars by a third rail. This third rail ran parallel with the running rails but was heavier and slightly higher. It rested on insulators that were on every fifth tie. The trains picked up the power from the third rail from a "shoe" attached to each set of tracks.

The Interurban was quickly accepted by everyone as a convenient means for getting around. There never had been anything like it. It was taken traveling to school, to church, to shop, to sell produce, to visit friends, to go "out on the town" on Saturday night, to catch the passenger train in Seattle for a major cross-country trip, and even to one's own wedding. Freight transported on the Interurban included coal, bricks, milk from farms and dairies, fresh slaughtered meat, market garden vegetables, flowers and rock from the Riverton Quarry.

"WATCH OUT FOR THE THIRD RAIL!"

The third rail was mighty dangerous and the residents along its route had a healthy respect for it. Nevertheless, there were many human fatalities, and countless numbers of animals lost their lives on the powered rail. To lessen the danger, the company eventually fenced nearly all of the right-of-way and went underground with the power at intersections. Through the city streets of Seattle, Tacoma, Kent and Auburn, the train was powered from overhead wires and called the trolley. The trolley lines ran as far south as the Meadows station, where the power switch to the third rail took place.

People living near the Interurban tracks constantly admonished each other, and particularly the children: "Watch out for the third rail! Be careful of the third rail! Don't step on the

TUKWILA—COMMUNITY AT THE CROSSROADS

third rail!" Nonetheless, tragic deaths on the third rail occurred over the years in the valley communities. A few years after the train service began, a young woman from Duwamish was making her way over the train tracks in an area where the third rail was exposed, carrying her infant son in her arms. Mindful of her precious burden, she was trying to be particularly careful as she stepped over the powered rail—but her long skirt suddenly tangled around her legs and she fell forward. The baby flew from his mother's arms and landed safely on the ground. There he lay wailing in vain for his mother, who lay dead beside him, her foot still across the third rail.

Parents could warn their children until their voices were hoarse, yet out of sight children will do as they will. One day early in the 1920s, a six-year-old boy tagging along behind the "big boys" watched them playing a very dangerous daredevil game—jumping onto the third rail with both feet simultaneously. Since the jumper was not grounded, he would not be electrocuted. Wanting to be grown-up, the little tad also jumped onto the third rail—but one foot slipped off the rail and onto the ground. No one played that game again for a long time.

Each year untold numbers of animals died on the third rail. So many small animals—rabbits, raccoons, foxes and domestic cats and dogs—were electrocuted on the third rail that the motorman kept a long wooden pole in the front of the car to clear the tracks. Large animals also met a quick death on the third rail. In the 1900s and 1910s many people let their cows and horses roam at large, and they found their way onto the tracks in spite of a fenced right-of-way and cattle guards at crossings.

There are numerous instances of tragedies, such as the day that Archie Lynch, Warren Wing's stepfather, drove his team over to the Riverton Quarry for a load of crushed rock. The matched team was unhooked from the wagon to rest, eat and drink while the wagon was being filled. Suddenly startled by a loud noise, the horses tossed back their heads and bolted right onto the Interurban tracks, a metal chain that was part of their harness dragging—right across the third rail. Receiving a heavy electrical charge through the chain, the big animals simultaneously dropped to the ground dead. Lynch lost not merely two expensive draft animals, but also two loved and trusted work companions. People frequently filed claims for such losses with the Puget Sound Electric Railway Co., but with little satisfaction. Frequently, when large electrocuted animals fell onto the third rail they shorted out the system, the power was cut, and the entire system shut down while the track was cleared. People were expected to "be careful" about the third rail.

THE "SKY RIDE" OUT OF SEATTLE

The Interurban left the Seattle terminal at Occidental Ave. and Yesler Way every hour for Tacoma and Renton. The Renton trains handled the local traffic betweeen Seattle and Renton Junction, while the Tacoma trains traveled nonstop from Seattle to Renton Junction, providing local service between Renton Junction and Tacoma. Normally the Seattle-Renton train had one or two cars, and the Seattle-Tacoma route had two or three cars.

The train left Seattle via First Ave. S. just south of Spokane St., where it went up on a high wooden trestle over tide flats and railroad yards to the present-day Airport Way and Lucille St. This trestle and others in the valley carrying the tracks over areas subject to flooding gave passengers the illusion of "riding in the sky." More than one passenger felt a tightening of the stomach as he or she gazed out the window with apprehension at the possibility of the train jumping the tracks. Roy Henderson, Interurban motorman from Duwamish-Allentown from 1914 to 1928, recalled that after his first swaying, bouncing "sky ride" on the First Ave. trestle he wondered if he really wanted to keep his job.

Turning south through Georgetown, the Interurban tracks paralleled the tracks of the Northern Pacific almost to the south end of present-day Boeing Field. At this point the train

OPENING THE VALLEY

left the steam railroad tracks and went southwest through the area occupied by the Associated Grocers' warehouse in 1990, and crossed the Duwamish River just east of East Marginal Way at S. 115 St. on a drawbridge designed to open for river-boat traffic. The cement footings of this historic bridge could still be seen in 1990. There were three such Interurban bridges over the Duwamish River. According to one conductor, Horace Rumery, he "never saw an Interurban drawbridge opened for the ship traffic in [his] 18 years as brakeman and conductor." Once across the river, the train traveled south alongside present-day Interurban Ave. through Duwamish-Allentown, Foster and Tukwila to Renton Junction.

Renton Junction was one of the busiest stops on the line. The tracks and station with the telegrapher's office were all located on a trestle. In 1990 this site is above and west of the old red barn topped with Fred Nelsen's prancing horse weathervane. It is just north of I-405 where Interurban Ave. becomes West Valley Highway at the intersection of Grady Way. At this place 90 years ago the Tacoma trains went south on a single track, while the Renton trains climbed an even higher trestle over several sets of main-line tracks and traveled east.

The Tacoma trains took 65 to 90 minutes for the 36 miles, while the Renton trains made the run in about 30. The train stopped at a station only if passengers or freight were to be taken on or dropped off. Passengers were on their own at unattended stations to raise the flag signaling the motorman to stop.

There were locals and limiteds. Limiteds would respond to the upturned signal flag with a shriek of the whistle that meant "I'm a Limited, stand back, I'm going through!" And the train whizzed by with a low roar and a gust of wind that made people standing on the platform shut their eyes tight and hold their breath. If the oncoming train was a local, it came to a gentle stop at the platform and the genial conductor stepped down to welcome passengers aboard.

In the first years of the company many trains had parlor cars. Elegant ladies in tucked and ruffled black silk street dresses rustled aboard the ladies' parlor car, while harried businessmen settled into the tapestry-cushioned chairs of the smoker to relax with a cigar and a refreshing drink, discuss the news of the day, or debate real estate prices with fellow travelers. Although desired and appreciated by the gentry, parlor cars were deemed uneconomical because the passenger-to-space ratio was not sufficient to pay their way.

LIFE ON THE INTERURBAN

he train was run by the motorman and by the conductor, who collected fares and saw to the shipping. To many living in the valley, these men were very special. To Frances Codiga North and her sister Emma, who rode the Interurban daily to attend St. George's Catholic School in Georgetown, the conductors "were almost exalted rulers in a very exciting life. Most of them were handsome—to hear the village girls talk—and they were young." The conductors working on the Interurban in the 1920s from the valley included Frank Baker, Roy Henderson, Joe Bow and Horace Rumery. It was the conductor's job to keep order on the train, which included enforcing the county health department's order that all train passengers wear gauze masks during the influenza epidemic of 1918. One burly rider refused to put on a mask and was evicted from the car by the conductor and Georgetown police at the Georgetown station.

In addition to managing the train, the Interurban conductors performed another important service—providing the local news of the communities along the tracks. In a half-hour trip from Seattle to Riverton or Tukwila, a rider could catch up on the most recent events in the valley—the newborn babies, church and school doings, romances, job openings, new houses going up, trouble at the Quarry—and all manner of fascinating details told by some of the best story tellers around, the Interurban conductors. Riding the Interurban was a focal point of life in

Puget Sound Electric Railway cars number 600 and 511 in collision at Riverton, November 23, 1912. Courtesy Warren Wing.

the valley between 1902 and 1928. Frances Codiga North fondly recalls that for 26 years "romances bloomed, mothers nursed babies, the Cleveland High School girls giggled, and then the Interurban was gone forever."

While the Interurban was normally highly reliable, there were problems, mainly from wrecks and flooding in the valley. Heavy wet snow and flooding of the roadbed shut down the train for a few days almost every year. After automobiles became common there were numerous "fender-benders" involving cars and the Interurban, and there were several serious wrecks.

One such accident occurred at the Riverton Station on July 26, 1912, when an express train hit an automobile stopped on the tracks. Apparently the chauffeur failed to hear a warning electric gong until the car was almost on the tracks. Dr. E. M. Rininger, noted Seattle physician, was killed instantly as the Interurban hit the automobile broadside. In the 1920s the valley communities were shocked and mourned together when well-known Riverton businessman O. C. Thompson's daughter Rivera, a teacher at the Duwamish School, was struck and killed while crossing the tracks at the Riverton station. A girl with the surname Zick was also struck and killed at the crossing.

The Interurban was intended to be mainly a passenger train, and 80 percent of its revenue came from passenger fares. However, a good deal of revenue was realized from running express coal trains from the Seattle Electric Company's coal mines in Renton, hauling milk cans from the many dairies scattered along the route, and hauling seasonal produce into Seattle from the Duwamish, Green and Puyallup river valleys. In addition, lumber and logs, and occasionally other heavy loads, were hauled on the Interurban. The Interurban also carried the morning and evening newspapers as well as the mail. It was all transported by Interurban—the lifeline of the valley.

BATTLES WITH THE INTERURBAN

In 1902 the Interurban fare was 15 cents, which included a transfer good for travel on the Seattle trolley system. Attempts to raise fares always brought vigorous protests from the valley's commuting population. Once, when the company attempted to raise the fare to 25 cents, commuters boarding the train handed over only 15 cents. When efforts were made to collect the additional dime at the next stop, the passengers resorted to passive resistance, throwing themselves on the floor or hanging onto their seats to avoid eviction. The biggest battle in the history of the Interurban occurred in 1909-10, when fares were raised from 15 cents to 40 cents in October. The entire Duwamish Valley cried out against this outrageous increase, and the railroad commission decreed that Puget Sound Electric Railway had to return to the original fare of 15 cents. Rejecting this, the railway appealed the case in Thurston County Superior Court.

An organized protest was planned during the winter. In the spring of 1910 a pamphlet written by an anonymous pamphleteer, allegedly living in the newly incorporated town of Tukwila, appeared at every Interurban Station in the valley. In *Tukwila Devastated—A People's Plea for Their Homes*, the author demands the return to the original 15-cent fare. The crux of the pamphlet's argument was "balancing the home budget":

Our work is in Seattle; our homes in Tukwila. We cannot pay 40 cents a day car fare to go to and from our work. If we give up our work we cut off our means of livelihood and we lose our homes. If we leave our homes and go live in Seattle we lose them. We cannot pay rent in Seattle and make payments on our property. We simply cannot avoid losing our homes with the 40-cent rate in effect.

Saturday, August 28, 1910, over 500 residents of the Duwamish Valley turned out for a mass meeting held at Foster. State Railroad Commission officials presented the railroad's compromise offer: nontransferable commutation booklets good for 16 round trips a month with a 35 percent discount, which made the fare 28 cents. The compromise was rejected. However, the Interurban gradually won out, and by 1918 graduated fares for valley communities were Renton Junction, 28 cents; Tukwila, 25 cents; Allentown, 21 cents; Duwamish, 19 cents; and Quarry, 17 cents. The fares continued to climb to the end of the service in 1928.

From time to time the people fought back by switching to alternative forms of transportation, mainly buses. During a battle with the Interurban in the early 1920s a high-masted boat was put into service on the river offering transportation to commuters from South Park to Renton Junction. However, in the end nothing could compete with the Interurban for speed and reliability.

The Automotive Era Begins

The Interurban was basically forced out by automotive vehicles—buses, affordably priced cars and heavy-duty trucks. As the train was phased out the Puget Sound Electric Railway initiated bus service along much of the Interurban route. Popularly known as "jitneys," the buses around 1930 were rectangular vehicles with a round window in the back and carried 30 passengers. The jitneys had five doors on one side of the vehicle, and at each stop the bus driver jumped out to let passengers out. These buses frequently broke down on the road and required constant repairing. Service was discontinued and river boats were tried for a short time, but with little success.

Better buses were designed that performed reliably, and by the 1930s a fleet of buses known as the "alligator buses" carried the valley commuters. These buses served until about 1948, when the Greyhound Bus Co. provided service for the Duwamish and Green river valleys. In 1990 Metro was providing bus service. The bus service has never approached the Interurban, which was used by almost 100 percent of the valley commuters.

The Kent Stage, a jitney bus. When valley residents had conflicts with the Interurban over rates, they turned to buses. Buses were first pressed into service in 1912, but breakdowns ended the experiment after a few weeks. In the 1920s determined valley commuters fought back by procuring two hard-rubber-tired buses, which they named the Duwamish and the Tukwila. Courtesy Warren Wing.

It has been said that the Interurban "never made a dime." That may well be true. The company had to pay taxes to every city and town it served, and had to live by the rates fixed by the local governing bodies. Not a dime in tax money ever went to improving service or equipment. It was a private enterprise venture that functioned in many ways like a public utility. As the era of the private automobile as the main means of transportation draws to a close at the end of the twentieth century, the Interurban is the focus of unprecendented interest, as the Northwest searches for transportation that is fast, frequent, economical, reliable, and does not damage the natural environment. The twentieth century began with the electric train, and the twenty-first century may begin in a similar fashion.

A mudslide covered the 1916 Pacific Highway and the Interurban tracks just south of the Riverton drawspan about 1918. The highway is built of planks in this section. The 1903 Riverton drawspan near 124 St. is in the background at right. Courtesy Warren Wing.

GOOD ROADS COME TO THE DUWAMISH VALLEY

> When I came to Foster in 1897 there were no roads leading out anywhere, just paths....you could walk or ride horseback or go in a wagon around stumps and one thing and another, and it was a mile—at least a mile—to any road that led to Seattle or along toward Tacoma.
> — Tom Clark, Foster, 1954

Tom Clark recalls that Military Road, the only road from Seattle to Tacoma when he came to Puget Sound, "was bad in those days. It was an old dusty, crooked winding road....two teams, and later after cars came in, two cars couldn't pass at the same time without sidetracking each other." For the next decade community roads everywhere in the valley continued to be less than satisfactory, with some being simply dirt and others being made of puncheon or wooden planks. The valley roads were basically on a par with other places in the country.

Gradually, the county rebuilt the existing roads as gravel roads, which drained quickly during wet weather and were less dusty in the summer. Most of the county road work in the Duwamish and lower White river valleys from the late 1890s into the 1920s involved widening, regrading, graveling and improving drainage of existing roads. The road construction activity in the Tukwila area in the first decades of the twentieth century was under the direction of James Nelsen, who served as County District Road Supervisor for 15 years.

The Duwamish Valley has a unique place in King County public works history because of its long, proud tradition of having good roads. The

OPENING THE VALLEY

active interest in good roads began in 1855 and continued in the twentieth century. The King County Commissioners' records often note petitions tendered from Duwamish Valley residents.

Population growth and booming local development across King County greatly increased road usage. Even before the appearance of the automobile, it was clear that the gravel roads that were replacing pioneer puncheon were not fully satisfactory. It took serious citizen action in the form of the Good Roads Association (GRA) to improve the entire regional road system. The Duwamish Valley figured prominently in this movement, since it was the test site of several improved road-building techniques. The GRA, predecessor of the American Automobile Association, had been formed in 1899 by Sam Hill, well-known wealthy Northwest land developer who had recently completed his mansion at Maryhill (now the Maryhill Museum) overlooking the Columbia near The Dalles. Hill gathered together men who shared his interest in improving Washington's roads, which as a whole were abominable. Among this visionary group was an energetic farmer from south of Renton Junction named Frank Terrence.

Hill had spent time in Europe, where he had learned of a hard road-surfacing system recently developed by John Loudon McAdam, a Scottish engineer. The Good Roads Association approached King County with the idea of trying the McAdam road-building system. The county engineer agreed and in 1905 undertook a landmark road construction experiment—macadamizing an existing gravel road. The Riverton Road that ran down the Duwamish Valley from Riverton to Renton Junction was selected for the experiment. The construction of the historic macadam road was overseen by D. W. Randall, Assistant Engineer of the Federal Office of Public Roads.

The construction of a macadam type of road is quite simple. After the soil is rolled and sloped for drainage, a three-inch layer of crushed rock is put down. A second one-inch-deep layer of rock is placed on top of this and then topped

> **ROAD AND BRIDGE PETITION—BLACK RIVER, WASHINGTON, AUGUST 4, 1902**
>
> To the Honorable Board of County Commissioners of King County:
>
> We the undersigned Citizens of King County do petition your honorable board to build a wagon road from where the Foster Bridge crosses the Duwamish River to where the survey crosses White River at Peter Nelsen's Place, and build the bridge this year. And also relocate a portion of the west end of the Renton Road, which is known as the Jim Nelsen Petition. . . . The reason that we are compelled to change the west end of the old survey is because the Interurban Railroad built their track on that place and put the road out in the slough. . . .
>
> Signed
>
> | | | |
> |---|---|---|
> | A. Gaskill | John Anderson | Fred Mess |
> | D. B. Rose | E. Van deVanter | J. F. Costello |
> | Henry Miller | D. Campbell | B. W. Jacobus |
> | James Clark | Fred Nelsen | Jas F. McElroy |
> | James Nelsen | Hans Nelson | Chr. Jorgensen |
> | W. Badgeo | R. J. Cameron | Peter Nelsen |
> | G. M. Burke | Joseph Foster | J. Bow |
> | J. T. Foster | J. C. Peterson | E. E. Lee |
> | Thos. N. Clark | Herman Nelsen | E. J. Stutz |
> | C. Mathews | | |

with a layer of fine rock. The combined layers total approximately eight inches. The road bed is next rolled and consolidated to a thickness of about six inches. The finished road then hardens to a smooth surface under the pounding of traffic.

Appropriately, the model road was named the Macadam Road, and on July 7, 1906, a crowd gathered in the vicinity of the burgeoning community of Riverton to inspect and celebrate the completion of a section of the experimental road. The Washington Good Roads Association was out in full force with over 100 of its road enthusiasts on hand, including President Sam Hill. The regional interest in the model road was reflected by the presence of three King County Commissioners, as well as Snohomish County Commissioners and the County Road Supervisor. Many other Northwest communities sent representative citizens down to the Duwamish to inspect this new road-building technique. A clutch of newspaper editors and reporters were on hand, as was the famous Northwest photographer Asahel Curtis, himself a member of the Good Roads Association.

The introduction of the automobile intensified the need for hard-surfaced roads. Experiments were made with asphaltic types of materials such as Warrenite, Dolloway, and Amiesite. These surfacing materials were all basically bituminous mixtures, commonly known as "blacktop." After the macadam road, the King County Road Department continued experimenting with new road-building techniques. It was decided to blacktop a test road, and the James Clark Road, which was, in fact, a section of the Macadam Road, was selected for the experiment. The State Highway Department agreed, for the first time, to fund this type of road improvement.

In 1907 the James Clark Road was regraded and given a "black top" of oil. After observation of road performance over a trial period, the blacktopping was proclaimed a total success and began to be used throughout the county. Later blacktop surfacing changed to a three-step technique in which oil was the main ingredient rather than asphalt. The original surface treatment lasted for over 30 years. By 1990 all of these roads had been rebuilt or overlaid.

Local, county and state government recognized the need for road improvement, and in 1916 the first paved road, known as the Pacific Highway, was opened. The road provided an alternate route to the Military Road from Seattle to Tacoma. The section through the Duwamish Valley was surfaced with paving bricks produced by the Seattle Brick Company in South Seattle. The valley route partially followed the old 1855 Duwamish River Road and Interurban Ave. The two-lane road ran along the riverbank, which was lined with lovely large maple trees, making this stretch of the road among the most scenic in the region, on a par with the famous Chuckanut Drive from Mount Vernon to Bellingham. John J. Reddin, later a writer for the *Seattle Times*, whose Riverton house fronted on the road, recalls that in the first years after the Pacific Highway was finished "very few people traveled it. In fact, my boys often perched on the front steps of our home....and counted only five to ten cars going past in an entire day."

Twelve years after the original Pacific Highway opened, on October 28, 1928, US-99 opened, which was also known as the Pacific Highway. This road immediately became the major road through the Duwamish Valley. It was built on the hillside about a half-mile above the Macadam Road through Riverton, climbing out of the valley floor around S. 116 St., where it ascended Riverton Heights. With every major north-south road in the region being routed through the Riverton section of the Duwamish Valley, Riverton flourished. When later main thoroughfares bypassed Riverton, the community's significance as a crossroads diminished to the point that, at the end of the century, the formerly active commercial and social center languished with neglect.

BRIDGES ACROSS THE DUWAMISH RIVER AND OTHER PLACES

In the latter decades of the nineteenth century travelers had only one place to cross the upper Duwamish River after the ferry system shut down—via the Black River Bridge at Black River Junction. A bridge had long been needed in the central Duwamish Valley. In 1899 the Federal Government appropriated the funds for this bridge. Officially called the Riverton drawspan, the wood bridge was a swing-design drawbridge that operated by turning on a central pivot. It was put into service in 1903. In the next three years three more similar drawspans were built over the Duwamish at Renton Junction, Oxbow and Georgetown.

The construction of this set of bridges along the course of the Duwamish both reflected the growing development in the Duwamish Valley and greatly stimulated this growth. Regarding the construction of these important bridges

OPENING THE VALLEY

across the river, it was observed in the *Seattle Post-Intelligencer* (July 21, 1906): "These improvements suggest…that the Duwamish Valley is fast becoming the great center of manufacturing industry of the city…and that the whole valley will soon be a beehive of industry and activity; and that prices of property in this neighborhood will double up in value."

THE FOSTER BRIDGE

After 1906 the only long stretch of river lacking a bridge was at Foster. This was somewhat ironic in that the original crossing of the river had been at Foster in the form of the Lewis/Steele ferry. The Foster community waited until 1923, when the first Foster Bridge—a footbridge—was constructed. The original 240-foot suspension bridge was built by the Manson Construction Company.

In the spring of 1938 the same company began work on the first vehicle bridge across the river. This bridge was a wood Howe Truss design and cost $16,351. The bridge was dedicated in 1939. One day 41 years later, as a truck heavily loaded with dead animals was driving over the bridge heading for the rendering works located near the railroad tracks, the Foster Bridge collapsed. The driver escaped, as did dozens of animal carcasses, which astonished people for miles downstream as they floated out to Elliott Bay. For several years following this disaster people living on Foster Point could reach their homes only by means of a single-lane "back door" road, S. 130 Place.

Work on a new Foster Bridge began in 1984. This bridge is a concrete box girder construction, 34 feet wide, with sidewalks on both sides and 244 feet long. To improve the west approach to the intersection with Interurban Ave. S. at 52 Ave. S., the new bridge is located slightly south of the 1939 bridge. The 1985 bridge cost $1.5 million and was funded by the federal, county and municipal governments, with 80 percent of the funds from federal sources.

Duwamish River drawbridge at Renton Junction, ca. 1912. These wooden swing design drawbridges deteriorated rapidly. The large center concrete and wooden pilings were perfect foils for logs and river debris swept down the river. Henning Sundby of Quarry recalls that there were constant problems with "logs and trash coming down the river jamming up on the center pilings. Sometimes in a flood they blasted all night long to break up the log jams." The heavy timber structure to the left is a debris deflector, built upstream of the bridge to prevent jams. The King County Commissioners' records for the early decades of the twentieth century are crowded with notations of repairs to these Duwamish River swing bridges. Courtesy King County Public Works Dept.

THE ALLENTOWN COVERED BRIDGE AND THE DUWAMISH FOOT BRIDGE

New England is noted for its romantic covered bridges. However, such structures are rare in the Northwest. When the Union Pacific Railroad built a vehicle bridge over its tracks in Allentown in 1903, it put up a wood-truss covered bridge. The Old Red Covered Bridge on the Renton Road (County Road 57) became a landmark that for many years brought people out of Seattle on Sunday drives. (Also known as the Allentown or Steele Hill Bridge, for the pioneer Steele family, the new concrete bridge, erected in the 1960s, was renamed the Codiga Bridge for the nearby Archie Codiga Dairy Farm.) Over the years the bridge caught on fire a number of times from the sparks that spewed from the smokestacks of the steam locomotives passing below. As was common in early bridge design, the bridge had water barrels fastened to the outer rail for fire fighting; however, this did not prevent it from burning down in 1956.

TUKWILA—COMMUNITY AT THE CROSSROADS

In 1926 the county built a suspension footbridge over the Duwamish connecting Quarry to Duwamish. This bridge was located close to the Duwamish School. It was replaced in the 1940s with a truss design bridge and again in the 1980s, with a concrete box girder design bridge.

HISTORIC PRATT TRUSS BRIDGES

In 1987 the study area was something of a showcase of vintage bridges. Three of the ten surviving historic steel Pratt Truss bridges remaining in King County were located

HISTORIC BRIDGES IN THE DUWAMISH VALLEY

Date Constructed	Name	Location	Style and Comments
1867	Black River Bridge	Black River Junction	First significant bridge over a river in King County.
1902	Renton Junction Interurban RR bridge	100 yards south of vehicle bridge	Swing design drawbridge.
1903	Riverton Drawspan	300 feet north of S. 124th St. bridge	Wooden swing design drawbridge; one lane closed 1919; removed 1927.
1903	Steele Hill Bridge, or Old Red Allentown Covered Bridge	Old Steele Hill to Renton, Renton Road	Wooden Pratt Truss covered bridge built over tracks by Union Pacific RR; destroyed by fire, 1956.
1916 (1906)-1934	Duwamish Interurban	100 yards south of 115th and S.E. Marginal Way bridge (1990)	Steel Pratt Truss, camelback design.
1906	Georgetown Drawspan	Oxbow near Georgetown	Wooden swing design.
1923	Foster Footbridge	Foster Point at 56th Ave. S.	240' wooden suspension footbridge; replaced by vehicular bridge, 1938.
1927	Duwamish-Allentown Bridge	S. 124th St.	Steel Pratt Truss; in 1990, distinguished as one of three bridges of this historic design remaining in King County.
1934	"Interurban" Vehicle Bridge	S. 115th and E. Marginal Way	Steel Pratt Through Truss; destroyed 1988.
1939	Foster Vehicle Bridge	Foster Point and 56th Ave. S.	Wood Howe Truss vehicular bridge; collapsed 1979.
1985	New Foster Bridge	Foster Point and 56th Ave. S.	Concrete box girder.
1988-present	New "Interurban" Bridge	S. 115th and E. Marginal Way	272-foot, 3-span concrete girder bridge.

OPENING THE VALLEY

Foster Pratt Truss Steel Bridge and Heppenstall's Grocery Store on Interurban Ave., ca. 1939. In 1985 this bridge was replaced by a concrete box girder bridge. A time capsule containing historical notes and memorabilia was incorporated into the construction of the bridge. Courtesy Maxine Anderson.

in Tukwila. These bridges were the "Interurban" Bridge at S. 115 St. and East Marginal Way, the Duwamish-Allentown Bridge at S. 124 St. and the Highway US-99 bridge at approximately S. 116 St. Only two of the three remained in 1990.

Replaced in 1988, the most interesting of the vintage Pratt Truss bridges in the study area was the span in the old Quarry District at S. 115 St. and East Marginal Way, known as the "Interurban" Bridge. This bridge was a part of one of the biggest "bridge recyling" efforts undertaken by King County up to the 1930s. In 1934 King County needed a bridge over the Duwamish River for the Valley Highway, and rather than build a brand-new bridge, county officials decided to modify an old Interurban bridge. The bridge sat unused until 1934, when it was widened while still in its original location and then moved 300 feet downstream, where its north pier was rebuilt and its south pier revamped. The character of the truss was significantly changed from its original design with a new floor system, bracing and other alterations required for automobile rather than train use. Remnants of concrete piers on each side of the river upstream marking the original location of the Interurban Bridge were still visible in 1990. The bridge continued to be called the "Interurban" Bridge after it was modified for vehicular use. The historic "Interurban" Bridge was demolished in 1988 and replaced with a four-lane, vehicular, 272-foot three-span concrete girder bridge.

In 1927-28 the Washington Highway Department built a bridge across the Duwamish

TUKWILA—COMMUNITY AT THE CROSSROADS

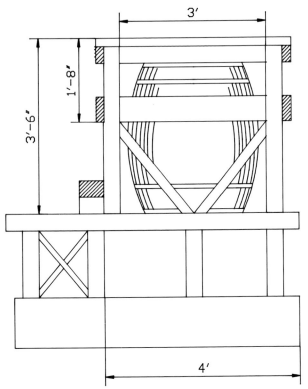

Water barrels were a standard part of many wooden bridges in the nineteenth and early twentieth centuries for fire fighting. The tradition was that whoever discovered the fire was to fight it by drawing on the water stored in the barrels. In the absence of a rural fire-fighting service, this practical and economical system saved more than one bridge. Original drawing by Patrick Brodin.

River for Highway 99. This bridge is a four-lane, vehicular, 200-foot steel riveted Pratt Truss with concrete abutments. It is an example of the later truss construction with heavier members. It was repaired and strengthened in 1971 and 1981. In 1989 the bridge came under the care of the City of Tukwila. In 1990 this bridge is historically significant because it is one of the few Pratt Truss bridges built before 1945 still in use in King County. Moreover, it is the only preserved bridge in the region with the distinctive camel-back truss design, which features an arched top chord with five slopes. This design allows for greater standardization of the structural units and gives better stress distribution. In the heyday of this design, 1920-40, it was often the most economical truss for railroad and highway spans, and once was very familiar throughout the Northwest.

WPA BENEFITS

Tukwila and the unincorporated Duwamish Valley communities greatly benefitted from the Works Progress Administration (WPA) program that was a key part of President Franklin Roosevelt's program for pulling the United States out of the Great Depression. With as much as 45 percent of the cost of road, bridge and sidewalk construction being underwritten with federal grants-in-aid, King County launched a vigorous program in the mid-1930s to renew and improve its transportation routes. This work included replacing the old wooden bridges from the nineteenth and early twentieth centuries with concrete culverts or other concrete structures, hard-surfacing existing gravel roads, widening narrow underpasses and building sidewalks.

Under the WPA program, sidewalks were constructed in Duwamish-Allentown, Quarry, and Tukwila. This work began in 1938 with the labor being supplied by the WPA and the county providing the materials, equipment, engineering and supervision. Road building in the Tukwila area used gravel from the county-leased Tukwila Quarry and the Riverton Quarry.

THE RIVER IS RISING!

I remember the word 'chinook' and the sinister way in which it was spoken. It told of floods caused by unseasonable warm winds melting snow in the mountains beyond the capacity of the river to carry it to the sea. Floods were heralded by swollen waters with flotsam and drift from mountain streams. Logs with great upturned roots plunging downstream swept everything before them.

Charlotte Dobbs Widrig, Quarry District

The history of Tukwila is heavily influenced by the region's rivers. Up to 1917, when the Lake Washington Ship Canal was opened, over 1,600 square miles of

OPENING THE VALLEY

Flooding in the valley, 1906. Looking east toward the Monster Farm (Brownell donation claim) and Metro hill. Flood waters fence-post-high were common. Courtesy Washington State Historical Society.

watershed fed the White, the Green and the Black rivers, which flowed together to make the Duwamish River. The Black River and Duwamish River systems drained both the Cedar River and Lake Washington. While Tukwila and its neighboring cities receive only 30 to 40 inches of rain annually, the headwaters of the White River receive around 100 inches of rain and snow, most of the precipitation falling during the winter months. Ideally, the precipitation falls as snow throughout the winter and the melting snowpack provides a good steady runoff during the dry summer months. But not infrequently warm moist air, called a Chinook, moves into Puget Sound during the winter, bringing rain instead of snow to the mountains. This rain, together with snow melted by the unseasonably warm temperatures, swells the mountain streams, causing flooding in the valleys.

Within a few decades of the first settlement, it was clear that the irregular but often devastating flooding would have to be controlled to make the valleys truly satisfactory places to live. Almost a century passed before an effective control system was accomplished in the form of the Howard Hanson Dam on the upper Green River. The radical changes made to the river by humans during the past 100 years, both upstream and downstream, have repeatedly guided the course of events in Tukwila.

THE BEGINNINGS OF FLOOD CONTROL

Beginning in the nineteenth century, valley farmers built dikes and drainage ditches, both individually and as community projects, to contain floodwaters. Never effective in holding back major winter floodwaters, they permitted the farmers to work their fields earlier in the spring and later in the fall by diverting the small rises in the rivers.

In October 1895 the local farmers took the initiative in focusing attention on the problem by creating King County Drainage District No. 1. The purpose of the organization was to resolve the flooding problem. A determined group, they immediately set to work to improve the drainage of floodwaters in the White River Valley. They dug a ditch from Kent to Renton Junction, 11 miles long, 28 feet wide and 14 feet deep, with numerous side branches up to 14 feet wide. This ditch can still be seen in 1990. While aiding the drainage problem, the ditch was not completely effective until the waters of the White and Black rivers were diverted from the Duwamish Valley in 1917 with the opening of the Lake Washington Ship Canal.

The federal government became involved and conducted the first flood control studies in the Duwamish and White river valleys in 1898 and 1905. The results must have been daunting, considering the magnitude of the problem. Local governments became involved with major changes to the Duwamish River when the young town of Seattle, cramped for space, decided in 1906 to level some of its hills and use the excavated soil to fill in the tide flats at the mouth of the Duwamish. At this time high tide brought the salt water to the foot of Beacon Hill, south to about Spokane St. and over to the steep hillsides of West Seattle. Nearly five million cubic yards of earth were sluiced into these tide flats, paid for in part by the sale of the newly created dry land. Before 1906 was over, the local river system was to undergo a cataclysmic change.

THE WHITE RIVER CHANGES COURSE

In the fall of 1906 the autumn rains began early and did not stop. By November a particularly violent flood was raging down the White River and into the Duwamish. From Auburn to the present-day location of Boeing Field, and from the west hills to the east, the Duwamish Valley was a lake. In most places the water was deep enough to permit rowboats to pass over the fences. Just before the floodwaters crested, a massive log jam occurred upstream from Auburn, and the White River spilled over its banks into the nearby Stuck River to the south. The White River, which had frequently spilled some water into the Stuck River during floods, now had the force of the entire backed-up river. The powerful floodwaters quickly cut a channel to the Stuck River and nearly all of the White River waters changed course, roaring down the Stuck River channel, thence into the Puyallup River and across the Puyallup Valley, taking its destructive fury to Pierce County. The valley from Auburn to Tukwila was immediately relieved of the floodwaters, and the Duwamish Valley had only to deal with the floodwaters of the Green and Black rivers.

It took seven years for the political leaders of King and Pierce counties to recognize the change in river channels. In addition, King County had to compensate Pierce County residents by paying for some of the flood damage repairs and building flood control measures along the Puyallup River. With the change of river flows, it no longer made sense to call the river channel from Auburn to Renton Junction the White River. Col. H. M. Chittenden, the Seattle District Engineer for the Army Corps of Engineers, recommended the river now be called the Green River—which it technically was, since the waters of the Green River now flowed in the channel. The citizens accepted the renaming of the river channel, thus the waters flowing down the old White River channel have gone forward in history being called the Green River. So ends the story of the taming of the first of the three sources of valley floodwaters.

THE STRAIGHTENING OF THE LOWER DUWAMISH RIVER

As the flooding of the Duwamish River was partially controlled, the City of Seattle's program for creating dry land

OPENING THE VALLEY

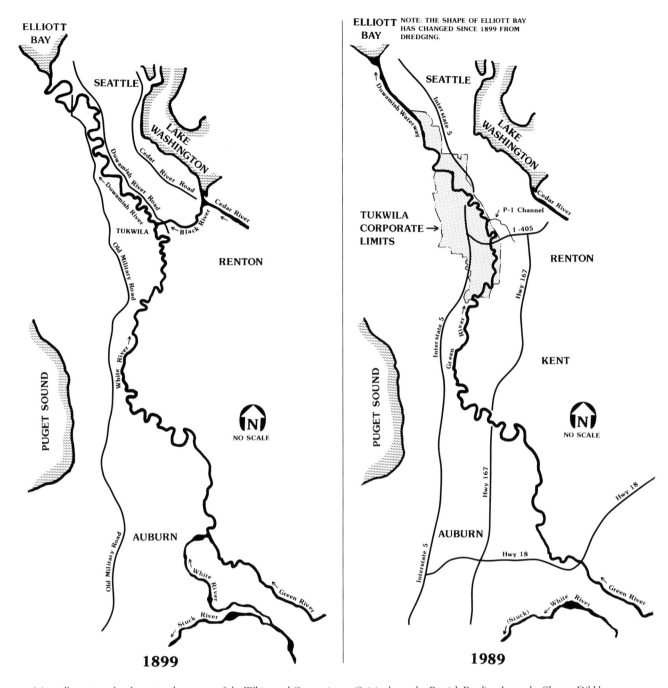

Maps illustrating the change in the course of the White and Green rivers. Original map by Patrick Brodin, drawn by Sharon Dibble.

began to work its way up the Duwamish Valley. The disastrous flood of 1906 was used as one justification for straightening the Duwamish. Shortly after the flood the Port of Seattle issued the following statement:

> It is to be hoped that the lesson of the recent floods that have destroyed so much property and some life in the Duwamish and other valleys near Seattle will not be lost, but that some earnest, aggressive and united action will be taken to prevent anything like that occurring again. The agitation for the straightening of the Duwamish that commenced some time back, and resulted in the appropriation of

thirty thousand dollars for preliminary survey, should now be recommenced with renewed vigor.

The building of the Lake Washington Ship Canal and the straightening of the Duwamish River would absolutely prevent the reoccurrence of floods in this section of the country.

The creation of Commercial Waterway District No. 1 was authorized by the state legislature in 1909 and established by King County on February 28, 1910. The district began organizing immediately and by May 1912 had acquired $160,000 worth of land for the right-of-way of the new river channel.

The project was not without opponents, however, as residents fought to save their farms and homes. The district predicted in 1912 that it would have to use court-enforced legal condemnation procedures to acquire 70 percent of the land. To the Port of Seattle it was a forewarning of what could happen when it tried to push Tukwila out of the way a few years later in its attempt to extend the Duwamish Waterway.

Nearly 20,000,000 cubic yards of earth was removed from the new river channel and used to build dry land upon the estuaries and tide flats at the mouth of the Duwamish River. The Commercial Waterway District was paid for in part by substantial property assessments. Thirteen and one-half miles of meandering river were shortened to four and one-half miles by the time the project was completed in 1917. The lower Duwamish Valley drained quickly and was protected from flooding, and industrial development spread rapidly.

The Port of Seattle now had control of the lower valley and began to look with renewed interest at the upper part of the valley, where the communities of Duwamish-Allentown, Foster, Riverton, Renton Junction and Tukwila lay quietly near the river's banks. The Port, determined to grow, and the small communities, determined to be left alone, had very different plans for the future. These differences would become the major issue in Tukwila's history in the 1950s and 1960s.

THE BALLARD LOCKS AND THE DEMISE OF THE BLACK RIVER

hile the idea of a Lake Washington Ship Canal connecting Lake Washington with Puget Sound had been discussed since the 1860s, it was in December of 1891 that serious planning got underway. The first of five alternative routes identified by the Army Corps of Engineers Ship Canal Board of Engineers was "By way of Duwamish Bay [Elliott Bay] and the valley of the Duwamish and Black Rivers to Lake Washington." Deepening the natural waterway system of the Black and Duwamish rivers, which already connected Lake Washington to the salt waters of Elliott Bay, appeared to be the most logical route for the ship canal. Following the river route required a 12-mile canal and included a series of locks to keep excavation to a minimum. Following a standard canal design, an estimated 7,000,000 cubic yards of excavation would be required to create the canal. Experienced civil engineers estimated that because of the flooding problem, the total excavation for the canal would realistically be more than double the basic estimate.

In spite of its initial appeal, the engineers quickly discarded the Duwamish-Black River alternative because of the high cost and work involved with maintaining this route:

> Owing to the large volume of water which, at the time of floods, enters the Duwamish River from the Cedar and White rivers, an enlargement of the canal to a very considerable magnitude would be required, that the current induced by the freshets would be reduced to a velocity that would not materially impede navigation or threaten destruction to the embankments of the canal; or such flood waters must be carried off in separate channels exterior to the canal prism.

Major H. M. Chittenden was sent in 1906 to study the canal proposal. In his report he favored the Salmon Bay route through Ballard,

The Howard Hanson Dam, completed in 1962, controls the waters of the Green River. The dam is named for Col. Howard A. Hanson who, from 1928 through the 1950s, dedicated his life to working for flood control in King County. Courtesy U. S. Army Corps of Engineers.

which ultimately won the approval of Washington, D. C. Construction began in 1911, and the canal opened in 1917.

Although the Black River was saved from being converted into a canal, it suffered a worse fate: Its waters were taken away and it ceased to exist as a river. Even at high tide, Lake Washington was 15 feet higher than Elliott Bay. It was decided that the lake level would have to be lowered by eight feet. This put the lake level below its outlet to the Black River. Now the lake would now drain exclusively through the ship canal, and not mainly through the Black and Duwamish river system, as it naturally had. In addition, it was decided that the waters of the Cedar River would be needed to make up for the water lost through the locks. The Cedar River was diverted into Lake Washington, and the Black River was reduced to draining only a small local area. Thus it was that by the opening of the ship canal in 1916 the second of the three sources of floodwaters in the Duwamish Valley was eliminated.

TUKWILA—COMMUNITY AT THE CROSSROADS

CONTROLLING THE GREEN RIVER— THE HOWARD HANSON DAM

Because of the foregoing events, from 1917 valley residents had protection from the floodwaters of the White and Cedar rivers. In addition, floodwaters from the Black River no longer bothered them, with the outflow of Lake Washington redirected through the ship canal. The remaining flood problem lay with the Green River—now flowing in the original White River channel. In April 1928 Duwamish-Green River valley residents requested a federal flood control survey of the Green River drainage area. After the survey was completed in 1938, a site six miles upstream from Auburn was chosen for the flood control dam. But there was a problem with this site. The proposed dam at this location would flood and destroy the river's primary fish spawning grounds. Once again the flood program became a battleground for conflicting interests. Fishing interests successfully fought the site near Auburn and forced the Army Corps of Engineers to choose Eagle Gorge as the alternative dam site.

Construction was authorized in 1950, but federal funding was delayed by the Korean War, relocation of the railroad, and measures to protect the City of Tacoma's water supply. Begun in February of 1959, the dam was completed in April 1962. The Howard Hanson Dam is a rock-fill dam, 235 feet high and 675 feet long at its crest. It fulfills the primary goal of flood control and floodwater retention, and provides the additional benefits of storing spring runoff and increasing summer flows to benefit fish habitat, irrigation and municipal water supplies.

Thus it was that after 64 years of dreaming, planning, lobbying, struggling and plain hard work, the third of the Duwamish River tributaries was tamed. Residents could at last look forward to growth without the repeated, severe flooding that had been the hallmark of the valleys. At long last the valley bottom was safe for development. While the residents of the Tukwila area were looking forward to a comfortable, safe future, the Port of Seattle was planning for heavy industry. This story is told in Chapter 12.

MODERN CROSSROADS

In the period 1950-80, the Duwamish Valley was the location of more major transportation public works. The effect of the crisscrossing of Tukwila and the Duwamish Valley by major road systems—Interstate 5 (I-5), Interstate 405 (I-405) and SR-509, and construction of the largest vehicle interchange in Washington, the Tukwila interchange—was not "opening up" as much as "cutting up" the valley. The importance of these transportation ways to the unincorporated communities and the City of Tukwila cannot be overemphasized. Unquestionably, the presence of these large-volume highways and the demands their construction made on the land changed the course of history of the area and contributed to the ultimate annexation of several unincorporated communities to the City of Tukwila.

CHAPTER 8
FOSTER—JOSEPH FOSTER'S LEGACY

Springtime on Brummer's Hill, Foster. By 1910 the old Foster community had expanded up the hill from Joseph and Martha Foster's homestead on the riverbank. This is the home of Charles Foster, Joseph's older brother. Center Charles Foster, his wife far left. Younger man and woman unidentified, possibly brother Leo Foster and wife, who also moved to Foster and lived nearby on the hill. Courtesy Wayne Weber.

The Joseph and Martha Foster family and the Joseph and Jean Campbell Steele family formed the nucleus of the original Foster community. The two homesteads were situated at an important Duwamish Valley crossroads: The Duwamish River Road crossing the river just north and east of Foster's homestead, on the Steeles' place. The road was the sole route down the valley for 40 years, and had a fair amount of traffic since it connected with the Military Road that linked Seattle with Steilacoom and Olympia.

The Steeles operated the original C. C. Lewis ferry, which became known as the Steele Landing when it came to be used as a public riverboat landing beginning in the 1860s. After Jean and Joseph Steele passed away, the youngest sons James and John farmed the land, and operated the ferry into the 1890s.

The home of the knowledgeable, helpful and hospitable Martha and Joseph Foster soon became the hub of community life. With Foster helping "run the territory" as the representative from King County, and Martha supporting the growing community as "wise woman and medical advisor," people naturally congregated at their home. Community gatherings, such as Thanksgiving dinner, were held at the Fosters', who had the largest house in the community. In the early years their house was frequently the Mox la Push precinct polling place. Because Joseph was widely known throughout King County and the Puget Sound region, the tiny community of Foster became known as well. A sketch of the Foster area and community in 1897 can be drawn from Tom Clark's oral history taken in 1955.

The pristine wilderness was gone. The bottomland was cleared except for some large cottonwood and cedar trees. It was now meadowland with some swamp grass. The hillsides had been logged off and were covered with second growth, punctuated by big stumps and felled trees that had been cut but never sent to market. There was logging activity on the top of Robbins' Hill, where there was a skid road built of one-foot-diameter timbers to skid logs down to the river to float to a downstream mill. The skids were greased, and it took a log about a minute to reach the river. The logs entered the river in the vicinity of the S. 124 St. bridge. There were no roads in the area at this time except the pioneer-built Duwamish River Road.

There were about six families living in the immediate area of the Fosters' homestead. The Fosters had a spacious, well-built, handsome, yet unpretentious home, with a large barn, a milkhouse and other outbuildings. The other homes in Foster were built of somewhat rough lumber and lacked the quality of the Fosters' place. Two of Joseph Foster's brothers, Leo and Charles, lived on the hill in the vicinity of where Showalter School was later built. James Steele, Martha Foster's brother, was still on the original Joseph Steele homestead, farming and keeping a dairy herd. He sold out around 1900.

The Interurban and Subdividing the Farmland

When the Puget Sound Electric Railway laid its tracks down the Duwamish Valley in 1902, Foster Station was one of the three original stations opened. The station was a stone's throw from the Fosters' house and the tracks came right through the Fosters' yard—less than 50 feet from the house—thus ending their half-century of quiet rural life. Always progressive and entrepreneurial, in September 1901 Martha and Joseph Foster subdivided a large acreage lying west of the Interurban tracks, calling it Foster's Garden Tracts. They surveyed home-sized lots and laid out streets, and began selling off parts of the old Stephen Foster donation claim for suburban home sites.

Elizabeth and W. N. Ladd bought a large piece that fronted on the Interurban tracks on the east and replatted it in September 1904 as Fostoria Garden Tracts. Another smaller section of the Fosters' subdivision was replatted as Fostoria Park. In March of 1907 two couples, Adolph and Mary Baker, and J. J. and Margaret Broomall, replatted the southernmost portion of the Fosters' subdivision, naming it Mortimer. The Mortimer Interurban station was established about one-half mile north of Foster station.

Although Tom Clark reported that there were only a handful of residents at Foster in 1900, this was probably an underestimate. In 1900 King County defined the Foster area as a separate voting precinct for the first time and listed 90 registered voters. It was named Sprague for the area's largest landholder at that time, J. M. Sprague. This name was used again in 1910; thereafter the precinct was known as Foster, as it remains. The geographic area encompassed by the precinct extended beyond the contemporary definition of the Foster community.

Two sources of population figures are available for 1910-11. The 1910 federal census reports 669 people for Foster. The 1911 *Polk's Directory* reports "about 500" residents for Foster. Comparing detailed information on occupations reported by residents of several valley communities at this time reveals more agricultural occupations in Foster than in the others. This is undoubtedly because Foster was a well established farming community before the Interurban came in.

The Foster Store

The first business in Foster was the Foster General Mercantile, which Joseph Foster built northwest of his place around 1895. The building had a second-floor hall intended for community use. Foster's first post office was established in the store in 1902 with Adam Held as postmaster. Around 1904 Foster sold the building, which changed

Sons of Martha and Joseph Foster, Hillory (left) and Joseph T. Foster (right) in the Foster Mercantile, ca. 1895. Joseph Foster put up a building northwest of the Foster home, approximately at the intersection of Interurban Ave. and 56 Ave. S. The Foster boys tended the store. Tom Clark observed that "they didn't have enough business to keep a cat alive, but Uncle Joe wanted to keep the boys busy and learn business." On the second floor was Foster Hall, the first community hall. Courtesy Museum of History & Industry.

hands about a half-dozen times in the next decade. When Interurban Avenue was built in 1916, the store, which was in the right-of-way, was moved a short distance. The road construction crew used it as a bunkhouse, and while the road was being built, it burned down.

1912 GENERAL MERCANTILE PRICE LIST

Macaroni, package	3¢
Vermicelli, package	3¢
Soda, package	5¢
Cheese/lb.	20¢
Butcher's lard/lb.	10¢
Matches/box	3¢
Tomatoes, 3 cans	25¢
Canned peas/can	10¢
Canned corn/can	10¢
Shaker salt/package	3¢
New potatoes/lb.	2¢
Mason fruit jars, quarts, doz.	59¢
Mason fruit jars, pints, doz.	49¢

The Valley News, July 2, 1912.

For a few years after the Foster Mercantile closed there was no store. However, Lena Swanson, whose husband Fred farmed the river bottom, operated Swanson's Bakery and Confectionery near Foster Station in the 1910s and gained quite a reputation for her fragrant breads, light golden cakes and juicy berry pies.

Edward Heppenstall went to Alaska during the Gold Rush in 1897 and stayed 24 years. In 1921 he moved to Foster to join his five brothers, who lived in the area. He also planned on starting a business. With the six brothers, their wives, and more than a dozen children, there were so many Heppenstalls around Foster that they used to joke about changing the name to "Heppenstallville."

Ed Heppenstall decided to build a grocery store and put up a two-story wood frame building. For the next 16 years the building was both business and home for the Heppenstall family. Orders were phoned in on the 10-party telephone line and delivered to customers twice daily by family members. The store mostly

Heppenstall's Grocery Store. Ed Heppenstall, prop., in the doorway. Being located across from the Foster station, the store enjoyed brisk trade throughout the 1920s and 1930s. Grocery orders were telephoned in to the store and deliveries made twice a day. Courtesy Elsie Rinehart.

stocked groceries. Sugar and flour came in 100-lb. sacks, as did beans and dried peas, all of which had to be weighed, wrapped in brown paper packages and tied with string. Cookies came in large boxes and were displayed in a rack. Customers purchased the amount they needed. Overhead, hanging from the ceiling were buckets, coal scuttles and lanterns. In the back room were a drum of kerosene and the "scratch" feed for chickens.

EARLY HOUSES ON BRUMMER'S HILL

Soon after Tom and Nellie Clark built their home on the lower side of the hill rising above the Joseph Foster homestead, Annie and James Wilson found a spot to their liking at the top of the next hill, which came to be known as Brummer's Hill. The James and Annie Wilson home at 4617 S. 144 St. was built of lumber barged up the river and then hauled up the roadless hill covered with brush and downed timber. There Wilson, a bricklayer by trade but handy with all forms of construction, built his family a home on a sturdy brick foundation. Son Harvold remembers the pride his mother took in the handsome front door with a beveled glass window that still graces the home's entrance. They shared the hilltop with Leo and Charles Foster, Joseph Foster's older brothers.

After a few years of solitude, the Wilsons were entertained by the spectacle of the construction of a 24-room stucco mansion across from them at 4420 S. 144 St. The house was built by Herman Linset, who had a saloon under the old Interurban depot on Yesler in Seattle. James Wilson built five fireplaces in the saloon owner's mansion. Harvold Wilson reports that all the young men in the community were impressed with son Arthur Linset's fancy car.

In 1909, with the house barely finished and as yet unfurnished, Linset died, followed in a few months by Arthur. Mrs. Linset suffered a mental breakdown from which she never recovered and spent the next several decades living in the mansion with her daughter Ethel, preoccupied with the notion of preparing for grand parties—which never took place. The two women lived in the basement so as to not disturb the main quarters, which were kept spotless for that day's guests—who always had simply not yet arrived!

After Mrs. Linset died Ethel sold the mansion, and it was converted to the Arcade Rest Home, a tuberculosis sanatorium. The house's bad luck seems to have been transferred

The Linset Mansion at 4420 S. 144 St. (now site of community swimming pool) was built around 1908 by Herman Linset for his wife, who, while the couple made their fortune in Alaska operating a saloon during the Gold Rush, had dreamed of such a house and the gay social life she would lead one day. The mansion had a library and music room, many parlors, a grand dining room, and a ballroom on the third floor. Oil paintings hung on the walls and thick Persian rugs cushioned the floor. Courtesy Corinne Johnson.

TOM AND NELLIE STARR CLARK—
FOSTER LEADERS 1915-1959

Thomas N. Clark came to the Foster area in 1897 from Cherry Grove, Kentucky, looking for a teaching job. He met Joseph Foster, who took an immediate liking to the young man and hired him on the spot. In the next 12 years Foster, then 70, and Tom Clark, 21, were to become close friends.

In 1902 Clark married Nell Starr, his childhood sweetheart, who came out from Kentucky. Both Nell and Tom were graduates of Indiana Normal School. The couple settled in Foster, where they worked teaching school and farming their hillside land and the Steeles' homestead river bottom. In the 1910s Tom taught at Tolt, Washington, and traveled over 30 miles, much of it on foot, back home to Foster every weekend. Nellie rode horseback up and down the valley teaching at various schools. By 1906 they were milking 40 cows and putting up 200 tons of hay a year for winter feed. The Clarks developed a large vegetable garden on their land, and the day the Pike Place Market opened, August 17, 1906, Tom took in baskets of their nicest vegetables and came home with his pockets jingling.

After Joseph and Martha Foster passed away, in 1911 and 1926 respectively, Tom and Nellie Clark became the center of Foster community life. Nellie Clark taught at the community schools for decades. She also was a founder of the Foster Study Club and Christian Science Church. She was an active member, and often a leader, in a branch of the Delta Masonic Lodge No. 172 in Riverton and Delta Chapter 109, Order of the Eastern Star.

Tom Clark, like his friend and mentor Joseph Foster, distinguished himself for his civic leadership and community service. Tom filled most of the community posts at one time or another, including Foster School Director, Community Club President and Community Constable. Over the years Clark's work activities included being a teacher, farmer, downtown Seattle hotel desk clerk, and realtor. He is perhaps best remembered as the Foster Justice of the Peace, an office he held from 1924 to 1954. By his own account he performed over 3,000 marriages.

Mary Ellen Anderson Whitehead remembers frequent conversations with Tom Clark, when, as a child, she walked past his house each day on her way up the hill to the Foster School. He always seemed like "an Abe Lincoln" to the little girl—tall, with a bony, angular build and an unruly shock of dark hair. He had a remarkably deep voice with a gentle Kentucky accent, and was always interested in the children and their cares and dreams. Neighbor Gerry Brooker Young remembers Tom Clark as "a very nice person and always ready to be a helpful, kind neighbor."

Tom Clark and Nellie Starr Clark, Foster community leaders, place ballots in the wooden ballot box used for 50 years in the Foster precinct. Courtesy Evelyn Koch Santora.

Tom Clark was famous for his keen sense of humor and love of joking and story telling. One of his favorite stories was the time he was reported for dead back in Foster while he was up north in the Alaska Gold Rush. The community held a memorial service for him. His fiancée Nellie was there in mourning, and each friend stood up and spoke in laudatory terms of the 25-year-old who had met such an untimely death. Tom would finish the story by gleefully describing everyone's shock, not the least his own Nellie's, when a few months later he walked into Foster just before Christmas.

The Clarks lived in Foster their entire lives and saw it grow from the small, close-knit group of neighbors to a larger community with organizations and civic services, many of which they helped bring to the community. Their lives bridged the early pioneer era of Martha and Joseph Foster, and the highly technical, post-industrial era ushered in by World War II. Tom and Nellie Clark both died of tuberculosis a few months apart in 1959. The Foster community was joined by people from up and down the Duwamish Valley in mourning the loss of this prominent and beloved couple from Kentucky.

with the ownership: One of the new owners became ill with TB, which he had contracted from the patients. The South Central School District acquired the property and demolished the mansion in 1968, making way for the community swimming pool built by the county Forward Thrust program.

THE POPULATION IN 1920

Foster flourished between 1910 and 1920, with 1,025 residents reported in the 1920 King County census. In 1920 the extensive enumeration district reached across the valley and up the hills to include part of Riverton Heights. The only detailed population information for this date comes from the voter records. Since the record includes only registered voters, it is not conclusive. Forty-six percent of the U. S.-born residents were from the Midwest, with Illinois leading, followed by Iowa, Minnesota and Wisconsin. As in 1910 Foster residents gave Washington as their place of birth more often than did residents of other valley communities—a reflection of Foster's nineteenth-century roots. Farming still dominated, but there were more laborers in Foster by 1920. Twenty-five percent of the men listed skilled occupations, with carpenter being the top trade.

FOSTER POINT

From the early pioneer days, people coming into the Foster area had mostly chosen to make their homes on the west side of the river. However, Steele's Ferry made it convenient to cross the river, and at least one pioneer homesteader settled on the east side of the river on the loop of land known as Foster Point. In the first decades of the twentieth century, deteriorated pioneer buildings could be seen on the east riverbank near the Point. With the ending of the ferry service and the closest bridge being the Black River Bridge, about one and one-half miles upriver, living on the Point became very inconvenient unless one owned a boat. The situation improved with the completion of the Riverton drawbridge in 1903, located north of the later location of the S. 124 St. bridge.

The area had been known as Foster Point since the earliest pioneer days; however, around 1905-06 there were several attempts to connect it first with Riverton, then Allentown. In 1905 William P. Patten subdivided the land, naming it East Riverton Garden Tracts. The only street built was Foster Ave. (56 Ave. S.), a rough road that ran the length of the finger of land that is the Point. In 1906 Joseph and Flora Allen named the area on the north side of the river Allentown Addition and Allentown Acres. The name Riverton never caught on, but some people do refer to the Point as Allentown. Generally, it is known simply as Foster Point.

Not having a bridge to Interurban Ave. was a frustration to Point dwellers, since the Foster Interurban station lay directly across the river. The situation eased a bit when John Anderson moved his family and rowboat onto the Point in 1922 and built their house close to the river, bank. Being a friendly, neighborly man, Anderson frequently provided transportation across the river for his neighbors on the Point. In 1926 the county built a footbridge connecting Foster Ave. with Interurban Ave. In 1939 a vehicle bridge was built connecting 56 Ave. S. to Interurban Ave. This bridge was replaced in 1985. These bridges are discussed in Chapter 7.

John Anderson was a bricklayer—a tradition that has carried on in the family for three generations, with his daughter Mary Ellen's husband Bill Toon taking up the trade as well as Anderson's grandson Bill Toon, Jr., who also learned the art of bricklaying from Anderson. The Andersons and the Toons built many of the brick homes in the valley. The house at 13335 56 Ave. S. was built by Bill Toon, Sr., for his family and was his first house.

The quiet country solitude afforded by the Point's geography is contrasted with the presence of the nearby railroad and animal carcass processing plant. Throughout most of the

John Anderson preparing to take his neighbors across the river. Before the Foster footbridge was constructed Anderson, who lived next to the river, would paddle across to carry home his neighbors living on Foster Point. Naturally, there was no charge for this community service. To avoid sliding down the slope during the rainy season, steps were cut into the riverbank leading to the water's edge from the Foster station. Artist's conception by Don Paulson.

twentieth century, five sets of railroad tracks have run by the northeast side of the Point—the route of the Northern Pacific, Milwaukee Pacific Coast, and Union Pacific Railroads. John Needham, who lived on the Point from 1933 to 1990, recalls that when the old steam engines came through in the 1930s they shook his house, which rested on wooden blocks, so severely that "about twice a year [he] had to crawl under the house and jack it up."

In the 1940s quieter diesel engines replaced steam engines. However, the community continued to live with the passing trains. Because there was a railroad crossing on the Point until the 1960s, the passing trains would give a long warning whistle as they sailed through. For a number of years it was considered great sport by some to put dynamite caps on the railroad tracks near the crossing. The report of the caps as they were set off by the train wheels sounded remarkably like gunshots. The crossing has been the scene of a number of tragedies over the years including numerous accidents, with at least one person being killed. One winter evening in the 1940s a woman who was tired of life went to the crossing and lay down on the tracks just before the evening express was due. The engineer never saw her.

Around 1950 the Seattle Rendering Company, locally known as simply the "rendering works," moved from a location in South Park to east of the Foster Golf Links. For more than 40 years residents on the Point have lived with the odor that wafts down into their yards and, when a southeast wind is blowing, permeates the entire area. This disagreeable situation was

Many people living along the river had boats. In 1933 Foster Point was completely covered with water, and John Anderson with neighbor John Needham rowed Anderson's boat down the middle of 56 Ave. S., looking into every house. Water was flowing through the houses as high as the doorknobs. It appeared that everyone was gone until they came to a house where they found a solitary woman who had just gotten out of the hospital and thus had been unable to leave on her own. Helping her into their boat, the men continued checking the houses and also rescued a young mother with three children that day. Courtesy Washington State Historical

improved around 1985, when a new rendering system was installed as a result of state anti-air pollution legislation. However, the problem has not been resolved and continues to be an issue with the valley residents for many miles around.

Upper Foster, 1900-1930

The flat valley bottom land along the banks of the Duwamish was preferred by the pioneers for farming as well as for the convenience of water travel. As population grew, with the opening of the valley by the Interurban and construction of bridges and roads, the community expanded up the hillside, and areas became informally designated as Lower Foster and Upper Foster. The higher location was favored by many because of the safety from flooding it offered.

About halfway up the long steady hill directly above Joseph and Martha Foster's homestead, three roads came together—Macadam Road, S. 144 St. and 51 Ave. S. This crossroads became the hub of Upper Foster, beginning in 1910, when businesses and community institutions sprang up. According to Tom Clark, the Foster Community Club was built first, followed by Brummer's Store, the Foster Presbyterian Church and Foster Fire Station.

Of the various businesses that flourished at this place, Brummer's Store was the first one opened, one of the last to close, and the best known. Located at the base of the very steep hill which came to be known as Brummer's Hill, the Brummer store was on the northwest corner of the intersection. The store was operated by Henry and Maria Brummer, who moved to Seattle in 1902. After keeping a store in Seattle for a few years they decided that they wanted to live in the country, and in 1909 they bought land in the Foster area and built their store and rooming house.

Many of the teachers at the nearby Foster School, such as Dorothy Corrigan from Minnesota, found lodgings at the Brummers' comfortable rooming house. In the evening, after Mrs. Brummer's typical delicious dinner, the roomers would gather in the parlor and converse, play cards or games, and sing. With a little persuasion Dorothy, who possessed a beautiful voice, would sing her rendition of "Alice Blue Gown." Dorothy stayed in the valley and married Bill Wiese, who operated the community gas station. Bill served the Foster community as the first commissioner of Foster Fire District No. 18 and the water commissioner.

The Brummers were from New York City. They had a definite flair for quality merchandise and made a point of stocking the best gourmet and even luxurious goods. Helen Nelsen recalls being sent as a child to Brummer's Store by her mother for that "special something." She would walk along Macadam Road on her way to the store "because there weren't any streets along the base of the hill… until the Interurban went in; it was just all fields." The Brummers successfully operated their store to the time of Henry's death at the age of 79 in 1944. Maria Brummer lived on for many more years and was described at age 82 by community chronicler Emma Curtiss as "enjoying all the activities that many of us younger ones do. She is always planning a party or going to one, keeps house, has lovely flowers and has no intention of a humdrum existence."

The square yellow-brown Foster School stands at the top of Foster Hill. Doris Heppenstall Hanset recalls "A pungent odor of oil-soaked sawdust used to clean the hallways greeted us at the door as we marched inside. Patient teachers presided over chalk-dusty classrooms as a large clock ticked off the hours until we could escape outside." Brown's chicken farm is in front of the school. Courtesy Elsie Rinehart.

The Chapmans operated a grocery store across the street from Brummer's Store in the 1920s. Over the years this store was operated by Weatherbee, Glithero, Johanson and Kilburg. To the north of the Chapman store was a gas station operated by long-time resident Andrew Dunbar. In 1934 he sold the business to Mel and Beulah Edwards, who moved into the attached living quarters. Earlier Edwards had rented a service station in lower Tukwila from Minnie Lutz. Mr. Edwards expanded the business to include vehicle repair along with the sale of gasoline. The Edwards family lived here for 13 years and were active members of the community. In 1947 the George Wilson family purchased the station.

For a short time in the 1920s there was an ice cream shop at the crossroads that was much frequented by the children. Henry Johnson, the town barber, affectionately known as "Barber Johnson," had his barbershop in his home a little way north of the gas station, and cut both men's and women's hair. An hour at Johnson's shop was a guaranteed way to catch up on the community news. Two physicians, Jack R. Morrison (Foster High class of 1935) and Alan L. W. Gunsul (Foster High class of 1944) grew up in the homes on either side of the Henry Johnson barbershop. Each established medical practice in nearby communities and actively served the medical needs of a good number of local citizens.

Winters with good snow found the Foster children gathered at Brummer Hill for sledding. Dusty toboggans were pulled out for the exciting fast ride down the hill. Jim O'Sullivan, Edwin Doty's grandson, recalls that sometimes a large bonfire was built at the bottom of the hill—for warming up cold hands and feet—and sledding would go on late into the night.

Building a Community

Many people struggled to get established in the community at this time. For example, the Walter and Anna Jorgensen family moved to Foster in 1918 because Walter wanted to raise the children in the country. Daughter Alice Jorgensen Wood recalls how her mother, Anna, pined for the nice modern house in Greenwood in Seattle that they had left to live in a tent for months while Walter built their house.

When someone in the community needed the labor of a strong team in the 1910s and early 1920s, they called upon Bill Hammer, who would trot over his pair of big brown horses with their brass-trimmed harnesses gaily jingling to plow the garden, haul in building materials or move the family to their new home. He also blasted out stumps and cleared land. The children loved to watch the large horses respond to Bill's whistles and calls as they plowed, harrowed and leveled the ground. The Terrace Apartments, at 13705 56 Ave. S., stand on the site of Hammer's place. West of the Foster School was the Brown and Mann chicken farm, a thriving enterprise in the 1920s. The farm

In the 1910s Riverton and Thorndyke children walked to Foster to attend school after the fourth grade. A two-plank boardwalk was built through the woods for the children's path. Courtesy Museum of History & Industry.

FOSTER COMMUNITY DOCTOR—JESSE L. RAINS, M.D.

Jesse L. Rains was born in a mining camp in Warren, Idaho, in 1878. His father was killed in an Indian attack when he was three and his mother moved the family to Grangeville, Idaho. He attended the newly opened University of Idaho and served in the Spanish-American War. He received his Doctor of Medicine from Jefferson Medical College in Philadelphia, Pennsylvania. He married May Wildenthaler in 1908 and practiced medicine in Grangeville and Oakley, Idaho, until he moved to Foster in 1923. The family settled in the Clemans' house, a half block from the Foster School. Daughter Mary recalls that because they lived so close to the school Dr. Rains was called on for all emergencies, and every autumn he examined the football team players before fall practice began.

Dr. Rains had an office in his home, but most of his practice was done as house calls—as far away as Black Diamond. Mary remembers that "he never refused help when needed. After going into people's homes and seeing firsthand their economic condition, he seldom sent bills for his services. He was often paid in produce, such as vegetables, chicken and fruits." Dr. Rains died suddenly in 1937 of complications from an operation. The Rains children are Mary, Dorothy, Lewis and David. Mary taught at the Foster School 1935-36, married Edgar Giboney, and still lives near the community. Daughter Dorothy married Marvin Robbins of Riverton.

supplied many stores in Seattle with fresh chicken and also sold poultry at the Pike Place Market.

Around 1900 Edwin and Emma Doty came out to Foster from Minneapolis with their daughter Jennie LaVera. Doty opened a lumber yard on the river bottom near Joseph Foster's place. He barged in loads of lumber and had millwork and special woods brought on the Interurban. Around 1905 Doty built his house on the hill at 14711 57 Ave. S. It was the community's model "modern house" in its day, with flush toilets and a pressurized water system provided by Doty's own wooden water tank behind the house. It had a grand circular drive where Doty parked his shiny black 1922 Buick.

Around 1909, Doty built a two-story frame building across the road from the Foster School and about a six-minute walk from the Upper Foster crossroads, to serve as the community hall. Built in a triangular lot at 52 Place S. and S. 136 St., for over a decade Doty Hall was used as a part-time school gym and for meetings and

> ### A Foster Childhood in the 1920s
>
> *Jim O'Sullivan*
>
> I remember joyous summers running around like a wild Indian—to paraphrase my mother—tattered overalls, rotten sneakers and my best friend in the world, Ned, there every day of the year. We slept out. We picked wild hazelnuts by the bushel and ate them on the spot. We investigated thoroughly all of the garter snakes and assisted in their birth and death—depending on the fear level.
>
> We talked for days if anyone were to see a Sheriff's car tour through our neighborhood, speculating wildly. There was no crime, no violence, no media distraction. The weather always seemed just right for the plans at hand and chores were not onerous. It was a good life.
>
> Later there were bicycles—mine were reconstructed from scavenged parts. This gave us mobility to go to Angle Lake and to visit girls in other neighborhoods (the local girls were unsuitable). Then came old rattle-trap cars and farther afield we went.
>
> And finally, despite all odds, we grew up. My days at Foster seemed very ordinary, but only now do I realize how ideal they were.

public events, amateur theatricals, singing clubs, debates, and community potluck dinners. Doty's daughter Jennie was a skilled elocutionist and delivered dramatic recitations of the Gettysburg Address, the poetry of Henry Wadsworth Longfellow and other popular works. Tessie Henke recalled struggling to get home from an evening event at Doty Hall—clambering over logs and brush in the dark, since the hill was still very wild and without roads. Old-timers remember Doty Hall being used at different times as overflow space for the grade school and as a feed store.

Foster Community Club

he Ladies' Improvement Club of Foster was organized June 4, 1906, and incorporated with 17 members. Nettie Olson was the first president and the meetings were held in members' homes. The next year, with Annie Wilson as president, the group began to actualize their goal to enrich the community with educational, social and physical improvements. The first major project successfully undertaken by the women was the founding of the Foster Community Club. In 1907 the women built a small one-room community hall with lumber that Tom Clark hauled by team to the site from Georgetown. Initially known as the Foster Auditorium and later as Foster Hall, the building was later enlarged. It was an important addition to the community, for it provided a meeting place to conduct community business and hold parties.

In the 1920s and 1930s the hall was also the local movie theater. First were the silent pictures with Mrs. Uttendorfer accompanying the picture show on the piano, and then the talkies. Jim O'Sullivan recalls that the picture shows were brought out to Foster Hall by a traveling showman who traveled by bus, bringing his own film and projector. The hardwood hall floor was often used as a dance floor as well as a basketball court. The community's young people spent long hours having fun and getting healthy exercise during the wet winter months at the Foster Community Hall. The hall served as the school gym during the time between the destruction of Doty Hall—which was used as the school gym—and the building of a new gymnasium at Foster School.

In 1918 Mr. Brummer organized the Community Hall Association of School Dist. 144 to manage the building as a service. For many years the Foster Community Club women put on dances and card parties to pay off the loan and finish the interior of the hall. In 1928 the community's men organized the Foster Improvement Club and elected officers. On November 24, 1931, the two community clubs agreed to merge under the name of the women's club.

On March 8, 1932, the Foster Club became affiliated with the Renton district as a member of the Associated South End Clubs, which had about 54 active member clubs at this time. Each club in the association elected a queen,

Foster Community Hall, 1938, near the upper Foster crossroads on Macadam Road. Built in 1907 by the Foster Ladies Community Club the hall was enlarged and improved over the years. The hub of community life for 52 years with activities ranging from basketball and dances, to Center for Community Relief Program during the hard Depression years, to civil defense training during World War II. The beloved hall was destroyed to make way for the I-5 freeway in 1959. Courtesy Washington State Archives.

and Foster was no exception. A queen was elected each year from 1934 to 1958, usually a student from Foster High School. Presidents during this period include Wesley Welsh, Tom Clark, Neal Day, Carl Yeast, Robert Greene, Kenneth Morrison, Chas. Smith, Roy Latimer and John R. Walkup. In addition to Foster, many of the club members lived in nearby Riverton Heights.

During the Depression the community club assumed a very dynamic role in the community. The year 1933 is an example of the activity during this era. During the winter months community members put on a play. In the spring the men organized a singing group, and neighbors from Tukwila, Riverton, Duwamish and Allentown turned out for a "home-grown" minstrel show. Throughout the fall and winter months there were regular Saturday night boxing bouts. However, the reality of the hard times many were living through was brought home every Monday morning as unemployed people formed long lines outside the community hall to receive food vouchers good for flour, rice, dried beans and milk.

As the community grew the building became decidedly too small, and right after the Depression a large two-story building was erected that glowed with activity in the coming decades. The Foster Volunteer Fire Department had a small building beside the community hall where they kept the fire truck and other equipment. When Fire District No. 18 was formed in 1943, the station continued in this location until the freeway was built.

During World War II the Foster Community Club was a center for Civil Defense (CD) activity. A major CD activity carried out at the hall was registering, classifying and fingerprinting every adult in the district. Civil Defense volunteers staffed the community hall day and night until the end of the war.

After the war the community club happily shifted to peacetime activities, including providing a library and a polling place on election day. The hall was in much demand as a meeting place by organizations and clubs, including ones from neighboring communities such as Riverton and Tukwila. Organizations that regularly met there include the Boy Scouts and Girl Scouts, the Royal Neighbors, Foster Christian Endeavor Society, Foster Parent Teacher Association (PTA), Townsend Club, King County Election Board, Foster Friendly Garden Club, and the Musicians' Union and Square Dance Clubs.

Gene Ives recalls a humorous prank pulled by Foster High School boys on a group of Rawleigh sales people meeting in the hall. As the people left the hall at the end of the evening they were astonished to find a little Austin-Healey car neatly parked on the front porch—about 10 steps up from the ground. It had been put there by the group of grinning young men who were sauntering by and satisfied with their trick, were willing to lift the vehicle back down to the ground.

FOSTER—JOSEPH FOSTER'S LEGACY

When I-5 cut through Foster, the Foster Community Club Hall was condemned for the freeway right-of-way and demolished in 1964. After this event the Foster Community Club continued, but without a hall it was very limited in its activities compared to previously. The loss of the Foster Community Hall was a serious blow to community cohesiveness, for the institution had brought old-timers and newcomers together, and had welded neighbors into a mutually supportive community that helped each other, worked, celebrated and played together. As the well-used and cherished Foster Community Hall collapsed under the blows of the wrecking ball, many turned their heads away with tears in their eyes—more than a building was being destroyed. It would be much harder to maintain their special Foster community spirit without the Foster Community Hall.

THE FOSTER LIBRARY

n important community service performed by the Foster Community Club was to provide space in the Community Hall for a public library. Sponsored by the Foster PTA, the Foster Library, a branch member of the King County Library system, opened on February 5, 1945. In 1952 the Foster Library Board was formed with representatives from various community groups. The board assumed responsibility for maintaining and equipping the library. Bernice Scoones was the first librarian and served a dedicated 22 years at the Foster Library.

In April 1960 the Foster Library was moved to an old house behind Foster High School that was rented from the School District for $1 a year. The King County Branch Library system installed an expanded book collection at the new facility, and library service to the Foster community was greatly increased.

Over the years the Foster Library Board worked hard raising funds and soliciting Foster organizations to support the library, but there was not enough money for a new building.

Finally, in 1966 funds from public and private sources allowed construction to begin. The completed 2,400-square-foot, $46,000 library, situated on the Foster High School grounds, was dedicated on September 13, 1967. State Sen. Robert C. Ridder, a South Central District vice principal, addressed those who had gathered to mark the important achievement, reminding them of Joseph Foster's dream of education for the community's adults and young people. At the 40th anniversary of the opening of the Foster Library, February 12, 1985, the director of the King County Library system presented a certificate of recognition to the Foster Community Club. Mrs. Marjorie Latimer, 91 years old, a charter member of the Foster Ladies' Improvement Club, accepted the award. The director observed that the evening's events grandly demonstrated "the place the library has in the hearts of Foster residents."

FOSTER FRIENDLY GARDEN CLUB

The Foster Friendly Garden Club was organized in May 1933 by Marjorie Latimer, Kate Naylor, Anna Chapman, and Bessie Cartner, who was the first president. The club selected the dogwood as its flower. Initially held in women's homes, the club meetings shifted to the Foster Community Club until it was destroyed. Since that time the club has met at the Thorndyke Community Club and the Foster-Tukwila Presbyterian Church.

During its more than 50-year history the garden club has successfully undertaken many projects, including Arbor Day community tree plantings and landscaping the Foster High School and Southgate Elementary school grounds. The club's activities have varied over the years. The club has built a float celebrating plants and flowers for a local parade, held plant sales, and occasionally made floral wedding decorations. With a revival of interest in gardening under way in the 1990s, the Foster Friendly Garden Club continues to offer community members the means to share their horticultural knowledge and joy in plants and gardening.

THE SUNSHINE GRANDMOTHERS CLUB

In 1955 the Sunshine Grandmothers Club No. 9, an affiliate of the national association, was formed in the Foster-Tukwila area. The Amiga Club, a similar club, formed in Allentown-Duwamish, joined the Sunshine Grandmothers Club. Objectives of the club are to support the Grandmothers Charitable Trust Fund, to establish better living conditions for the aged, to assist in community hospitals and to encourage membership growth by organizing clubs throughout the state. The club has met at the Foster Community Club Hall and at the Foster-Tukwila Presbyterian Church.

THE FOSTER-TUKWILA PRESBYTERIAN CHURCH

The Foster-Tukwila Presbyterian Church is an evangelical congregation that has served the people of Foster, Tukwila, Duwamish-Allentown, Riverton, and Riverton Heights for over 80 years. The purpose of the church is stated in its weekly bulletin: "To Know Christ And To Make Him Known." Pursuing this goal in 1990, the church offers home Bible study groups along with regular Sunday education classes for adults and young people.

The church was founded in 1907, when Mr. and Mrs. George Chandler and Mr. and Mrs. Fred Starbard of the Cherry Street Presbyterian Church, Seattle, moved to Foster. They purchased property on the corner of S. 144 St. and 53 Ave. S. in 1908 and built the first small church building in 1909. Although it was unfinished, the congregation held its first Christmas service in the church in 1909. The church building was used for public school classes for two years after the Tukwila School burned in 1920.

Instability in the early years was resolved by Dr. Mark A. Matthews in the 1920s. Dr. Ezra P. Giboney became pastor in February 1930, and during his term the congregation built a manse and enlarged the church building to its present size. Many members of the community have good memories of the Sunday evening Christian Endeavor gatherings led by Mrs. Giboney for many years that were a happy combination of inspiration and fellowship. Rev. Giboney, along with members of the congregation, started Riverton Heights Presbyterian Church, now Fellowship Bible Church, at S. 160 St. and Military Road S.

Reverend Harold Lang was the pastor from 1949 to 1963. In 1942 major alteration and expansion of the building was completed. The 1990 building consists of additions that have been constructed around the original building, which serves as the pastor's study and the church narthex. The old roof of the first building can be seen between the ceiling and the roof of the present building.

The construction of I-5 displaced many church families, as well as taking the church manse and parking lot. The congregation voted to move the church building to a new location at the corner of S. 144 St. and 56 Ave. S. rather than construct a new building. On August 26, 1969, the whole community turned out to watch as the old landmark church slowly moved up the hill. It took the entire day. Church members contributed to the work of establishing the old building on its new site.

After several years of declining membership, in 1973 A. Taylor Dunlap, a Bible preaching pastor, came to the church. He infused a fresh spirit into the congregation and many new people joined the church. Nick Krantz, a former teacher, came to Foster-Tukwila Church in 1978. Pastor Krantz's dynamic leadership resulted in successful ongoing programs, such as the weekly Women's Ministry led by lay women. Sunday evening services came about as a result of Pastor Nick's emphasis on prayer. Music has always been an important part of the life of the church members. From 1940 to 1980 Mrs.

Virginia Radnich and Mrs. Mildred Heppenstall served as church organists.

Just as in its early days, the congregation retains its community character. The 1990 congregation of 165 members is diversified and includes people from backgrounds other than Presbyterian. In addition, it attracts members from beyond the immediate area. In 1990 the church continues to provide meeting space for community activities including Love Church Services, an interdenominational outreach supported by numerous south end churches to help needy people, as well as Boy Scouts, training classes for the Tukwila Fire Department, and two AA groups. The congregation helps support many international missions and local missions including the Union Gospel Mission and Teen Challenge.

St. Joseph Mission and St. Thomas Catholic Church

Up to 1912 Catholics living in the Duwamish Valley took the Interurban to Renton or Seattle to attend Mass. In September of 1912, Fr. Robert Ryan, Pastor of Our Lady of Lourdes Parish in South Park, established a mission church to serve the 20 Catholic families in the new, small communities that were growing along the upper Duwamish Interurban route. Masses were said in Robbins Hall and the Riverton School until a little frame church was built near Mortimer station.

Dedicated in 1914, the mission church was to serve the valley Catholics for 50 years. Initially, Franciscans of St. George's Parish were in charge of the St. Joseph Mission Church, with Frs. Bartholme, Berberich and Trabert providing ministerial services. In 1929 St. Joseph's was attached as a mission to St. Anthony's Parish, Renton, with Fr. William Carey, Pastor. The mission congregation was very proud when William and John Shaw, born and raised in the community, said their first masses at St. Joseph's as newly ordained priests. The Shaw brothers were the grandsons of Joe Koenig, known in the community as "the Chicken King" because of his large poultry farm.

By 1946 the church had grown to 600 families and on November 16, 1946, was recognized as a parish. A brick rectory was build adjacent to the church and Fr. John C. O'Connell became the first resident pastor. In 1948 the name was changed to St. Thomas, to avoid confusion within the Archdiocese of Seattle with St. Joseph's church on Capitol Hill. In 1957 Fr. Anthony Palmasani replaced Fr. O'Connell.

The route of I-5 through Foster passed over the site of the original church, and in 1963 St. Thomas Parish built a much-needed new church at 4415 S. 140 St., on the old Gaskill farm site high on the hill overlooking the old mission. The 600-seat church and parish complex includes a Sunday school, parish hall and rectory. To celebrate a half century of the community worshiping together, and giving thanks for the new home for the church, the parish served a fall harvest dinner in the newly constructed parish hall in 1964, exactly 50 years to the day after the first worship service was held. St. Thomas Parish has a regular Sunday School and summer classes; however, it has never maintained a regular parochial school.

In 1977 Fr. Palmasani was replaced by Fr. Walsh. Next Fr. Jarlath Heneghan came to the parish. In 1979 the original sanctuary was remodeled to better reflect the liturgy changes brought about by Vatican II. Fr. Ibar Lynch began as pastor in 1990. St. Thomas Church members participate in a wide variety of spiritual and community outreach activities through church organizations including:

- Parish Council—15 members who work in union with the Pastor making decisions guiding the church.
- Religious Education Program—to consider the spiritual needs of youth and adults.
- Parish Club—to foster community spirit and to assist in parish needs.

TUKWILA—COMMUNITY AT THE CROSSROADS

St. Joseph Mission/St. Thomas Parish Church at Mortimer. The original 1912 church had 12 pews on either side of the aisle. The church's name was changed to St. Thomas in 1948 when it achieved parish status. Courtesy Dorothy Miller McCarthy.

- Outreach—to channel charitable contributions to assist the needy within the parish and to promote good will among neighboring churches and the community.
- 50-Plus Group—to serve senior members in activities of a social, religious and community nature and to contribute to parish needs.
- St. Thomas Adults Reflecting Christ (STAR)—to experience and share a vision of a fuller life in Christ and Church through community and fellowship.
- Welcoming Committee—to assist new parishioners.

THE FOSTER STUDY CLUB

In 1926 a group of women from the Foster-Tukwila area decided to form a discussion group which they named the Foster Study Club. The number of members was limited to 14, which was the number of meetings originally held annually. The members were drawn from an area that was within walking distance from the members' homes, cars being scarce. The founders of the study group chose for their motto "Study to Show Thyself Approved unto God." From its beginning, each year a theme has been chosen by the program committee. At the biweekly meetings there is a brief business meeting, and a prepared paper is presented by a member.

There is an annual meeting open to all interested women to enable them to learn about the aims and requirements of the club. The club has a yearly outing, which may be to the theater or a cultural/historical field trip. The club's twenty-fifth and fiftieth anniversaries were celebrated with special activities. In the 1980s the club assisted in establishing a King County Branch Library in the historic Tukwila Schoolhouse. Over the years the group has had luncheon meetings as well as evening dessert meetings.

The Foster Study Club is a valuable community institution that originally arose from the women's "self-improvement club" movement of the early twentieth century. For 65 years it has provided a means for intellectual inquiry, dialogue and growth for women living quiet lives characterized by hard work and limited ready opportunity for intellectually stimulating activities. The continued vitality of this club testifies to the ongoing need it fulfills, as well as the commitment of the women of the community to intellectual and cultural growth.

FOSTER VOLUNTEER FIRE DEPARTMENT, FIRE DISTRICT NO. 18 1943-1989

In the early days the outbreak of a fire in the Foster community generally ended when the building was reduced to ashes. After King County Volunteer Fire District No. 1 was organized by the people of Duwamish-Allentown in 1935, Foster called upon them to fight community fires. In addition, fire fighters from Renton and Burien would assist with large fires. Determined to form their own volunteer fire department, School Superintendent Wesley Crum, Bill Wiese and Arthur Kassner canvassed the community with a petition for a Foster Volunteer Fire District area, and easily obtained sufficient signatures. On July 20, 1943, the King County Commissioners established King County Fire District No. 18, Foster.

With little cash at the outset, the price of the first pieces of equipment was right—$1 for a 1936 front-mount pump and hand-cranked siren. Edwards' Garage and Gas Station in the Upper Foster business district at the foot of Brummer's Hill was the temporary fire station. Notice of a fire reached the station, which did not have a telephone, by a call to Brummer's Store or one of the other nearby businesses having a phone. Whoever received the fire alert call ran to Edward's Garage and hit the fire siren on the roof, and within minutes the volunteer firemen began arriving at the fire station on the run.

Under Volunteer Fire Chief Arthur Kassner's able leadership, a group of about 30 enthusiastic volunteers received professional fire fighting training and worked together to improve their equipment. Win Gallacher became fire chief in 1949, followed by Ernie Robertson, Charley Godfry, Jim Angle, Walt Kassner, Larry Juno, Tony Ruffino and Ed Davis. Eventually the volunteers received token payment of 25 cents for drills and 50 cents for fires. The men put the money into the Foster Firemen's Fund used to pay for additional equipment and the annual Firemen's Dinner. In 1963 a new fire station was built on S. 144 St., across from Foster High School, and a larger 500-gallon pump truck and a radio dispatch alarm system were purchased. In 1974 the department bought an aid car and EMT training became standard for all fire fighters.

In the history of the volunteer department one of the most memorable experiences occurred in 1974. Fifty percent of the volunteer firemen were out of town on a firemen's retreat when smoke was reported at Showalter Junior High School. With a new 15-minute Scott Air Pack fire detector, Fire Chief Jim Angle quickly found the source. This was a serious fire at a key community institution and a mutual aid alarm was sounded throughout south King County. Fifteen engines and one ladder truck quickly responded. The school was saved, but the damage was heavy.

For 45 years trained volunteers fought fires at home and in neighboring communities, as Fire District No. 18 expanded its area to include Riverton and Thorndyke. The Foster Community and nearby communities were proud of and grateful for the volunteer fire department, which saved property and lives and reduced insurance premium payments. The men of the community gave generously of their time at weekly training sessions and often risked their personal safety for the lives of others.

Prior to Foster being annexed to the City of Tukwila in 1989, Fire District No. 18 elected to close its doors at the Foster location and join forces with White Center Fire District No. 11. The volunteers and all equipment were moved from the Foster area. After the annexation, Tukwila remodeled the old building and now mans it for 24-hour fire service.

SPENCER POTTERY

In 1949 Ralph Spencer, chemist, and Lorene Spencer, artist, acquired the Charles J. Erickson house at the Upper Foster crossroads across the street from Brummer's Store. In the next few years the husband-and-wife team became leaders in the Northwest Craft Movement as they developed high-quality original pottery made of local natural materials. Ralph combined native clays he mined himself and created glazes to chemically "fit" the clays. Lorene trained herself to be a potter, using a specially designed potter's wheel developed by Ralph, and evolved a functional pottery style making use of the clays and glazes created by Ralph.

They worked with the new arts programs that were introduced into the Seattle public schools in the 1960s, teaching the youth the art of making pottery with native materials. The Spencers enjoyed success from the beginning with the public, who appreciated both their pottery of native clay and the creative school program. They exhibited as a team for many years at art galleries, museums and fairs in the Pacific Northwest. In addition, their pottery was displayed and sold at the prestigious America House in New York, a gallery dedicated to uniquely American arts and crafts from across the United States. Ralph Spencer died in 1973, and a few years later Lorene moved to Olympia, where she continues to make Spencer pottery. Lorene sold the Blue Gallery, and since 1985 Bonsai Northwest has occupied the building.

The annexation of the Foster community to

The Blue Gallery was the studio and home of Lorene and Ralph Spence, who developed original pottery using native clays. They remodeled the building, originally the Charles Erickson house, in 1972, making a portion of it five stories high. Painted cobalt blue, the building was their studio, sales gallery and home, where they raised their four children. Original drawing by Barbara Vaughan.

the municipality of Tukwila is a logical move, since the history of the two communities is closely intertwined. The entire original town of Tukwila lay within the borders of Joseph Foster's land. For decades Tukwila residents have actively participated in and been an important part of Foster's institutions, most notably the Foster School District No. 144 (South Central since 1942), the Foster Presbyterian Church, the Foster Community Club, the Foster Study Club and many others. On the other hand, Foster owed its original public water system to Tukwila. The historical record clearly shows much mutual support from the communities over the decades. The oldest of the upper Duwamish communities, Foster has a long and proud history as Joseph and Martha Foster's own community.

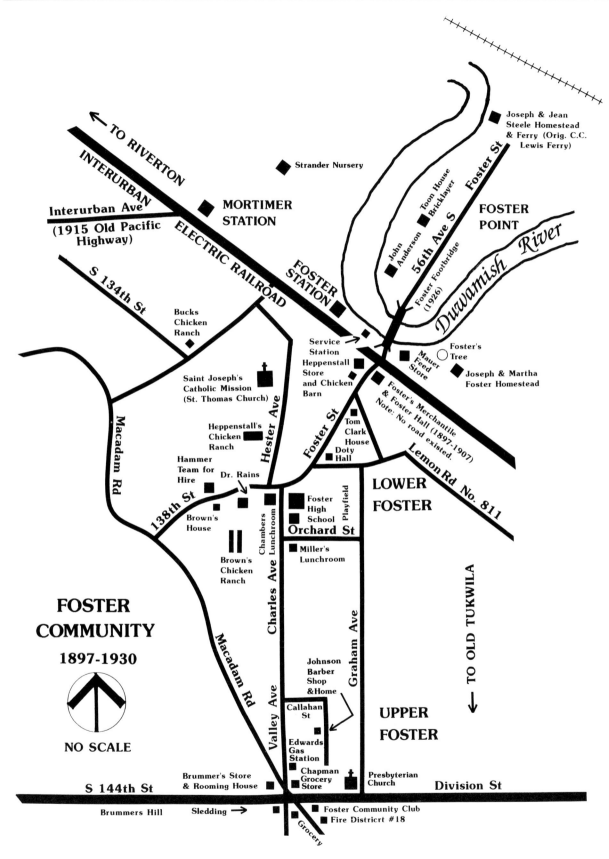

Map by Patrick Brodin with assistance of Mary Ellen Anderson Whitehead, Maxine Anderson, Kay Reinartz. Drawn by Sharon Dibble.

CHAPTER 9

RIVERTON ON THE DUWAMISH— SEATTLE'S MOST PICTURESQUE SUBURB

Panorama of Riverton, ca. 1907. Looking northwest across to Riverton from above present-day 4357 S. 135 St. The Macadam Road flows through the center with the Riverton School in the center of the photo. Between 1902 and 1910 this area of the Duwamish Valley was transformed from the Robbins donation claim to a thriving suburban community—thanks to the Interurban. Courtesy Elizabeth Springer.

I am convinced that Riverton is destined to become the main city in this area of the Duwamish Valley.
    Dr. Frederick Nichols,
    Riverton physician from 1913 to 1956

The area of the original Milton and Susannah Steele Robbins land claim was the focus of intense subdividing activity in the seven years following the establishment of the Interurban station in 1904. From this activity emerged the unincorporated community of Riverton. Of all the early twentieth-century upper Duwamish communities in the study area—incorporated or unincorporated—Riverton was the most promoted, grew the fastest and became the largest early on. Careful study of the plat records shows that, unlike other nearby areas, the majority of the subdividing was done by community residents rather than outside investment firms, although a few developers did have large holdings.

The community name, Riverton, appears to have its origins in the plats filed by George H. and Hattie M. Nichols, and the Robbins family. In December 1904 the Nicholses joined forces with their friends Charles and Maude E. Lincoln and subdivided an area as Riverton Acre Tracts. Reflecting the lush beauty of the natural landscape, they named the boundary streets Glenwood (S. 130 St.) and Fernwood (40 Ave. S.). This plat is historically significant since it marks the first official use of the name Riverton in the community.

In the next three years the Nicholses used the word Riverton in the names of all of their plats: Riverton Acre Tracts, 1904; East Riverton Garden Tracts, 1905; Riverton Addition, 1906; and Riverton Macadam Road Tracts, 1907. Following the Nichols' choice of the name Riverton, between 1907 and 1919 the Robbins family used the name Riverton in their three plats: Robbins' Springbrook Addition to Riverton, 1907; Robbins' View Tracts Addition to Riverton, 1909; and Robbins' Orchard Addition to Riverton, 1919. And so it came to be that the community was Riverton. The establishment of the Interurban station at Riverton helped solidify the name.

The Selling of Riverton

The deluge of people surging into Seattle in 1900 with every train from the Midwest created a high demand for homesites. In February 1902 the large real estate firm Crawford and Conover reported: "The market has been remarkably active for this time of the year. We have made a large number of sales, almost all of them in residence properties. Business has been fine and the outlook unusually bright."

The vigorous market also resulted in a sharp, steady rise in the prices of Seattle home lots and houses. In 1902 the prices of lots on Capitol Hill ranged from $800, in the area of 12 Ave. E. and E. John St., to $4300 at E. Aloha and 16 Ave. E. Lots on 10 Ave. E. went for $1000. Lots on the north side of Queen Anne Hill were priced at a modest $330 to $700, and lots in Ballard could be had for $300 to $700. The cost of having a house built on a lot ranged from a few hundred dollars to thousands, with the average being around $2,000. For example, a "nice" eight-room house cost $3,000; a six-room story-and-a-half mission cottage on Queen Anne Hill cost $1,500; and a four-room bungalow in the Observatory area of Capitol Hill was a modest $400. With the exception of Ballard, Seattle property was soon beyond the reach of many people, particularly those in the trades, clerical jobs and industry.

In contrast, in River View Tracts in the heart of the thriving Riverton community, a large cleared homesite, with a view and pure spring water piped to the tract, cost $375. In the Robbins' Springbrook Addition to Riverton, mountain view lots located five blocks from the Riverton Station and supplied with piped water could be had for $250 and up. The size of the lots varied from one-quarter of an acre to the coveted five-acre tracts. The Interurban made these homesites a mere 30 minutes from downtown Seattle.

A number of "downtown" real estate brokers also offered Riverton tracts, such as J. F. Ord who, from his well-appointed offices overlooking the solemn tusked walruses gracing the front of the new Alaska Building, made home tracts in Riverton available as cheap as they came—$200 for a quarter of an acre. "Fine Soil—Fine Location One Mile West of Riverton. Terms: $20 down and $20 a month."

Local unofficial sources report Riverton's population in 1906 to be around 400. However,

The home of Charles and Maude Lincoln, Riverton, at 13209 40 Ave. S. is among the best-preserved examples of the country farmhouse style in the upper Duwamish Valley. A broad front porch with simple straight brackets reinforcing the porch posts maintains the country flavor. When the house was built in 1908 Riverton had already been logged off. The lush woodsy setting for the home in 1990 is more in keeping with the natural appearance of the area. Courtesy Tukwila Historical Society.

TUKWILA—COMMUNITY AT THE CROSSROADS

it was more likely between 150 and 200. Around 1908 a number of the enterprising valley boosters got together and put out an attractive booklet, *Riverton on the Duwamish—Seattle's Most Picturesque Suburb*. The booklet extolls the perfection of the suburban community which is described as, "Purely a residential place where peace and rest are enjoyed. There are no railroad yards, shops or tracks of steam roads within one mile. Nor are there factories or 'other noisy concerns.'"

Naturally, the local land developers were squarely behind this promotional piece and ran display advertisements. The Riverton Realty and Building Company, the enterprise of partners McCoy, Whitcomb and Morrison, announced that it was ready both to help homeseekers find a suitable lot and to build the home on the lot. Watson and Shirley Squires of the Union Trust Co. announced that their lots ranged from a low $175 to $500 for a quarter of an acre. In addition to land developers, the local builders and associated craftsmen were boosters. In small, neat notices they offered all manner of materials and skills needed to build homes including finished lumber, fireplaces, windows, brick and terra cotta ornamentation, doors, sashes and glass, and specialty cabinetry.

> **RIVERTON**
>
> **The Mecca of the Homeseeker**
>
> Do you want to build a home in a locality where the sanitary conditions are perfect?
>
> Do you want to build your home where all the modern conveniences are at hand?
>
> Do you want to build your home where there are more natural building spots than can be found in any other locality in the neighborhood of Seattle?
>
> Then come and see for yourself a place combining all of the requisites for the building of a country home practically in a city.
>
> From *Riverton on the Duwamish—Seattle's Most Picturesque Suburb*, ca. 1908

EVERYTHING IS UP TO DATE IN RIVERTON

hile the promotional literature engaged in the usual exaggeration, in fact, the old Robbins homestead and hop farm was being transformed into a suburb. Being situated on the steep hills that rose on the west side of the Duwamish River, the community was high enough above the river to escape all but the worst flooding. The slope was also favorable for a sanitary sewage system. The

Macadam Road looking north toward Riverton Station. Note the 1903 Riverton drawspan in the background and the Beck house on hill on the left, at 13136 42 Ave. S. O.C. Thompson and Ellen Thompson are shown in front of their original furniture store on Macadam Road, ca. 1909. Courtesy Olive Thompson Hozack.

community boasted it had modern conveniences normally only found in good-sized cities: graded streets, a pure piped water system, the telephone (Independent and Sunset service—same as Seattle) and wooden sidewalks from the depot all the way up the hill to what is now 32 Ave. S. From the beginning Riverton was very progressive, with electric street lights installed by 1924. There was a light in each block and property owners were charged $15 a year for the convenience.

Among the services of which the community was proud was a good piped water system developed and managed by the Robbins family. Riverton Water Company, Inc., was a gravity-fed system that drew upon the large springs located on the Robbins farm in the vicinity of 40 Ave. S. above Southgate Park. Water was stored in two large storage tanks and piped to the village below. By 1929 over 130 families were being served by the system. Emmett L. Robbins was the corporation president and the family retained the controlling interest, although there were other stockholders.

The Population

The opening of the valley to suburban residential development coincided with the peak of the historic "Great Migration" of immigrants into the U.S. The year 1907 marks the peak of the flood. Unlike the period 1880-1910, when Scandinavians and other North Europeans dominated, after 1910 the Great Migration was dominated by people from southern and eastern Europe, and Japan. The influx of immigrants was evident everywhere in Riverton. The 1910 U.S. census reveals that every other person in the community was an immigrant. In addition, 80 percent of the American-born people were children of immigrants, i.e., second-generation Americans. In the entire district only a dozen people reported that they were "old stock" Americans, i.e., third-generation or more. In terms of national origins, the census enumeration district, which includes river bottom to the north, reports 28 percent Italians, 15 percent Japanese, 10 percent Germans, 7 percent Swedes and 3 percent Danes. Reflecting the fact that the vast majority of these immigrants were young singles or newly married, the majority of the children were born in the United States.

Contradicting the image promoted by the realtors that the new "Interurban communities"

Home of Emmett L. Robbins with family on porch. Courtesy Tukwila Historical Society.

Emmett Robbins

After Milton and Susannah Robbins passed away the homestead was divided. Eldest son Emmett, born after the family settled in the area, had a 70-acre farm next to his parents' place and kept a herd of 30 dairy cows. Emmett spent his life in the community and was known to his friends and neighbors as a man of marked strength of character. He maintained a leadership role in the formation of the community of Riverton in the 1910s and 1920s, and was very active in community affairs, including serving on the Foster School Board and founding the Delta Masonic Lodge No. 172. He built Robbins' Hall, which served as the community hall for many years, being used for school meetings and social gatherings. As a community elder he was fondly known as "Grandpa Robbins." Direct descendants of Robbins remaining in the community include Bill, Milt, Agnes and Marvin.

MAKING A LIFE IN *AMERIKA*

Like many of their neighbors, Thomas Scibor and Rozalia Wolotzyn Scibor, who moved to Riverton in 1919, had immigrated to America to make a life for themselves. Rozalia and Thomas had emigrated separately from Poland around 1905. Scibor was attracted to the Northwest because he was told that Portland was a place where roses bloomed at Christmas.

Scibor found work in the sawmills and logging camps in Oregon, saved his money and made new friends. But he felt lonely and wanted to "settle down" in his new life with a girl from the Old Country. Not finding a suitable mate in Portland, Scibor took two weeks off from his job and traveled back to Chicago, which had a large Polish community, to find a wife.

In the following days he was introduced to one young woman after another; either he was not interested or they were not interested. All he had to offer was his commitment to the marriage and a chance to live in the Northwest. With only a few days left, Rozalia Wolotzyn was recommended to him as being intelligent, beautiful and a hard worker. Scibor went directly to the foundry where Rozalia worked and found her covered with graphite and sand. Scibor introduced himself to the startled nineteen-year-old woman and asked her to take the day off—he would pay her for her lost wages—because he wanted to ask her to marry him.

Eyeing the man standing before her presenting his suit, the spunky Rozalia later told her son, she thought to herself "she was born once, she was going to die once, that she would take a chance once." She agreed to marry Scibor—providing they solemnized the union with a proper Catholic wedding.

Since Scibor's two weeks off were almost over, there was no time to post the Catholic marriage banns and the couple, now betrothed, caught the train back to Portland the next morning, spending three days and two nights sitting in the day coach looking out the window, exchanging small talk, and casting shy glances at one another. In Portland the banns were posted and on January 25, 1909, the entire Polish community turned out to put on a first-class Polish wedding to get the adventurous young couple started in their new life.

Photo and story courtesy Thomas Scibor, Jr.

were being populated by business and professional people seeking quiet suburban living, the occupations most frequently given in the census are farming, ranching and laboring. Further reflecting the agricultural focus of the area at this time, nursery and livestock dealing are commonly reported.

Polk's Directory 1911-1912 reports a total population of 425 for Riverton and Riverton Heights and reveals an interesting representation from a variety of trades and professions. The building trades predominate and include carpenter, plasterer, bricklayer, electrician and lather. Occupations characteristic of commuters are also evident and include motorman, actor, bookbinder, photographer, cigar maker, court reporter, dressmaker, painter, watchmaker, woodworker and fisherman. There were eight teachers in the community, six women, all of whom taught at the Riverton School. Because of the Riverton Pulmonary Sanitarium in Riverton Heights, there were a number of health-care

RIVERTON ON THE DUWAMISH—SEATTLE'S MOST PICTURESQUE SUBURB

Riverton Interurban Station and S. D. Goff Mercantile, ca. 1904. S. D. Goff built his mercantile next to the Riverton station in 1904 and immediately enjoyed brisk business from the traveling public. When Rosenberg took over the store around 1919, he built his loading dock between the store and the Interurban tracks and received and shipped his goods directly from the Interurban loading dock. Riverton drawspan, 1903, in background. Building behind man waiting is a store. Courtesy Olive Thompson Hozack.

professionals including physicians, nurses, an osteopath and a dentist.

In the 1920 U.S. census, the Riverton enumeration district, which includes Riverton Heights, reports 1,035 residents. Details such as nationality origins are not available. The voter registration records, naturally limited to those who vote, show that the American-born population was largely from the Midwest, with the top states being, in order, Illinois, Iowa, Minnesota, Missouri and Michigan. The most common occupation given is laborer, followed by machinist, carpenter and farmer.

Tom and Rozalia Scibor, like many other immigrants, bought land in Riverton because they wanted to live in the country where they could garden and raise their children in a healthy environment. In the 1920s they opened the You and Me Restaurant in South Seattle, taking the Interurban to and from their business. Second son Thomas Scibor, Jr., nine when they moved to Riverton, remembers: "When we came to Riverton in 1919 it seemed that each and every household was of a different nationality and religion. Everyone was very cooperative and helped each other and mixed very well. They shared and bartered with what they had and it was a real good neighborhood to live in."

The same rich soil that had earlier provided bumper crops of hay and hops now produced a variety of vegetables, berries, fruit trees and flowers in abundance. Many homeowners kept chickens and even a milk cow, or a few pigs or goats if they had more acres. During "berry time" there were places for the children to go pick to earn a little extra money. Processing and preserving food was a part of almost everyone's summer and fall activities, with many women canning hundreds of quarts of vegetables and fruit. Extra eggs and raw milk were sold to neighbors.

BUSINESS GROWS IN RIVERTON, 1905-1910

hortly after the Riverton station was opened in 1904, S. D. Goff built his General Mercantile, Hardware and Feed Store next door to the station building. The

133

TUKWILA—COMMUNITY AT THE CROSSROADS

Riverton Postal Station was located in Goff's store, with S. D. as Postmaster. Around 1905 Emmett and Margaret Robbins opened a general store up the hill at S. 132 and 37 Ave. S., where they sold a full line of groceries as well as hardware, clothing, confections, cigars and tobacco, and all kinds of building materials. In business until 1922, they offered free home delivery of orders. The second floor was Robbins Hall, which had a good hardwood floor for dancing and a stage for performances. The Riverton Heights School often used the hall for school affairs. Later the Sorensen and Hasper Meatmarket occupied the building offering for sale fresh meat which the partners Martin Sorensen, a Dane, and Herman Hasper, a German, slaughtered on the premises.

Except for the Robbins', all of the early businesses clustered around the Riverton Station, which also enjoyed the advantage of fronting on Macadam Road, the best road up the Duwamish Valley in that era. Henry and Clara Rosenberg, Jewish German immigrants, bought Goff's store and made their home in the back. In 1912, after Dr. Rininger was killed at Riverton Station Crossing, Puget Sound Electric Company paid Rosenberg $100/month to help watch the train crossing until an overpass could be built. In 1920 the Riverton Postal Station was closed and the community's mail came from Georgetown. However, most people brought their outgoing mail down to the Rosenbergs, who gave it to the Interurban conductor, who, in turn, deposited it at the Seattle Post Office.

When the Interurban pulled into Riverton Station, it not only carried people but brought supplies, the mail and the news. Farmers hauled the results of the morning milking down to the station in shining steel cans that were lined up on the dock ready for the early train. Often fresh eggs and other produce for the Pike Place Market were sent along with the milk. The Seattle morning papers were delivered at Riverton station at 6:45 a.m. and the evening papers at 5 p.m. Lucky was the boy—girls were rarely paper carriers in those days—who had a paper route. In the early 1920s Nevelle (Bill) Robbins had the paper route for all of Riverton. On Sundays, when the newspaper was always large and heavy, he borrowed Ozzie Springer's horse and buggy to haul the papers around.

Mr. Larson, a Swedish immigrant, opened a shoe repair shop just south of the station. Larson lived in the back of the shop and in the first few years was almost always available for quick repairs; later he was open 8 a.m. to 5 p.m. Mr. Larson helped young Algot "Gus" Gustavson immigrate and, upon his retirement, turned his business over to Gus. As Gus worked on shoes and learned to speak English he became well known in the valley. He eventually took over Mr. Larson's place and later moved to O. C. Thompson's building at the crossroads.

Just south of Rosenberg's on Macadam Road, Ole C. (O. C.) and Ellen Thompson operated a general mercantile and feed store. They had come to Seattle in 1898 and taken up residence in a boarding house on Capitol Hill. O. C. became a bookkeeper for Malmo Nurseries, and the thrifty couple were able to save enough to buy a tract in the new suburb of Riverton in 1905. Determined to get established quickly, the Thompsons moved onto their land immediately, where they lived in a tent while they built a chicken house. They moved into the chicken house and took in boarders with whom they shared the house. Thompson continued to commute to Malmo's while building the grocery and feed store on the lower end of their tract at 12812 Macadam Road. Ellen managed the store and the boardinghouse while also caring for the children. One old-timer recalls that O. C. Thompson was a "W. C. Fields type of character, with a dry sense of humor that could have a sharp edge." He liked to wear a bowler hat and, like Dr. Nichols, was devoted to Riverton.

Around 1912 the store burned to the ground, but the Thompsons rebuilt immediately and, in spite of heavy debts from the winter supply of feed and grain that was lost, they did not go bankrupt. In 1918 they sold the store to

RIVERTON ON THE DUWAMISH—SEATTLE'S MOST PICTURESQUE SUBURB

McCoy Hall on Macadam Road was built by Charles McCoy, founder of the Delta Masonic Lodge No. 172, to serve as the first Lodge Hall. The street-level part of the building was rented for commercial activities. After the hall burned in 1909 Delta Lodge did not have its own hall until 1926, when a new brick lodge was built at 13034 41 Ave. S. Courtesy Olive Thompson Hozack.

A Historic Crossroads

As more people moved into Riverton in the late 1910s, a real business district formed around the intersection of S. 130 St. and a road locally known as Valley Highway (later East Marginal Way). The hub of the community's business life for 70 years, this landmark intersection has seen many businesses come and go.

One of the largest enterprises was O. C. Thompson's two-story commercial building constructed about 1922 on the northeast corner of the intersection at 12924 East Marginal Way. This building has been the site of active business enterprises throughout the entire twentieth century. Originally operated by Thompson as a general mercantile, hardware and used furniture store, the store gradually shifted to a catch-all second-hand store that achieved the status of a community institution. Larry Linnell recalls that in the late 1920s and '30s the basement was a pool hall and card game area not to be nosed into by small boys.

The second floor was a large hall with a solid hardwood floor that served well the Saturday night community dances. Over the years many clubs met there, such as the Modern Woodsmen of America and Royal Neighbors. In the 1930s "Miss Salmon" came out from Seattle every week to teach dance classes—which were relished by many a young lady and detested with equal vigor by boys in knee breeches sent over to learn a few dance steps.

The building saw many uses over the decades. In 1950 Thompson sold his hardware-junk store to Roy Henderson, who operated it

A. W. Flesch and built a hardware and furniture store several blocks west, where a new business district was forming. Charles K. McCoy built McCoy Hall near Thompson's store.

Most of the businesses were also the homes of the owners. The favorable location by the station put them on the edge of a ravine which led to the river and did not allow for a family garden, but it did make a great place for childhood adventures. When the heavy rains came, the older Riverton boys headed for the ravine, which filled up with floodwaters teeming with steelhead salmon. Sometimes they made a raft and poled over the river-spearing salmon with pitchforks.

It was not long before the community established another important community institution—the public dump. Riverton residents hauled their throw-aways part way up Robbins' Hill (40 Ave. S.) and off to the west, where they threw their trash down the high creek bank. The dump eventually closed, and Southgate Park occupies this area in 1990.

THE RIVERTON CROSSROADS

Photos courtesy Washington State Archives unless otherwise indicated. Clockwise, from above:

In 1990 the three adjoining wooden frame buildings facing on East Marginal Way have undergone considerable alterations, yet retain the flavor of the originals. Douglas's Blacksmith Shop and Automobile Repair Garage was on the right. After the Interurban closed down the building immediately left of the garage served as the bus station. The building left of this began as an annex to Stutz's Mercantile which was first occupied by Clara Musselman's Dry Goods and Miscellanea.

Charles Stutz built his store on the corner of S. 130 St. and East Marginal Way. The building left of the annex on 130th served as a slaughterhouse for a time in the 1910s. Villard and Frances Linnell operated the store from 1924 to 1941, and then Lee Markland took over.

O. C. Thompson built this block around 1920 and operated his business on the right-hand side. In the 1920s and '30s the left side of the building, facing on East Marginal Way, housed Naylor's Bakery. Johnny Dennis's Barber Shop was located around the corner on the S. 130 St. side. The second floor was often used as a community hall for meetings, dances and boxing matches with local talent.

Harley Knapp's Garage on the northwest corner of the Riverton crossroads provided fuel and auto repairs from 1925 to 1975. Knapp's is distinguished as the longest-lived business in Tukwila under the same ownership. Courtesy Phyllis Knapp Storvick.

Gus's Shoe Repair shop on Macadam Road was first developed by Mr. Larson, a Swedish immigrant. His assistant Gus eventually took over the business and in the 1930s moved the shop to the north portion of O. C. Thompson's block at the Riverton crossroads.

until 1962. Henderson's Hardware Store was described by *Seattle Times* columnist Byron Fish as "a public service for pack rats. Roy Henderson keeps all the things a man would like to save, but doesn't have room for in his shop or basement." In later years the building was occupied by Gus's Shoe Repair and a rock shop. In 1990 the landmark building, now Jake's Antiques, stood little changed and was back to its original use—second-hand furniture.

In the 1930s Stuart Naylor, who operated a bakery in the building next to Thompson's, arrived every morning at 3 a.m. to bake his hearty wholesome bread and to create the cream puffs, custard fills, bear claws and "rubbernecks" (maple squares) that were highly esteemed by everyone for miles around. Assisted by his stepchildren Charley and Winona, Naylor sold his bread through most south-end stores and eventually built a new bakery near Southcenter.

The Hultzes operated a bakery, confectionery and ice cream parlor on the southeast corner of the intersection. Around 1922 Charles E. Stutz and his wife Marie took over the space and converted the shop into a grocery store, which Marie ran with the help of their three sons and daughter. Soon they added a butcher shop, doing the butchering and dressing out of the meat in a long building located directly east of the shop on S. 131 St. One day the King County Health Inspector appeared at Mr. Stutz's door asking to see his slaughterhouse. Walking through the butchering building the inspector frowned, pulled a form and a pencil out of his black leather case and, while Stutz watched, wrote out an order closing him down—failure to meet county sanitation code. Giving up butchering, Stutz used the building as a garage. It was still standing in 1990.

Still committed to diversification, in 1923 Stutz added a 12-by-8 foot wing on the south side of his building for a dry goods store. Later that year Clara Musselman, an enterprising widow, moved to Riverton and leased Stutz's annex as Musselman's Dry Goods. Musselman's was also a miscellanea, and one of the children was usually on hand to help find "that special item" from one of the hundreds of boxes that lined the walls, floor to ceiling, in the narrow shop. Eventually Stutz expanded this wing into a full-sized one-story building that connected with Douglas's two-story garage building directly south.

In 1924 Stutz sold the grocery business and was leasing his north building to Villard and Frances Linnell. The Linnells made their home above the store with their children Larry and Janice from 1924 to 1933. Both Mr. and Mrs. Linnell were very active members of the community from 1924 through 1941. Frances, in addition to working in the store, was a member of the Royal Neighbors of America, and Villard of the Riverton Improvement Club and Modern Woodsmen. Frances Linnell was a Grand Matron of the Eastern Star, Delta Chapter 109.

For many years Catherine Buck and Ben Schwartz were lucky enough to have jobs all through high school working at Linnell's grocery. As they grew up, the Linnell children took over the store work. Mr. Linnell sold his store in

Ky Fox's Frisky Four kept hearts light and feet dancing all over south King County from 1931 to around 1960. The original band was made up of Foster High School students Ky Fox, leader, and banjo and saxophone player; Elmer Lindgard, piano and trumpet; Bob Fuller, saxophone and vocal; and Jack Ramage, drums. Ky says, "They were all good musicians. Elmer was particularly talented—he picked up from the radio many of our arrangements. He also played trumpet, lead or harmony, while simultaneously playing piano chord progressions with his left hand." Ky Fox's band was very busy playing at the dozens of popular lakeside resorts in south King County in the 1930s and '40s, all of which had dance pavilions. They also played at the Spanish Castle Ballroom, Highline, and Dick Parker's in north Seattle. Ky Fox, son of well-known area builder F.G. Fox of Riverton, changed band members and the band name over the years, but he kept on bringing the joy of dancing to the community. In 1990 he was still at it, being the musical coordinator for the Seattle Banjo Club. Photo is the Dixielanders, in 1959, Fox at left. Courtesy Ky Fox.

TUKWILA—COMMUNITY AT THE CROSSROADS

> ### THE LINNELL GROCERY STORE IN THE 1920s
> *Larry Linnell*
>
> A grocery store in those days was an amazing establishment. Not only were there the regular shelves of canned and packaged foods, but there were bins of bulk foods to be sacked upon order. Dried beans, granulated sugar, brown sugar and rice. Barrels of kerosene, molasses, dill pickles, herring, sauerkraut and cookies were on the floor. Bundles of dried codfish, 100-lb. sacks of sugar, chicken feed and flour were in the storeroom; other items—barbed wire, galvanized buckets, bolts of cloth and hardware. Behind the meat counter was a 4 x 4 chopping block where halves of beef were carved to steaks and roasts. Sugar was 5 cents per pound, hamburger and hot dogs 19 cents, potatoes 10 lbs. for 25 cents, milk 7 cents per quart with cream "that thick."
>
> Along one wall was a marble-topped soda fountain with four wire-legged stools. Malts, sundaes, sodas and banana splits were served up with a dollop of whipped cream—5 and 10 cents, please! A great selection of candy and confections. Jars of mints, both pink and white, peppermints, "Big Oscar" candy bars, and don't forget the "Lucky Bite" mints! If you bit into a pink mint you would win a big candy bar.
>
> The most important fixture in the store was a great metal-page ledger with 18 springs per page, each of which held a customer's account bills. Most everyone charged their groceries. During the Depression the Linnells carried many people's accounts for a long time. Some of them took many years, but almost everyone settled up the debt eventually. The neighborhood grocers, such as my father, the Heppenstalls, Brummers, Chapmans in Foster, Fredericksons in Allentown, and Bert Foreman in Tukwila carried many families through the Great Depression.

1941, when ration coupons became a headache and Larry went off to war. Next Leonard L. Markland bought the corner store and opened Riverton Foods, known to everyone as Lee's Market for over 20 years. From 1946 to 1960 Bob and Lou Carson operated Hometown Hardware in the central building. In 1960 they moved their business to S. 144 St., off Pacific Highway.

One of the best-known businesses starting up in this era and staying in business for over 40 years was Johnny and Gertie Dennis's Barber and Beauty Shop. Open every day, the shop was always crowded on Fridays and Saturdays with Johnny and Gertie briskly clipping, trimming and marceling the Rivertonians in the 1920s and '30s in preparation for Saturday night parties and Sunday morning church. In the early 1920s a haircut for a man or boy cost 25 cents, a fashionable lady's marcel (finger wave) 30 cents, and a permanent $1.00. A young couple just getting established in 1922, the Dennises lived in the back of the shop with their children Gladys and Jack. They closed the original shop after the Depression, and Gertie operated a restaurant on the north side of O. C. Thompson's building, while Johnny opened Johnny's Barber Shop on the southwest side of the building. After the war Mike Yellam took over the shop, operating it as Mike's Barber Shop. Mike was still keeping the community trimmed in 1990.

Back in the 1920s, competition appeared as Gelino, an Italian immigrant, put up another striped barber pole in front of his home on Robbins' Hill on 40 Ave. S. near the Robbins Water Works. Naturally, the large Italian-American community in the river flats patronized him, as did many others who soon learned that he really knew his barbering and gave a real good close shave, too. Another enterprising Italian immigrant was Lacava, who opened a shoe repair shop just south of the Riverton crossroads. The shoe shop has been demolished, but Lacava's house built next door at 13012 40 Ave. S. was still in use in 1990.

BUSINESSES DOWN THE ROAD

hile the community was becoming less agricultural all the time and cars were replacing horses, there was still a call for feed and seed. Miller Feeds opened in the 1920s on Valley Highway and was in business for over 50 years, with son Don keeping the family business going to the late 1970s. The feed store really boomed after Longacres Racetrack opened near Renton Junction in 1933, since the track bought a large portion of their animal feed from Miller's. Competition arose just north of Miller's on the Valley Highway when Burdick's opened their feed store in the late 1920s.

Next door to Miller's, the McBreens opened a service station in the 1920s. The Verhoef brothers took it over and operated a tavern and service station into the early 1930s. Subsequently, Bill Quealey and then Ray Warren operated the place. Barney Schwartz, who provided skilled repair and gas for 25 years, is best remembered. Widening of East Marginal Way (known earlier by local residents as Valley Highway) in 1978 forced Schwartz to close. In the 1980s-'90s the old tavern portion of the building has been a restaurant where good, home-cooked lunches have been available, first as Connie's, then as Vi's. Four blocks up the hill west of Miller Feeds was the Riverton Machinery Works, owned and managed by Harley Graves. An ambitious young man could get a start in the machinist trade, learning welding, milling, machining, boring and riveting.

CROSSROADS FUN

The Riverton crossroads was also the scene of young boys' highjinks and other fun. Living at the Riverton Hospital on the south side of the crossroads, Dr. Nichols' sons and their friends occasionally played tricks on the passing motorists. The favorite game with the drivers involved placing Victoria Nichols' old purse in the middle of the road. A wire was attached to the purse and the boys hid under the bushes beside the road, wire in hand, waiting for a likely car. It was Depression time and soon an alert driver would spot the purse, slam on his brakes and leap out to pick it up. At that moment the boys would jerk the wire and the purse would disappear from under the outstretched hand of the motorist.

One Fourth of July there was a display at the intersection that people are still talking about. South of Linnell's the Kerrs opened a novelty shop. An incident that helped the Kerrs decide to retire began when May McLaughlin's sizzler firecracker got into their fireworks stand. Everything went from ladyfingers up to 5-inch salutes. Roman candles were shooting fireballs, and skyrockets were zooming 300 feet up and down the highway. This was probably the most exciting, colorful event in the whole history of Riverton, chortles Larry Linnell.

KEEPING THOSE MODEL TS RUNNING

The advent of the automobile, which coincided with the development of the Riverton community, spurred the opening of engine maintenance and general automobile services. Daniel Van de Water (he later changed the name to Vanderwater), an enterprising Dutchman, opened a general machine shop and repair works around 1907. Progressive minded, in 1911, when automobiles were still scarce, he listed his business in *Polk's Directory*: "Automobile, pump and general repair work, gasoline and coal oil engines bought and sold, distance no object, agent for Lambert Gasoline Engines."

By 1919 W. R. and Mabel Douglas had bought the building south of Stutz, where they operated Douglas's Garage and Repair, which eventually was a combination blacksmithing shop, gas station, auto repair and bus station after the Interurban closed. During Prohibition, County Sheriff Matt Starwich stored impounded bootleggers' cars at Douglas's garage. Since they had a nice warm sitting area, it attracted the local constabulary and soon became a favorite gathering place for the local men to catch up on the community goings-on.

The Douglases had an apartment above the auto repair shop, where they lived with their four daughters, Maud, Gladys, Margaret and Dorothy. Every year there were more cars passing through

Riverton, and one summer day little ten-year-old Dorothy was run down while she was trying to cross the street. The entire community mourned with the well-known family. It was clear to everyone that Riverton was no longer a quiet residential community, but was becoming a part of the hustle and bustle of nearby Seattle.

As more people got cars, more service stations opened in Riverton. On the northwest corner of the crossroads Bill Robbins built a large auto repair garage and gas station where he pumped "Flying A" gasoline. Throughout the 1920s the Nolan brothers—Bruce and Vern—could be seen all hours of the day and night bending over the engines of Model Ts and Chevys as they kept the cars running. People with the taste and pocketbooks for fancier cars drove in Oaklands and Veleys. Harley Knapp took over the station around 1925 and for 50 years provided quality auto service at the Riverton crossroads. In addition to pumping gas and repairing cars Knapp operated a Ford dealership with a neat showroom that could display a single car. Beginning with a classy Model A tow truck, towing cars stuck in the muddy side roads and stalled on the highway was an important part of Knapp's service for decades.

The closing of Knapp's Garage marked the end of an era that reached back to the period before World War II. A few years later the station was torn down and the underground tanks unearthed and hauled away, leaving a great gaping hollow on the northeast corner of the intersection, like the grave of a great beast—a mute testimony to the end of the era when the Riverton crossroads hummed with community life.

Saturday Boxing and Sunday Outings

In this era of prize-fighter heroes, the greatest being Gene Tunney, boxing was very popular across America. The Nolan brothers were professional boxers, and when O. C. Thompson's second floor was empty they rented the hall, brought in a large mat and held public boxing matches, with a friend collecting two bits at the door. Nights when the Nolans were holding a boxing match in Thompson's Hall were always exciting, and the local men and women jammed into the hot upstairs room to cheer on their favorites. Impressed with the Nolans, soon many local boys like Glen Schwartz and his brothers, Tom Scibor, Charlie Lakin, and Don Springer took up wrestling and boxing, and these amateur matches became a part of the evening's entertainment with either Bruce or Vern refereeing. Glen Schwartz trained hard and became good enough that the Nolans used him as their standby and at times he boxed Bruce or Vern. It was boxing just for the fun of it, but the excitement was as great as if wagers had been made and prizes awarded to the winners. Following in this tradition, 20 years later Otto "Skeets" Krueger, known in Riverton as the "Oil Man" because he operated the oil service, became well known for television wrestling.

In the 1920s and 1930s social life in the community involved a lot of visiting and gatherings at the school, church or one of the lodges. Community picnics were held in a field by a bend in the river behind Bancheros' place, below the Red Covered Bridge. This was also a local favorite swimming hole for the Riverton youth. The Interurban made it easy to travel over to Renton and even into Seattle for excitement, especially Saturday night dances and the movies for young and old alike. Parents were not always quick to approve of these Saturday night jaunts to the nearby watering holes. The last car back to Riverton left town at midnight, and it was a long walk back if the revelers missed it.

People who could "get away" in the summer generally went camping for a vacation. A favorite place was Angle Lake Grove, where the popular camping place was at the southeast end of the lake. Alki Beach in West Seattle was another favorite beach outing. The Interurban was taken to Spokane Street, where travelers transferred to a streetcar "on stilts" that carried

From 1900 to 1930, Miller's Beach, (now Normandy Park) was the favorite summer vacation place for people in all the river communities. People brought tents and bedrolls and long hours were spent digging clams, walking on the beach and just soaking up the sunshine. Courtesy Sunnydale Museum.

them to Alki Beach and Lincoln Park, where the endless steps leading to the beach always seemed more numerous on the way home than on arriving.

Probably the most popular place was Miller's Beach. Helen Stougard recalls one such summer vacation: "My mother drove our Model T Ford to Miller's Beach on the Sound, which is now Normandy Park, holding onto a short rope attached to the halter of our cow as she walked along beside the car. It cost 25 cents to get in and stay as long as you liked. We stayed 2 weeks. Needless to say, all the campers in their tents had plenty of milk, cream, butter and cottage cheese. It was there I learned to swim in the cold, cold water."

DR. FREDERICK G. NICHOLS, COUNTRY DOCTOR

The Riverton community was unique in the Duwamish Valley for many reasons, one of which was the presence of Frederick G. Nichols, M.D. A dedicated physician and active member of the community, Dr. Nichols committed himself to caring for the health of both Riverton and the entire Duwamish Valley. Frederick Nichols was born at Clyde, New York, on September 24, 1873. Having completed school through the eighth grade in New York he moved to Manistee, Michigan, where he took a teacher's training course and taught grade school. Nichols made his way to Puget Sound around 1900. Arriving during the building boom, he worked as a lather in Seattle and then as a mill hand for the Port Blakely Mill on Bainbridge Island. Saving his money, he brought his mother and sister Hope out to live with him.

Around 1908 Nichols married Ella Wadell, a trained nurse from Canada. In 1909 Ella and Frederick Nichols moved to Portland, Oregon, where Ella ran a rooming/boarding house to support the family, while Fred attended the University of Oregon Medical School. Disaster nearly struck when the rooming house caught on fire; however, they threw the furniture out the windows and managed to save the building, too. Nichols received his Doctor of Medicine degree in 1913.

From the first moment Nichols saw Riverton and the Duwamish Valley he loved the area, and he was confident that Riverton would grow into a major community. Dr. Nichols, now 40, decided to establish his professional practice and his home in Riverton. He rented a house on S. 128 and opened an office in the Cobb Building in Seattle. After they moved to Riverton, Ella and Frederick Nichols decided to share their lives with children and adopted their daughters, Bonnie and Winnie, shortly after they came to the community. Sons Fred and James were adopted in 1920 and 1923.

When Dr. Nichols came to Riverton there were several doctors residing in the community. However, they were on the staff of Riverton Pulmonary Hospital and did not practice locally. Soon Dr. Nichols and his pinto pony, Pat, were a familiar sight in the valley as he made house calls at all hours of the day and night. In 1921 he got his first car, a Chevy, and Pat went to the Schwartz family to be petted and loved by the children. Dr. Nichols's house-call schedule wore

THE RIVERTON HOSPITAL

The Nicholses bought several tracts of land in Riverton, and 1918-19 they built a three-story combination hospital and home at the Riverton intersection (13041 East Marginal Way). For several years before this, they had been caring in their home for sick people who needed hospital attention. Dr. Nichols designed the building himself. The second and third stories were built of wood, with the lower hospital level being constructed of attractive fieldstones gathered in the immediate area and hauled to the work site by Nichols himself. The large fireplace in the family living room was made of the same type of fieldstone. Being a skilled plasterer-lather, Nichols did all of this work himself.

The hospital is approached by way of a fieldstone walkway that leads up the hill from East Marginal Way to the large glass door of the waiting room. The doctor's office was to the right, with the operating room behind. A private room, a three-bed ward, bathroom, laundry and space for an x-ray room completed the hospital facilities. Dr. Nichols and Ella cultivated beautiful gardens around the building, including first-class roses that can still be seen blooming in the summer. Dr. Nichols became known as the "Rosebud Doctor," for every morning he paused in the garden to select a fresh, perfect rosebud to wear in his buttonhole. The family's quarters on the second and third floors were spacious and beautifully appointed. The second floor consisted of the kitchen, formal dining room, living room, solarium, two bedrooms and a bathroom. The top floor had two more bedrooms and a sewing room.

In 1962 the Nichols family sold the house, and in 1990 it was being utilized as low-income housing. Tenants for some years have reported that, on occasion, as they enter a room on the hospital level of the building a man in an old-fashioned suit and starched white shirt, carrying a small black bag, turns away, disappearing into the walls. Dr. Nichols returning to his hospital, perhaps?

Dr. Frederick Nichols with wife Ella Wadell and Pat, his pinto pony, in front of their first home-office in Riverton at S. 128 and E. Marginal Way, ca. 1913. Dr. Nichols and Ella, a licensed nurse, built and operated the Riverton Hospital located at 13041 East Marginal Way and 40 Ave.S. They made their home and raised their children in living quarters on the second and third floors of the handsome building designed by Dr. Nichols, who also built parts of it himself. Still standing, the Riverton Hospital is of great historic value to the Tukwila community. Courtesy Fred Nichols.

out a lot of cars. Over the years the community saw him behind the wheel of a Graham-Paige, a Packard and a Studebaker Star, as well as later model Chevys. At times when the fog was very dense, Ella would walk in front of the car with a lantern guiding him to his night call.

Eldest son Fred Nichols recalls that "making house calls was a very big part of his work. My brother and I would accompany him on his calls… he enjoyed a cigar after dinner and he would drive to a call putting his smoking cigar in the [car] ash tray. We [boys] saw to it that it was kept lit until he got back [to the car]." Sometimes his house calls included operating right in the patient's home, with Ella assisting.

An excellent manager, Ella ran the Riverton Hospital throughout the 1920s while Dr. Nichols traveled about making house calls and seeing patients at his offices in Seattle, and later in Lake Burien and White Center, in addition to Riverton. After Ella's death in 1929 Dr. Nichols closed the hospital and struggled to raise his sons alone, the daughters having left home. In 1932 he married Victoria O. Belaire, a nurse, from Moxee City, Washington (near Yakima). Dr. Nichols, having experienced very bad health after Ella's death, took an extended trip to Alaska with son Fred and came back with his health restored. The Riverton Hospital was reopened under the competent management of Victoria in 1933, but was closed by 1936 because of a shortage of good help. Dr. Nichols' wives—both registered nurses—assisted Dr. Nichols with office procedures, treatments, deliveries and operations in addition to managing the hospital and their own home and family.

The Nicholses literally lived with the hospital, with Mrs. Nichols preparing or overseeing preparation of the patients' meals in the family kitchen and the hospital laundry alongside the family wash. Typically, Mrs. Nichols had a small staff to assist with the hospital work. Occasionally the staff members lived on the third floor. The family was very accustomed to the cooing and crying of babies, since newborn babies were routinely brought up to the Nichols' dining room, where their bassinets were put on the floor by the warmth of the furnace register.

Delivering babies naturally was a large part of Dr. Nichols' work. Many people, living in the valley were delivered by Dr. Nichols. All told, Dr. Nichols delivered over 3,000 babies, including triplets—which he was very pleased about and considered a highlight of his career.

Fred recalls one incident that convinced him he was not interested in becoming a physician himself. One hot, muggy summer day Dr. Nichols announced that he was going to remove

Fred Nichols' birthday party, 1923 picture taken beside the Riverton Hospital. Every child in Riverton was invited to Fred Nichols' birthday party. Fred is fourth from the left in the first row. The girls are wearing the party-favor hats popular in that day. Courtesy Beth Lovegren Gjersee.

his wife Victoria's tonsils and invited their sons to watch the operation. Garbed in robes and surgical masks, the boys drew close and watched as their father, attired in his white sleeveless undershirt and a fat cigar clenched in his teeth, leaned over their mother sitting in a chair in the operating room of the hospital. Victoria opened her mouth wide; Dr. Nichols stuck a long needle down her throat, injecting the local anesthetic; she gagged and the boys bolted from the room.

The community was glad that they had their own doctor. Although Dr. Nichols was a Rivertonian, he was the doctor for the communities up and down the valley including Tukwila, Foster, Duwamish-Allentown and Thorndyke. The words "fine" and "dedicated" came to everyone's lips when asked about Dr. Nichols. Dr. Nichols was very successful in treating pneumonia, a serious illness of the day. When Dr. Nichols made his house calls most people tried to give the doctor a lunch or other refreshment. For example, Mrs. Carrossino always had a glass of wine for Dr. Nichols, and a glass of milk and a plate of cookies for his boys, who often accompanied him on his calls.

Dr. Nichols was paid $3 for an office call and $5 for a house call—same price day or night. Like all country doctors in that era, Dr. Nichols often accepted goods or services in exchange for his medical expertise. For example, Mr. Voss, who worked for the Riverton Laundry, did Dr. Nichols' shirts without payment whenever his family received medical care. The way they did his collars always elicited an irritated "so damn much starch," from Dr. Nichols. People would pay him with vegetables, or by working in the garden or chopping wood. Dr. Nichols delivered all 13 of the Gotts' children. With all the mouths to feed, Forrest Gott, who was in the fuel business, had more wood and coal than cash. A few days after the birth of each baby, Mr. Gott's truck would back up to the Riverton Hospital and he would unload a supply of fuel for the doctor.

> ### THE COUNTRY DOCTOR DURING THE DEPRESSION
>
> The practice of paying the doctor in work or home produce was especially prevalent during the Great Depression, when many people had no money to their name. As Dr. Nichols said, "People got sick and needed a doctor's care even when they had no money," and during that time Dr. Nichols dispensed medicines from his operating room and accepted whatever payment the patient could manage. For example, one pregnant woman saved pennies in a milk bottle. After he delivered the baby Dr. Nichols was given the full bottle in payment. The Nicholses themselves experienced very hard times during the Depression. With almost everyone in the community paying "in kind," there was very little cash coming in. Around 1933 Dr. Nichols gathered his family around the fireplace and burned over $100,000 in unpaid accounts receivable—thereby canceling payment obligations for his services. Moreover, Nichols lost $20,000 in savings when the bank he patronized failed.

In addition to his work caring for the valley people, at various times Dr. Nichols was on the staff of Columbus (now Cabrini) Hospital in Seattle and later the West Seattle Hospital. When World War II called up all of the younger doctors in south King County, Dr. Nichols, then 67, covered the entire area from West Seattle to Renton Junction to Skyway, to Des Moines and Puget Sound.

In practice 43 years as a general practitioner, Dr. Nichols never retired. He was still working the day he died at age 83, on April 12, 1956. Victoria died on April 2, 1960. Dr. Nichols was a lifetime member of the American Medical Association. In addition, he was a 32nd Degree Mason, Delta Lodge No. 172, and a Patron of the Southgate Lodge in Burien. He was also active in the Rotary and Lions. In spite of a busy professional life, he served as a Boy Scout leader in Riverton for many years. Dr. Frederick Nichols is remembered with great affection and admiration for the dedicated professional and caring neighbor that he was.

A Snug Little Bungalow in Riverton

With the valley experiencing a boom in housing construction in the 1910s and 1920s, many of the businesses starting up in Riverton were geared to meet the needs of the new homeowners. General contracting was offered by M. S. Arbogast; P. Scott did plastering and cement work; and Fidlier and Walters were lathing and shingling specialists. The Riverton Realty and Building Company, run by partners C. K. McCoy, C. L. Whitcomb and D. A. Morrison, had their shingle out and were enjoying brisk business selling homesite tracts for as little as $375 and building houses to go on the lot with "plans furnished and houses built to suit purchasers." In addition to this partnership, Whitcomb operated his own business as a designer and builder. His advertisements announce: "High-class work my specialty. Give me your idea; I will do the rest." Among his projects was the Riverton Heights School.

Up on Military Road in Riverton Heights, brothers Walter and Valdemar Lassen, Danish immigrant carpenters, opened the doors of the Reliable Ladder Works, where they manufactured stepladders, fruit extension ladders, window ladders and painter's trusses (scaffolding). Homeowners could have window screens and screen doors made to order as well as fancy turned wood. The brothers would also contract general construction jobbing.

The builder who is best remembered is Ben Kaiser. Kaiser moved into Riverton in the 1910s and soon established a reputation throughout the area as a good builder, with his homes being found in Seattle on Capitol Hill and Queen Anne Hill, as well as in the Duwamish and Green river valleys. In 1914 the O. C. Thompsons hired him to build their home at 4049 S. 128. With roomy three bedrooms to accommodate the Thompsons' growing family, the house has corner bay windows and an inviting porch across from the front. The Thompsons had Kaiser build window seats in all of the bays. In a floor plan typical of the period, sliding pocket doors on either side of the entrance hall close off the living room on the left from the dining room, kitchen and sewing room on the right. Further graciousness is provided by a beamed ceiling in the living room. The work of restoring this gracious historic Riverton home had been undertaken by Terry and Chris Bitzig and their family in 1990. Other examples of Kaiser's houses still preserved in 1990 may be seen at 4128 and 4136 S. 130 Ave.

Community Institutions Grow

The people who came to make their homes in Riverton were not only seeking attractive home sites and snug houses, but, like the pioneers who came into the valley 50 years earlier, they wanted to build a community that had solid, good institutions—churches and schools to give the community strength and guidance. The first church founded in the community was Methodist—the church of the Northwest frontier.

The Riverton Methodist Church

The Riverton Methodist Church sits on the hillside overlooking Riverton, the graceful spire of its bell tower rising bravely above the roofs of the homes that surround it like a country church at the center of the village. This church evolved from a community meeting held in Riverton on October 24, 1907, at McCoy's Hall. The church was incorporated on November 1, 1907, built by the Riverton community with little financial help from the Methodist Church. The first money, $500, came from the Ladies Aid, organized in 1907.

Ground was broken in spring of 1908. Lumber companies sent over timber, boards and shingles. Hardware stores donated kegs of nails, nuts and bolts, and hinges. And the people came. The men came with their ladders, saws and hammers. The women brought endless baskets of food to feed the workers—potatoes, roast meat and fish, loaves of homemade bread, biscuits, doughnuts, pies and cakes, and gallons of coffee and cream. The children helped with the chores, like refilling nail pouches and carrying water, and enjoyed the festive atmosphere that characterized the work parties. The church was completed in April 1909.

In 1912 the original one-and-one-half story building was enhanced with a gable-roofed addition on the north side when the bell tower was added. Simple bracketed bargeboards enhance the gabled roofs. The lower double-hung windows are distinguished by peaked lintel surrounds. Small single-paned diamond-shaped windows are found in each gable end and in the bell tower. When the church announced it could not buy a bell, a devoted church member donated the bell. By the end of 1912 the church had only a $300 debt remaining, which Emmett Robbins paid off, putting the church in the black.

Rev. Cyrus L. Gilbert, the church's first pastor and Sunnydale schoolteacher, also served the Sunnydale church. On Sunday he walked the five miles between the two churches twice to provide morning and evening services at each place. Protestants living in the community who did not affiliate with the Methodists held a Union Sunday School every Sunday at Robbins' Hall.

In 1918 the Riverton Methodist Church was without a minister. Having the still-new church dark saddened the community. However, no minister appeared who was willing to take on the pastorate. Then, in 1921 two dynamic women moved to Riverton who knew how to "get things done." Clara Mae Musselman, proprietor of Musselman's Drygoods, and Belva Mann bought houses close to the little white church. Ignoring community residents who shook their heads with despair that Riverton would ever have a pastor again, the determined women put on their hats and caught the Interurban to the Methodist Church offices in Seattle. Mrs. Musselman and Mrs. Mann negotiated with the regional director to share a minister with the Sunnydale Methodist Church. Once again a minister held Sunday morning services at the Riverton Methodist Church and then walked over the hill to Sunnydale for afternoon services.

Ministers came and went with regularity. Larry Linnell recalls Rev. Wolfe, whose tenure was very short-lived. He was rather thin, with pince-nez glasses, a high starched collar and a soft, low voice. The older ladies were not happy with Rev. Wolfe, as they could not hear him well. A complaint was forwarded, and Rev. Wolfe was replaced by Rev. Rhinehart. He was stocky with a great mustache and jowls that shook when he got "wound up." He made the rafters and windows shake! Everyone was happy.

In the Depression years the church was a very active community focal point. In 1932 the church celebrated its 25th anniversary. Two years later Rev. Frank C. Abbott came to the church for a year, and in 1938 he returned with his wife Edith Gjersee Abbott to make their home in Riverton. Rev. Abbott was an energetic young leader, and under his guidance the Riverton Methodist Church during this period hummed with community activity, with very active youth and singing groups, as well as much community outreach.

As a reaction to the economic and social troubles of the Great Depression, the Technocracy movement developed, proposing a plan for industrial recovery and permanent economic equilibrium on the basis of production control by trained engineers. Its adherents proposed modification of the market economics of capitalism and the use of labor in factories. The theories were widely discussed, although they received little concrete support by the established political parties. Interest in Technocracy swept through the Duwamish Valley during the Depression years and 30 to 40 men met regularly at the church to discuss Technocracy. After Rev. Abbott caught them smoking at their meetings in the church, however, they had to find another place to meet.

Beginning in 1955 the congregation acquired property in Riverton Heights and began to hold classes there, in addition to the old Riverton Church. By 1966 a new church had been built, and Riverton Methodist Church congregation joined the Riverton Heights Methodist to form the Riverton Park United Methodist Church. The old church was sold. The bell was removed from the bell tower and taken up the hill to the new church, where it can be heard throughout the valley Sunday mornings.

BETH HA SHOFAR MESSIANIC CONGREGATION

In 1968 the Gospel of Peace Tabernacle acquired the old Riverton Methodist Church building. The nondenominational group from Seattle are strong supporters of Israel and the Zionist Movement, and dedicated to spreading the vision of Israel's place in prophecy for the twentieth century. During the next 12 years, this group of worshippers grew in knowledge and understanding, and became part of a nationwide and worldwide movement to return to the first-century form of worship called Messianic Judaism, which was established by Yeshua of Nazareth (Jesus).

In keeping with this vision, in 1980 the group revised their name to Beth Ha Shofar, a Hebrew name which means "House of the Trumpet." Rabbi Roger A. Ludington leads the community of Jewish and non-Jewish believers in Messiah Yeshua. Rabbi Ludington has travelled extensively in over 35 countries, including over 20 trips to Israel, telling of the Restoration of Israel, Zionism and the Messianic vision. In its 10 years in Riverton the group has grown into a small thriving community and has expanded to several lots adjacent to the synagogue.

THE CHURCH ON THE CORNER

In 1933 the Christian Science Church selected the corner of S. 131 Ave. and Macadam Road for their building, and an active church has occupied the site ever since. The Christian Science Society of Tukwila, organized initially in 1920 with Nellie Starr Clark as a key organizer, received official recognition on May 10, 1920, from the Mother Church in Boston. For over a decade the group met in each other's homes and the Tukwila Community Hall until they opened their church on December 20, 1933. The name of the congregation changed to Christian Science Society, Riverton, in 1948 when the Mother House decided that since the Riverton Church was in an unincorporated area the name should be changed to Christian Science Society, Seattle. The Mother House withdrew recognition from the congregation on September 19, 1956, and the local church was closed.

In the years following the Christian Scientist Church's leaving Riverton, the little church on the corner became the home of a number of congregations. Other than their names, little is known about these organizations. The Riverton Heights Christian Church was next to occupy the building. From 1976 to 1982 Pastor Everett Barker lead the Bethel Baptist Church, and from 1982 to 1984 the Victory Baptist Church made its home here.

The Primera Iglesia Bautista began holding services in the church building in 1984 under Pastor Leon. In 1988 B. P. Hartl became the pastor. The church is a Spanish-speaking Baptist congregation. Although most of the adults speak English, Spanish is spoken in their homes. This as well as the desire to actively maintain the language, is the basis for the Spanish-language church. The congregation has been affiliated with the Southern Baptist Convention since the early 1980s.

THE RIVERTON SCHOOL

The homeowners flocking to Riverton tended to be young couples with school-age children. In 1909 the community asked Foster School District 144 for a grade school in Riverton. That year Charlie

The Riverton School, built in 1923, S. 130th Place. Entering the door, the children left their wet coats and galoshes in the cloakroom at the entrance. In the basement were a playroom for rainy days and the washrooms. Later the Southgate School was built on the site. This school became the Tukwila Community Center in the 1980s. Courtesy of Olive Thompson Hozack.

McCoy provided the district with a house to be used as a school. The next year Emmett Robbins, a former member of the Foster school board, rented Robbins' Hall to the district for a nominal fee. As families moved in, the need for a school became greater, and the district finally bought a building site above Macadam Road (14101 S. 130 Pl.) from G. H. Nichols for $1,800 in 1911.

The pupils reached the schoolhouse by a footpath from Macadam Road. The school was essentially a large two-room house topped by a belfry. In the 1910s the school typically had 40 to 50 children attending grades one through four. The classrooms were about 20 by 20 feet and the students sat at wooden desks with bench seats. Each room was heated with a potbellied stove tended by an older boy.

On fair days the children played tag, ball games and jump rope in the playground behind the school. Around 1914 a covered play shed was built to provide shelter from the winter rains. Near the school lived Mr. Swanson, an inventor, with whom Bill Boeing, who founded the Boeing Airplane Co., collaborated. There was a hangar in the back yard, and the school children used to sneak over during recess and stare in wonder at the small aircraft Mr. Swanson was building.

In 1923 the first Riverton School was replaced with a larger building. In the 1920s and 1930s the teachers included Miss Myers, Miss Landon and Mr. Cook. Among the best remembered are Miss Lula Bacon, who ruled the third and fourth grades, and Miss Anna Peterson, who presided over the first and second grades. They ruled their classes of 25 to 40 students with a strict but loving hand. The children were called from the playground by the ringing of a handbell. They lined up in columns of two to march into the building to the beat of an iron triangle being struck by a steel rod. To "beat the triangle" was a position of honor given only to deserving students.

From fifth grade through high school Riverton children walked one and one-half miles to the Foster Central Elementary and High School. A special honor and responsibility for a Riverton school pupil at that time was to deliver the "money bag" to the District Superintendent's office on "Bank Day." Only mature fourth graders qualified. It was quite a step toward self-confidence and independence to be selected. To help parents understand how their child was doing in relationship to classmates, during the 1920s report cards showed the number of students in each class. Also shown was a breakdown of the number of students that received As, Bs, Cs, Ds, or Fs. The teacher would circle the grade received.

COMMUNITY CULTURAL AND SOCIAL LIFE

Community halls are important because they provide space for communal gatherings and promote social and cultural life. The earliest community hall in Riverton was Robbins' Hall, 1905. For a number of years after 1910, every other Tuesday night the Riverton Pleasure Club held its popular dances at Robbins' Hall where members learned and practiced the latest dance steps. Around 1907 Charlie McCoy built a community hall down on Macadam Road. This burned down in 1909, and once again Robbins' Hall was the only public hall. However, the Methodist Church made its hall available for community events. In the 1920s O. C. Thompson's hall and the Delta Masonic Lodge No. 172 provided alternative sites for community gatherings.

Riverton in 1910 was a landscape denuded of much of its natural vegetation as a result of logging the native timber and a "cut, slash and burn" approach to clearing the land for construction. However, Riverton's new subdivisions were soon beautified with gardens overflowing with roses, sweet peas, pansies, daisies, spirea, cornflowers, cactus dahlias, poppies, and a host of other flowers. Flower gardening was a favorite pastime and Riverton rapidly developed a reputation in the Duwamish Valley for its exceptionally beautiful gardens.

Around 1910 the Riverton Women's Civic Club was formed with the expressed goal of improving the quality of life in the community. The women undertook many projects to advance their goals. In 1912 they sponsored a Riverton Flower Show with the intent of stimulating community floral beautification. The show was held at the Methodist Church, with President Nellie Levy declaring the objective being to "encourage the valley communities to vie with one another over who would have the prettiest places, yards and hothouse plants that can only be grown in our equitable Puget Sound climate."

Eighty-five gardeners from the community took their best blooms to the Methodist Church, where Gertrude Blair of Riverton judged them with two horticultural experts invited in from Kent, Mrs. Marshall and Miss Knapp. Entries were brought by a wide variety of people, ranging from young children to 85-year-old Susannah Steele Robbins. Jane Fenton Kelly's congenial husband, Michael Kelly, was the Master of Ceremonies for a grand evening program of music, refreshments and prize giving. The community's awareness that it was transforming the wilderness was expressed in the newspaper observation that "considering that ten short years ago in the very spot where the lovely floral display was shown, there was a forest primeval, [the] effort at Riverton is nothing short of wonderful."

Another organization which led in shaping and guiding the Riverton community was the Riverton Improvement Club. Founded around 1920, the club was active into the 1940s. Originally a men's club, the group merged with the Riverton Women's Civic Club in the late 1920s. The Riverton Improvement Club was influential in guiding the Riverton School and often represented the school's interests before the Foster school board. The records of this community organization are not available at the time of writing; however, scattered information indicates the club sponsored a small community library in the late 1920s. In the late 1930s the group sponsored a fast-pitch softball team with players coming from nearby communities—including Tukwila and Foster. The team was very good and made it each year to the "Knockout Tournament" sponsored by the *Seattle Post-Intelligencer*.

Lodges were a very popular form of affiliating at the turn of the century, and these groups flourished in Riverton. Between 1910 and 1920 six lodges were founded including Modern Woodmen and Woodwomen, Modern Brotherhood Lodge, the Freemasons, Delta Masonic Lodge No. 172 with the Order of Eastern Star, and the Royal Neighbors of America. The latter group, a mutual aid society, was founded in 1925 by 31 women with leadership from Clara Musselman and Mae Robbins.

Delta Masonic Lodge No. 172, Community Landmark

Among the first organizations formed in Riverton and also the longest lasting is the Delta Masonic Lodge No. 172, whose lodge hall is a historic landmark. In June 1908 a group of Masons living in and around Riverton resolved to form a lodge in the district. They secured the support and recommendation of the St. Andrews Lodge No. 35 at Renton and petitioned the Grand Lodge of Washington, which granted dispensation that year. At the first meeting of the Riverton brethren, the question of a name for the Lodge was discussed, and Worshipful Brother Eugene Sandahl, who was destined to be the longest lived of the Charter Members, said, "As we are living in the Delta of the Duwamish, why don't we call it Delta Lodge," and this was agreed upon by all the brethren.

Delta Lodge No. 172 was chartered on June 8, 1909. The charter officers were Samuel D. Goff, George H. Nichols, Edwin H. Benedict, Eugene Sandahl, Emmett L. Robbins, Valdemar Lassen, James Monroe and Charles K. McCoy. Other community leaders who were charter members included Charles Whitcomb, Lester M. Adams, Charles Lincoln and Martin Christianson. Shortly thereafter Joseph Foster became a member by affiliation.

At first the Lodge used Brother Charles McCoy's hall near the Riverton station for meetings until it burned down on November 11, 1909. Then the Lodge met in Emmett Robbins' old hops house. During this "rustic" period, fir logs were used for pedestals for the Master and Warden as well as the altar. A hand axe served as the official gavel, and two Lodge Wardens carried a hammer and mallet as symbols of their roles as guards. Robbins' Hall served as the meeting place from June 1910 until the Lodge built a new temple in 1926, for a rent of $5 a month, which later went to $7.50.

Delta Chapter No. 109, Order of the Eastern Star, was instituted on November 30, 1908, at McCoy Hall in Riverton. Hattie Nichols and Frank Dayton were the charter Worthy Matron and Worthy Patron. For the next 17 years meetings were held at Robbins' Hall until the new Masonic temple was built. Eastern Star is a benevolent fellowship group helping one another and striving to be of service to others and the community. Soon Delta Lodge No. 172 and Eastern Star members came from the nearby communities including Foster, Tukwila, and Duwamish-Allentown.

The Lodge members were very involved with local concerns. For example, in 1911 the Lodge gave its support to a Masonic Labor Bureau to assist men finding work. During World War I the Lodge helped sponsor a bulletin for servicemen at the YMCA in West Seattle. Delta Lodge grew slowly until 1918 when it began to rapidly gain members. Emmett Robbins was presented with a silver trowel in 1922 in appreciation of his many years of service to the Lodge. In 1923 Delta Lodge No. 172 incorporated. During these years the Lodge was very popular with Masons around the country, with Superior Court judges, police chiefs and prominent Seattle lawyers visiting frequently.

By 1925 the group had 200 members and undertook building a new temple at 13034 41 Ave. S. Local builder Fred Fox built the hall, which was dedicated in December 1926. A handsome two-story red brick structure, it evokes a temple feeling by the classical details of its design. For example, the cornice frieze features classical dentils. The building has a hip roof on the west side and a gabled roof on the east with an 18-inch roof overhang that is supported and enhanced by pairs of corbels. The front of the building is both classical and graceful with a gable-roofed dormer featuring two pedimented returns. Tall arched windows on the second floor include a double arched window in the central portion and a fan light high in the dormer pediment. Many of the wooden, double-hung windows have leaded glass. The east side of the building has a plain boxed cornice and plain frieze.

The building has a number of meeting rooms, an auditorium, and a full banquet hall in the daylight basement. The building has been well maintained over the years and little altered. The second-story windows on the south side have been enclosed with bricks. Beginning in the 1940s, almost each year was marked by a substantial improvement in the Lodge, including an organ, carpeting, handmade lights (gift), a remodeled rear kitchen and other furnishings.

During the 1920s and 1930s Delta Lodge was the focal point of social activity in the community. Upon receiving his Master's Degree a member provided a dinner for the Lodge members. The Eastern Star Women were particularly active in combining fund raising and having a good time, and often sponsored community dances with the music provided by local bands Ky Fox's Frisky Five and Ramage's Rhythm Rascals. During World War II members raised money to purchase a sewing machine for sewing bandages for the Red Cross. Members also manned booths selling War Bonds.

Delta Lodge's activities have always included assisting in the formation of other Masonic chapters and lodges, including Delta Chapter No. 109 and the Joseph Foster Chapter of De Molay. The latter was disbanded in 1966 because of insufficient members.

On June 27, 1948, 22 girls, many daughters of members of Delta Lodge No. 172 and Delta Chapter No. 109, met at the Delta Lodge Temple and formed International Order of Job's Daughters Bethel 33. From the beginning Bethel 33 was very active in Lodge ritual and community service activities, as well as providing social expression for the members. Over the years the young women have been energetic and successful in fund-raising by putting on car washes, garage and yard sales, bake sales, dime-a-dip dinners before the meeting and cake walks after meetings, and in helping at Lodge dinners. In the 1960s Bethel 33 won awards for performances of its Rhythmic Choir.

From the early years the Lodge has been famous for its community meals. In 1977 the Lodge's traditional "crab feed" was dropped because of the price of crab, and the Delta pancake breakfast was instituted as a tradition.

The Lodge's involvement with community activities continues in recent time. For example, on April 15, 1978, at the request of Brother Edgar D. Bauch, Mayor of Tukwila, Delta Lodge, together with state representatives, was invited to lay the cornerstone of the new Tukwila City Hall. With a good turnout of Lodge members and Tukwila citizens, the Ancient Ceremony of laying the Cornerstone was held at the entrance to the new building. In 1980 the Lodge initiated an award program for Foster School students. In recent times Delta Chapter 109 has given funds to the Tukwila Police Department's DARE (drug prevention program) and to San Francisco earthquake relief in 1990. A continuing program is collecting clothing and money for the Riverton Park United Methodist program distributing these items to those in need. In 1984 Delta Lodge observed its 75th anniversary with the striking of a commemorative coin.

Riverton on the Duwamish sprang forth after the building of the Interurban. The construction of major county roads through the community in the 1910s and 1920s increased its appeal. The construction of new transportation ways, notably SR-599 and I-5, made it possible to bypass Riverton in the 1960s, and the community's businesses gradually closed.

1990 Riverton is a quiet place. In the early morning residents are no longer wakened by the high, cheerful whistle of the 5:05 Interurban. The clang of the bell atop the Riverton School no longer calls young people to their lessons. But late at night, after the fog has drifted up from the valley floor, if you listen carefully you might hear the clip-clop of Pat's hooves as he carries Dr. Nichols on a midnight house call.

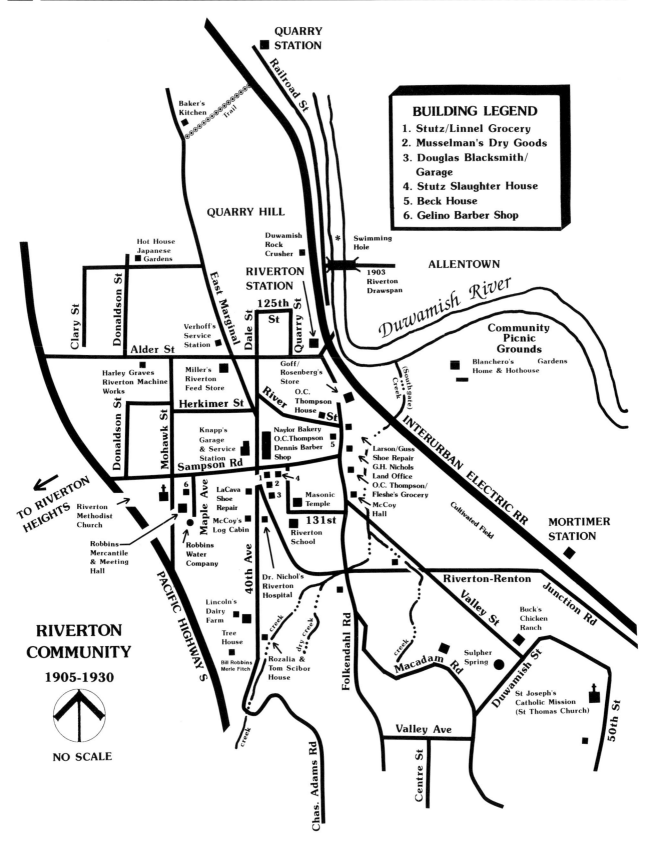

Map by Patrick Brodin with the assistance of Tom Scibor and Kay Reinartz. Drawn by Sharon Dibble.

CHAPTER 10
COMMUNITIES FLOWER ON THE RIVER BANKS—
DUWAMISH-ALLENTOWN AND QUARRY-NORTH RIVERTON

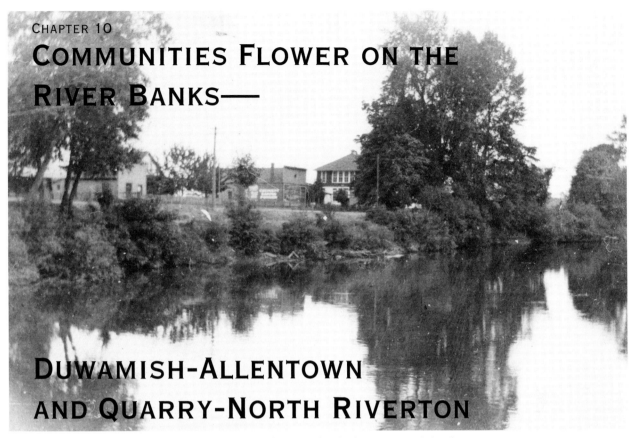

Duwamish River from the road near the bend looking toward Duwamish School. Courtesy Mabel Nelson.

The River was a pattern woven into everyday life. In summer it was a place to swim and boat, in fall a place to fish for salmon.
  Charlotte Dobbs Widrig, Quarry District

Of all of the communities that formed in the upper Duwamish Valley, the Duwamish-Allentown, Quarry-North Riverton communities lie most directly on the very banks of the Duwamish River. Because of their close proximity to the river these communities historically enjoyed the greatest convenience of river travel and suffered the most severely from the river flooding. Records tell that in the 1880s and 1890s it was not uncommon for houses to be built on stilts to avoid flood damage.

The first residents of the area were the Bennett Johns family. Johns, a widower, came in 1854 with his eight children and built a homestead on the east side of the river. The exact location of the home is not known. The Johns' closest neighbor was the Polly and Cyrus Lewis family, which included six children, who lived to the south just northeast of Foster Point near the Duwamish River Road. Timothy and Elizabeth Johns Grow, with one son, were the closest neighbors to the north. There were no donation claims filed on the land along the Duwamish from Johns to Tim Grow's land. However, early in the 1860s David Graham and wife Susannah Mercer, daughter of Seattle founder Thomas Mercer, claimed this area under land-grant law.

THE THOMAS RAY FAMILY

With the breakup of most of the large donation claim acreages in the 1870s, the Grow land and the Johns land were sold off. Details of the residents during this period are unknown, with the exception of the Thomas Ray family. Thomas Ray came to the Duwamish Valley around 1882 and built a farmhouse and outbuildings on the north side of the river in the area of 11269 East Marginal Way. He cultivated a thriving market garden and orchard. By this time the commercial ferry

153

service on the river had ended and the closest bridges were at Black River Junction or Georgetown. The Rays provided ferry service for their neighbors living on the south side of the river as well as travelers passing by.

The Rays were very sociable people who enjoyed company. Thus, when Ray built the house he made several of the main-floor rooms large enough for the many parties and dances that his numerous daughters put on each year. Throughout the 1880s the brightly lit house, with a collection of teams and wagons outside, resounded into the wee hours of the morning with the strains of fiddle music, singing and merriment as parties, dances, weddings and christenings were celebrated. Neighbors up and down the river put on their "Sunday best" and paddled, walked or rode for an hour or more to join the fun. Sometimes a woman who traveled astride a horse an hour or more to reach the Rays carried her party dress and changed in the Ray girls' upstairs bedroom. Dancers, flushed and warm from the fast reels and mazurkas, spilled out onto the porch to enjoy the refreshing air off the river.

In the late summer large parties of Indians from Vancouver Island traveling up the Duwamish to the White River and Puyallup Valley hop fields routinely camped in a thicket of cedar trees across the river from the Ray house. The children would put baskets of apples in the boat and row over to visit with the Indians and sell them apples.

The Ray house retains many of its original features. It is a one-and-one-half story L-shaped house with an intersecting gable roof. There is a one-story hip roof addition in the rear (west) side. The roof line has a boxed cornice and plain frieze. Plain surrounds trim the window and door openings. Most of the windows are tall, narrow and double hung, and come in pairs. On the front (east) facade is a 6-by-14 foot hip roofed porch. Turned posts support the roof. The ornate brackets on the posts have been removed.

Around 1915 the house was bought by Joseph and Teresa Carrossino, Italian immigrants. The Carrossinos put in a bocci court in the garden between the house and the river, where they played the popular Italian game. The bocci court may be seen in a photograph in Chapter 13. The house has been modified over the years. A rustic siding was replaced with "brick" composition siding in 1946. On the south facade a 6-by-16 foot shed roof porch was enclosed with multiple paned windows in 1965. The kitchen was also remodeled at this time. The 1965 earthquake destroyed a brick chimney on the south side of the house.

Considering that the house is around 110 years old, it has undergone minor alterations. With the old Duwamish River still flowing peacefully by on the south side, the immediate house setting remained very much as it had always been through the 1970s. However, by 1990 the house was somewhat isolated by encroaching commercial development.

Known as the Ray-Carrossino house, it is one of the few nineteenth-century farmhouses still standing in 1990 in Tukwila and the environs of Seattle. It is significant for its representation of the style of house of the settlers of the 1880 period and their life, as well as that of the Italian immigrants of the early twentieth century.

Near the Ray-Carrossino house, at 3914 S. 115, is the Torres-Siccardi house, which Prof. Victor Steinbrueck, Seattle historian and architecture expert, dated as built between 1860 and 1890. Its builder is unknown, but it was designed to be a general mercantile and originally had a false front, which was removed by Torres, who bought the house around 1920.

The one-and-one-half story house, measuring 18 by 32 feet, is built in the pioneer farmhouse style with a gable roof and boxed cornice. The exterior walls are covered with shiplap siding, and have a plain frieze and cornerboards. Shelf surround molding trims the double-hung windows. The kitchen was located on the rear (north) side of the house in a characteristic pioneer shed-style 12-by-12 foot addition, which had a cat slide roof porch on the west end. Originally, a porch supported by turned posts ran across the front (west) side of the house, the porch roof forming a balcony enclosed by a simple vertical wood railing. This porch has been replaced with a partially enclosed entry. Unfortunately, nothing is known of the early residents of this old house.

THE NAMING OF THE TWIN COMMUNITIES

Throughout the twentieth century people coming to the Duwamish Valley have often asked why an area known as Duwamish and Allentown, or more commonly, Duwamish-Allentown, has two names, since the "communities" are really a single community. The names come from history. In the beginning of white settlement the entire Duwamish Valley was known throughout Puget Sound as simply "Duwamish." As the original donation claims were broken up by the sale of parcels of land, the new landowners tended to cluster—as much as possible—around the original pioneer enclaves. The communities that evolved acquired names that originated with the name of the first pioneer family—for example, Van Asselton, Maple Town and Foster—or, in other cases, from natural features, such as Oxbow, Mountain View and South Park. The five-mile area lying between Van Asselton and Foster Point continued to be called Duwamish—until 1906, when Joseph and Flora Allen subdivided two large tracts of land in the Duwamish district, naming them Allentown.

AMBITIOUS DREAMS SHAPE THE COMMUNITY

The Duwamish-Allentown area was subdivided by two developers, the Allens and the Hillmans, as investment ventures. Both concerns undertook various promotion schemes to attract buyers. In October and December of 1905 Clarence Day Hillman and Bessie Olive Hillman platted a portion of the old Duwamish district as Hillman's Meadow Gardens and Meadow Gardens Addition.

On March 9, 1906, the Allens, who owned the northeast corner of Bennett Johns' donation claim, filed the plat for their subdivision, Allentown Addition. It was bounded by a sharp turn in the river to the west, bordered on the Hillman's Meadow Garden-Addition on the north, and the right-of-way of the Northern Pacific, and the Columbia and Puget Sound Railroads on the west. Two months later, May 16, 1906, the Allens platted the balance of their landholdings in the valley as Allentown Acres Addition to Seattle. Flora named many of the streets for family members—for example, Paul, Robert and Florence. The area was soon known by the plat name, Allentown. The Hillmans' subdivision continued to be known by the historic name Duwamish. The Hillmans' and the Allens' subdivisions were about the same size.

One of the original Interurban stations established in 1902 was Duwamish. By 1906 a second station was opened and named Allentown station for Allens' subdivision. Joseph Allen built his land office directly across the tracks from the station at the corner of First (44 Ave. S.) and Allen Ave. (S. 124 St.) on which he had painted in large letters on the front: ALLENTOWN. The 1903 Riverton drawspan may be seen in the background. Courtesy Warren Wing.

TUKWILA—COMMUNITY AT THE CROSSROADS

JOSEPH ALLEN

Joseph Allen was born in Carlington, England, in 1836. He immigrated with his wife to the United States in 1879, and soon became involved in coal mining. In 1881 the couple came to the Northwest, where Joseph delved into railroad contracting. He associated with the Great Northern, Rio Grande, Chicago, Milwaukee, and Puget Sound and North Bank railroads. In 1890, several years after his wife died, he married Flora Moore. Allen had four children by his first wife—Florence, Rosetta, Robert D. and H.M. Allen.

Joseph and Flora Allen never lived in their Allentown subdivision but made their home on Capitol Hill. Allen died March 22, 1909, at Minor (Providence) Hospital of complications from an appendicitis operation performed three years earlier. He was 73 years old.

EARLY YEARS IN DUWAMISH-ALLENTOWN

When Ernest and Delia Merkle came to Allentown in 1908, there were only a half-dozen other houses in the district. All of the Duwamish Indians were gone, having been moved by the federal government to a reservation near Auburn. A single native family remained in the Duwamish-Allentown community. Duwamish Chief Mike Williams, an old man, lived with his son Michael in a small house across the railroad tracks near the covered bridge. Michael attended the Duwamish School and was friends with the other children in the neighborhood, and distinguished himself as a player on the Duwamish Community Baseball Team in the 1910s. Chief Williams, who refused to live on the reservation, was buried in the Renton Cemetery, where his grave is marked "Mike Williams, Chief of the Duwamish people."

The Merkles bought their Duwamish Valley home when they attended a homesite auction Joe Allen held in the fall of 1908, in an attempt to move lots in his Allentown subdivision during a sluggish market. They found a perfect site on the very banks of the meandering river and made their $20 down payment—the balance to be made in $20 monthly installments. Merkle built the family a three-bedroom house on their lot on Riverside Ave. (12244 42 Ave. S.). On moving day the entire family packed up their bags at their Brighton Beach home and took the trolley to the Occidental and Yesler Street station, where they caught the Interurban for the Allentown station. The furniture came later by horse-drawn dray. At first they had only one close neighbor along the river.

The children loved the environment and had a great time playing hide-and-seek and run-sheep-run among the great stumps remaining from the logging off of the virgin forest. The cattle and horses roamed freely among the stumps and low brush that covered the land.

As more people came into the community, objections began to be raised to the animals wandering freely through yards and in the roads. Many people talked to Delia Merkle about this, and she took the initiative to draw up a petition for the enforcement of a Herd Law. The effort was controversial, since most families kept one or more horses and cows, and there were two dairies. The pro-Herd Law forces insisted that it was a hazard to the safety of the community to have the animals at large. Mabel Nelson recalls how the children worked hard to make a new Norwegian immigrant girl, who did not understand English very well, understand that she should not wear a red dress to school because the bull might chase her. The con forces were concerned with the loss of the convenience and economy of feeding their animals by simply letting them graze at will throughout the community. In the end, the petition was successful. People built pens and sent the children out to stake Bessie in patches of green grass.

In the 1911-12 *Polk's Directory*, the population of Duwamish is listed as 150 and that of Allentown as 100. Describing the twin communities as Interurban stations, the *Directory* provides insight into their image in that era: "largely a residential district for Seattle businessmen, being easily accessible to the city and being so prettily situated on the Duwamish

DUWAMISH-ALLENTOWN AND QUARRY-NORTH RIVERTON

River." By 1911 Duwamish-Allentown enjoyed telephone connections with Seattle and Renton through Pacific Telephone & Telegraph and the Renton Telephone Company. Mail came out from Seattle by R.F.D. Route 5. The closest post office was Georgetown. *Polk's Directory* indicates that the most common occupation in 1911 was laborer, followed by carpenter. Other occupations frequently mentioned include bookkeeper, gardener, miner and electrician. A number of professional women made their homes in the community, including eight teachers and four nurses.

A major shortcoming for homeowners in the community was the lack of a public water system. This situation continued until 1935, at which time the community became a part of Seattle Water District No. 25. Moreover, up to the time of annexation to Tukwila the community did not have a public sewer system, and homeowners maintained septic tanks. Indeed, many people had piped their raw sewage directly into the river until anti-water pollution legislation of the 1960s and '70s outlawed this practice.

From the opening decade of the twentieth century, when the Riverton drawspan was built, Duwamish-Allentown enjoyed the stimulation of being on the main road connecting Seattle to Tacoma. In 1912 the pioneer Ezra Meeker, already a legend in his own time, traveled over the road with his famous ox-drawn wagon to visit the Duwamish School. It was reported that "he had interesting and friendly ways in talking to the school children." In 1904 Barney Oldfield, with his Stutz Bearcat, came through on his way to take part in the auto races at the Meadows Racetrack. The valley residents lined the road to get a glimpse of him and his automobile. That was some car!

The 1916 Pacific Highway brought travelers through the community, and during World War I soldiers marched through Duwamish-Allentown on the Pacific Highway. The construction of the second Pacific Highway, U.S. 99 in 1928, changed Duwamish-Allentown's position from being at the hub of valley transportation to being a side-road community.

> **GRANDMA MERKLE'S HOME REMEDIES**
>
> **Mustard Plaster**
> 1 level tablespoon dry mustard
> 1 tablespoon flour
> Mix with cold water to make a soft dough. Spread between 2 pieces of cotton material. Put on the chest and back of the sufferer.
>
> **Cough Syrup for Children**
> In a small granet [sic] cup or pan cut one big onion, add 1/2 cup sugar, 1/2 cup water, simmer on back of cookstove and keep warm and give a teaspoon at a time for cough.

Most people tried to treat illnesses with home remedies and good advice from experienced women like Delia "Grandma" Merkle. For a short time in the 1910s the community had a doctor. Dr. Fletcher maintained a general practice from his home on the hillside above the Allentown station on the Quarry side of the river. When Dr. Fletcher moved out of the community, Dr. Frederick Nichols of Riverton became the community's physician and delivered many of the community's babies. However, Allentown had its own midwife, Mrs. E. M. Hale, a competent black woman who had moved to the Northwest from the Old South some years earlier and lived up by the covered bridge. In their search for "cures" some people consulted the gypsies who passed through the community every spring.

FRONT STREET BUSINESSES

he street along the river was platted as Riverside, but it was always called Front Street. The village businesses all opened up here, with the area just south of the bend in the river being the focal point of community activity from around 1910 through the 1930s. On the southeast corner of the intersection, at approximately 11602 42 Ave. S., the Gilmans operated a hotel with a dance hall upstairs. Nearby was Jones Saloon, which enjoyed brisk trade from the quarry workers,

TUKWILA—COMMUNITY AT THE CROSSROADS

> **A 1911 JUNGLE DANCE**
>
> In the 1910s costume dances were popular. In 1911 the community "live wires" staged a Jungle Dance. Fredricks' Hall was transformed into a temperate jungle with small cedar and fir trees. The musicians played under a cedar branch canopy and dancers in the guise of animals of all types pranced and capered around the hall. Some of the men sported deer antlers and others had bear skins slung over their shoulders. Community seamstresses put together seagull, fox, rabbit, lynx, wolf and even salmon outfits using fabric from old garments, bark, leaves, hazelnuts and anything else they could find that was free. Great ingenuity went into many costumes, with a piece of old grey hemp rope becoming a tail, and a discarded fishnet being transformed into a bird's coat with hundreds of turkey and goose feathers sewn to it. The children sitting on the sidelines were frightened at the strange antics of these "animals." The adults had a marvelous time and people were still talking and laughing about it 70 years later.
>
> *Story from Lona Schwartz Sweeney.*

who would drop by for a shot of whiskey or glass of beer after a long dusty day hauling rock.

The first grocery store was Mac Mahill's Grocery, where Ransome Bigelow and Frank Nelson worked. Bigelow came over in his rowboat from the Quarry District to work. The work of delivering grocery orders up Poverty Hill was often given to neighborhood children who would receive a nickel's worth of candy for their effort. Mabel Nelson recalls that despite the hard work climbing the steep hill toting heavy sacks and boxes overflowing with groceries, the children enjoyed the chance to go up on the hill and meet the people who lived there. The only telephone in the community for a few years was in Mac Mahill's store.

Around 1912 Mac Mahill's store closed and Mr. and Mrs. Oscar Fredricks opened a general mercantile with a hall upstairs, just north of Mac Mahill's old place. Fredricks' original building (demolished) stood where S. 116 St. met Front St. The Fredrickses lived in the back of the store. They stocked all the essentials used by the homeowner. Many a mother sent a young child over to the store with a list of her needs early in the day. Fredricks would "put up" the order, and father or big sister or brother would pick it up after work or school.

Eventually Fredricks sold the store to Dorothy and Elmer Stanford; Dorothy, the daughter of Clarence and Lily Sweeney, operated the store until the late 1950s, when the building changed hands again and was made into apartments, which it continues to be in 1990.

The second floor of the building was the community hall through the Depression years. The dances at Fredricks' Hall were famous, and people came from up and down the valley. Music was more typically provided by a collection of musicians than by a "regular" band. Often the musicians who assembled had not played together until that very evening. On any given evening the instruments could include fiddles, piano, drum, concertina and accordion, and occasionally a horn, clarinet or saxophone. Paul Monroe, who lived just a few doors from the hall, was not only a first-class builder, but also an accomplished musician, and taught the violin as well as frequently playing for dances. He was often joined by Charley Fullerton, who packed up his fiddle and caught the Interurban from Seattle to the Duwamish station. Years later Fullerton's nephew Warren Wing moved to Duwamish to live by the side of the river and publish a series of books relating the history of the Interurban in King County.

Over the years the frequency of dances varied, but many winters they were weekly. Often a bountiful community potluck dinner was shared before the fiddlers tuned up. During the late 1920s, Mr. Weber, who had been the state fiddling champion, organized very popular dances that were held alternately at Fredricks' Hall and in Renton. The community dances were attended by everyone. Parents typically brought their children. Little ones were left sleeping in baskets or among the coats in the cloakroom with mothers popping in every so often to check on the baby.

Older children watched from the sidelines and at a young age tried the dance steps themselves, often with a kind adult providing guidance through the complications of the waltz, schottische or polka. Twelve-year-old Mabel Nelson had such a teacher in Mr. Holmquist, who "danced Norwegian style which was very fast…and he swung [her] off [her] feet many times." As they grew older the children mastered many of the dances, and by the time courting days arrived most young men and women were passably good dancers, which was important since dances and dancing were the chief recreation of the era.

The Duwamish Community Church was cared for by the women of the community, who saw to the general upkeep of the building as well as raising funds and maintaining community closeness by putting on innumerable church suppers and other community events from the time of the church's founding in the nineteenth century. In the 1920s and '30s the dedicated women looking after this important community institution included: First row, l. to r., Mabel Lawrence, Alethea Henderson, Nellie Swartout, Resa Murray, Mrs. Stout, Mrs. Bass; second row, l. to r., Frances Elder (behind post), Dorothy Sweeney, Mrs. Albright, unidentified, Mrs. Launstein, Cozy Smith, Muriel Clearsby. Courtesy Mabel Nelson.

Shortly after the Fredrickses opened their store, Bill Goldsmith opened a grocery and hardware store across the street at 11520 42 Ave. S. When automobiles became more commonplace Mr. Goldsmith put in a couple of gas pumps. A bachelor, Goldsmith lived in this store that was packed to bursting with merchandise. Folks used to say, "If Goldsmith doesn't have it, no one has it!" Often a request led to Goldsmith, a very large man weighing over 300 pounds, slowly making his way through the crowded aisles, sorting through women's pointed buckle shoes, horse liniment, cartons of oil of clove, and kegs of 10-penny nails.

Goldsmith had a warm spot in his heart for children and cats, and many a child left his store happily sucking on a red-striped candy stick. One day when business was slow and Mr. Goldsmith was sitting in his big rocking chair, his tabby cat jumped into his ample lap and gave birth to a fine litter of mewing kittens—with Goldsmith not moving the maternity ward an inch during the proceedings. How the children loved that story and recounted it to their children and grandchildren—so that at the end of the twentieth century the community was still laughing about Goldsmith's "cat maternity."

Another important business in the community was Archie Codiga's Dairy located on the riverbank near the covered bridge. Codiga began dairying around 1910. In 1918 he married Anna Hadeen, Duwamish School teacher. The Codigas' five children all worked on the farm and delivered milk. The presence of the neat Codiga farm imparted a serene rural atmosphere to the community that is fondly remembered as development encroaches on the community. Son James Codiga continues to live on the farm and was keeping a small herd in 1990. Daughter Frances, who married Jim North, All-American athlete from Tukwila, served in the Washington Legislature for a number of years.

THE BEND IN THE RIVER

The sharp bend in the Duwamish River had been a landmark from the early days of the pioneers and continued to be the location of many interesting activities in

Tukwila—Community at the Crossroads

From before 1900 into the 1920s large herds of cattle and sheep were regularly driven down the Duwamish Valley from Wenatchee and Ellensburg to the Frye Packing Company on Airport Way. The herdsmen traditionally stopped to water the animals at the bend of the river in Duwamish near S. 116 St. At that time the riverbank sloped gently and the animals safely walked to the water's edge to drink. Courtesy Mabel Nelson.

the twentieth century. Early in the 1920s Frank Goodale, Justice of the Peace, made his home with his wife Violet down at the bend of the river. Many a young couple walked along the Duwamish River from the Interurban station to Goodale's house in their wedding finery and came back married for life. So many people came from all over south King County to be married by Justice Goodale that he became known as "Marryin' Sam." Later, after Frank passed away, Violet Goodale took over as the Justice of the Peace and continued the family tradition of helping couples tie the knot. A community leader, Frank served as the Duwamish Fire District No. 1 secretary for many years.

As well as a place for happy events, the sharp bend in the river became the site of repeated tragedies over the years as many automobiles and trucks, traveling too fast for the road, landed in the river, with a number of the drivers drowning.

THE DUWAMISH IMPROVEMENT CLUB, 1915-1916—TO INCORPORATE OR TO NOT INCORPORATE

Around 1915 the Duwamish Improvement Club was formed. It immediately initiated action to incorporate the community as a fourth-class city. Throughout the fall and winter, weekly mass meetings were held discussing the pros and cons of incorporation under the chairmanship of Mr. Washington, with O. H. Putnam keeping the minutes. People from nearby communities came to discuss incorporation. From Riverton came Morrison, Kaiser and Lewis. From Georgetown came E. M. Harris, and Mayor Stevens came from Tukwila. Mr. Dobbs from Quarry provided expert information about the laws governing fourth-class cities. The pro interests carried the November 11, 1915, vote with 28 for and 5 against. The enthusiastic community briskly formed committees to take care of the details: information committee, resolution committee, boundary committee and finance committee. A census was taken and 350 residents counted.

The text of the Incorporation Petition clarifies the motives behind the determination to incorporate. It appears that community members felt that they were not "getting their just dues" at the hands of King County. Among their specific complaints was the county's application of bridge and road tax money, collected in the community, to improvements located elsewhere in the county. It was believed that incorporating would allow the community to escape paying this tax. In addition, the totally inadequate water system was an issue. The petition preamble states:

> By incorporating we can place the incorporate officers [sic] in a position whereby we can secure a water supply that will be satisfactory to our daily use, both as to quality and quantity, and at a cost of less than one half what is being paid under the present conditions.

On December 10, 1915, the official notice of Petition to Incorporate Duwamish, Allentown, and vicinity appeared in the *Duwamish News*, together with the names of the 41 signees from Duwamish and 21 from Allentown. The larger number from Duwamish reflects the larger population living in that district. The community leaders who assumed responsibility for the various activities involved with this important political move were Alex Washington, Dr. W. E. Olmstead, W. E. McKee, E. J. Thurber, O. G. Roseburg, Oscar Fredricks, J. H. Oyen, O. F. Nelson, Mac Mahill, Mr. Schuenemann and O. H. Putnam.

By January all of the steps necessary to establish an incorporated municipality in Duwamish-Allentown were completed, and the Improvement Club minutes make little further comment on the action until May 4, 1916, when the record notes that it was "moved and seconded [that] we drop this incorporation discussion." Unfortunately, not a single explanation is provided for this decision.

In addition to incorporation, the Improvement Club took up other activities and issues, such as assisting destitute families living in the community with money generated by the women of the club with "cake and coffee" fund-raisers. A Spring Box Social was held at the Duwamish School May recital, with all proceeds donated to the Duwamish Baseball Club. In addition to transacting business, the club enjoyed entertainment at their meetings. For example, in January of 1916, the Duwamish School teachers put on a musical program with numbers sung by Anna Hadeen and Misses Kyle and Mann.

1920s POPULATION

hile the old Duwamish district was commonly known as Duwamish-Allentown by 1920, King County still recognized it as Duwamish. In 1900 when the lower Duwamish, i.e., Georgetown, was included in the census, the total population was reported as 1913. The 1910 census, taken after Georgetown was annexed to Seattle, gives the population for Duwamish as 652. Ten years later the community had increased by 75 percent, and the total population was reported as 860 in 1920 and 951 in 1930.

The voter registration books for 1921-23 provide population details for the period. Twenty-seven percent of the voters were naturalized citizens. Top countries for immigrants were England, Germany, Sweden, Canada and Norway. Of the American-born voters, only six percent gave Washington as their state of birth. The other 94 percent came principally from the Midwestern states, with Illinois accounting for 16 percent. Ohio, Indiana, Montana, Iowa, Missouri, Pennsylvania and Wisconsin each account for about 5.5 percent. The most commonly listed occupation is laborer, followed by carpenter, farmer, painter and miner. Over 80 percent of the women stated that they were occupied as homemakers, although four were teachers and several more office clerks.

From the 1920s on, a number of businesses came and went in Duwamish-Allentown including a small dairy at 11854 42 Ave. S. Bertha Monroe, Paul Monroe's wife and formerly Fredericks' clerk, now operated a grocery store of her own. The elder Torres operated a slaughterhouse at the base of Poverty Hill. Mrs. Evelyn Jarvis Forrest operated a candy store on the riverbank at the foot of the hill until the early 1940s with the help of her daughter Aileen, who liked sampling the freshly made candies "to see how they were." In addition, Mrs. Forrest provided free postal service for those living on Poverty Hill until mail delivery began around 1943.

Poverty Hill has been the site of significant paleontological finds in the 1980s. University of Washington researchers have been studying the finds with great interest for knowledge of prehistoric conditions in the area. Mary Gaviglio, long-term resident of the hill, recalls her children bringing home fossils they found while digging in the rock cliffs of Poverty Hill. They found petrified birds' beaks and clamshells, as well as arrowheads.

The community's best and busiest builder in the 1910s-1930s was Paul Monroe. Monroe developed a construction company from his carpentry expertise and built hundreds of homes in Seattle, particularly on Capitol, First and Queen Anne hills. His own stucco two-bedroom house at 11616 42 Ave. S., Allentown, is an example of his building craft.

THE LITTLE WHITE CHURCH ON THE DUWAMISH RIVER

Some time in the nineteenth century the people living in Duwamish built a small frame church, which still serves as the community church from its picturesque location facing the Duwamish River at 11659 42 Ave. S. The early history of the church is clouded. Prof. Victor Steinbrueck states that the style and construction of the sturdy building suggests between 1860 and 1890. If it was built in the 1860s, it is among the oldest churches preserved in King County. This could be the little Methodist church that Jane Fenton Kelly talks about attending around 1870.

A number of legends are associated with the old church that are linked to the 1850s-1860s, again suggesting that the church is over 120 years old. According to one story there was an Indian massacre near the church during the

"Our Duwamish Sunday School bunch" at Woodland Park: Florence Smith, Mabel Bigelow, Mabel Nelson, May Wolbert, Dorothy Jackson, Amy Merkle, Agnes Smith, Nora Merkle, Bertha Wright, Annette Personetta, Lucille Smith, Catherine Merkle, Neva Roseberg, Russell Roseburg, Viola Merkle, Kenneth Wolbert, Hobart Smith, John Clark, Ragnar Brandon, Elsie ?, Vira Biglow, Nellie Nelson, Nomi Wright, Olga Holmquist, two little Wright girls, Ray Wolbert and Ralph Clark. Courtesy Mabel Nelson.

DUWAMISH-ALLENTOWN AND QUARRY-NORTH RIVERTON

DELIA AGNES FINUCAN MERKLE
COMMUNITY LEADER 1908-1950

Delia Agnes Finucan Merkle moved to the tiny new community of Allentown in 1908 with her husband Ernest and five children. In the coming years Mrs. Merkle was to assume the role of community leader and organizer, home medicine expert, and community wise woman. As she grew older and her own children were grown and gone, Delia came to be fondly known throughout the community as "Grandma Merkle."

Born in 1876 in County Clare, Ireland, Delia emigrated to America alone at age 16. She joined her sister in Iowa, where she first worked as a housemaid. Having taught school in Ireland, she was soon certified to teach in the U.S. At this time she met and married Ernest Merkle, whom she met when he bought her dinner basket at a box social.

Delia Merkle had excellent organizational skills which she applied in initiating community action. Lona Sweeney recalls: "Grandma Merkle played a really wonderful part in this Duwamish Valley because it was her idea to get the Duwamish School here." She served as the precinct committee representative from Allentown for 35 years. Over the years she initiated many ordinances, such as the early Herd Law. She was behind most citizen action movements in the 1910s and 1920s.

For three decades the Merkle house was a focal point of community activity. In the absence of formal community institutions people tended to take their problems and concerns to Mrs. Merkle, who was always interested and inevitably helped work out a solution. People who knew her said that "she had a unique understanding and could help you see your problems with a different perspective than other people."

Grandma Merkle gained a reputation for being a "good listener" and providing advice and guidance that often resolved the problem. Many a woman and man sought her out for a private conversation about problems that she or he was facing, ranging from dealing with shortages of money and marital conflicts to depression and loneliness.

Delia Merkle. Courtesy Roger Baker.

An intelligent, creative woman with a warm, caring attitude toward her fellow humans, and a great store of practical knowledge on the diagnosis and treatment of common maladies, Delia Merkle was ever ready to help the young mothers moving into the community who came to her filled with anxiety over their feverish children.

Perhaps it arose from the same genetic source that had prompted her father to counsel others as an attorney in Ireland, but Delia Merkle had words of counsel, comfort and guidance for all who came to her. In this era before the advent of personal counselors and with no resident minister or doctor who might provide community members with emotional and psychological support, Delia Merkle was a key person in providing community structure and stability. Three generations of the Ernest and Delia Merkle family have made their lifetime homes in Duwamish-Allentown: Viola Merkle Baker, daughter; Roger Baker, grandson; and Roger Baker, Jr. and Buddy Baker, great-grandsons.

1855-56 Indian War. This is unquestionably fiction, since there is no record of any of the Duwamish settlers being killed during the 1855-56 conflict. A second story is that a large hollow tree near the church was used as a hiding place for Indians who set upon river travelers. This is also an unlikely story, since the native Duwamish people were, with few exceptions, friendly and cooperative with the Duwamish Valley settlers. A final, verified, story is that the gavel for the early Duwamish School PTA was carved from a tree that stood near the church. Earlier the church was set back from its present location, about 20 feet from 42 Ave. S.

TUKWILA—COMMUNITY AT THE CROSSROADS

Verified records of twentieth-century activities at the church begin with the 1911-12 *Polk's Directory* listing of the Duwamish Chapel with regular Sunday Services at 10 a.m. The chapel was a branch of the Westminster Presbyterian Church of Seattle. On Sundays the visiting minister conducted Sunday School as well as preached. On Sundays when no one came out, Roy Henderson led the service.

Since 1951 the church has been the Duwamish Community Presbyterian Church. The reestablishment of an active congregation in the community was "a dream come true" for the 43 community members who gathered together with Rev. Charles Parrott to charter the church. The church has been ministered to by four ordained ministers, three student pastors, and two retired ministers. For over 20 years Frances Eder served the church as pianist and Cherie Berg as organist.

In 1962 Rev. James L. Unger came to the little Duwamish Church with instructions to persuade its few members to join another congregation and close the church. Upon first sight Rev. Unger saw why they wanted it closed, as it was in great need of repair. In the coming year Rev. Unger was astonished by the all-out support of the entire Duwamish-Allentown community to restore the church and establish it as a viable community institution. Rev. Unger has written about this experience, which he feels was one of the greatest influences in his life on his career:

> Though most of the members were older and retired, their enthusiasm spilled out into the community. Young people began to attend with their children. The offerings increased to the point where we began to talk of making some necessary improvements in the church building. With the announcement of the project and the pounding of the first nail, money began to come in, even from people whom we had never met and were not church-going people! The more work that was done, the more funds came in. This little congregation [possessed] faith, courage and love.

Rev. James Unger and the entire community worked together to save the old historic church. The sanctuary ceiling was lowered, another classroom added, and the entrance enclosed. Regular church pews replaced the chairs formerly used. The church then took on a completely new fresh look, with new paint inside and out. It was built as a single 20-by-40 foot room, its doors opening onto the river on the west side, where an elegantly simple spire reaches toward heaven. It stained-glass windows were dedicated as a memorial to Roy Henderson, church mainstay for 35 years.

COMMUNITY ORGANIZATIONS

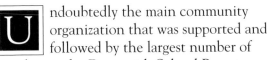ndoubtedly the main community organization that was supported and followed by the largest number of people was the Duwamish School Parent-Teacher Association (PTA), followed by the Duwamish Improvement Club. By the 1920s the Duwamish Garden Club was well established and neighbors worked together to maintain a beautiful community noted for its neat, colorful gardens. The Goat Owners Club and the Bee Keepers Club also flourished at this time. Masons affiliated with the Delta Lodge No. 172 in Riverton. Members of the Veterans of Foreign War associated with the White Center-Burien Chapter of the VFW.

From 1912 into the 1950s Duwamish had good ball teams. The longest-lasting was summer baseball, which rallied community spirit around games played with teams from other places in the valley including South Park and Tukwila through the 1950s. In the 1930s Duwamish had a football team that played at the South Park playfield. There were uniforms or other frills, but a good time was had with much camaraderie and community loyalty built. In 1933 a Boy Scout Troop was sponsored by the Duwamish Improvement club, with Roy Henderson serving as Scoutmaster. With the onset of World War II the group disbanded.

An early community rallying point was the Duwamish Baseball Team, organized around 1912. In the early days it was a champion team and not only played on home ground, but often traveled to challenge teams from other communities, with a good turnout for games at home and away. The boys played ball and the girls went along as the "rooting section." The team played in the valley near the railroad tracks. To show her support and provide a gastronomic incentive for good hitting, "Ma" Jones, who operated a local saloon with her husband, gave an apple pie to the player who hit the most home runs in a game. Courtesy R. C. Smith.

THE DUWAMISH IMPROVEMENT CLUB REAPPEARS

In the early 1930s a new Duwamish Improvement Club was organized for the purpose of promoting the welfare of the community, improving material and social conditions, encouraging community spirit, and cooperating with other community clubs for the mutual good. While this group was not a continuation of the original club from 1915, its interests and goals were the same as those of the early group, and the organizers voted to retain the original club's name. The club always followed a nonpolitical, nonpartisan and nonsectarian policy, thereby retaining the right to endorse anyone, because of his or her qualifications, to benefit the community. Founders were Bill Swartout, Frank Goodale, Francis Eider, Walter Bigelow, Clarence and Lily Sweeney, Hazel Menalia, Harold and Muriel Cleasby, and Silas Murray. Initially about 25 families regularly attended meetings.

The first major accomplishment of the club, in 1933, was the creation of a Volunteer Fire Department consisting of a hand-drawn hose cart manned by volunteers. From this modest beginning, the community club grew and assumed the role of guiding the community and protecting its interests. In its more than 50 years, the Duwamish Improvement Club has successfully achieved many objectives in legislation, publicity, traffic safety and roads, public utilities, parks and playgrounds, zoning, and schools.

In the 1950s the Improvement Club temporarily disbanded. The near loss of the community school in 1963 sparked the reformation of the club. The reorganized club's officers were Warren Wing, president; Neil Bigelow, vice president; Harry Petersen, secretary; and Albert Gaviglio, treasurer. The group immediately attracted a large number of community members. Throughout its history the club has always operated on a sound financial basis. Since the 1980s the women of the club have held semiannual fund-raisers to support club activities.

An example of the Duwamish Improvement Club's community leadership role is its work in obtaining an access road from the community to Highway 99 when the West Marginal Freeway opened in 1962. Duwamish-Allentown's old access road—commonly called "the road through the bean field"—had been eliminated by the freeway. Through the combined efforts of the club, its officers, local merchants, and State Representative John Bagnariol, the Highway Department was convinced that an access road was needed, and S. 112 St. was constructed.

Installation of street lights in 1966 throughout the community was perhaps one of the club's proudest achievements. This was accomplished through negotiations with Seattle City Light, which provided the lighting, and Water District No. 25, which handled the monthly billing. In 1977 the Improvement Club acquired Water District 25 building for a club hall. Named Petersen Hall, in recognition of Harry Petersen's lifetime of community service, the hall sees good use for meetings, fund-raising and social activities.

Another achievement of the Duwamish-Allentown community spirit was the successful thwarting of Seattle's attempt to annex Fire District No. 1, which would have robbed the community of its important fire district tax base. The club had a bill introduced in the State Legislature to prevent the Seattle takeover. After much effort, including two busloads of residents traveling to Olympia to speak in favor of the bill, it successfully passed.

Growing Up in the Duwamish Valley in the 1910s-1920s

The young couples who moved into the new communities growing around the Interurban station in the Duwamish Valley had young, growing families. With an average of four children per household, the streets rang with the sound of children's voices and laughter as they went about the business of growing up.

It was always intriguing to stop by the village blacksmith's shop next door to the Duwamish Church and watch Mr. Scherrer repairing farm tools or shoeing a horse. Around 1911 young Bill Scherrer brought everyone to their front porches to see his high-stepping mare pass by, pulling the community's first rubber-tired buggy. Many children, like Lona (Sweeney), Glen and Benny Schwartz, spent long happy hours riding horseback. Later many children had bicycles; but how they hated having to push the bikes up the hills.

Often a child would operate a "little business" to raise spending money. In the middle 1910s Ernest Peters opened a candy stand on the riverbank in front of the Peters' home. One early summer evening when the children were playing hide-and-seek at twilight near Ernest's candy stand, little John Ward was struck by a car driving fast down the river road. Cars were infrequent in those days, and the younger children did not fully understand the danger.

The younger children rarely left the immediate village area. Teenagers' social activities included dancing, fudge parties, box socials and ice cream parties. Many of these events were attended by parents and younger brothers and sisters. Mabel Nelson recalls that "we danced in our homes, those that were big enough, and our parents joined in with us.... We used the Edison phonograph, with the cylinder records and my, how we all enjoyed it!" Around 1910 Peter Cerini sold his big barn and it was turned into the Barn Dance Hall. Viola Merkle Baker recalls: "It was a joy to go over there. No drinking, no drugs, and no drunk drivers. Those were good days filled with fun and friends." A real lark would be meeting at the Merkles and walking to Cerini Station (Duwamish Junction, 1990) and back, "singing the entire three-and-one-half-mile trip."

> ### The Duwamish Bulletin
>
> In 1965, under the able hand of long-term community leader Harry J. Petersen as Editor, a monthly community newspaper, the *Duwamish Bulletin*, appeared and received immediate acclaim from the community. Published regularly for over 30 years, it has been an important factor in maintaining Duwamish-Allentown community spirit by keeping the residents informed of events and happenings important to the community, thereby generating community pride and support for important issues such as traffic lights. The *Duwamish Bulletin* is funded by members' dues, advertisements by local merchants and club funds.

Roy J. Henderson
Community Builder 1930-1960

Roy J. Henderson was born in 1891 in Duluth, Minnesota. In addition to Duluth, his family lived during Henderson's childhood years in Yakima and Seattle, Washington, and Eagle Point, Oregon. At age 15 Roy Henderson experienced a miraculous recovery from a life or death bout with typhoid fever. His mother had a strong religious faith and continuously prayed for her son's recovery. Henderson did recover and experienced a deep spiritual awakening as the result of his ordeal, which he maintained throughout his entire life.

Roy Henderson, community leader from 1935 to 1960, with his daughter Mary. Courtesy Mary Henderson George.

Between ages 17 and 20 he did all types of farm work. At 20 he was stricken with malaria and came to Seattle. Recovering from the disease, he took a job with the streetcar company and from there went to work for the Interurban. As a motorman and then conductor he was well known for his helpfulness and cheerful outlook. Later he operated a coal business. In 1917 he married Coral Hoskin. Their daughter Maxine was born in 1919, and Coral died the same year from complications from childbirth. In 1922 he married Alethea and the couple moved to Allentown where their daughter Mary was born at their home at 4815 S. 124 St.

From the beginning Roy Henderson was active in community life, and assumed leadership roles in almost every community activity and organization for almost 30 years. Shortly after their arrival in the community he and Alethea became mainstays of the Duwamish Garden Club. In 1930 they joined the Duwamish Community Church and in the next 35 years Henderson served as Sunday School teacher and superintendent, church elder and treasurer. He was a leader in the chartering of the Duwamish Presbyterian Church that took over from the non-denominational National Community Church in 1951.

In 1933 he ran for the Duwamish School Board with the slogan "Take the school out of politics and elect Roy J. Henderson." Elected, he served for 13 years. In 1933 he became the Scoutmaster for the Duwamish Boy Scout Troop. Most memorable for the boys were the many day and weekend camping trips the Scoutmaster took them on in his coal truck which would haul 15 boys and all of their gear.

When Fire District No. 1, Duwamish, was formed in 1935 Henderson, as Duwamish Fire Commissioner, had the distinction of being the first County Fire Commissioner in the State of Washington. In 1960 he served as the Chairman of the Board of Fire District No. 1.

When Roy Henderson died October 1, 1970, his home community and the entire valley mourned his passing. Longtime friend John Needham's sentiments express those of everyone: "Roy Henderson—they didn't come any better." Henderson's daughters, Maxine Henderson Champion and Mary Henderson George, live in the Puget Sound region.

Helping at Home

While there were many hours of play in most children's lives, there were also many hours of work, beginning at a young age. Chores were typically divided as "girl's and boy's work." Girls often began looking after younger brothers and sisters, as well as neighbor children, when they were 10 years old or even younger. Girls were also expected to take on cooking responsibilities at an early age. In many homes bread was baked daily and there were always three ample meals served. Beginning helping at age five and six, many girls could handle all the cooking for the family by age 15. To the boys usually fell more of the outdoor work, not the least of which was keeping the eternally empty woodbox filled, and later the coal bin.

Girls and boys both equally helped mother and father with chores around the house, churning butter, bringing in water from the pump in the yard and caring for the chickens, ducks, cows, horses, pigs, and sometimes sheep or goats. After the Herd Law went into effect, younger children's chores included taking the cows to pasture and fetching them at milking time. Young people made good friends with many of the family's animals, who were an important part of their childhood. Mabel Nelson writes: "I remember one time going to get the cow, but couldn't find the baby calf. The cow had tears streaming down her face and I felt sorry for her, so I hunted for the calf. I found it and she was so happy and inspected it to see that it was alright."

Children spent hundreds of hours in the summer hoeing and weeding the garden on their hands and knees, and then harvesting and assisting in preserving the vegetables. Everyone helped with shucking peas and snapping beans in preparation for canning. A household of six or seven would normally home-can 500 to 800 quarts of food for the winter food supply. Frances LaFranchie Menalia remembers her mother, a Swiss immigrant, canning hundreds of quarts of meat and fish, as well as vegetables, fruit and pickles. She also made sausage, cheese and specialty foods for holidays.

Lacking a public water system, most families relied on a back-yard well for water. However, some families did not have their own wells. The Nelson family demonstrates people's inventive approach to solving such basic problems as the need for laundry water. Nelson built a platform on the riverbank and rigged up a pulley system under a big tree across the road from their house which assisted the children in pulling up buckets of river water for the family washing. On washday a fire was built under the big copper boiler and the children were busy tending the fire and stirring the laundry.

Drinking water was obtained from a public pump near the Allentown station. It was the Nelson boys' job to haul the water home in a metal can they carried in the wheelbarrow. This water was poured through a charcoal filter into a storage barrel in the kitchen. Everyone had to be conservative in using the drinking water, never drawing more than could be drunk.

A few of the young people had paid jobs. At 14 Frank Nelson went to work for a can company in Seattle. He rode eight miles on his bicycle morning and night in order to save more of his $1.25/day pay. Eventually he took the Interurban, although it cost up to 60 cents a day.

Christmas

Wintertime brought special activities. Christmas was looked forward to by children and adults alike—but there was no "rushing" of the season. The focus was not on gifts, but on breaking the routine. Traditional activities included special baking and cooking, and visiting in one another's homes. The Christmas holiday meant time off— children from school, and adults from the often hard and monotonous schedules required to make a living. Most people had a Christmas tree, which went up between December 20th and 24th. Since candles were used to light the tree, people lucky enough to have a covered porch often put the tree outside—just in front of the living room window. Everyone kept a bucket of water and sponges nearby in the event that the tree caught on fire.

Christmas gifts were generally simple and inexpensive. Many people made the gifts they exchanged at Christmas. The emphasis was on usefulness, and often a child's gift was a new pair of stockings or hand-knit mittens. In most families gifts such as toys, skates or wagons were not given to a single child, but were a group gift to be shared and enjoyed by all.

Winter Play

Winters were cold—as they had been in the nineteenth century—and most winters all of the ponds and standing water froze over, providing great ice skating for over a month. In the 1910s it was often possible to be able to ice skate down a stream that ran out of the Codiga pond through the Duwamish

Ice skating on the Codigas' pond, 1915. Bonfires were kept burning close by the ice for light for night skating and to warm up by. Often someone like Roy Henderson would set up a hot dog stand. Looking back, Lona Schwartz Sweeney happily remembers: "Everybody would be there and everyone seemed to look out for each other and if anybody got hurt there was somebody to help." In the photo are the Nelsons with the Bigelow boys. Courtesy Mabel Nelson.

Playing in the River

The meandering Duwamish River was a main focus of summer fun for the community's youth. Roger Baker recalls: "We used to swim probably every day during the summer time well up into September. You might say we practically lived in the river. We used to get on an inner tube or log and float downstream with the current however far it took us—often beyond South Park. When the tide came in, the current reversed and we'd float back home—swimming along the way, playing in the water and hunting golf balls that were rolling on the river bottom." Most of the riverbed in the Duwamish-Allentown-Quarry district was very shallow at low tide—perhaps three feet. But there were

district, around and behind Poverty Hill and beyond S. 116 St., almost to Georgetown. Mabel Nelson remembers the younger children being given fast sled rides on the ice by the older kids, like her brother Frank: "We sure had to hold onto that sled tight or fall off once he got started."

The winter fun at Codigas' pasture pond was a part of growing up for several generations of Duwamish Valley children. In the 1930s Roger Baker remembers that "it was always a big time because we would have a big campfire and we'd bring over stuff to roast....and we kids got out and played on the ice with ice skates, sleds and inner tubes and anything that would slide." By the late 1960s the Burlington Northern Railway owned the old pasture land. The company filled up the pond and eventually established their piggyback freight car operation on the site, which continued in 1990.

deep holes, and woe to the child who did not know how to swim who stepped into a hole. The big kids would rescue little ones in these cases," remembers Baker. Very young children were usually forbidden to go down on the riverbank, but the goal was for every child to learn to swim early in life. Yet there were close calls and many drownings over the decades in the communities along the Duwamish River.

The favorite swimming hole, shared with kids from Riverton, was at S. 124 St. and 42 Ave. S., where the 1903 Duwamish bridge had been. In the 1930s, on a sandbar that had formed downstream from the center pilings remaining from the demolished 1903 bridge, Curt Sweeny, Jr., Bud Fander, and the Baker brothers, Ernie and Roger, improvised a diving board from which they leapt into the deep channel that flanked the sandbar on each side. The "skinny-dipping" place was up towards the

TUKWILA—COMMUNITY AT THE CROSSROADS

The Duwamish School in 1922. From 1911 to 1973 the Duwamish School served as a place of learning for the children and a community center for everyone, with the public library being located in the school as well as the school hall being used for community gatherings. Always noted for its beautiful gardens and neat lawns, the work of the custodian, Mr. Grezech, who put love and pride into his work, the school received an award for "the most beautiful school grounds in the county." Courtesy Washington State Archives.

old Black River bed near Renton Junction, where young people from nearby communities would join in the fun.

THE DUWAMISH SCHOOL

In the 1890s children in the Duwamish area attended school in the little one-room Sunday School building adjacent to the Duwamish Community Church, with Mrs. George, from Boston, as teacher. When the first and second grades filled up this building another small one-room building was built nearby, across a ditch, where the third and fourth grades were taught. From the fifth grade on, children walked to the Foster School. Eventually a one-room schoolhouse was built on Front St. for grades 1-4. After 1900 grades 1-8 attended classes held in two two-room buildings fronting on the river near the later site of the fire station.

By 1900, with the old school closed and the children having to walk three miles each way to the Foster School, Delia Merkle organized a campaign to establish a separate school district. Delia, together with Mrs. Nelson, Mrs. Jones and others, canvassed the community door-to-door with a petition for establishing the Duwamish School District for grades 1-8.

In 1911 Duwamish withdrew from Foster District 144 and became independent School District No. 175. The Duwamish School was held in portable houses in the center of the village next to Hammer's Dairy. In 1911 a large new school building was erected facing the river on Front St. Over the years community members who devotedly served on the school board include Delia Merkle, Nellie Spleen, Mr. Bookmyer, Clarence Sweeney, Mabel Lawrence, George Smith, J. H. Caffrey and O. G. Roseburg.

The children were proud of their new school and happy to have the large basement to play in on rainy days. Mabel Nelson recalls that the first graduating class in 1912 consisted of five girls and four boys. Miss Nora Kelly was a very popular principal and lived next door to the school. Two beloved and well-remembered teachers were Miss Anna Hadeen and Miss Caffrey.

The tradition of excellence applied to the school's staff, as well as pupil performance. Mr. Grezech, the school custodian for years, not only took excellent care of the school building, but kept the grounds immaculate and over the years developed exceptional gardens around the school. The entire community proudly joined Mr. Grezech in accepting a Citation of Recognition for having "the most beautiful school grounds in the county" handed down by the King County Board of Education.

The PTA was a key community organization and was very effective in equipping the school over the years, for example, buying heavy gold velvet draperies for the stage in 1929. The Duwamish School was always a major focal point of the Duwamish-Allentown-Quarry community. It was a community institution that people worked together to establish and maintain over its 60 years of history, and it was a favorite gathering place. Almost everyone was interested in the school, whether or not they had children in school. For example, Spring School Graduation Exercises was a community event attended by one and all—whether they had children graduating was not important.

THE DUWAMISH LIBRARY

The 1940s brought several changes for the Duwamish School. In 1945 the dream of a community library was fulfilled when a King County Library branch was established in the Duwamish School for school children and adult use. From the beginning the library was much used, with book circulation for the opening year being 5,071 and increasing to 13,855 the peak year of usage, 1956. Circulation dropped after that year, probably as the result of the presence of television in homes. The announcement in 1961 that the county was planning to close the Duwamish Branch Library brought vigorous community protest. In spite of considerable community effort, the library service was changed from branch to book mobile in 1962.

KEEPING THE SCHOOL OPEN

In 1942 the Duwamish School became a part of the consolidated South Central School District. However, this change did not greatly affect the school's place in the community. In 1963 a calamity befell the venerable old school when it was abruptly closed for being out of compliance with fire safety regulations. The community's children watched

> ### THE VALLEY'S SONGSTRESS ANNA HADEEN CODIGA
>
> Anna Hadeen, the child of Swedish immigrants, was the Duwamish Valley's own "Swedish Nightingale," being gifted with an outstandingly beautiful contralto voice. Recognizing their daughter's outstanding talent, her parents provided her with a good musical education and Anna Hadeen sang professionally at the famous Pantages Theater in Tacoma and in the Northwest concert circuit in the 1910s and '20s. After her marriage to Archie Codiga she no longer traveled on the concert circuit, but frequently had singing engagements in Seattle at concert halls and churches, where she was in high demand for the beauty of her lilting, strong, sweet voice. Among her best pieces were "When You Come to the End of a Perfect Day" and "Somewhere a Voice Is Calling."

as their school desks were moved to their new school—Central Elementary School in Foster.

At the school board meeting held the following week, over 100 irate Duwamish-Allentown residents crowded into the hall. After much heated discussion a committee was set up consisting of community leaders Neil Bigelow, George Gomez, Chet Hartsock, Harry Petersen, Warren Wing, Melvin Schley, Roger Thrall, Lydia Merkle, and school board members Mike Yellam, George Drew and John Skeel. State Representative from the 31st District C. G. Witherbee and Duwamish School Principal Stanley Whitehead also served. After many meetings, petitions and hard work, a proposition for the necessary improvements and a school levy for $22,750 passed by 85 percent in the local polling.

Once again the community's children could walk to their school. But all was not tranquil for long. In November 1967 the *Duwamish Bulletin* questioned: "Duwamish School to be Closed Again?" A committee was formed by the School Advisory Council to study the problem and everyone waited anxiously for the outcome. An inspection by the fire marshall called for only

TUKWILA—COMMUNITY AT THE CROSSROADS

minor repairs. Another reprieve for the old school. Every year after this, the subject of the school's condition was brought up and with relief the school continued to operate.

In the spring of 1973, the school's need for repairs, together with low enrollments, prompted the informal decision to close the Duwamish School. The following September the South Central School Board voted "to pursue the closing of the Duwamish School next year, to provide space at Southgate and look into the aspects of leasing or renting of Duwamish School and grounds." This time there was to be no reprieve. The steady decline in the number of children in the Duwamish-Allentown area in the 1970s, and the necessity of busing in additional students to make adequate-sized classes, in addition to the cost of maintaining the 1911 building, made it difficult to justify keeping the building open as a school.

On June 8, 1973, 62 years and 2 days after it had opened, the Duwamish School was officially closed with a farewell ceremony attended by hundreds of present and past graduates of the beloved school. Tributes to the school, its teachers and principals, and the education gained there were given. Memories of the enthusiastic rallying of the community around the school time and again to save it were recalled. Childhood memories and lifelong friendships made at the school were celebrated. Tears were shed and hearts were heavy with the pain of loss. It was with great sadness and regret that the Duwamish-Allentown community saw their school—to which they had dedicated so much energy and love—close its venerable doors forever as a place where the community's children were educated. The community had lost not only its own school but also a major focus of community life and activity. It would be harder to retain the special identity that had always characterized Duwamish-Allentown without the Duwamish School.

After discussion of the possibility of converting the school property into a community center it was concluded that the cost was too high, and the old building was razed. The site is maintained as Duwamish Park. During the summer months the area is used for family gatherings, and once again there are children playing on the grass.

KING COUNTY FIRE DISTRICT NO. 1— DUWAMISH

round 1900 a man named Johnson built a magnificent mansion overlooking the Duwamish Valley from high on the hill near S. 114 St. and 41 Ave. S. One foggy night the house caught fire and burned to the ground. Up and down the valley people came out of their houses and stood staring at the brightly lit sky in wonder as charred shingles and burning embers drifted down to the river to be carried to Elliott Bay with the outgoing tide. There was no system for fighting fires, and decade after decade wooden buildings went up in flames.

After years of discussion of the fire problem, in 1932 the Duwamish Community Club founded the Duwamish Volunteer Fire Department. The call for volunteer fire fighters quickly brought in 32 men including a number of 17- and 18-year-olds. A hand-drawn hose cart with 100 feet of one-and-one-half-inch cotton hose was obtained from the City of Seattle Water Department and stored in a tiny "station" building on the riverbank next to the Duwamish footbridge (near S. 120 St. and 42 Ave. S.) An old Studebaker that had been converted to a motorized hose truck by the Works Progress Administration (WPA) was bought for $25 and stored in Bill Goldsmith's general store.

Early in 1935 legislation was passed empowering communities to form volunteer fire districts and levy taxes to support their operation. Following the tradition established in 1855 by Duwamish Valley residents in taking the lead in King County in achieving significant community improvements, the first fire protection district in the county was King County Fire District No. 1, Duwamish, established on July

King County Volunteer Fire District No. 1, Duwamish, never lacked volunteers from the day it was organized in on July 21, 1935. In addition to working together the men also joined in fellowship together with card playing at the Fire Station and the annual banquet being tops. Here the firemen enjoy dinner at the China Pheasant, October 4, 1949. First row, l. to r., Gil Bates, Chief Curt Sweeney, Commissioner Silas Murray, Ken Phelps, County Fire Marshall Jay Thomas, Asst. Chief Clarence Sweeney, Lt. George Kozlinsky, Capt. Bob Hore, Don Mercer, Gene Howlet; second row, l. to r., Bud Larson, Ted Dawson, Ben Hoffner, Harry Smoyver, Roy Carter, Lt. Elmer Stanford, Curt Sweeney, Jr., Capt. Chet Hill, Sect. Charles Shultz. Roger Baker not in picture. Courtesy Roger Baker.

21, 1935. This was also the first volunteer fire district in the State of Washington. The first commissioners were F. H. Smith, chair, and W. D. Swarthouse and Roy J. Henderson. This small group chose Bill Goldsmith as fire chief, Henry Washington as assistant chief, and Curtis Sweeney and Hobart Smith as captains. Other volunteers included Harold Cleasby, Leo Sweeney and George Smith. With tax money and community contributions Fire District No. 1 built a fire station in 1940 and bought a well-used 1918 American LaFrance 500-gallon pumper and a Wisconsin motorized hose cart. After the war a Civilian Defense pumper trailer was acquired. Originally encompassing Duwamish-Allentown and Quarry, in the early 1940s boundaries were extended to the area north of the Boeing Access Road at Highway 99.

This enlarged the district to four and one-half square miles and it took in half of the Boeing Administration Building.

Shortly after the formation of the fire district, the volunteer fire fighters had a chance to test their skill when the Codiga barn burst into flames one autumn from spontaneous combustion of the stored hay. The volunteer fire fighters came running from every direction, as did the rest of the community to see the biggest blaze in recent times. The Renton Fire Department joined the Duwamish Fire Department, and working most of the day together they saved part of the barn, which the Codigas rebuilt.

Over the 53 years that Fire District No. 1 existed as a key community institution, a number of men distinguished themselves for long-term service. Joining the volunteer department in 1938, Chester Hill served in all positions including fire chief and fire commissioner. In 1988 Hill received the Washington State 50 Years of Faithful Service award for his volunteer activities. Curtis Sweeney supported the district for 39 years, first as fire captain and then as fire chief. With the annexation of Duwamish-Allentown by the City of Tukwila in 1989 King County Fire District No. 1, Duwamish, disbanded.

QUARRY-NORTH RIVERTON DISTRICT

The area of land lying across the Duwamish River from Duwamish-Allentown and directly north of Riverton developed along with the nearby communities in the 1910s. Because of plat names and its location adjacent to Riverton it has come to be called North Riverton. However, the community's history is more closely tied to that of Duwamish-Allentown because of its physical proximity and the sharing of community institutions, especially the Duwamish School. The Quarry District was originally developed by the Union Trust Corp., formed in 1892 by Watson Squires, Washington's last Territorial Governor. The Quarry District area was subdivided in 1903-1907.

THE RIVERSIDE QUARRY

It had been long known that the large hill in the center of the Duwamish Valley on the banks of the river was of high-quality rock. The river's meandering course was partially determined by the bedrock underlying the alluvial fill deposited by flooding. The bedrock protruding up through the otherwise flat riverbed was visible as rapids at low tide. The river channel straightens and then makes a pronounced right-angle turn between the former Quarry and Poverty hills.

Watson Squires recognized the growing need for good-quality crushed rock in King County and developed the rock deposit as a quarry, naming it the Riverside Quarry. Around 1906 Squires leased the quarry to Bell & Scott Contractors, who began blasting immediately and built a rock crusher. In 1912 Bell & Scott undertook massive improvements, including the installation of a larger crusher with a much greater capacity than the previous one. The operation switched to electrical power, which permitted the construction of a tramway to the top of Quarry Hill. In addition to being clean and quiet, riding the electric train was very scenic because it almost totally encircled the large hill as it made its ascent. Local residents were delighted with the company's decision to install transformers and furnish electric current for lighting the homes in the area that were without access to electrical power, although high power lines ran through the community.

Around 1913 Bell ran the quarry alone for a time and then took on a new partner, Price. The partnership employed some 25 men. The rock was blasted loose, but removal was done by hand with wheelbarrows and small carts. The rock was loaded into cars provided by an Interurban spur to the site. The quarry operation originating on the northeast side of the hill, changed to the west side because the blasting was disturbing homes. In the next 50 years the quarry operation continued, with the great rock hill gradually being blasted away and hauled off to all parts of King County for the citizens to drive over for centuries to come. A barge loading ramp and facility was built on the Duwamish River, near where Highway 99 and East Marginal Way intersect, for scow deliveries. Watson Squireses passed away and his sons reorganized the investment firm as Squires Investment Company. Mr. Romano leased the quarry from the Squires around the end of the 1930s and operated a rock-crushing plant on the property. By now the quarry was known as the Riverton Quarry.

Around 1947 a protracted labor dispute between the Operation Engineers Union and the Teamsters shut down the quarry. Puget Sound Bridge and Dredging Company and Romano negotiated a joint venture. The quarry was operated under this arrangement from 1949

Duwamish-Allentown and Quarry-North Riverton

Riverside Quarry, later known as the Riverton Quarry, ca. 1910. Original rock crusher built by Bell & Scott, who leased the Quarry mine from 1906 to 1912 from owner Watson Squires. Drawing by Patrick Hill from an old photograph.

to 1970. The operation required about a dozen workers. Over 5 million tons of rock products were taken from the land during the 65 years of operations.

Quarry-North Riverton Neighborhood

In addition to leasing the quarry, the Squireses sold homesites. Located east of the quarry, this residential neighborhood became locally known as the Quarry District, although the Squireses named the plat Riverton Addition. The name North Riverton was given support as the official name in 1924, when King County established the voting precinct under the name North Riverton.

Blasting, which was a key tool in breaking up the solid rock, was a daily activity at the quarry operation. Between 1906 and 1963 the residents of the Quarry District and Duwamish-Allentown lived with the repercussions of the blasting, with windows rattling and dishes falling off shelves being a regular occurrence. In the 1950s plate-glass picture windows were known to shatter. Many people said that they had an earthquake every day at 11:00 a.m. and 3 p.m., the time of the daily blasting. Studies have revealed that a geological fault line running throughout the area was responsible for transmitting the shock of the dynamite explosions over a wide area.

Every so often an incident occurred that caused the entire community to get up in arms over the danger to life and property caused by the blasting. Normally people would talk it over and a couple of spokespeople were selected to talk to the quarry management about the flying rocks breaking windows or damaging the gardens. One such incident was the day in the 1920s when a shower of rocks flew across the Duwamish River hitting homes in Duwamish-Allentown. To make matters worse, the area pelted was the route regularly taken by the school children. The quarry manager was soon facing Delia Merkle and a community contingent in his office. Numerous lawsuits cropped up over the years from blasting damage. Sometimes damages were awarded; however, generally everyone just lived with the situation.

The Quarry District was not a quiet place. In addition to the blasting and quarry operation traffic, there were the trains. Henning Sundby, lifetime resident, recalls that "the biggest shakes came from the huge 6-by-6 driving wheels of the big steam locomotives. They would shake me almost out of my bed." The noise ended when diesel engines were introduced in the 1950s.

The Bigelow Shingle Mill

Among the earliest residents in the Quarry District were Frank and Lewis Bigelow, brothers, who came in 1905 before the quarry was opened. In 1909 Frank built a shingle mill on the bank of the river, just north of where the footbridge was later built. The mill was operated for a number of years, fed with all of the available cedar timber in the Duwamish Valley and on Quarry Hill, which was naturally heavily wooded. Working full tilt it took four to five cords of cedar a day to keep the mill productive. When these nearby sources of wood were exhausted, timber was hauled in from Lake Burien, which was being logged off. After all of this wood was gone, logs were brought in from the Cedar River. By 1916 most of the accessible timber in the area had been cut. That winter was the winter of the famous Puget Sound "Big Snow" and the mill roof collapsed under the weight of three feet of heavy, wet snow. Bigelow dismantled the mill, selling off the equipment. The shingles for the 1911 Duwamish School were handmade at the Bigelow Shingle Mill.

By 1915 Quarry had more than a dozen houses scattered on the rough dirt streets. Residents at this time were the McGees, Lutes, Sakumans, Halls and Dobbses, whose daughter Charlotte Dobbs Widrig became a writer. The neighbors were glad to have James and Nellie Blair living in the district, since Nellie was a trained nurse who worked for Dr. Frederick Nichols of Riverton for 25 years.

Typical of the people who moved to the Quarry District were the Sundbys. Barnhard and Mary Oien Sundby had emigrated from Norway as single people and had met and married in West Seattle. Barnhard, a shipwright by trade, began building houses when the demand for wooden boats diminished. The Sundbys moved

Brother Horn
Larry Linnell

Near the Allentown Bridge, adjacent to the Interurban Station, on the banks of the river were several two- or three-room shanties inhabited by older folks. An enchanting character lived there known only as "Brother Horn." He had long, red shoulder-length hair and a full, wonderful beard. We were always welcome to hear stories of his life, which I'm sure were embellished for our wide-eyed benefit. Occasionally he would don a pair of oversized black bloomers given to him by his neighbor, "Lady of the Lake." He would sit in his large innertube float, with his clothes bundled on a long stick, and set forth down the river with the outgoing flow to Seattle. He would be accompanied by his black-and-white dog, Rockaway. Because Brother Horn was unable to whistle, he would call Rockaway by smacking his lips loudly. What a sight! Brother Horn was well known along Seattle's Skid Road for his soapbox oratory during the Depression.

to Quarry in 1918. Between 1920 and 1940 Sundby built many fine large houses on Capitol Hill and Queen Anne in Seattle, as well as in the Duwamish Valley. Houses built by Sundby still remaining in 1990 can be seen at 11918 Interurban Ave. S., 3924 S. 117 St., 11605 40 Ave. S., and 4037 S. 119 St. Sundby loved building boats, however, and built at least two boats in his backyard in Quarry, launching them into the Duwamish for their trip to Puget Sound.

Like the other children in the Quarry District, the Sundby children went to the Riverton Grade School and then to the Foster School for grades five through eight. It was about two miles from Quarry to the school and the children normally walked. They were given a booklet of Interurban tickets with strict orders to take the train, but only when the weather was very bad. The young men of the Quarry District were a close-knit group of pals. Henning Sundby recalls that the Quarry boys were different from the Allentown-Duwamish fellows across the river in that they did not smoke cigarettes.

After the new Duwamish School was opened, parents in the Quarry District wanted their children to attend this school, which—except for the presence of the river—was very close to their homes. Going to the Duwamish School broke the ice between the Quarry and Duwamish young people. To get over to the Duwamish School the Quarry pupils had to walk either south to the Allentown Bridge (124th) or north to the drawbridge at S. 115 and East Marginal Way—both routes being about two miles. Parents began ferrying the children across the river to school in a rowboat. The "School Ferry" crossing was approximately where the community footbridge is located in 1990.

Favorite places for the children to play were the parts of Quarry Hill that were abandoned by the quarry operation and the hillside that was still in its natural state. There was a "hobo jungle" on the hill, and the children were told to "keep clear" of the area and its residents. More than once between 1920 and 1940 the hill was burned over from bonfires started by the

Riverton Quarry piers. After the quarrying operation moved from the northeast side of the hill to the west side there were two "plateaus" of rock left that the district children found perfect for "war games," with a pair of huge concrete piers serving as forts. The piers were also used by the Mountaineers Club for rappeling practice in the 1930s and 1940s. Here Robert Rinehart of Tukwila trains for climbing Mount Rainer. Wife Elsie Anderson Rinehart, also an avid climber, is on the other end of the rope. Courtesy Elsie Anderson Rinehart.

children playing with matches or by the hobos who stayed there, who were numerous during the Depression years.

The Riverton Quarry provided work for many living in the district. The Stanleys, Duwamish residents, worked there for years, with Mr. Stanley serving as the quarry foreman and Mrs. Stanley as the quarry cook. High-school boys often worked at the quarry. In the summer of 1922 Henning Sundby and Glen Schwartz built up nice sets of muscles breaking up rocks. Schwartz also worked the local boxing and wrestling circuit, and trained at the same training camp near Quarry Hill that turned out George "Bearcat" Baker. Bearcat was the son of a retired railroad chef who operated Baker's Kitchen restaurant at 1206 East Marginal Way, near the Interurban station. Mrs. Baker's fried chicken made the restaurant famous. Bearcat doing his early morning roadwork was a familiar sight to the community in the early 1920s. When a "smoker" was held at the White Center boxing arena, many people from the Duwamish-Allentown-Quarry area who knew Bearcat and his family would go over to cheer for the hometown favorite. Dr. Frederick Nichols was the arena doctor.

Over the decades Quarry Hill diminished in size and, with the removal of the main outcropping of rock, further excavation became too expensive. In 1963 the 70-foot-high tower of rock that had supported the old rock crusher, long out of use, was blown up. The destruction of this landmark that had distinguished the area for over half of a century marked the end of an era. The land in 1990 is occupied by the Metro bus barn.

The Duwamish-Allentown and Quarry-North Riverton community did not regret the end of the daily blasting. However, the community has not been left in peace. The air is filled with a continuous low roar as trucks and automobiles flow by on several freeways west of the community.

In those early days of peaceful rural living the community woke up to the sound of birds chirping and the mooing of the cows at the Codiga farm. Throughout the day they would hear the one long and two short blasts of the West Seattle Fauntleroy ferry whistle, signaling that it was getting ready to pull out. People would check their watches. "There goes the 2:25 ferry," they'd say. And then there was the sound of the Duwamish School bell and the laughter of

George "Bearcat" Baker in 1925, at age 17, won the Northwest Heavyweight boxing title. Later Bearcat worked as a youth boxing trainer at the Jackson Street Boys Club. In 1990 Bearcat Baker, at age 82, was given a place in the Northwest Athletes Hall of Fame. Courtesy Ben Schwartz.

the children playing in the schoolyard during recess. These memories remain and strengthen the community as it continues in its resolve to preserve its special way of life on the banks of the Duwamish.

Duwamish-Allentown and Quarry-North Riverton

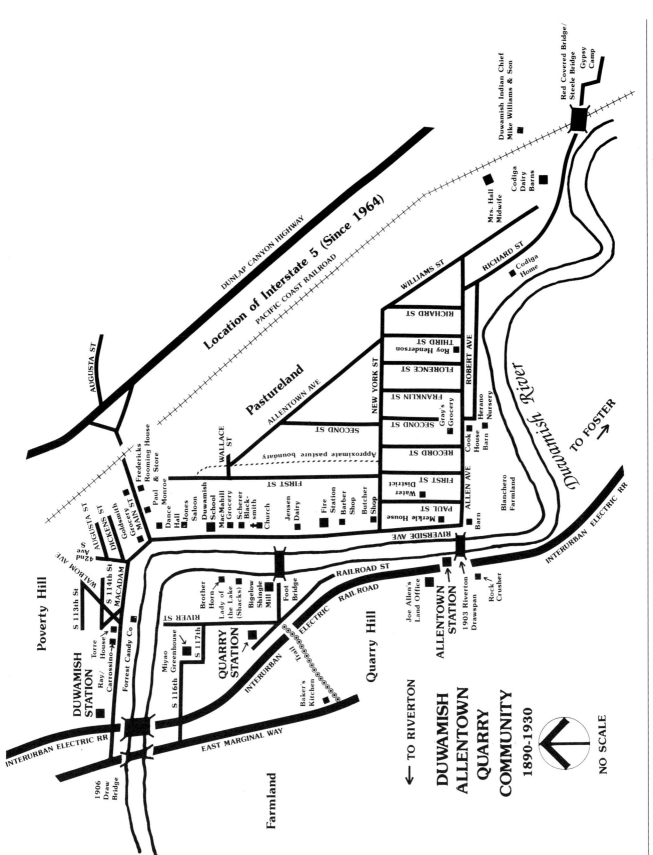

Map by Patrick Brodin with assistance of Roger Baker, Viola Merkle Baker, Lona Schwartz Sweeney, Henning Sundby, Kay Reinartz. Drawn by Sharon Dibble.

The Garden Station stop of the Interurban opened in 1904 at the bottom of Tukwila Hill. Across the road was Hull's General Mercantile with the Garden Station Post Office alongside. Courtesy Tukwila Historical Society.

CHAPTER 11

TICKET TO TUKWILA, TOWN ON THE HILL—1902-1928

When the Interurban began service up the Duwamish Valley in 1902, it established three stations—Duwamish, Foster and Renton Junction. In 1904 Garden station was opened between Foster and Renton Junction. This station was located at the base of a steep hill where hazelnut trees grew in abundance. On November 29, 1904, the Garden Station Post Office was established in a small building next to Hull's General Store across from the Interurban stop with Mrs. Minnie M. Lutz as postmaster. A widower with three children, Hull recognized in the attractive Minnie a good business partner as well as life partner, and the enterprising couple were married. The Post Office was moved into the rear of Hull's store so that Minnie could tend both the shop and the Post Office. The second floor of the building doubled as community hall and Presbyterian Church meeting place. In 1906 the Interurban erected a depot at the foot of 58 Ave. S. and renamed the stop Tukwila Station.

It is popularly believed that the name Tukwila is Chinook jargon. However, careful study by native language expert Dr. Nile Thompson suggests that this is not accurate.

According to Thompson, who since 1971 has researched Puget Sound Salish—the language of the region that includes the Duwamish dialect—the local word for hazelnut bush is *k'ap'ux^wac* (roughly, "kapowhats"). In Thompson's opinion the word Tukwila has the appearance of being a local term, rather than Chinook jargon. The prefix *tx^w* (pronounced like the "tw" in twilight), meaning "place of," is found in many regional place names. This prefix seems to be the first syllable of Tukwila. However, no completed etymology has been achieved.

THE FIRST FAMILIES

William J. Fouty was probably the first Euro-American to come to live on Tukwila Hill who remained into the era of the municipality and development of the valley. Originally from Minnesota, in 1877, at the age of 12, Fouty traveled to Puget Sound. He worked in a logging camp and floated logs down the Cedar and Black rivers to a shingle mill on the Black, close to the confluence of the rivers. Later this mill would serve as the Fouty family home. In June 1889 Fouty saw the dark billows of smoke and flames over Seattle as he watched the city burn from Tukwila Hill.

Returning to Minnesota, he married Constance Bennett in 1895. Fouty made his way back to the Duwamish Valley where the family made their home first on the hill around 58 Ave. S. and S. 144 St., later moving to the old shingle mill (across the river from S. 143 St.). Ben, the eldest of the Foutys' three sons—F. B. (Ben), Almond and Joseph—became good friends with Joe Moses, Chief of the Black River Duwamish, who lived across the river from the Foutys. As an expression of friendship Chief Joe Moses made Ben Fouty an honorary member of the Black River tribe.

The Fouty children grew up on the Black River. Before the Lake Washington Ship Canal was opened in 1917, ships traveled from Lake Washington to Elliott Bay via the Black and Duwamish rivers, which were somewhat shallow, with many treacherous sandbars and snags. Often the Fouty children, who knew the river well, helped pilot boats to the junction. Young Ben Fouty put himself through high school at Renton and Queen Anne by salmon fishing in the Black and Duwamish rivers.

Soon after the opening of the Duwamish Valley by the Interurban, a cluster of homes appeared near and on the hill above Garden Station. Among the first were Bernard and Mary Kassner from Kenaunee, Wisconsin. Kassner was a blacksmith by trade and worked in the logging and mining camps, shoeing horses and making drills and tools. The young couple's first camp in 1901 was on the Nooksack River near Mount Baker, where they lived in a tiny shack on the riverbank. When the heavy spring rains raised the river up to their front door, Mary, holding her baby to her, lay awake all night putting her hand down on the floor every hour to see if the water was coming into the house. In addition to the dangers from flooding, the shy young woman from Wisconsin was bothered by the loud carousing of drunken loggers at night. Bernard worked hard at blacksmithing, and after a single year they had saved enough to buy land and moved to the Duwamish Valley.

Kassner immediately built a cabin for his family and a small blacksmith shop next door. Sons Walter and Arthur were born in the little cabin in 1904 and in 1907, with midwife Mrs. Grooms, a neighbor, in attendance. In the snug, functional smithy, Kassner installed his bellows, anvil, forge and smithing tools brought out from the shop he had operated in Wisconsin. This was the first business in the community. The Kassners and most of their children and grandchildren remained in the community and were community mainstays throughout the century.

Walter Kassner often saw Indians when he was growing up. The Duwamish natives had been forced out of their ancestral valley to a federal reservation near Auburn in the 1860s, but a few had continued to come back to their home territory. A brushy Indian trail lay close to the Kassners' place, heading east down to the Duwamish River. One day young Walt was gathering hazelnuts near the trail when a pair of Duwamish men came up the path. Frightened, the lad dropped everything and ran for home. Another time, while Mary and the children were eating at the kitchen table, Mary saw two Indians, their faces cupped against the glass, looking in at the family. Not wanting to alarm the children, she said nothing until they had disappeared.

In the first years after the opening of the Interurban station about a dozen families moved in, including the Wallenbergs, 1905, the Klines from Illinois, 1906, the J. A. Smiths, 1906, and the T. S. Unos from Japan, 1907. In 1905 Samuel and Agnes Myers, from Ohio, moved to Garden station and opened Myers' General Store to the south of Hull's Mercantile. Operating the store on the first floor of the building, they rented the second floor as a home.

In the next 50 years the general store changed hands from time to time or went out of business to be reopened later. Mr. Waltz built a garage south of Myers after automobiles came into common use, and this business changed hands periodically. However, Tukwila's business district never expanded beyond this small commercial enclave until the 1960s. The community remained essentially a residential place, with people traveling first on the Interurban and later by bus and automobile to the nearby communities of Riverton, Foster, Renton, Kent, or into Seattle for shopping, banking and church. Conducting business outside of the community was, in fact, quite convenient since the community was a place of commuters. From the very beginning most households had one family member who was near a commercial center every day, and necessities were picked up by the traveler.

Hull's store, located at Interurban and Main St., Tukwila, opened around 1904 and operated until the 1960s. With the Tukwila Post Office located in the store, this store was a community meeting place. Courtesy Washington State Archives.

THE DEVELOPERS

The opening of Garden station in 1904 attracted homeseekers; however, developers had already been interested in the area for some time. In the autumn of 1890 R. J. and F. H. Graham launched a real estate venture on the west side of Tukwila Hill. The Grahams offered their home tracts in the area from S. 152 St. north to S. 144 St.

Early in 1902 a number of local property owners in the Duwamish Valley began subdividing land along the river, and on September 30, 1902, the first large commercial interest appeared. The South Seattle Land Company, incorporated in 1890 with over a half million dollars capital, was headed by C. D. Stimson, owner of the largest lumber milling operation in the Seattle area, the Stimson Mills of Ballard. The corporation had been quietly buying land throughout the south end of King County since 1890. C. D. Stimson's associates were his brother Thomas Stimson, H. G. Struve, J. F. Eshelman and Maurice McMicken, corporate secretary. The South Seattle Land Company named its Duwamish Valley subdivision Brookvale Garden Tracts.

TICKET TO TUKWILA, TOWN ON THE HILL—1902-1928

Other ambitious developers were Clarence D. Hillman and Bessie Olive Hillman, who acquired a large tract along the river and up the hill, which they platted as Hillman's Seattle Garden Tracts on August 11, 1903. The Hillmans' land was the most favorably located for immediate development since it included the Interurban station.

At this time Hillman and his wife were involved with numerous land ventures including Pacific City, Algona and Hillman City. In the next decade C. D. Hillman was to become a notorious character in the region, whose shoddy land dealings eventually would lead to criminal charges. Convicted of U.S. mail fraud by mailing false advertising to real estate customers, in 1911 Hillman was sentenced to the federal penitentiary at Walla Walla, but received a Presidential pardon in 1912. Legacies of Hillman's unscrupulous land dealings in Tukwila and elsewhere in the Duwamish Valley crop up occasionally in the form of legal irregularities in plot boundaries.

The Town of Tukwila was not originally platted as a town, but was formed by merging sizeable tracts from Brookvale Garden and Hillman's Seattle Garden, in addition to tracts from Interurban Addition to Seattle (1902), Colegrove's Acre Tracts (1904), Richard's First Addition to Sterling (1907), and the Seattle Land Company's Five-Acre Tracts (1890). Tukwila's original borders encompassed approximately three quarters of a square mile lying on the valley bottom and up the hill, then called Profanity Hill (Tukwila Hill) because of all the swearing at the horses by drivers struggling up the hill.

JOEL SHOMAKER'S DREAM AND VISION

round 1902 a newspaper man from Kentucky, Joel B. Shomaker, came to Puget Sound. While working as the farm editor for the Seattle *Post-Intelligencer*, Shomaker bought a tract from C. D. Hillman in the area of Garden Station and built a house for his wife and children. Shomaker commuted into Seattle daily on the Interurban, which passed directly beneath where his house sat on the hill. When the great flood of 1906 shut down the Interurban, Shomaker rowed to Seattle.

An energetic dreamer, Shomaker was destined to influence the history of the entire Duwamish Valley for the remainder of the century. Reports vary, but at this time there appear to have been about 100 families in the area. Soon after coming to the Tukwila station community, Shomaker began promoting the idea of incorporating the community. He saw the potential for industrial development in the Duwamish Valley and felt that it would be to the community's advantage to establish itself as a municipality at an early date.

Shomaker had a flair for the dramatic and enjoyed getting attention. His daily attire consisted of a black cutaway Prince Albert coat, fresh pleated-front white shirt, black string tie, broad-brimmed black felt hat and walking stick. His best friend in the community was Del Adelphia, whose only known occupation was magician. Like Shomaker, Adelphia favored the cutaway Prince Albert coat and broad-brimmed hat. Old-timers recall the two men as inseparable friends who used to cut quite a figure as they briskly walked down the dusty roads of the valley, their coat tails flapping and brass heads of their twin walking sticks glinting in the sun as they discussed politics, development of the valley and the supernatural. A gypsy at heart, Shomaker found a perfect foil for his ideals, dreams and schemes in the magician.

Together with Adelphia, Shomaker generated community interest in incorporating. All that was needed was a town name and sufficient "ayes" in the community vote. A clever promoter, Shomaker schemed to draw the community in by holding a "Name the New Town" contest. Tradition has it that Katherine Sheperd won the prize, a handsome leather-bound volume of classical literature that Shomaker took from his private library, for her suggestion of *Tuck-Wil-La*.

Tukwila was hardly an original name considering that the Duwamish natives had

> ### COME TO PUGET SOUND
>
> A Puget Sound booster from the beginning, in 1908 Joel Shomaker wrote and published several songs extolling its attractions, among them "Burn the Mortgage" and "On Logged-off Land—Come to Puget Sound." The latter, which Shomaker called "A Song of Prosperity," expresses his great enthusiasm.
>
>
>
> *Joel and Luella Shomaker and children at home. L. to r.: Blaine, Luella, Winfield, Nancy with dog Spot, Joel. Luella was pregnant with daughter Laura when picture was taken. The original Shomaker home may be seen at 14241 58th Ave. S. The house is in good condition, with the only major alteration being the removal of the porch. Courtesy Laura Shomaker Bateham.*
>
> Would you like to have a home in the land of the free,
> Where the big pine-cone meets the waves of the sea?
> Then come to Puget Sound, where happiness is found,
> And buy you a farm on logged-off land.
> Do you want to live at ease on the bright sea-shore,
> Where the ships fan the breeze from the wide world o'er?
> Then come to Puget Sound, the evergreen ground,
> And buy you a farm on logged-off land.
> Do you want to chase game on the wild wooded hills,
> And hook the fishes tame in the brooks and rills?
> Then come to Puget Sound, the sportsmen's ground,
> And buy you a farm on logged-off land.
> Chorus:
> Oh, if you would be happy and live a long time,
> Have credit at the bank and friends in every clime,
> Then come to Puget Sound,
> Where all the year 'round
> You can pick crops of dollars on logged-off land.

called the area by this name for ages and it had been readily adopted by the early settlers. In addition, Puget Sound Electric Railway had been calling the closest Interurban stop Tukwila Station for more than two years, and the school had already been named Tukwila by the Foster School District.

Interest in incorporation mounted during the winter months as Shomaker called public meetings at Hull's Hall, where he told the community of the advantages of incorporating. Then the effort received a heavy blow. In March 1908 the Garden Station Post Office was closed and Georgetown became the community's post office. Shomaker was livid, and the postmaster for King County began to regret that he had closed the little post office as he found the black-hatted Kentuckian in the Prince Albert coat haunting his waiting room. Nothing would do but to reopen the Garden Station Post Office, which happened May 28, 1908—just in time to sway the incorporation vote. Eighty-one people cast their votes, with 61 ayes and 20 nays for incorporating. Formalities required for incorporation completed, the petition was registered and other tasks completed for fourth-class municipal status.

The Town of Tukwila's incorporation became official on June 23, 1908. The first Town Council meeting was held on June 29 at the home of the appointed mayor, Joel Shomaker. Councilmen were Del Adelphia, John M. Hall, R. H. Heath, J. Wilson, and John O. Wold. Ernest M. Engel was treasurer and E. G. Green clerk. A police magistrate, marshal, city attorney and health officer were appointed. Reflecting a great interest in quickly establishing an official image defining the town, the first ordinance of the Town of Tukwila was the design for the official corporate seal. The second Tuesday of each month was set as the regular council meeting date.

The *Duwamish Valley Tribune* was adopted as the town's official newspaper. While this newspaper served as the official paper for a only few months at this time because a local paper started up in September, for most of the first half of the twentieth century the *Duwamish Valley Tribune* and its successors served as Tukwila's official newspaper. Shomaker's confidence in Tukwila had won supporters and in September 1908 F. W. Sears launched a weekly community newspaper, the *Tukwila Hazelnut*, which lasted until 1914.

Tukwila celebrates its founding. On July 4, 1908, Tukwila marked its incorporation with a grand party. The Seattle Post-Intelligencer *reported: "[In the] morning the citizens gathered to hear the reading of the Declaration of Independence and a patriotic address by Mayor Joel Shomaker. In the afternoon there were a number of athletic events for the boys and young men. [In the] evening there was a display of fireworks. Tukwila people entertained handsomely for besides the local citizens there was a large sprinkling of people from neighboring communities who came to join in the fun." Courtesy Laura Shomaker Bateham.*

TUKWILA FOR PROGRESS

Officials elected for 1909 were mayor, Joel Shomaker; councilmen, Del Adelphia, John M. Hall, J. Wilson, Frank W. Johnson and J. G. Hopkins; Treasurer, Ernest W. Engel. Lots were drawn to determine which councilmen would hold one- and two-year terms. Salaries were fixed for clerk, $120 a year; marshal, $80 a year; treasurer, $25 a year; attorney, $150 a year. At the end of 1908 Tukwila's assessed valuation was $168,565.

Filled with enthusiasm and dreams for the future of the Town of Tukwila, Mayor Shomaker arose to address the town council and citizens who crowded Hull's Hall. "The town is noted at home and abroad for its industrious, active and progressive inhabitants," he told them. "It is made up of working men and women who place the sanctity of home above the corrupting influences of commercialism." Shomaker told the assembly that they "represent all political parties and religious creeds, and stand united on the platform which declares 'Tukwila for Progress,' and perfect harmony in all matters pertaining to the upbuilding of the Town of Tukwila." Looking ahead, Shomaker shared his vision of the future of the area: "The agitation for deepening, widening and straightening of the Duwamish River will result in the transfer of much property within our borders and in the vicinity. Industrial activity will be apparent in all directions.…We must be ready to grasp whatever opportunities are presented for the assistance of our people and the uplifting of the rural home as the ideal of American citizenship."

The drive for progress appears to have been uppermost in Shomaker's mind at this time and he exhorted the community to make public improvements as "fast as funds will permit." At the top of his list were roads and streets, a public water system, a drainage system and electric

TUKWILA—COMMUNITY AT THE CROSSROADS

lights, an independent school district, a public park and town cemetery, and a town hall, public library and "place of amusement." He recommended the cultivation of plants and flowers, especially those native to the Northwest, to beautify the town and to be a source of "pleasure and profit" to the people.

A good start fulfilling the beautification goal took place in the spring of 1909 when the mayor issued a proclamation making May 6 Holly Day, in response to the Tukwila Improvement Club's request. Club members distributed two sacks of holly seeds. Undoubtedly some of the large holly trees found in Tukwila at the end of the century got their start on Holly Day, 1909.

Under Shomaker's focused and progressive leadership the newly founded town started with much energy and sense of purpose. For the first few years the community and town council favored deciding important questions at mass meetings, a practice that eventually disappeared, suggesting waning community interest in the municipal government. The first such meeting was held in August 1909, when the tax rate was debated. Consensus was finally reached and the rate was set at 10 mills/$1 on all taxable property.

The summer of 1909 was a big one for all King County. The Alaska-Yukon Pacific Exposition was held on the campus of the University of Washington. Upper Duwamish Valley dwellers flocked to the fair. Boxer Fred Nord, who was to move to Tukwila in 1911 with his bride Ellen, placed second in the Golden Gloves Tournament.

Joel Shomaker found the fair very exciting and visited several times. One day he entered the tent of a fortune-teller, who read his life line and informed him that he was to die soon. Shomaker believed the prediction and, wanting to live out his final days in the wilderness, he resigned as mayor on October 16, 1909, sold his house in Tukwila to Mr. Schuer, a gold-leaf artist, and moved his family to the Olympic Peninsula.

After Joel Shomaker left Tukwila in October 1909, Councilman John M. Hall filled out Shomaker's term as mayor pro-tem. The founding of the town had been largely Shomaker's idea, and without his presence the municipality felt adrift. However, new leadership emerged and the town struggled to establish itself in fact as well as name.

From the beginning, much of the Tukwila town council's business dealt with roads—building new roads and repairing old ones. In his final summary of the first year's accomplishments, Mayor Shomaker proudly pointed out that several blocks, representing five local improvement districts, had been improved by the erection of good substantial wooden sidewalks. In 1909 one new street was opened and a surface storm drain dug on Main Street. However, when the year's-end reckoning came, the books showed that Shomaker's zeal for improvements had overdrawn the town by $517.

The drain on the town's finances from street and sidewalk work went on for decades. Grading and drainage problems were particularly severe on hillside locations. Stumps had to be blasted out of the streets. Streets were often impassable. Wooden sidewalks had to be replaced and repaired frequently. At first all road work was done with available tools and local teams. Eventually the town purchased new equipment including several two-wheel scrapers and rented a barn for storage.

TUKWILA SCHOOL

In the early years children traveled on the Interurban to attend school either at Foster or at Renton's Old Central. In 1907 the Foster School District decided to hire a teacher and open a school at

"Tukwila for Progress," Mayor Shomaker's seal.

186

TICKET TO TUKWILA, TOWN ON THE HILL—1902-1928

Tukwila Grade School class of 1909 with Mrs. Lamb, teacher. Mayor Joel Shomaker donated a school site on the northwest corner of Main St. and Tukwila Ave. In 1910 the Foster District built a community elementary school. Courtesy Maxine Anderson.

"Tuckwilla." Joel Shomaker offered a corner of his property as a temporary school site and a portable school building was put on the northwest corner of Main Street (58 Ave. S.) and Tukwila Ave. (S. 144 St.) This building subsequently became a home and was moved to 14488 58 Ave. S., where it remains, in good condition.

In 1910 the Foster District paid John M. Hall $850 for four lots for a school site on Tukwila Ave., later the site of the Tukwila Volunteer Fire Station. Initially it was a one-room school, where grades one through four were taught by the first teacher, Mrs. Lamb. The next year a second room was added onto the little building and the site was improved by walks, grading and fences. In 1910 there were about 30 students. Eventually grades one through six were taught, with Mr. Dimmitt as principal.

THE POPULATION IN 1910

The federal census for 1910 reported 412 residents, with essentially equal numbers of adult men and women (adults defined as those 15 and over). Tukwila was a community of young people, with 44 percent of the population being between 15 and 40 years old and another 23 percent being under age 14. In short, only one out of every three people was over age 40. The majority of the children were born in Washington, with only 10 percent being foreign born.

Tukwila had noticeably fewer immigrants than communities located on the river bottom, and only one person out of five was foreign born. Fifty-three percent of the foreign-born were from Northern Europe, with two out of three immigrants being from Sweden. Other countries of origin, in order of largest representation, were England, Canada, Germany and Scotland. While most of the people were not foreign born, three out of four were second-generation American, i.e., at least one parent was foreign born. Putting first- and second-generation Americans together shows that four out of five people in the community had direct immigrant ties.

Almost all of the U.S.-born adults had come to Puget Sound from other states, with one in three hailing from a Midwestern state; Wisconsin, Minnesota and Illinois are the most frequently listed states of origin. An additional interesting characteristic of the population suggested by the 1910 voter registration is that 40 percent of the males qualified to vote had been in Washington a decade or longer.

While most of the women reported that they were homemakers, most of the men reported they made their living in nonfarming occupations, reflecting the suburban quality of life even at this early-twentieth-century date. Two out of five men were in skilled occupations, with carpentry leading the list. Other trades in the community included tailor, jeweler, barber, shoemaker, cook and florist. There were three blacksmiths. Many of the men were skilled in the building construction trades that were in high demand because of the regional building boom— for example, mason, tilesetter, paperhanger and painter. Only 12 percent gave farming as their livelihood, while 15 percent were unskilled laborers. A number of the farmers specialized in table crops including mushrooms, fruit and poultry.

The community's largest business that served the region was William A. McIntyre & Sons, Building Contractors. McIntyre operated his business with sons Arthur B., George E. and Benjamin N., all of whom made their homes in Tukwila and maintained the company office at W. A.'s home. The building boom in the Duwamish Valley and Seattle kept the McIntyre men out at construction sites in all seasons.

THE COUNTY VILLAGE, 1910-1920

Town officials in 1910 were Ernest W. Engel, mayor, and councilmen Northrup, Wold, Johnson and Wilson. When Engel was elected, some newspapers reported that a socialist had taken over the town's government. However, Engel was an avowed Populist and not a Socialist, as some have thought. In this period it was common to label candidates from the People's Party, which was Engel's party, as Socialists, with the hope of casting a shadow over their Populist platforms.

The Tukwila that Engel oversaw was basically a rural place, and the issues brought up to the town council often focused on removing the thistles and brush in the streets and the problem of cows roaming at large through the town. The controversy over cows was settled by allowing the animals to run free at night, but forbidding this from 6 a.m. and 8 p.m. A nonconforming animal would be impounded by Town Marshal Lutz, and its owner could repossess it only upon paying for the feed Bessie had consumed while incarcerated at Lutz's.

In August 1911 Engel resigned as mayor for unknown reasons, and Councilman Miller filled out the term. Officials elected for 1912 were Jacob Guntert, mayor, and councilmen Eugene Lutz, D. A. Williams, Eugene Sandahl, J. R. Gilliland and Edwin F. Doty.

The new town officers faced a community demanding street lighting. Since 1910 citizens' petitions had been regularly presented to the town council requesting this lighting. Finally, disgusted with delays, in 1912 the Ladies Improvement Club offered to assist the Town Council in building street lighting and a mass meeting was held to discuss the issue. Because of the cost of installing electric lights, it was agreed to settle for a few kerosene street lamps as a practical temporary solution. This was done and discussion of an electrical system continued. As another economy it was decided that the King County jail would serve very nicely as Tukwila's official jail for the time being.

Looking south from approximately the south end of Foster Golf Course, ca. 1915. In view are several Tukwila store buildings, the Tukwila Interurban station and a freight shed. Note the long wooden stairway up the hill to the right of the power line poles. Courtesy Warren Wing.

TICKET TO TUKWILA, TOWN ON THE HILL—1902-1928

FOSTER NO. 1 COAL MINE IN TUKWILA AND THE TUKWILA QUARRY

The first coal deposits in King County were discovered in the area of the Black River in 1853 by Dr. M. Bigelow and Luther Collins. In 1873 Eramus Smithers discovered good-quality coal on his land on the Black River, and coal mining became a major factor in the regional economy for the next 40 years.

In 1901 the Seattle Electric Company developed a drift of coal that began from an outcropping at the base of the hill south of and parallel to 56 Ave. S., naming it the Foster No. 1 Coal Mine. In 1905 an Interurban siding was built at Foster where cars were loaded with coal. The 6-by-8 foot mine opening led to a coal bed approximately five feet thick. The coal was found to be mixed with "bone," which in fact, was realgar (arsenic sulfide), which produced arsenic gas when burned. Hand sorting the coal to clean out the "bone" proved to be too costly, and the mine was abandoned after about 800 feet of slope had been developed.

In 1910 Eric Peterson leased the mine from Seattle Electric and resumed mining activities, extending the drift another 400 feet. Only about 410 tons was mined and sold locally for about $5 per ton. The coal had very high ash content and while it burned with a hot flame, it tended to form clinkers, so it could not be used commercially, and the mine was closed in 1916. Between 1932 and 1935 the mine was operated by the Foster Coal Company. During these three years 824 tons of coal were removed from the mine, which consisted of three underground water-level prospects. The mine was reportedly abandoned because the inflow of water into workings became
too rapid.

In 1990 the City of Tukwila ordered a careful investigation of the remains of the Foster mine. Field reconnaissance and discussions with long-term residents suggested that the hillside below 56 Ave. S., and the properties between 55 and 56 Ave. S., should be examined before new or re-development of this historic mine is attempted.

About ten years after the Foster Mine was opened, rock began to be quarried from a location on the side of Tukwila Hill west of Interurban Avenue and below Main Street (S. 144 St.). The quarry was worked fairly regularly for the next 30 years. For years the county drew on the Tukwila Quarry for rock. The quarry was deemed a hazard in the 1940s and eventually closed permanently.

THE LADIES IMPROVEMENT CLUB

Shortly after the incorporation of Tukwila two improvement clubs formed. The men organized as the Tukwila Improvement Association, headed up by W. H. Webster, president, and John M. Hall, secretary-treasurer. The women formed their own organization—the Tukwila Ladies Improvement Club, with Agnes M. Hall, president, and Minnie Lutz, secretary-treasurer.

From the historical record it is clear that the Ladies Improvement Club was the more active of the two clubs in actually improving the quality of life in the community. After the Holly Day observance in 1909 the men's group does not come up in the historical record. In contrast, from 1910 on the women appeared regularly at town council meetings proposing improvements, offering to take over projects that were floundering, and buying land, needed buildings and equipment for the town. For example, after moving the street-light issue from discussion to actual installation of temporary kerosene lights the women pushed on, and when the 25-pole electrical system was installed in 1916, a good deal of the credit goes to the women's work in raising the needed money. They solicited local cash contributions and convinced the County Welfare League and others outside the community to donate money to the municipal cause.

The club developed and maintained Tukwila's first park from 1909 to the closing of the Interurban in 1928, in the area between the Tukwila Interurban station and the river. In 1912 the club sponsored its first dance in Hull's Hall. From that time on, the club was the focal point of community social activities, with dances, box socials, potluck dinners, theatricals, card parties and children's parties being regularly scheduled throughout the year. Ben

TUKWILA—COMMUNITY AT THE CROSSROADS

Kassner played the fiddle for dances. William Fouty was on hand every Saturday night to call the square dances—it is said that he could call all night without repeating a set.

Tukwila was still a very natural place, Walt Kassner remembers, with the backwoods "full of rabbits, quail, ducks and pheasants, and the Duwamish and Black rivers full of salmon and other tasty fish." Around 1915 a herder moved into the community with about 50 goats which he grazed north of the area that became Tukwila Park. During the night a black bear came into the camp and killed several goats. The herder dispatched the bear with his rifle. This is the last time a bear was seen in the community.

Pacific Highway accident. By 1918 there were enough automobiles driving down the new Seattle-Tacoma Road, built in 1916, to warrant regulation, and the town council set the speed limit at 12 mph. Tukwila hired a motorcycle patrolman in August to enforce the Tukwila Reckless Driving Ordinance, and by December about $1,000 had been collected from speeders on Pacific Highway—and this with a motorcycle without a speedometer! Tukwila street improvements were funded by these fines. Courtesy King County Public Works Dept.

HARD TIMES AND BOUNCING BACK

s John Hall took the reins as mayor in 1913, Tukwila was in a crisis. The streets were in great need of repair—actually impassable in places—and the municipality was broke. Ernest Engel Jr. and a Mr. Quivist loaned the town $100 to grade and improve Tukwila Ave. Later that year a petition for disincorporation was tendered for the first—but not the last—time. A check of the signatures on the petition revealed an insufficient number to be valid.

The election of 1915 in Tukwila brought some surprises. A publisher, Stephen H. Stevens, was elected mayor and three women received votes for council positions, Etta Frost, Tessie Henke and Mary Kline. Undoubtedly, their effective work for the community through the Ladies Improvement Club had brought attention to their leadership abilities. A new Tukwila weekly, the *South End News*, put out by editor-publisher Robey G. Banta, became the town's official newspaper until it folded in 1918. Under Mayor Stevens' able leadership, the town achieved stability.

Tukwila began to complete some improvements. In addition to the Ladies Improvement Club park down by Tukwila station, Puget Sound Traction, Light and Power Company was granted a five-year contract to install and maintain 25 street lights. Pacific Telephone & Telegraph extended their system into Tukwila and many homes put in telephones. A city dump was developed, and the Main Street Viaduct, funded partially with assessments to abutting property owners, was installed.

THE FIRST PACIFIC HIGHWAY, 1916

ith pride Tukwila was looking forward to the completion of the new Pacific Highway linking Seattle and

TICKET TO TUKWILA, TOWN ON THE HILL—1902-1928

JUDGE DURBIN

Joseph L. Durbin came to Seattle around 1900. A watchmaker by training, Durbin was young and adventurous and looking for a more exciting job. He found it with the Pinkerton Detective Agency in Seattle, where he met W. J. Fouty. In 1904 both Durbin and the Foutys moved to Garden Station. Durbin supported the formation of the municipality and soon was closely involved with the town management, working first as a part-time deputy marshal in 1914 and then as Tukwila Superintendent of Lights and Police Justice in 1915. In the coming decades Durbin was continuously involved with the town government, holding various jobs including town magistrate, police justice and justice of the peace.

Soon Durbin was well established as Tukwila's justice, and he became known to everyone as Judge Durbin. Serving as the Tukwila Justice of the Peace almost to the time of his death at age 91, Durbin went on record as the oldest living active justice in the United States at the time. As a community elder Judge Durbin was regarded with affection and respect for his age and long service. People chuckled over his antics, such as stopping traffic on Interurban Ave. with a shake of his cane so that he might cross.

Tacoma. The section through the town was called Interurban Ave. The highway immediately became the major north-south road in western Washington, and put Tukwila and all the valley communities at the hub of activity. However, a major battle ensued between Tukwila and the King County Commissioners over the paving of Pacific Highway. Mayor Stevens claimed that in 1915 the Board of Commissioners had promised that the section of the highway that passed through Tukwila was to be paved with first-quality brick and not concrete, as the Commissioners seemed determined to use. Mayor Stevens obtained a temporary restraining order, asking the County Commissioners to show cause why a permanent injunction should not be issued. The stretch of road was Interurban Ave. from Riverton to Renton Junction. Tukwila, working together with other interests in the county, won out, and the road was constructed of brick; the stretch up the Duwamish Valley was known for many years as the "Old Brick Seattle-Tacoma Highway."

E. G. Green served as mayor from 1918 through 1923. During this time the town changed its approach to financing improvements and established more revenue-raising systems. The first of these was requiring that all businesses pay a $5 license fee to operate in Tukwila. When the mayor and council realized that the town was out of money in 1918, a mass meeting was held to determine whether the community supported the idea of a bond issue to finance street improvements. After much heated discussion, a $7,000 bond was agreed upon and later passed formal vote.

The beginnings of expanded homeowner services appeared about this time, when the municipality

For decades the Fourth of July was the annual community event. In July 1920 the celebration included the installation of electric lights in Tukwila. The bald man at the second table is the president of PSP&L. Picture was taken at foot of Main St. across from Mr. Foreman's store. L. to r.: Walter Kassner (seated), Ben Kassner, Tessie (Kline) Henke (standing), Franz Henke, Emma Engle Lovejoy, Frank Lovejoy, Gertrude Engle, Mary Kline (seated). Courtesy City of Tukwila.

made its first attempt at public garbage collection. There was no regular service at this point, just a one-day collection; citizens were admonished to "have their garbage ready."

TUKWILA'S CHURCH AND SCHOOL

Tukwila was without a church, and many in the community went over to the Foster Presbyterian Church for Sunday services or to the Riverton Methodist Church. Catholics went to St. Joseph's Mission at Mortimer Station in Foster. In 1918 Rev. Reed of the Foster Church held Sunday services and Sunday School in the Tukwila School until it burned in 1919. In the 1920s and 1930s various church groups met in the community. Around 1929 Nellie Clark of Foster and Mrs. Friberg of Tukwila organized a Christian Science Church group that met regularly in the Community Hall.

Carl and Agnes Gustafson, Swedish immigrants, were active in the Swedish Tabernacle Church (now First Covenant) in Seattle. While they took their three children to church every Sunday, they saw that, lacking a church in the community, many young people were growing up without religious training. Committing themselves to filling this need, the Gustafsons held a Sunday School in their home once a week for neighborhood children, with Agnes Gustafson teaching the Sunday School, writing gospel tracts, playing the guitar and leading the children in singing hymns. In the summer Mrs. Gustafson managed to run a Bible school in her home, in addition to her usual work during this busy season of the year.

On February 24, 1919, the Tukwila School burned. For the next three years school was held at the Presbyterian Church in Foster. During this time of change in the school, the Municipality of Tukwila filed an unsuccessful petition requesting its own school district separate from Foster. In July 1920 Tukwila town council representatives informed the Foster School District what Tukwila wanted in its new school.

Mrs. Grooms, community midwife who came to Tukwila from Canada around 1915, delivered many babies throughout the 1910s and 1920s. Neighborhood children loved Mrs. Grooms, who rewarded them for helping her with saucer-sized sugar cookies, each with a huge raisin in the center. For years she maintained the English tradition of serving tea every afternoon for the immediate neighborhood. Courtesy Alvin Henke.

Hoping that construction costs would drop, the School District delayed building a new school until May 6, 1921, when $10,000 was approved for "a new school at the Tukwila site, with all necessary furniture, apparatus and equipment and improvement of the grounds." The school opened in 1922.

COMMUNITY IMPROVEMENTS

The 1920s began with stability in the government and improved living for the community homeowners. Frank Kline, who had come to Tukwila in 1906 with

Inside Foreman's Tukwila Grocery, 1929. Mr. Foreman, who took over the Tukwila grocery on Interurban Ave. from Hull, had good help from son Bert and daughter Eileen. Courtesy Eileen Winters.

his wife Mary, was a building contractor and laid out most of the town's streets. As a means of cutting municipal expenses, responsibility for repair and maintenance of the wooden sidewalks was placed with the property owners, and the street superintendent set out to notify all recalcitrant citizens of their duty in this regard.

Susanne Minkler McVeigh remembers regarding with childhood wonder the six-foot-wide sidewalks with wooden cleats that ran up the steep sides of the hills. Jim North recalls that during the 1910s and 1920s "Tukwila had the best wooden sidewalks for miles around—this offset the road system which was notoriously bad. For many years the hill roads were one-way streets. Main Street, running up the hill, was the only two-way road." There was a wooden viaduct at the bend of 58 Ave. S. that connected the street with Interurban Ave.

During the dry summer days gutters and drains were installed on Main Street and the street dragged for graveling. By September 1920 the heavy cost of this work had drained the town's coffers, and a six-month $500 bank loan was taken out to meet necessary expenses.

In 1919 those living down on the Tukwila flats—the area around Interurban Ave. and 58 Ave. S.—organized themselves as the Citizens of the Flat District of Tukwila and in the coming years repeatedly brought their needs to the attention of the government. In February 1922, recovering from bad flood damage, citizens of the flats appeared before the town council to discuss their plan to control future flood damage. The self-sufficient group of citizens—mostly farmers—had designed a system built of pipes and fencing reinforced with rocks and brush that they believed would prevent further washing away of their land. They estimated that the project would cost approximately $600, half of which the residents had already raised. Moreover, the residents were prepared to do the construction work themselves, but they wanted the council to contribute an additional $300. Impressed with the group's initiative and determination, the council appropriated the money.

THE LADIES IMPROVEMENT CLUB HALL

In 1921 the Ladies Improvement Club bought a building site on Tukwila flats and soon raised the money to build a neat frame hall in 1924, which immediately became the center for all municipal and social activities including town council meetings, card parties, weddings, political rallies, amateur theatricals and monthly community potluck dinners. Frank Kline planned, supervised and worked alongside community volunteers who built the hall. In the 1920s the highlight of the community's week was the Saturday night dance at the Ladies Improvement Club Hall. Ellen Nord would play the fiddle, with Bernice Larson on the piano. Ellen and husband Fred loved to dance and were at a dance almost every Saturday night—often both playing and dancing. A highlight of the evening would be when John Kline led the group in the Virginia Reel.

Harriet Bergquist Tombs remembers that when she was a teenager her set loved the community hall, for they always had someplace to go Saturday night for very little money. Many of the young couples who courted at the Tukwila Saturday night community dances later enjoyed their wedding dances and receptions at the beloved old hall, and still later silver and golden Wedding anniversary celebrations. For decades Tessie Henke oversaw these and many other community occasions. The old hall was still standing on Interurban Ave. in 1990.

Special dances were held during the year that marked the seasons. In October corn shocks were put in the corners, and red and yellow leaves rustled on the walls. Carved jack-o'-lanterns, their smiles and grimaces waxing and waning from the flickering candle stubs inside, glowed around the entrance to the hall, where inevitably Franz Henke, the town marshal, stood by the door making sure that unwelcome guests did not enter. Some years it was a Harvest Moon Dance, others a Halloween Masquerade with prizes given for the best costumes. The community saw out the old year and welcomed in the new at the annual New Year's Eve Dance, which was a dressy affair.

THE TUKWILA LIBRARY

The Ladies Improvement Club was very interested in making books available to the community and succeeded in building a public library in the 1920s. The driving force behind this important community institution was Ramona Scott Minkler. Ramona Scott, a professor of literature who taught at Bradley University in Peoria, Illinois, came to Seattle around 1920, where she met and married Clifford Minkler. They both wanted to live in the country and moved to Tukwila in 1922. As a part of her advanced higher education, Ramona Scott had acquired a large private library which she brought with her. Her collection included complete sets of Shakespeare, Charles Dickens and other classics. Eventually she and her mother, Mae Scott, a high school teacher, gave their personal libraries to the Ladies Improvement Club to be used for a public library.

The women of the club raised money and added more books including popular young people's literature such as *The Bobbsey Twins*, *The Rover Boys*, Louisa May Alcott, Zane Grey adventures and nature books. The Agricultural Dept. *Annual Reports* were acquired for the benefit of the valley farmers. The little building the club built beside the Community Hall was only a few feet wider than the large PUBLIC LIBRARY sign that hung on the front.

Two afternoons a week Sarah Kassner was on hand at Tukwila's Public Library to loan out volumes to book lovers from up and down the valley, as well as Tukwila. The landmark library on Interurban Ave., which became famous as the smallest library in the state, burned down early in the 1930s. Some of the books were salvaged and were available to readers in the Community Hall.

TICKET TO TUKWILA, TOWN ON THE HILL—1902-1928

The Bergquist house at 14455 58 Ave. S., the home of Mayor George C. and Catherine Bergquist, originally a four-room bungalow built in 1900. The Bergquists, like many others, remodeled their house over the years, transforming it to a large stylish house reflecting the tastes of the period. Between 1924 and 1926, a full second floor was added and the living room expanded the entire width of the house. Avid gardeners, the Bergquists designed, cultivated and maintained extensive landscaped grounds and gardens around the house for over a half a century, giving beauty to the street and pleasure to all who passed by the gracious home. Courtesy Patrick Brodin.

POULTRY FARMS AND OTHER ENTERPRISES

Allen Erickson, who came with his parents John and Augusta to Tukwila in 1912, recalls that by the 1920s the dense forest covering the hills had been logged off enough to allow grazing and small farm plots. The valley bottom was all farms. Close to the Ericksons' was the Baker chicken farm, which covered a large tract between 57 Ave. S. and the Tukwila School grounds; Hamlin Myers also farmed. However, farming was mostly confined to operations requiring small acreage. There were two strawberry farmers on Tukwila Hill—Wiederman and Heinz. Rev. Koenig, a minister, had a raspberry farm on the flats, and nearby Mr. Wyzurich raised turkeys and sold them commercially.

With a ready market in Seattle, poultry farms flourished. The Martin Mathiesens, who came in 1928, had over 1,600 chickens some years. Mayor J. P. Walkup raised turkeys. On the south side of the hill Michio and Hisako Kato, Japanese immigrants, raised poultry and sold eggs in Seattle. They also raised vegetables and contracted beans to Libby's canning company, as did many other small-acreage farmers in the area.

Land prices continued to increase. In March 1923 Ben and Gota Anderson came to Tukwila to join Gota's sister Anna Landstrom. The Andersons paid $1,050 for their place, which included more than one-half acre, a house, garage, woodshed, chicken house and rabbit hutches. While farms were numerous, the majority of the residents, like Ben Anderson, commuted on the Interurban to Seattle or Renton and worked for wages.

In the 1920s and 1930s the old businesses down on Interurban Ave. changed hands several times. Bert A. Foreman took over Hull's Grocery Store in 1926 and Foreman became the Postmaster, a position he held until 1938. The tradition of a lighted Christmas tree above the Tukwila Post Office began about this time. Next the Carstensons had the store. In the 1950s Roy Rector built a second store with a gas station and frozen food locker next door where a box in the subzero building could be rented for a modest fee. Later Al Heemink, son of German immigrants, took over the business. From 1961 to 1980 Jim and Lilly Locke successfully operated the Tukwila Grocery. Locke's parents were pioneers from China in the Olympia area, who had come to Washington in territorial days. The Lockes' store was an important continuing community institution during this difficult period of transition.

When Prohibition came in, Tukwila had its share of bootleggers. The town's location on the

Pacific Highway (Interurban Ave.) made it mighty handy to pull onto a back road to pick up a bottle or two on the way to a party. When Sheriff Matt Starwich or one of his eagle-eyed deputies axed a bootlegger's still, neighbors chuckled over the tipsy ducks and geese that wandered through their yards.

Town Government in the 1920s

In the early years of the 1920s there was growing dissatisfaction among the community residents with the municipality. There was the constant cost of maintaining the streets, to say nothing of trying to build new ones. Moreover, people living in an incorporated area expected improvements such as functioning sewers, street lighting, public water supply, police protection, and help with flood damage. There was widespread frustration with the interminable delays in getting things done and the recurrent "bankruptcy" of the town.

E. G. Green, who was mayor in 1923, managed to get all of the street repairs required by the heavy rains that year completed by September. In addition, the long-awaited concrete sidewalk on Interurban Ave. was finished after two years of delays. However, these improvements were not enough to quell the disgruntled citizens. Perhaps the "last straw" was the 1924 spring flooding that once again was cutting into the bank near Second Ave., requiring the town to spend its last dollars hauling rock to the site in an attempt to reduce the damage. On June 12, 1924, a "Petition to Disincorporate" was presented to the town council.

Petitioners were convinced that dissolving the municipality and functioning as a community in unincorporated King County would reduce their taxes. They were also against the bond issues that the town was floating to pay for improvements. Tukwila had long been rife with political factions, and some claimed that antagonism between the pro and con disincorporation forces was so great that neighbors on opposing sides did not speak to one another. A signature check proved the petition legal. The formalities required for disincorporation were taken care of over the summer, and the issue was placed before the voters on the November ballot. Disincorporation was defeated and the Town of Tukwila stayed on the map.

G. C. Bergquist held the reins of government as mayor from 1925 to 1927. Under Bergquist's energetic leadership Tukwila tackled its old problems of street maintenance and paying for improvements. In an attempt to check speeding on the highway, signs were placed at each end of town announcing the speed limit. Mayor Bergquist was determined to bring a public water system to Tukwila and worked tirelessly to achieve this goal by writing letters, attending dozens of meetings with Seattle officials and talking personally with Seattle's Mayor Brown about Tukwila's tapping into the Seattle water system after the completion of the Lake Youngs project. During this time two of Bergquist's next-door neighbors lost their homes to fire. He responded to these tragedies with renewed determination to establish a municipal water system with sufficient pressure to support fire fighting. Noted for his conscientiousness, one night Bergquist caught the engineer whom the Town had hired to drill a well pouring water into a dry shaft.

Bergquist was not to have the satisfaction of seeing the water flowing into the homes while he was still mayor, but as a result of his efforts and those of his successor J. R. Walkup, Tukwila had its water system by the end of the 1920s. The valuation of Tukwila at the end of Bergquist's second term was $188,900, the highest on record. However, in the coming years the town's valuation would drop until the late 1940s. Under Bergquist Tukwila began a period of stabilization that was cemented by its next two mayors, John R. Walkup and John P. Walkup.

TICKET TO TUKWILA, TOWN ON THE HILL—1902-1928

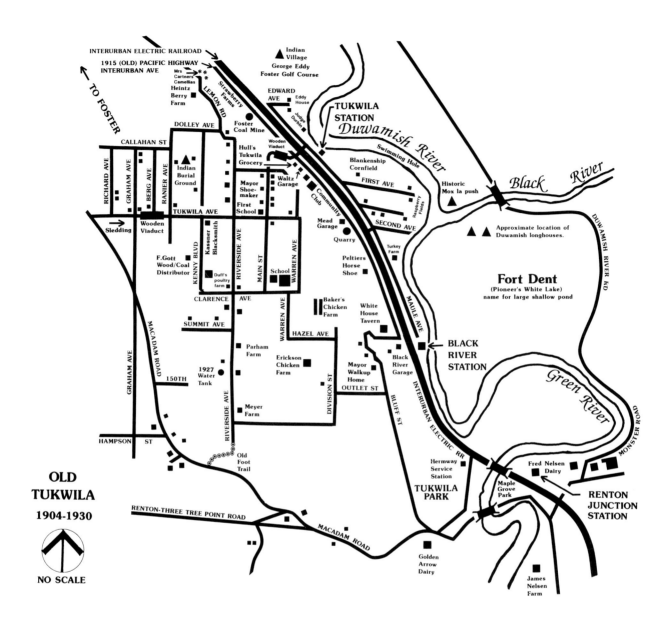

Map by Patrick Brodin with assistance from Elsie Rinehart, Freda Leahy and Kay Reinartz. Drawn by Sharon Dibble.

CHAPTER 12
TUKWILA, CROSSROADS OF COMMERCE 1928-1990

The Tukwila School, built in 1922 at 14475 59 Ave. S., was used as City Hall from 1947 to 1978. Recently the building has served as the Tukwila Library. In 1979 this historic school building was added to the National Register of Historic Places. L. M. Dimmit, Foster School District Superintendent, is on the steps of the school. Courtesy South Central School District.

In 1928 John R. Walkup became mayor—an office he held for five years. His son John P. Walkup then held the mayor's post until 1946. The Walkups maintained continuity in government and brought stability and long-term planning to the municipality. These elements had been missing from the beginning with leadership changing frequently.

The Tukwila that Mayor J. R. Walkup took charge of was not a pretty place. Council minutes for this period mention willows, thistles and other brush growing in the streets. Vandalism, the breaking of windows and other property damage, comes up as an issue, as does some residents' habit of regularly throwing garbage and refuse in the streets. In the spring of 1928 it was discussed at council meeting that "a rumor is afloat that certain citizens wished to bring up the matter of disincorporation again."

Led by the outspoken Hiram Blankenship, who appeared everywhere with his pet monkey on his shoulder, the disincorporation faction reiterated that the community would be better off as a part of unincorporated King County. Disincorporation would reduce taxes. Once again complaints focused on the cost of improvements and bond issues, which they maintained did not sufficiently benefit the town to justify the cost. They angrily pointed to the planned water system that allegedly was to cost the town $43,000. It was felt that the municipal budget of $1,265 for 1928 was too high.

Undaunted, the mayor and council, committed to the best interests of the town, forged on. Walkup tackled the need to reunite the community with dedicated zeal. In keeping with his years of experience as a Populist and labor organizer, Walkup visited his constituency, walking from house to house and talking to the citizens in their living rooms and kitchens about community issues.

Determined to get the public water system initiated by Mayor Bergquist flowing, Mayor Walkup negotiated with Seattle for access to Cedar River water. In July, $14,000 in general negotiable coupon bonds of the City of Tukwila were provided for by ordinance. Finally, in November 1928 Tukwila was granted its water franchise, pipes were laid and a water storage tank was built at the south end of 57 Ave. S. The water system was completed. Collecting the water bills was put in the hands of the city clerk.

Homemakers all over Tukwila turned on their spigots and filled the tea kettle—without going to the back-yard pump. This was a major improvement! There were indeed advantages to living in the incorporated municipality. Emeline Gott, who had hauled thousands of gallons of water over the years caring for her 13 children and the Gott orphanage, had vowed that if Tukwila ever actually got a public water system she would let the faucet run all day; and she did. The disincorporation forces were silent.

Within the year the nearby unincorporated communities of Foster and Thorndyke requested access to the Tukwila system. Eleven years later the Foster and Thorndyke hookups were in effect.

THE DEPRESSION YEARS

Tukwila experienced the hardships of the Great Depression along with the rest of America. Acknowledging the dire straits of many, in November 1930 the town council voted that needy residents in the community be allowed to cut wood found growing on unimproved streets, for personal use only.

The stress of the national economic collapse was intensified for those living in the upper Duwamish Valley by a rash of midnight fires that, without a local fire-fighting force, burned freely until the buildings were reduced to a heap of smoldering ashes. The typical fire broke out at night during the winter months. Word of the fire spread rapidly on the party line telephone system and the community, filled with horror, flocked to the fire and attempted to control its spread with garden hoses. The homeless family was taken in by neighbors, and for weeks many in the community did not sleep well from apprehension of the midnight fire call. Many people who lost their homes this way

The Tukwila municipal water tank, built in 1928 at 57 Ave. S., was a part of the new public water system. The old landmark was torn down in the 1950s. Courtesy Washington State Archives.

lived in tents for months or even years until they could afford to rebuild.

Between 1930 and 1934 the Tukwila Public Library, the shoe repair shop next to the Tukwila grocery store, and a half dozen homes along the valley road all burned. It was soon concluded that the fires were the work of an arsonist, but in spite of the men of the community taking turns at night watching, the firebug was never caught. The fires were not confined to Tukwila but included the neighboring valley communities of Foster, Duwamish-Allentown, Quarry and Riverton. A positive benefit emerged from these Depression fires: the formation of the various community volunteer fire departments.

The community pulled together during the Depression, with children's clothing being routinely passed around. Mothers developed

TUKWILA QUILTING CLUB

The Tukwila Quilting Club was formed early in the Depression by Bess Neil as a way for members to socialize while helping others, with a minimum outlay of cash during hard times. Meeting in each other's homes once a month, members donated scraps from their sewing baskets to make quilt tops, and purchased material for backs and cotton bats to fill the quilts. The club made popular patterns including double wedding rings, flower basket, Texas star, broken windmill, nine blocks and others.

Soon after its formation, the club members agreed to dedicate their skill to making gift quilts for newlyweds to help them get started in life. Each bride who was raised in Tukwila received a quilted covering and each Tukwila groom a tied quilt. If she looked carefully, a young bride might find a scrap of the material her mother had used to make her last dress. A beautiful baby quilt was given to the firstborn child of each couple in Tukwila, including newcomers.

In a short time the women developed a systematic approach to each quilting project including selecting the pattern, cutting the pieces and piecing the quilt top. The quilt was set up on a frame at a member's home and the sewers dropped by to work whenever they had a few hours to spare. As well as expert seamstresses, the women were excellent cooks and often shared a potluck lunch. A generation of children remember hurrying home after school hoping to find leftovers. Quilting was done in the fall and winter months when the women were not busy gardening and canning.

Membership in the Quilting Club dwindled to five women and it was disbanded in 1966 with the last quilt made to commemorate Tukwila's 50th Anniversary. While most of these sewing women had died by 1990, working together making quilts for the community is a significant symbol and expression of their community spirit, and caring for their friends and neighbors. The Quilting Club provided the skilled homemakers of Old Tukwila with a focal point for their social lives, and an opportunity to express their artistic and creative impulses. They left the community rich memories of the period when Tukwila was a small, rural, close-knit, mutually supportive community. Lucky are those who received one of the women's quilts—a gift of love from nimble fingers.

The Tukwila Quilting Club members spent many hours around the quilting frame socializing and making tiny, even stitches and gifts of love from the scraps of many sewing baskets. L. to r.: Emma Walkup, Emeline Gott, Mrs. Knudsen, Mrs. S. H. Stevens, unknown, Ura Brewer, unknown, Alpha Klein, Mrs. Bess Neil, Lelah Stevens, Mrs. Charnell, Mrs. Bates, Jan Knudson, Leonard Klein and Barbara Klein. Courtesy Freda Leahy.

skill in "turning coats" and remaking adult clothing for young people. Those who had cars stopped driving them—no money for tires or gas. Men worked together repairing the houses and community buildings using whatever materials they could find. Family groups expanded as relatives out of work moved in. In most homes at least one or two people had some kind of work, and the others raised food in the garden and took care of the cow and chickens. Teenagers lucky enough to have work gave all of their earnings to their parents to help support the family.

Looking back, many people remember the Depression with good feelings because it was a time when people worked together. Many remember happy family and community gatherings playing cards and board games, eating popcorn and homemade fudge. Sunday picnics at People's Park at Renton Junction or Angle Lake were potluck dinners with lots of dishes made of fresh garden produce. People remember being happy and optimistic as everyone "was in the same boat."

Politics in the 1930s

1932 began with a focus on school needs. As a result of petitions from councilmen Walkup, Fredrickson and Thies, the Foster School District board restored the sixth grade to the Tukwila School.

In October 1932 a petition with 142 signatures was presented by citizens to the town council calling for a special election for the purpose of disincorporation. This was a large percentage of the population—things looked bad for Tukwila. However, only 95 of the signatures proved to be valid. This drastic move had been prompted by the terrible conditions of the streets and the inability of the town to keep things up before they went broke again. Many citizens were convinced that they would be better off under the jurisdiction of King County.

It was Depression time and the town struggled on. The Tukwila Ave. viaduct was condemned and dismantled. The town still had a problem with domestic animals, cows, horses and goats as well as dogs running about freely, and yet one more ordinance was passed strictly forbidding this nuisance. Another nuisance that was forbidden was "children coasting on Main Street." Just a couple of years earlier two children had had a close call when their sled collided with an automobile driven by the county deputy sheriff on Interurban Ave. The town council was alerted of gambling activities in the community and quickly passed regulations controlling slot machines and gambling devices. On the other hand, pinball machines and games of skill were licensable.

At the end of 1932 John R. Walkup stepped down as mayor and his son John P. Walkup became the mayor. John P. appointed his father as the city clerk. Land was acquired for Tukwila's official public park, which came to be known as Tukwila Park. Progressive minded, J. P. Walkup brought Tukwila into the Association of Washington Cities, a significant organization formed to assure that Washington cities got their fair share of gas tax, beer licenses and other revenue-sharing taxes. The town council began considering reducing the water rates.

> ### Foster Golf Course
>
> Located on the original Joseph and Martha Foster homestead, the Foster Golf Course occupies a significant historic site in the Duwamish Valley. The large maple tree at the north end was planted by Joseph Foster near his cabin around 1865. Foster's maple tree is highly valued as a legacy from the Duwamish Valley's foremost territorial days citizen and a commemorative plaque rests on the tree. When the Foster family sold the property in 1925, the deed contained the condition that the Duwamish native people were guaranteed a perpetual right to cross the land to fish and get water from the river.
>
> George Eddy opened the Foster Golf Course on February 13, 1925, with nine holes, later expanded to 18 holes. In 1940 son Robert W. Eddy took over and operated the course until 1950. Joe Aliment, who had caddied at Foster Links since 1925, bought the course on January 1, 1951, with his wife Hazel. The couple operated the course and continuously improved it until they sold it to the City of Tukwila in May 1978. It was the Aliments' desire that the site always remain a golf course. The Aliments were outstanding members of the community, known for their generosity toward the town's young people and community at large.

Growing Up in the 1920s and 1930s

Most children only occasionally had a few pennies or a nickel in their pockets. Parents expected their children to work in and around the home without receiving any kind of money for their work—which was often quite substantial. However, these traditions motivated many enterprising children to earn their own money. Among the most common work for young people was picking berries at "Old Man Wiederman's" and Heinz's strawberry farms on the hill. The children went over to pick for Mr. McDonald with a mixture of fear

Stanley Gustafson, 17, earned money the summer of 1938 cutting, splitting and delivering firewood, $2/cord. Young people looked hard for jobs and were glad to get a start someplace. Courtesy Stanley Gustafson.

and curiosity, since McDonald claimed that he was an old-time trapper and dressed the part. Koenigs, who had a raspberry farm down on the flats, between the Interurban station and the river, paid school children 35 cents a crate with a bonus of a nickel a crate if they finished out the season. Koenigs, like many others, sold their produce at the Pike Place Public Market. Older children walked five to seven miles down into the Kent Valley to pick peas and beans for the vegetable farmers.

While there was work aplenty, most mothers saw that the young ones also had time to play. Swimming was about the most popular summer activity, with the favorite "swimming hole" for Tukwila youth being at the back of the Blankenship place across from the golf course. Diving for golf balls around the Foster Golf Course occupied the Tukwila youth, as it did all the children in the valley. Often Helen Cumming would go with the Tukwila children to watch over them. Her son Bill would take pad and pencil and sit on the riverbank sketching. Energetic young people would walk to Angle Lake or even Seward Park in Seattle to swim. Tragedies occasionally occurred, such as when ten-year-old Richard Gilbert drowned while playing with companions in the river around 1926.

Every season had its special fun for the children. Halloween brought out the mischievous spirit, and November 1 always found many soaped and waxed windows, log-barricaded streets, and outhouses pushed over or put someplace unusual, such as on the roof of a shed. When winter brought snow, it was sledding from the top of Tukwila Ave. and Main St. It was a thrilling ride with telephone poles whizzing by on one side of the narrow sidewalk and barbed-wire fences on the other; a sharp turn down the hill at Main Street and then over the wooden overpass and across Interurban Ave., coming to a stop before the third rail was reached.

WPA FOR TUKWILA PROGRESS

Every year the City of Tukwila had a longer list of projects and improvements than it had resources to meet. In 1935 the Washington Works Progress Administration (WPA) came like the answer to Mayor Shomaker's prayer to achieve PROGRESS, and stayed enough years to substantially improve the town. Some of Shomaker's dearest dreams were fulfilled—the completion of the community park, major improvement of all the streets, construction of concrete sidewalks, and modern street lighting throughout the community.

TUKWILA, CROSSROADS OF COMMERCE—1928-1990

EMELINE AND FORREST GOTT COMMUNITY LEADERS

The Gotts loved children, and in addition to their own 13, they established a Foundlings Home, where they cared for orphans from 1911 into the 1930s. In addition, they always had time to take community children on outings. Forrest Gott was in the fuel business, and provided wood and coal for most people in the upper Duwamish Valley during the 1920s and 1930s. Many times a month Mr. Gott filled the back of his truck with children from all the valley communities, taking them to ball games, swimming at the Y.M.C.A. in Seattle, school picnics at the Woodland Park Zoo in Seattle, and camping at Echo Lake. The Gotts were active in the Foster-Tukwila Presbyterian and the Riverton Heights Presbyterian churches. Emeline cooked daily for 15 to 25 people, serving her tasty meals on a long table in the Gott kitchen. She was also served as president of the PTA for many years and was active in Ladies Aid, Quilting Club and Mothers Club.

Every September the Gotts drove up and down the valley collecting children standing by the side of the road clutching sacks of lunch and jackets, and headed for the Puyallup Fair, where they stayed until dark. Mrs. Gott always took a shopping bag filled with sandwiches, cookies and fruit for the youngsters who forgot their lunches or got "extra hungry." Most of the children slept all the way back home and Mr. Gott lifted the drowsy children down from the truck bed to their waiting parents. For weeks to come the children's heads were full of the wonders of the fair and the thrill of the midway rides.

Forrest and Emeline Gott. Courtesy Frances Gott Hopper.

To assist in the WPA work, the town bought a Chevrolet dump truck for hauling gravel and dirt.

In 1938 a number of changes took place in Tukwila. Lois Newton, the town treasurer, kept the town's financial records in her living room desk. She issued and recorded payment of water bills, kept in a coffee can. The bills were delivered by her daughter Florence. In 1938 the Tukwila School was closed and the town council bought the building for $100 to use as Tukwila's first official City Hall.

The Tukwila Post Office was a 4-by-6 foot area in Foreman's store, as it had been since 1926, with 60 rental mail boxes and barely enough room to turn around. In 1938 Helen Walkup became the Tukwila Postmaster. She found a larger space in Roy Rector's store next door at 14211 Interurban Ave. S., and moved the Post Office to that location where she added rental boxes. The Post Office remained at this location until a large office was opened in Southcenter in 1965. At this time Walkup retired, and because it was a third-class post office, mail was delivered in the community.

THE TUKWILA COMMUNITY CLUB

fter many years of building the community and maintaining a central focus for community social and cultural life, the Ladies Improvement Club slowly began to fade. By 1937 membership had declined and financial difficulties raised concern about the future of the land and the club's Interurban Ave. building.

Under Tessie Henke's able leadership a reorganization effort was successful. The club now became known as the Tukwila Community Club and, like the original club, it played an influential role in local government. In the 1940s and '50s the club exerted a strong political influence at the local and county levels. The weekly meetings were attended by the mayor, who gave a report on the town council actions. In order to keep close touch with the town council, the community club appointed members to represent their interests at council meetings. The club communicated its regional concerns in the form of resolutions sent to the South End Associated Clubs, which was highly influential with county and state government.

In the next three decades the club was involved with and charted the course of many issues affecting the town, including flood control on the Duwamish and Green rivers, WPA projects, animal control, Lake Sammamish State Park development and April Clean-Up Day. Each decade the Tukwila Community Club supported many community improvement projects including the illumination of 58 Ave. S., speed control on Interurban Ave., and water and sewer system improvements.

One of the most significant achievements of this citizens' action organization was the realization of an effective fire-fighting system that included fire hydrants placed throughout the community and a trained volunteer fire department. The Volunteer Fire Department significantly reduced fire insurance rates in Tukwila.

Once again the Community Hall on Interurban Ave. hummed with activities, including dances, card parties, potluck suppers and luncheons. By the late 1940s the club boasted a membership of 130, in a town with a total population of 400. In the 1950s the community received a private library of 1,000 volumes from the estate of Mr. Yoder, and the Community Club reopened the Tukwila Public Library.

Over the years the club helped the schools and youth by contributing uniforms to the Foster High School basketball and baseball teams, sponsoring a Brownie troop and helping clean up Tukwila Park, where playground equipment was placed for the children. In addition, the members also took a keen interest in the status of their fellow townspeople, and families and individuals in times of need received money or goods to tide them over.

The Tukwila Community Club—as both the early Ladies Improvement Club and the reorganized club—was among the most significant cultural and social forces in the community, showing committed long-term leadership, continuity over the decades and achievement of goals for the community's growth. During the 1970s the club began to decline, a trend that continued through the 1980s until the club was basically inactive. However, interest exists in saving the building and reviving the club as a community focal point for residents to participate in local government.

In 1934 a WPA work force improved Tukwila Park by building a tennis court, four log cabins, a wood storage shed, an outhouse, and a large cook house with a sink, tables and a large wood-burning stove. Three of the cabins burned down in the 1950s and were not rebuilt. The original gazebo was rebuilt in September 1986 and continues to be the park's centerpiece. For many years the park was maintained by community volunteer groups such as the Community Club and Boy Scouts. Courtesy Pat Walkup Hopper.

TUKWILA, CROSSROADS OF COMMERCE—1928-1990

TUKWILA'S ARTISTS

In 1937, at age 20, William "Bill" Cumming, born and raised in Tukwila, met Morris Graves, who was working for the Federal Art Project, a WPA effort. Cumming soon became a part of the circle of artists that had been brought together by the WPA, which became known as the Northwest School and was among the most talented of this group. Cumming's impressionistic figurative paintings became well known and sought after by regional and national art collectors. In his book *Sketchbook, A Memoir of the '30s and the Northwest School*, Cumming writes of his growing up in Tukwila, and his life and work. Cumming works hang in major galleries throughout the United States and abroad. Cumming's painting of the old Tukwila School and former City Hall may be seen at City Hall.

About the time that Cumming was finishing Foster High School, another artist was growing up in Tukwila. Don Paulson spent his Tukwila childhood roaming the woods-covered hills and walking along the riverbank, often spending full days fishing and sketching. Paulson was painting watercolor before beginning grade school. A naturalist painter, Paulson possesses unusual sensitivity in his shared relationship with his environment, and a sense of immediacy and intimacy with the Northwest scene. Paulson's works may be seen in the Seattle and Anchorage Art Museums and in many regional private and corporate collections. Paulson painted the scene on the cover of this history book. In addition, he contributed many of the illustrations.

WORLD WAR II

Tukwila and the other Duwamish Valley communities were close to a strategic spot with high potential for enemy bombing during World War II—the Boeing Airplane Plant. Because of this hazardous location, an air raid siren was put on Town Hall and in October of 1942 a resident night watcher moved into the Town Hall for air raid warning. This was discontinued in March 1944. Ben Fouty, community air raid warden, organized volunteer wardens to oversee various districts of the town. The town council purchased $1,500 in War Bonds.

The impact of the war was evident everywhere in the community. In February 1941 the old Riverton School became a USO club for soldiers stationed at Quarry Hill and the Riverton community sponsored dances for servicemen at Delta Lodge. Young women were admonished that it was their "patriotic duty" to attend the dances. In January 1942 the Foster Community Hall was designated the local Civil Defense Office, and in October Dr. Nichols talked to the Civil Defense Medical Corps there. In the fall of 1943 the senior class at Foster School had only six boys remaining, the others having enlisted. Many of the male teachers were drafted or enlisted. Air raid drills were added to fire drill: school bus routes were shortened to save gas, and children walked farther. During the war years many community men and women voluntarily enlisted in the armed forces. Others went to work in war industry, particularly at Boeing as the regular employees left to fight in the war.

Japanese-American families living in Tukwila were sent to Tule Lake internment camp in northern California, where they were detained for three years. Many of their sons and daughters later enlisted in the U.S. military and served throughout the war. Most of the families, such as the Unos, who had come to Tukwila in 1907, the Mich Katos, the Hanadas, the Nobuyamas, and the Mikamis, returned to Tukwila after the war. In some cases their property and belongings were safeguarded by neighbors and trusted friends. In other cases people had simply taken the Japanese-American people's goods without a cent of compensation. With little complaint, the hard-working Japanese-Americans took up the task of reestablishing themselves, in many cases with help from their old friends and neighbors.

The war changed the community. Many gave up the commercial poultry operations or other agricultural livelihoods that they had pursued earlier in favor of jobs at Boeing or other companies. Tukwila experienced growth with the postwar building boom.

TUKWILA—COMMUNITY AT THE CROSSROADS

Tukwila Community Club Hall on Interurban Ave. Built and maintained by the Tukwila Ladies Improvement Club from 1924 to the late 1930s, the hall was inherited by the Tukwila Community Club which emerged from a reorganization of the earlier group. For over a half a century the hall has been the focus of community, social and often political activity. With only occasional use in the 1980s, the old historic hall was deteriorating. Courtesy Washington State Archives.

TUKWILA VOLUNTEER FIRE DEPARTMENT

In June 1944 a committee from the Tukwila Community Club petitioned the town council to provide the citizens with fire protection by forming the Tukwila Volunteer Fire Department. The volunteer department was approved, and five mills were added to the budget in 1945 to buy firefighting equipment.

A fire truck could not be found because of wartime shortages, so in 1945 an ordinary truck was modified for fire fighting. A 1918 American LaFrance fire truck was purchased from Duwamish Fire District No. 1 by the firemen with their own money. The old Tukwila School play shed was converted into a fire station with fire trucks on the first floor, a hose tower at one end and meeting rooms on the second floor. Most of the work was done by the volunteer firemen and the women's support group called the Firemaids, who helped raise the money needed for equipment and construction.

Vic North served as the first Volunteer Fire Chief. Over the 24 years of the volunteer department, many men gave freely of their time and energy to make Tukwila a safer place to live. The fire-fighting force averaged 21 to 28 active volunteers who were young, well trained and good at their jobs. Over the years they saved lives as well as property.

The volunteers practiced fire fighting on

TESSIE KLINE HENKE
TUKWILA COMMUNITY LEADER 1910-1960

Tessie Kline Henke came to Tukwila in 1906 from Chicago with her parents Mary and Frank Kline, Americans of German descent. Tessie, 16 at the time, eventually married Franz Henke, and the couple made their home on 58 Ave. S. with their son Alvin, who still resides in the community in 1990.

Tessie Henke's life and volunteer work in Tukwila is an expression of exceptional community spirit. Tessie dedicated her energy, good humor and organizational skills to the community, and furthered its interests and needs through work with the churches, schools and clubs. A charter member of the Ladies Improvement Club, she guided the club through its reorganization in the late 1930s and served as the treasurer of the Tukwila Community Club for years. During the "down" years she single-handedly maintained the focus and energy of the Community Club.

Tessie Kline Henke. Courtesy Elsie Rinehart.

In addition, she frequently helped people as a concerned and caring neighbor and friend. For more than 40 years she was the social and cultural mainstay of the community. She welcomed newcomers and helped them get acquainted, oversaw weddings, organized showers and celebrations, saw that community traditions were kept. She visited and looked after the elderly and ill, attended all funerals and provided support for the bereaved.

She was a good listener and informally served as counselor for many people. She believed that "there is something good in everyone." She had a ready smile and her sense of humor was contagious and healing. The community honored Tessie at the time of her 71st birthday, February 21, 1961, with a "This is Your Life" program attended by 200 people. With Tessie's death, Tukwila, community and individuals, lost one of the best friends it had ever had.

Wednesday evenings and Sunday afternoons, and worked on maintaining the building and equipment in between. On sunny days or summer evenings these practices sometimes ended with a good old-fashioned water fight—life could not be all work and no play.

The firemen and Firemaids raised a good deal of the money for equipment with carnivals, bingo games, dances and bake sales, since there was very little to spare in the town budget. Soon the Volunteer Fire Department began sponsoring community events, one of the most popular being the annual Easter Egg Hunt in Tukwila Park for the community children. Another eagerly anticipated annual event was "Santa Claus Coming to Town"—in the Tukwila fire truck with sirens screaming. This traditionally occurred the Sunday before Christmas. Each wide-eyed child who turned out to see the fire truck Santa Claus received candy and oranges, and, best of all, a ride on the fire truck. Lucky was the child who stood closest to the bell—he or she got to ring it as they rode through town.

The Tukwila volunteers had mutual aid pacts with the nearby Duwamish, Foster, McMicken Heights and Burien fire departments, thereby assuring the area's residents excellent fire protection. As more funds were available, the firemen were given token payments for each practice and fire they attended, which they signed over to the Fire Department to buy more equipment and supplies. When the old 1918 American LaFrance was sold, many memories went along with it. In 1954 the town purchased a Kenworth fire truck, and a year later a new American LaFrance. This equipment was lost when the fire station burned.

In 1970 the City of Tukwila established a paid professional fire department. With the annexations of 1989 Tukwila's fire service area increased by eight and one-half square miles. To provide the necessary fire protection for this area, the City added 50 full-time firemen. In 1990 the Fire Department headquarters was located at 444 Andover Park East. Three satellite stations are located in Duwamish, Tukwila Hill and Foster.

Aftermath of World War II

In 1947 J. P. Walkup stepped down from the mayor's chair and Charles O. Baker, who was on the town council, became mayor of Tukwila. The next 12 years of the community's life under the inspired and progressive leadership of Mayor Baker were the most critical in its history. The town had become a third-class municipality, allowing it to annex land. Another long-awaited change, which was the key to the enormous growth that was to take place in the following decades, was about to happen: substantial flood control through the construction of the Howard Hanson Dam on the Green River. Joe Aliment, as the representative from Tukwila, joined the Washington Flood Control Committee and participated in the special conference on local participation for the Green River Flood Control Dam Project.

The postwar building boom was on. In 1947, 35 building permits were issued, 22 in 1948, and 27 in 1949. As a result of the new construction, water mains were laid, streets constructed and all the requirements of new residential districts met. The valuation of the town in 1949 was $217,393. This was the highest it had been since 1927.

However, Tukwila was still a small town with 800 residents in 1950. In the 1950s the municipality experienced a decline, as the improvements completed by the WPA were not adequately maintained in many cases. Tukwila somehow seemed out of the mainstream. The bus service on Interurban Ave. had been discontinued, and the closest public transportation was the Greyhound bus on Highway 99. Nora Nunan recalls that from their house, which was located where City Hall is in 1990 (6200 Southcenter Blvd.), they saw the light from only one other house. Their next-door neighbor had a commercial poultry business, and across the road, where Southcenter was built, the Mikamis raised prime vegetables for the Seattle market, and there was a mink farm. Much of the area was marshland where the men of the community went duck hunting in the autumn.

TUKWILA—COMMUNITY AT THE CROSSROADS

THE CITY OF TUKWILA SAVES THE UPPER DUWAMISH VALLEY FROM INDUSTRIALIZATION

In the postwar years Tukwila was destined to become involved in the major issues of King County and Seattle. Unquestionably, one of the most significant accomplishments of the City of Tukwila in the past half century is its halting the Port of Seattle's plan to turn the Duwamish Valley and possibly the Green River Valley as far as Auburn into a heavily industrialized area. This accomplishment has been a benefit not only to valley residents but to the entire region including Seattle. If the Port's plan had gone through in the 1950s—30 years before public recognition of environmental damage issues and controlling legislation—the damage to air, water, and natural flora and fauna would have been enormous and, in many cases, irreversible. The story is a fascinating one and shows how small does not mean without power or the ability to influence history. In winning its battle with the Port of Seattle, Tukwila shaped the history of King County and the region as few municipalities have in their history.

THE PORT OF SEATTLE

Since the early years of the twentieth century Seattle-area boosters had worked to make the city a large, heavily industrialized port city of national recognition. The Port Authority of Seattle was created to carry out much of this task and was highly successful in realizing its goals. By 1938 it had made plans to replace the quiet Duwamish Valley communities from Duwamish-Allentown south to the Tukwila crossroads with heavy industrial development.

In 1948 the Port of Seattle was an extremely large, powerful bureaucracy with a large revenue base that enjoyed the widespread support of business, the City of Seattle, King County and the Washington State Legislature. By developing sites for heavy industry, the Port had created more customers for shipping which, in turn, benefited the Port through shipping fees and allocations of a portion of the property taxes collected by the county. The Port was looking for opportunities to grow.

The Port had powerful allies with whom it had faced and overcome opposition on many of its past projects. Seattle and King County had benefitted from the Port's successes through increased sales and property taxes resulting from an expanded working population. The county assisted the Port with favorable zoning and Seattle helped in other ways. For example, while the Port was preparing to straighten the lower Duwamish, opposition from Georgetown and West Seattle was eliminated by Seattle annexing the communities in 1907.

The Port's scheme for industrialization in the upper Duwamish Valley was strongly sup-

> **MABEL J. HARRIS, CITY TREASURER AND CITY COUNCIL MEMBER**
>
> Mabel "Mae" J. Harris served 28 years as elected official for the City of Tukwila. Born and raised in Winthrop, Minnesota, Harris came to Tukwila in 1947. In September 1962 Mayor John Strander appointed Mae Harris Tukwila City Treasurer. In 1963 she was elected to the office and held it continuously until 1978, when the city adopted the Optional Municipal Code form of government, which abolished the elected treasurer position. Mae recalls that in those days, the greater part of the city budget was spent on streets and roads. There was a terrible cash flow problem. The greatest source of revenue was the real estate property tax. All bills of the City were paid by interest-bearing warrants held by Seattle First National Bank.
> Between 1978 and 1989 Harris served three terms as a member of the Tukwila City Council. Looking back on her nearly three decades in the Tukwila city government, Harris says, "I feel my greatest contribution as a council member of the City was in the field of transportation."

208

TUKWILA, CROSSROADS OF COMMERCE—1928-1990

ported by the Seattle business community and, considering that there were no alternative plans to develop the valley, the Port knew it could count on continued business support. With the city and county behind it, the Port received nearly unanimous support from the State Legislature to levy a property tax paying for the project. With these allies, plus the federal Bonneville Power Authority, which stood to benefit from increased utility sales to heavy industry that development would bring, the Port was virtually unstoppable.

THE PLAN

The Port's plan for the Duwamish Valley was to purchase large sections of land in the upper valley and then dig a new straightened river channel. The seven miles of meandering river would become a three-mile deepened and widened waterway. The abandoned riverbed and lowlands would be filled and sold as sites for heavy industry. Under the most expansive option in the plan, the project would continue up the Green River to Auburn, developing over 3,500 acres of industrial tracts.

As was stated in the 1946 Master Plan, the Port planned to initially create 920 acres of industrial sites on undeveloped valley land, "with an additional possibility of 200 acres, if and when industrialization of the area makes present rural communities on the river bottom undesirable for residential purposes."

Clearly the desires and interests of the residents of the small Duwamish Valley communities—North Riverton, Duwamish-Allentown, Foster, Riverton, Renton Junction and Tukwila—were of no concern to Seattle. Their lives, their homes, churches, schools and community life were not an issue. They were merely an obstacle. Just like the tiny community of Oxbow, which was erased from the map in 1914 when the lower Duwamish was straightened, the small river communities in the upper valley were destined to vanish.

HISTORY OF THE INDUSTRIALIZATION PLAN

The straightening of the lower part of the river between 1912 and 1917 had created four and one-half miles of excellent waterway serving a sizable industrial area, and this success stirred interest in the rest of the river. In 1943 the Bonneville Power Administration's "Western Washington Industrial Survey" discussed potential sites for industry near Seattle and said:

> When needed, it is expected that the Duwamish Valley for about three miles between the present head of the waterway…and Renton Junction will be developed for industrial purposes. At the present time the valley is cut up by the winding river, but plans are in an advanced stage for straightening the channel and dredging a waterway that will be navigable at least for barges and small vessels.…

This was followed by a report in 1946 to the Seattle Planning Commission that also emphasized the "essential need" to straighten the river.

By the early 1950s the Howard Hanson Dam on the Green River was approved and construction began. With flood protection thus assured for the upper Duwamish Valley, the Port prepared to take over the entire valley. In 1954 the Port of Seattle, the Seattle City Council and the King County Commission jointly hired the New York engineering firm of Knappen, Tibbetts, Abbett, McCarthy and Stratton to produce a feasibility study for straightening the upper Duwamish River and the territory which should be included in a new Duwamish Industrial District. This study completed, the firm was contracted in 1956 "to prepare drawings that will show the recommended locations of streets, railroad lines, utilities and sewers the Port will construct in that 4½ mile-long area." All was going according to plan and the Port was confident that the first 600 acres of industrial land would be ready for occupancy by 1959.

209

TUKWILA—COMMUNITY AT THE CROSSROADS

THE OPPOSITION UNITES

With the publication of the consultant's report to the Port in September 1954, the reality of the plan began to hit home in the Duwamish Valley. Many of the property owners were not interested in being bought out by the Port and looked for alternatives. It was a disparate group with a variety of motives. Some were property owners who wanted to limit their taxes; some were land developers and speculators who wanted to get the jump on the Port and make money. Some living in the heights feared that their pastoral views would be converted into stark, noisy, dirty industrial landscapes. Some were 1950s-style environmentalists who foresaw the pollutants pouring into the Duwamish's waters and noxious smokestacks creating smog to smother the entire Seattle region on stagnant winter days. Some wanted to make Tukwila stronger and others just wanted to be left alone.

The weapons they could muster were of four basic types: lawsuits, organized public support, obtaining representation through a governmental body, and time. Time to find allies. Time to stall the Port and disrupt its timetable. Time to think of a plan. The property owners realized that to wield power they needed to be represented by a governmental body, and they approached King County. Already aligned with the Port, the county declined.

TUKWILA BEGINS TO ANNEX

In desperation they turned to the nearby community of Tukwila, a gesture many must have thought futile. But Tukwila had come of age. As mayor of Tukwila, Charles O. Baker played a key role and demonstrated great skill in using strategy and timing, mixed with good fortune, to protect Tukwila and its sister communities from the destruction planned by the Port.

Mayor Baker and key community members began to quietly meet with area property owners and a few interested businesspeople. Baker began doing what good politicians do best—he created a coalition out of a diverse group with conflicting motives, guiding the self-interested actions of individuals in a direction and sequence that would further the larger goal. Many things began to happen quickly and simultaneously as the opposition to the Port's plan took on a life of its own. Mayor Charles Baker and future mayor John Strander, chairman of the Tukwila Planning Commission, were at times leading, and at other times merely responding to, the accelerating pace of events as they gathered forces to the opposition.

Annexation would be the key. The property owners would have a stronger position if they were part of an incorporated city and if the property were zoned for a different use than the Port's proposed heavy industry. In exchange for protection and its assistance, the City would gain an expanded tax base. In the summer of 1948 Tukwila annexed, its first new area: Herman C. Anderson's Golden Arrow Dairy. This was the beginning of 40 years of annexations during which time Tukwila would find annexation to be a powerful tool.

SOUTHCENTER AND ANDOVER INDUSTRIAL PARK—THE ALTERNATIVE TO THE PORT'S HEAVY INDUSTRY

In July of 1956 Mayor Baker appeared before the City Council to report that he had been contacted by a business interest which had just purchased 250 acres of land south of Tukwila, and that they desired to be annexed to Tukwila. The Council indicated they were favorable to such a proposal. Allied Stores, through its subsidiary corporation, Andover, Inc., had proposed the much-needed alternative to the Port's plan, and the unanimous support of the business community began to waver.

TUKWILA, CROSSROADS OF COMMERCE—1928-1990

BUILDING A COALITION

Mayor Baker knew that the Port's support needed to be eliminated if Tukwila was to have a chance to win. With this appealing alternative to the Seattle area business community causing division therein, Tukwila now sought support from other governmental agencies.

With Tukwila's encouragement, other agencies began to question the Port's plan. The Washington Fisheries Department, having barely finished forcing the relocation of the Howard Hanson Dam to protect the fish spawning grounds, again found the fish run threatened. The Washington Highway Commission, hard at work to construct the federally financed freeways, found that the Port's plans were creating a financial and planning nightmare by requiring higher, longer bridges and major roadway relocations. Mayor Baker's friendship with the head of the Highway Commission, Bill Bugge, enabled Tukwila to coordinate smoothly with the State. Baker's leadership in organizing the Valley Industrial Planning Council added the opposition of nearby communities Kent, Renton and Auburn to the fight.

In July of 1956 the Port had its first official meeting with the Tukwila City Council and received a lecture from the council about the Port's lack of consideration. The Tukwila City Council made it clear that part of the Port District would be within the city limits of Tukwila and that the Port would have to comply with Tukwila zoning and Tukwila-issued building permits.

The Tukwila Council moved quickly to block the Port's plans. It created the City Planning Commission and the Annexation Committee in September. Someone was assigned to keep an eye on the group studying the Metro Plan. A portion of the proposed annexation was rapidly moving along and on September 30, 1957, the City of Tukwila expanded.

After July's unsuccessful meeting, the Port sent its chief engineer, Mr. Treadwell, to the October meeting with the Tukwila Council. The Council listened with narrowing eyes as he explained that the "improvements" to the Duwamish would reach up to Renton Junction within three years. Within six weeks, on November 25, 1957, Tukwila annexed another large parcel of land which the Port had planned to develop, once again removing land from the jurisdiction of the King County Planning Commission. The following day the Tukwila City Council formally voted to oppose the Port plan and on December 16, 1957, the Council adopted a zoning plan directly opposing the Port by limiting development to commercial and light industrial business.

Shortly after Andover, Inc. had acquired a total of 550 acres and expressed interest in acquiring another 250 acres, the Port of Seattle complained to the newspapers that the Duwamish industrial development plan would not be economically feasible with only the remaining 500 acres. The Port threatened to force Andover to sell the newly acquired property by using the Port's powers of condemnation. Then came the most serious blow to the Port's plans.

THE STATE SUPREME COURT CASE

The Port had sought and received authorization in 1957 from the state legislature to levy a two-mill property tax to finance the Duwamish industrialization program. But as the King County Assessor prepared to implement the tax, a lawsuit was filed in Superior Court on October 22, 1957. Seventeen valley residents had joined together as the plaintiffs in the suit: Helen Nelsen, Archie and Anna H. Codiga, Joe and Hazel Aliment, John and Louise Strander, Shannon and Lucille Houge, Paul and Beatrice Wieser, Harlan and Ruby Bull, the Harmses and the Listons. The plaintiffs stated "on behalf of all other taxpayers similarly situated" that they chose to oppose the increase in property taxes because the levy "provides funds to condemn property for private purposes, in violation of the State Constitution." At issue was the Port's right to use the governmental power of eminent domain to take land from the present owners and then sell it to other private individuals and corporations, after preparing the land for industrial use.

The case went before the Washington State Supreme Court in 1959 and the Court concluded that, whatever the merits of the Port's plan, the Port did not have the legal authority to condemn and purchase land under its existing authority. The tax was thrown out.

Mess family farm, Southcenter area, ca. 1920. The valley had been thoroughly cleared and secondary growth was becoming established on the hills. A sawmill still operated on the western hillside at this time. Courtesy King County Public Works Dept.

The Port now found that its support at the state level was divided, as was the business community. The county's jurisdiction had been eliminated by Tukwila's annexations, and three other cities had joined the fight. Now both the Port's funding and its power to condemn had been blocked. The Port's support was too weak to get new legislation from the State. The Port was never able to regain the initiative.

TUKWILA WINS

The independent, feisty Duwamish Valley communities had fought to preserve themselves from the Port's plans and had won. While all the communities entered into battle, being unincorporated units they lacked political legislative power. Only the municipality of Tukwila possessed the tools to save the upper valley and its sister communities. But there was a bitter irony in victory: One of the communities' allies, the Federal Highway Commission, would soon build I-5 through their valley. Saved from annihilation by the waterway, the communities would lose homes, churches, businesses and a portion of their identities to the broad freeway and its roaring river of cars. In the coming decades, Andover Park and the Southcenter retail center would provide Tukwila with a tax base that would have been inconceivable 10 years earlier, but there would be a historic price to pay—hundreds of acres of farms and the quiet rural life would be gone forever.

THE CITY OF TUKWILA FROM 1957 TO 1990

Unquestionably, the prolonged battle with the Port of Seattle consumed the majority of the time and energy of Mayor Charles Baker and the Tukwila City Council, but somehow they managed to bring about major changes at home. In the first years of his tenure as mayor, Baker and his fellow public officials worked diligently with an annual budget of $12,000 to build Tukwila into a city. The streets were improved, the water system was upgraded, building codes were enacted and

Tukwila, Crossroads of Commerce—1928-1990

financial stability grew. With this growth came Tukwila's attraction to investment and development.

In order to be assured of a prosperous future, the City expanded to encompass several square miles and, with more land, a plan was developed that proved to be both unique and economically sound. A planning commission of 12 was formed with John Strander as chairman. The John Graham Co. was hired as consultant to draw up the master plan. Among the many community innovations was the placing of all utilities, old and new, underground by 1972. It was agreed that land use was to be restricted in order to preserve the clean, uncluttered beauty of the city. In addition, plans were made for architectural design, landscaping and signage controls. A balanced zoning plan was developed, with the area divided 70 percent commercial and 30 percent residential.

The Crossroads of Commerce

ndoubtedly the most significant change facing the City was in the area of transportation. Anticipating the development of two freeways—Interstates 5 and 405—that would put Tukwila squarely at the crossroads of commerce, the Tukwila Planning Commission included transportation access as part of its plan. With other improvements being considered and the assessed value of the City increasing, Tukwila came to the attention of a very imaginative and innovative developer, Rex Allison, Director of West Coast operations for Allied Stores Corp.

As the originator of the concept of regional shopping centers, Allison and Allied Stores had already successfully built the Northgate Mall, the Tacoma Mall and numerous others around the United States. Tukwila offered an opportunity for another mall with its ideal location at the interchange of two major freeways. After several years of extensive negotiations by Mayor Baker and Marvin Boys, representing Allied Stores, mutually agreeable terms were reached. Three years in construction, on July 31, 1968, the Southcenter retail center opened with 116 stores enclosed within a 30-acre covered area. Over 7,200 parking spaces surround the mall. Sharing the site are a variety of services including a full-service bank, a large Cinerama theater, an automotive center, service stations, restaurants and several hotels and motels. In 1961 the Andover Industrial Park was developed by Puget Western, Inc., and in the next 20 years this and other industrial parks provided space for over 1,000 business firms employing 20,000 people.

Changes in Tukwila's Arterial Circulation Plan were necessary to maximize the benefits of improved freeway design developed through municipal and state cooperation and to fit freeway revisions that developed as the State Highway Department details became more definite. An example of the

Tukwila leaders and policy makers who helped guide the city through the critical 1960s and early '70s gathered in September 1968. All of these men served their community as councilmen, and three led the city as mayor. L. to r.: Rudy Regel, Bill Crostick, John Strander (mayor), Dwight Gardner, Richard Bowen, Tom Forsythe, Arlie Radford, Charles Baker (mayor), Stan Minkler (mayor), Gene Ives. Courtesy Darlene Crostick.

213

Tukwila—Community at the Crossroads

improved Highway Department design is the bridging of the I-405 east-west freeway by the 57 Ave. S. extension and Christensen Road to preserve the existing arterials and connect the residential areas to the major industrial and commercial development. The grade separation of the I-5 Tacoma-Seattle freeway near S. 160 St. makes possible more direct access between the industrial-commercial complex of Tukwila and the area served by the westerly extension of I-405.

As each City administration under Mayors Strander, Minkler, Todd, Bauch and Van Dusen passed through the portals of the Tukwila City government, the improvements to the City continued. The assessed value continued to increase, and the guidance of Tukwila's future never faltered. Firms from almost every commercial sector are now represented in the ever-growing legacy that is Tukwila.

The City of Tukwila proudly marks its 75th anniversary. Mayor Gary VanDusen, City employees, and citizens ceremoniously erect a special commemorative sign placed on roads leading into the crossroads community in 1983. L. to r.: Ralph Trepanier, Mabel Schults, Michael Back, Kathyrn Ruhlman, Doris Cox, Mark Badten, unknown, Hubert Crowley, Maggie Schwindt, Mabel Gylden, Pat Lowrey, Doris Phelps, George Hill, Mayor Gary VanDusen, Byron Sneva, Don Williams (kneeling). Courtesy City of Tukwila.

Tukwila in 1990

By 1990, three decades after Mayor Baker led Tukwila into its present dynamic phase, the population had grown to 14,631; there were over 1,000 apartment units sprinkled throughout the city; over 8 million square feet of commercial and industrial buildings covered the valley; two of the busiest freeways in the state bisected the town; and the assessed value of the city reached more than $300 million (100 percent valuation).

In addition to this change in outward appearance, Tukwila's attitude had changed also. Denser living patterns, loss of natural beauty, noise and other problems which commonly accompany development sharpened the public's sensitivity to amenities, urban design and public services. In 1990 the City of Tukwila struggled with the typical problems of a rapidly growing West Coast city, and the days of small-town life recorded in this book fade into memory. From an idea in the mind of Joel Shomaker to the Northwest crossroads of commerce, Tukwila has emerged as a leading city in the Puget Sound area.

CHAPTER 13

DAIRY FARMS, NURSERIES AND MARKET-GARDEN FARMS FLOURISH IN THE DUWAMISH VALLEY

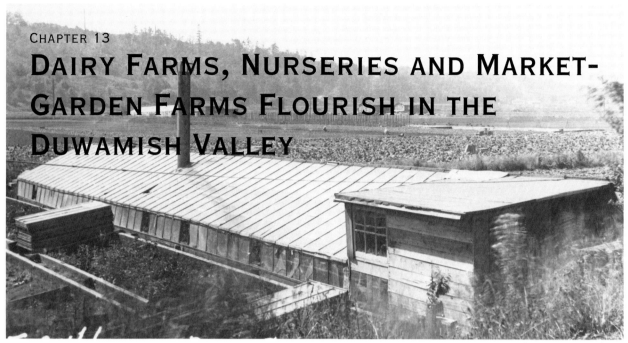

Courtesy Washington State Archives.

A photo essay by Kris Freeman and Kay Reinartz

From the beginning, those who immigrated to the Duwamish Valley had little money. Their capital was uncleared land and their own skills. Yet they had a distinct advantage over settlers in other areas—lush, rich soil. In addition, the subsoil, consisting of thick black loam over clay, retained moisture through the dry season. The fields near the river were especially fertile. In the same way that the Nile historically enriched Egyptian farmland, periodic flooding brought new soil to the valley, restoring the nutrients used up by dairy and vegetable farming. The *Washington Standard* of 1880 boasted of the Duwamish and White river valleys: "Ours is a much better dairy country in every respect than any part of California.... The farms upon the river bottoms produce a third more hay per acre and it costs one-half less to winter stock." The homestead farms of the nineteenth century gave way in the 1910s and '20s to market-garden farming with vegetables being raised for the Seattle market. Italian and Japanese immigrants were especially successful with these enterprises, while Danish and Swiss immigrants predominated in dairying. Many market-garden farms built greenhouses where seedlings were nurtured.

DAIRIES

LaFranchi dairy herd (below). The lush flood plain of the Duwamish attracted many immigrant dairy farmers in the first decade of the century. Among them was Joe LaFranchi, a Swiss, who purchased land in Joseph Allen's subdivision along the riverbank around 1905. The property included an old barn, surrounded by an orchard that was planted when the rail-

Courtesy Tukwila Historical Society.

road first came through. During the 1920s, the barn became a liability to Archie Codiga, who had purchased the property from his partner, LaFranchi. The aging wooden building was infected with bovine tuberculosis. Codiga's daughter Frances North recalls: "Dad had to get his herd out. Every time the inspector came by he lost half his herd....I remember driving those poor cows, and they looked so healthy, to the slaughterhouse." Codiga eventually accumulated 130 acres on both sides of the Duwamish. The family started bottling milk when it wholesaled for 10 cents a gallon. "We figured we could do better if we peddled it at two quarts for 15 cents," says Frances, who started running a 24-quart route when she was 12 years old. Cows still graze on a small portion of the property, operated by Codiga's son Jim.

Herman Anderson of Golden Arrow Dairy (right) liked to keep his milk on the move. He purchased the first insulated dairy truck in the area as well as the first electric pasteurizer. In 1922 Herman and Grace Anderson moved from Skagit County to Tukwila and started Hermway Dairy with 11 cows. By 1929 the company had 12 retail milk routes; by 1950 there were 30. The herd of 150 cows on 180 acres could not support continued growth, and Anderson bought milk from Consolidated Dairy Products in Burlington, hauling the milk the 90 miles to Tukwila early each morning. Anderson kept innovating to increase business, for a time selling kosher milk and ice cream. Son Wynn recalls: "During World

Courtesy Wynn Anderson.

War II, with gasoline shortages, dairies traded business. One of the Golden Arrow routes that traveled to Ballard traded equal quartage with another company whose route came to Burien." The farmland was sold to the Andover Co. and currently the land is part of the Southcenter and Andover Industrial Park site.

Courtesy Helen Nelsen.

James Nelsen (left) transports the Orillia Dairy Queen in a Winston 6, ca. 1916. James, who owned one of the area's first automobiles, was the eldest of the Nelsen brothers who became dairy barons in Tukwila. James purchased his first land in 1886 and initially sent milk to Seattle by riverboat. He used the Interurban electric railway after 1902.

Dairy Farms, Nurseries and Market-Garden Farms Flourish in the Duwamish Valley

Charlie Nelsen (right) delivers milk for the Fred Nelsen dairy. Fred, brother to James, operated his dairy at Renton Junction. Fred Nelsens' six daughters were drafted to run the hay fork and to process milk. "We girls got up at 6 a.m. every morning and washed and sterilized the bottles and bottled the milk before leaving for school," says daughter Alma. "We came home from school on the 3:30 Interurban and at five o'clock we bottled the milk. Evan, the only son, had a milk route in Seattle in 1918. He was too lenient with the young families whose husbands or fathers had gone to war and ran up such big bills for milk and cream that Father ultimately sold the route." The family still had time for playing baseball after supper in the summer. "We worked but we had fun and it was a good life," Alma recalls.

Courtesy Renton Historical Museum.

Milking time (below). "We played the radio, right in the barn. They always said cows give more milk when they listened to music. We played country western," says Rudy Bergsma, who worked as a hired milker in the Fred Nelsen and Ray Nielsen dairies for over 20 years. Herman Schoenbachler, whose dairy was in the Southcenter district, remembers how World War II civil defense measures made his barn a less-than-pleasant place for cow and milker alike. "The Defense Department came along and made us black out our barn and it was almost impossible to milk those cows in that barn because of the heat. The cows put off steam and here we'd put all that black paper over the windows." Most barns were built on the highest ground available, which still might be inundated by winter floods. "In 1933 our complete farm was covered with water," says Schoenbachler. "The plank-and-rail corral was floating. In those days the farmers looked after the dike. We'd walk the dike day and night and when there was a gopher hole, we'd fill it."

Photo by Asahel Curtis, courtesy Washington State Historical Society.

Courtesy Jim Bergsma.

The Bergsma family. Left to right: Sybil Bergsma James, Josephine Bergsma, Ada James, Rudy Bergsma, Joe Bergsma, Frank Bergsma, George Bergsma, John James. The family began milking for Fred Nelsen in 1934. About a year later sons Rudy and Jack hired on at Riverview Farm, although they continued to live at the Nelsens' with their parents. When Jack quit school in 1931 to work on a dairy farm in Ferndale, he was paid $15.00 per month plus room and board to milk 32 cows twice a day, seven days a week. Younger brother Rudy recounts the schedule at Nielsen's Riverview Farm. "We began at 2 a.m. After we got our milking chores done we had to bottle the milk and clean the barn. Then they put us out to work in the field until 11:00 a.m. Of course we were up at 1:30 a.m. in the morning. Then we'd go home and sleep for an hour, be back at work at 2:00 p.m. We got through about 5:30 p.m. We were sure busy. My mother was the best milker; she always got more milk out of a cow than any of us." Rudy says that milking hurt his hands at first, but that he got used to it. "I still don't have arthritis in my hands and I'm 73 years old. So I must have kept my fingers limber."

Riverview Farm. "Jacob Nielsen, who started in 1928 with 20 cows, was good natured and had a hard time collecting the money due on his retail milk routes during the Depression," says his son Ray. Even when milk cost just 9 or 10 cents a quart, "half of them wouldn't pay; half of them didn't have the money to pay." The Nielsens were thankful they had no worry about having enough to eat during those lean years, "but you get tired of drinking milk all the time," adds Ray. The Nielsens kept building their operation until they had 600 cows and seven routes. At its peak, Riverview employed 17 workers in the barns and bottling plant. Although there are no longer any cows at Riverview, the dairy still operates three wholesale routes in 1990.

Courtesy Ray Nielsen.

DAIRY FARMS, NURSERIES AND MARKET-GARDEN FARMS FLOURISH IN THE DUWAMISH VALLEY

VEGETABLE FARMS

The row on row of lettuce, radishes, beans and peas blanketing the valley were most often cultivated by hand. And many of the hands belonged to children and teenagers. "We children had to work from the time we were five or six years old," says Anna Jose, who worked on her father's and her husband's small farms. "We had to clean the chicken coops. We had to bring in the eggs, we had to bring in the wood. And when they were clearing land we had to carry stones to the wagon. That's how life was." Albert Gaviglio remembers how he and his brothers would put on two layers of clothes each morning—school clothes underneath, work clothes on top. A few minutes before classes began, they would take off their work clothes, leave them in the field and walk to the Duwamish School for the day's lessons. After school, they went back to the fields until it was time for dinner.

Courtesy the Carrossino family.

Bruno Carrossino (above) and a friend show off the hand tillers used at the Duwamish Gardens.

Teresa Carrossino (right), like many of the valley's farm wives, worked as long and hard as her husband and sons. To pay for the use of the house where they lived, which was on Duwamish Gardens property, Teresa cooked for 15 hired hands and the seven partners—three times a day—turning out homemade ravioli, fried chicken, french fries and doughnuts. "That's why we made so much wine, 1,500 to 2,000 gallons every year. We got the grapes from California," says Teresa's son Rinaldo. Anna Jose recalls the cooking schedule at the Jose farm, where her mother-in-law had a special bread-making trough made of new shiplap lumber, big enough to handle a 50-pound sack of flour. "The two of us would knead that bread.…We made our own cheese; she would even dry her own fruit." The Jose women would start their day at 5:00 a.m. by cooking a heavy breakfast for the field hands, and then make a

Courtesy Josef Scaylea.

hot lunch at 11:00 a.m. and a big cold lunch at 4:00 p.m. Between meals they picked beans and peas. Dinner was at 10:00 or 10:30 p.m., after the vegetables had been washed, bunched and loaded on the truck for early-morning delivery to the Pike Place Market.

219

Playing bocci at the Duwamish Gardens. The bocci court alongside the cornfield, was a center of social life for the valley's Italian community. (In the background of the photo is the historic Interurban Bridge at S. 115th and East Marginal Way.) "On Sundays we'd only work from 4 a.m. until noon. Then we'd have visitors—25 to 30 every Sunday. The men played bocci. The women sewed. If it was too wet to play bocci, they played poker," says Rinaldo Carossino. Irene Prandi Siccardi emphasizes that these community gatherings were very important to her family because her mother and dad "came over here [from Italy] all by themselves—each one separately so they had no family—no grandparents, no aunts and uncles or cousins. So friends meant a lot to us and we did have lots of friends." Other recreation centered around the river. "We had a real nice swimming hole with a sandy beach right across from where we lived. We'd go swimming…every day at 3:00," says Irene. "As busy as we were, every Sunday my mother would pack up a lunch and all the hired hands and everybody would go to Angle Lake and have a picnic."

Courtesy Josef Scaylea.

Photo by Asahel Curtis, courtesy Washington State Historical Society.

DAIRY FARMS, NURSERIES AND MARKET-GARDEN FARMS FLOURISH IN THE DUWAMISH VALLEY

Courtesy Akiko Mikami Shimatsu.

Blue Lake beans on the Mikami Farm, late 1930s
Even with eight children, the Mikamis didn't have enough labor at harvest time; they would pay neighborhood children half a cent a pound to pick peas and beans. Matsusuke and Tamayo Mikami operated a dairy farm near S. 180th St. in the 1920s, until passage of the Alien Land Law made it illegal for them to lease property. The Mikamis sold their cows to John Prandi and began farming vegetables on a 19-acre plot in the Southcenter district, eventually purchasing the land for $125 an acre when their children came of age. The Mikamis were interned during World War II, despite the fact that their eldest son, Matt, was already serving in the Armed Forces. Sons Takumi and Kiyoto were drafted out of camp, and Akiko volunteered for the Women's Army Corps (WAC). "It's real odd, they put us in camp, but they trusted us enough to put me into G-2, which is military intelligence," says Akiko. Neighbors of Japanese families were also dismayed by the internment. "We went to the train depot to see them off. There were lots and lots of tears," says Irene Prandi Siccardi. Left to right, Haruko, Yaeko and Masao Mikami.

Pike Place Market (facing page, below). While many of the valley's farmers had contracts with wholesale houses or canneries, some depended on the retail trade at Pike Place Market. Giovanni Gaviglio drove his wife to Pike Place every day to run the family's produce booth. Mrs. Gaviglio, like many farm wives, was a very hardy woman. She once went into labor while working in the family fields and delivered her baby there without help or medical assistance. When he was 18, son Albert got his own stall at the market and began putting in 15- to 16-hour days at $12 for a six-day week for Joe Desimone, an influential South Park Italian farmer and Pike Place merchant.

221

Courtesy John and Louise Strander.

NURSERIES

Aerial view of Strander Nursery. In 1911 two Swedish immigrants, John S. Strander and Peter Wessman, founded the Renton Junction Nursery. They had to shut down in 1918 when World War I and the influenza epidemic made business unprofitable. They started over in 1924 by purchasing a section of the Stephen Foster donation claim. "Part of the claim had been logged, but mammoth stumps remained and the clearing was done with dynamite caps, mule teams and just plain hard labor. John S. Strander had two severe hernias as reminders of this task," says Louise Strander, who married son John B. "Instead of a combined nursery, Wessman operated a separate rose nursery while the Stranders grew hardy trees and shrubs. It took many years to grow a sizeable inventory of nursery stock. Meanwhile the couple sold eggs to a restaurant route, produce at Pike Place Market and beans to the canneries in Kent. The two nurseries were operated during the 1920s and 1930s with the help living on the premises and a housekeeper employed to cook for them," she adds. Specialties raised by the nursery included a weeping pussy-willow tree. New varieties were developed. The Strander family operated the nursery until the construction of I-5 took 15 acres of the property.

DAIRY FARMS, NURSERIES AND MARKET-GARDEN FARMS FLOURISH IN THE DUWAMISH VALLEY

Miyao Nursery. Kaijiro and Ume Miyao raised chrysanthemums, tulips, hyacinths and Easter lilies on their 2.5-acre plot on 39th Ave. S. Ume and her daughters tied each chrysanthemum to the greenhouse roof to ensure straight stems. Aside from cucumbers and tomatoes raised for sale, the Miyaos grew no vegetables; instead they supplied their neighbors with flowers for funerals, births and weddings. "Then when they had vegies, they'd bring us crates of them," says son Bill Miyao. Like many other Japanese families, the Miyaos had to start over after World War II internment. Bill remembers his father cleaning blackberry vines out of the greenhouses the family purchased on 39 Ave. S. in 1947, on their return to Tukwila. "It hadn't been used during the war," says Bill. During the 1930s Kaijiro and Ume had owned a nursery at Renton Junction; since Ume had been born in the U.S., she was a citizen and able to buy land. Left to right above: Jerry, Sharon, Ume and Kaijiro.

Courtesy the Miyao family.

Courtesy the Miyao family.

Miyao greenhouse. As on other Tukwila farms, the Miyao children were a vital part of the family operation. During summer vacation their day started at 4:00 or 4:30 a.m. The annual job was painting one of the family's three greenhouses. "By 10:30 it was too hot in the greenhouse and we'd have an early lunch and rest. Then we'd go out and paint until evening. We lost out on play time all summer," says Bill. Left to right: Jerry and Sharon.

Chapter 14
The South Central School District

by Ron Lamb

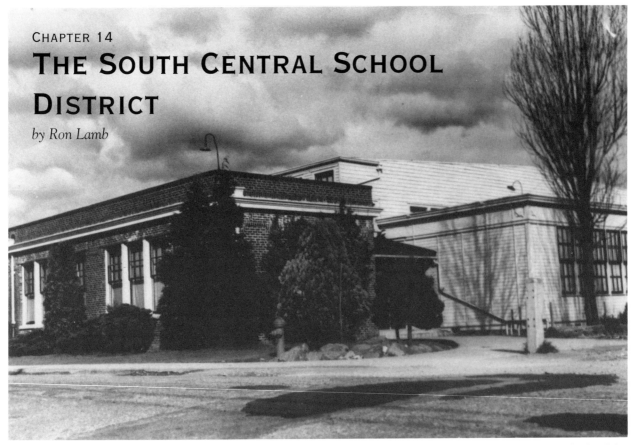

Built in 1922 on the site of the original one-room schoolhouse, this building served as Foster High School, Central Elementary School and the state's first occupational skills center during its 52 years of existence. Courtesy South Central School District.

Since pioneer times, the school district known first as Foster and then as South Central has defined Tukwila, Foster, Thorndyke, Riverton, and at times Duwamish as a single larger community. Its roots go back 100 years, to the first schoolhouse in the district—the one-room Foster School—built in about 1892.

The Black River School District No. 6, 1878-1904

The area that forms the South Central School District, as well as parts of the contemporary Renton, Highline, Kent and Vashon school districts, originally constituted Black River School District No. 6, established August 10, 1878. This district stretched from the west shore of Lake Washington to Colvos Passage on the west side of Vashon Island. The location of the Black River District school is unknown. Between 1878 and 1902 the Black River District was considerably reduced in size as smaller school districts were created.

Foster Builds a School and Forms a School District, 1892

School began informally in the Foster area in about 1891, when Joseph Foster began teaching his sons, Joseph T. and Hillory, and three other children from neighboring farms in the living room of his home. However, Foster soon realized that, despite his many talents, he was not a teacher. John Giblin was hired to continue instructing the pupils, and later John's brother Charles took over the home-based school.

About this time, a community meeting was held to discuss building a schoolhouse. Joseph and Martha Foster offered a tract of land on a knoll above the river as a site for the school. The land was officially transferred to the school district for a $1 gold coin on March 1, 1892.

The South Central School District

The people of the community built the Foster School at a site on the southwest corner of what became Foster Memorial Park, at 51 Ave. S. and S. 139 St. Simple yet solid, the school had only one room and a covered porch but was built of the best timber available in the area. It stood until about 1930. The first teacher, Henry Lung, welcomed the first students sometime during the 1891-92 school year.

Having built its new school, the Foster School District No. 104 was established on February 6, 1892. The original Foster School District was bordered on the east by the Duwamish River. The western boundary was at approximately 32 Ave. S., the southern boundary about the middle of Southcenter, and the north boundary near the intersection of Macadam Road and Interurban Ave. Joseph Foster, Emmett L. Robbins, James Clark and J.A. Gaskill were school board members in the early years.

In its first five years the Foster School District served only a handful of students. When Joseph Foster hired Tom Clark to teach in 1897, there were eight students: Joseph T. and Hillory Foster, Leigh and Chester Robbins, Glen and Roy McGloughlin, and Marion and Wiley Walters. In 1901 Clark left for the Alaska gold fields and Nellie Starr, Clark's fiancée, became the Foster teacher, with 15 students. As in the nineteenth century, the school year consisted of a four-month winter term and a three-month summer term, allowing students time off when their help was needed on the farm.

Consolidation and Growth

n April 7, 1904, the Foster School District No. 104, with three pupils, and Black River School District No. 6, with nine pupils, consolidated to form Foster School District No. 144. The consolidation and enrollment growth prompted the school board in 1905 to purchase another acre of land from Joseph Foster immediately north of the original acre, for $350. During the next school year, the district built a new four-room schoolhouse,

Foster's original one-room schoolhouse, built in 1892. Courtesy South Central School District.

moving the original schoolhouse to the southeast corner of the property. That same year, the district first provided free textbooks to its students.

Improved transportation coupled with immigration brought rapid population growth in the upper Duwamish Valley during the first decade of the twentieth century. Between 1905 and 1910 the enrollment grew from 61 to 397. Schools were opened at Duwamish and Tukwila in 1907 for grades 1-6. Foster continued to serve as the central school, offering grades 1-8. In 1909 district voters approved a $16,000 bond issue to purchase sites and new schools at Duwamish, Riverton and Tukwila. A basement was added to Foster School at this time.

Duwamish Departs

n November 7, 1910, Duwamish residents filed a petition with the county school superintendent for formation of a new school district. After failing to receive approval, the petitioners appealed the

TUKWILA—COMMUNITY AT THE CROSSROADS

L. M. DIMMITT

L. M. Dimmitt, Foster Superintendent 1913-22, had a special place in his heart for Foster/South Central schools beyond his years as Foster superintendent. Born July 5, 1884, in Jackson County, Missouri, Lorris Myrvin Dimmitt began his professional career there as a teacher. He became a superintendent, making his mark in consolidating and building programs. In 1910 he moved west to take a teaching position in the Renton School District, where he taught at the Sartori and Central schools.

In May 1913 Dimmitt became superintendent of Foster School District. When he first arrived in Foster, the area was remote and rural, he later recalled. Many students rode horses to school, staking them in a nearby pasture for the day. Since there were no telephones in the schools the first years, Dimmitt walked to schools in Riverton, Thorndyke and Tukwila to talk to teachers. Communication improved when he bought an automobile. Dimmitt built his home in lower Foster,

L.M. Dimmitt, superintendent of Foster School District No. 144 from 1913 to 1922 and later superintendent of King County schools. Courtesy of Charlotte Dimmitt Jaspers.

where he and his family resided until 1922 when he left the district. After serving as superintendent at several schools in the region, he worked in the office of State Superintendent of Public Instruction Noah D. Showalter. In the 1930s, Dimmitt and his family returned for several years to the house he had built in lower Foster. In 1946, he became King County Superintendent of Schools, a position he held for 18 years.

On his retirement as county superintendent, he told the Renton *Record-Chronicle* that he considered three factors when interviewing prospective new teachers: Does this teacher love and have an interest in children? Is he or she willing to do "that something extra" for each child? Will he or she be able to keep order in the classroom without resorting to force?

He and his wife, Emma, had five children, daughters Vannetta, Charlotte, and Helen, and two sons, Myrvin and Ellsworth, three of whom became teachers. L. M. Dimmitt died in January of 1981.

---

denial to the county commissioners, who overturned the earlier decision and established Duwamish School District No. 175 on June 6, 1911. Duwamish remained a separate district until it consolidated with Foster on July 7, 1942 at the insistence of the state school reorganization board and with a favorable advisory vote of the residents of both districts.

Tukwila attempted to form its own school district in 1909 and again in 1919, but both times the petition was denied.

POOR, BUT PROGRESSIVE

Despite population growth, the Foster School District remained poor in property valuation, a problem that haunted the Foster/South Central School District throughout the first six decades of the century. In a school district financial statement issued March 31, 1917, the Foster school board stated that "the high cost and decreased assessed valuation has made it necessary to ask an increased tax levy in order to continue our schools on their present basis...." Indeed, the financial statement shows that the assessed valuation of property in the district fell from $845,581 in 1911-12 to $663,000 in 1916-17. To make up the loss of revenue from the declining valuation, the school board increased the school tax by three mills.

In May 1913 the voters of the district approved a bond issue to enlarge the Foster and Thorndyke schools. The Foster building was roughly doubled in size by a two-story addition on the back (the main entrance faced north). Thorndyke also was doubled in capacity by adding a second classroom and a cloakroom/lunchroom. With the construction at the two schools, the district went to what was called a 6-6 plan: Students in the first six grades were in the grade schools, and students in the upper six grades attended the central school at Foster. This plan allowed the district to offer manual training (shop) classes to boys and home economics to girls in the eighth grade.

Beyond an Eighth-Grade Education—A High School

Early in the twentieth century, it was believed in rural communities that an eighth-grade education was adequate preparation for life. Eighth-grade graduation ceremonies were the culmination of schooling for most children, and in Foster this rite of passage was marked by commencement ceremonies at Doty Hall, northeast of the central school site. Some young people commuted on the Interurban to high school in Renton or Seattle. By 1912, the school board was beginning to think about adding high school classes to the Foster School District curriculum.

The district added the ninth grade in 1912 and tenth grade in 1913. High school classes were held on the second floor of the Foster School building, with Superintendent L. M. Dimmitt, Richard Clifton, and Madge Ware as teachers. Foster became an accredited high school for the 1914-15 school year and had its first high school graduate, Ava Sophia Adams.

A High School Building

With a high school course of study offered at Foster School, the district began planning for a separate high school building, starting with an adequate gymnasium. A 1916 bond proposal for a gymnasium at Foster and for purchase of additional school sites was defeated. The Foster Community Hall was rented in 1919 for use as a gymnasium. School dances and other school activities also were held at the community hall for many years.

In 1919, the school district obtained three additional acres at the central site through unusual circumstances. As the only public official for miles, Dimmitt was called in one evening to mediate a dispute between two bachelor brothers who owned property east of the school, which later became the lower playing field. He suggested that the two part company and sell their property—to the school district—to avoid future conflicts. When they agreed, he was quick to offer earnest money on the spot.

In the spring of 1920, a bond issue for a new school in Foster and Tukwila was defeated. Finally, in May of 1921 voters approved a bond for a high school building at the central site, a new

The 1917 Foster High School girls' basketball team. From left to right: Vera Hultz, Alice Swanson, Naomi Thompson, Florence Schmidt, Grace Chandler, Marie Swenson, Beulah Adams, Coach M. F. Odle. Courtesy South Central School District.

Chapman's school cafeteria at 13815 51 Ave. S., where students enjoyed 5¢ soup and 10¢ sandwiches in the 1920s and 1930s in the absence of a cafeteria in the Foster School. Another student spot was Hazel and Harold's Corner, a lunchroom and store at the southeast corner of S. 139 St. and 51 Ave. S., across from Foster High School. Courtesy Washington State Archives.

Tukwila School, and a new Riverton School. Architect William Mallis drew up plans for the new Foster building east of the old one, on what later became the lower playing field, but the school board voted instead to locate the new building south of the old one, on the site of the original one-room schoolhouse. Built by local contractor Fred Fox at a cost of $5,640, the three-room brick veneer high school building was completed in June 1922.

Improvements to the High School

Through the efforts of the students, the PTA, Superintendent Frank Laird, boys from the manual training program and volunteers from the community, a gymnasium was added to the high school in 1926. Somewhat later, a seating area, known as "the Chicken Coop" because of its chicken-wire enclosure facing the playing court, was added above the west end wall.

A few years after the gym was completed, the study hall portion of the high school building was purchased, already constructed, from O. P. Smith and was added onto the south side of the building. In 1929 Fox, working with Mallis, built a second addition at a cost of $20,865, and in 1933 the office was built by the WPA. High school students continued to attend some classes in the old grade school building for several years, but as class-rooms were added to the high school in the following decade, the old building gradually ceased to serve the upper grades.

High school at that time emphasized preparation for work after graduation rather than preparation for college, although it offered college preparatory and general studies plans as well as commercial. According to Alice Jorgensen Wood, a 1925 Foster graduate, "Most of us took the commercial course in high school so that we could be equipped to get a good job—typing, shorthand, bookkeeping, commercial arithmetic. Those students who did

Foster Publications

Student and community events alike were dutifully recorded by the *Klahowyah*, Foster High School yearbook, and the *Growler*, student newspaper. The first Foster yearbook was published in 1916, but the name *Klahowyah*, a Chinook jargon greeting of friendship, was not associated with the yearbook until 1921. *Klahowyah* also was the name of a student newspaper that appeared in the fall of 1920. The origins of the *Growler* go back to 1926, when a student named James Cumming, brother of artist Bill Cumming, started a community newspaper, which he titled the *Communicator*. Cumming had the paper published weekly in Renton and charged $1.50 for an annual subscription. In 1928, a teacher suggested that the school assume publication of the paper, and the name was changed to the *Growler*. Throughout the years, the *Growler* has often won critical acclaim for scholastic journalism, particularly under the advisorship of Grace Gylling, who introduced the photo-offset method of printing the paper in 1954-55.

The South Central School District

The staff of the 1916 Foster High student yearbook, Foster's first, on the steps of Foster School. Alva Wallenberg, third from the left, class of 1917, later became a teacher at Foster and lived in the area for many decades. Edward Cunningham, fourth from the left, class of 1917, left the University of Washington as an engineering student to fight in World War I and was killed in France in 1918. A maple tree was planted on the school grounds in his memory in 1920. L. to r.: Milton Reid, Elmer Frame, Wallenberg, Cunningham, unknown, Eugene Gilbert, Lois Sarver and Floyd Hampson. Courtesy South Central School District.

not take this course usually ended up attending a business school after graduation." In addition to her commercial classes, she worked on the *Klahowyah* school yearbook, was salutatorian of her graduating class, was on the debate team that took the county championship and was the first female student body president.

Showalter—The "Last" Grade School

Early in the 1930s the school board began considering a plan to close the four small grade school buildings at Riverton, Foster, Tukwila and Thorndyke, thus consolidating the grade school program to a single site. Fearing loss of their local schools, many residents of the four communities resisted the consolidation plan at first. But the mood of the time among state and federal officials clearly supported consolidation of schools and school districts. Through the efforts of Tukwila's Mayor John P. Walkup, State Senator Earl Maxwell, Governor Clarence D. Martin and State Superintendent of Public Instruction Noah D. Showalter, a federal grant of $40,000 and a state offer of $25,000 were secured for the school consolidation project. Local voters, won over by the considerable federal and state funds accompanying consolidation, approved 25- and 10-mill levies in successive years to complete the funding for the project. On the same ballot as the 25-mill levy, district residents chose the 7-acre site on S. 144 St. over another 5.5-acre site two blocks south of the central school site. Showalter School, considered at the time the last grade school the district would need to build, opened for the 1938-39 school year and was dedicated by Governor Martin Sept. 9, 1938.

The federal grants stipulated that the four old grade schools be demolished. However, high community interest in preserving the old grade schools as community centers led to the school board arranging for the sale of the old schools in Riverton, Tukwila and Thorndyke to the local community clubs. Foster Grade School was demolished during the winter of 1938-39.

In 1946 Showalter was substantially expanded with the construction of a two-story north wing containing 12 classrooms and the cafeteria. John P. Walkup secured the $269,000 to pay for the addition from the Washington State Development Board. Opening the new wing at Showalter ended double-shift schedules. Showalter School included grades 1-8 at this time.

The school's Advisory Council was organized in 1936 to foster communication between citizens and the school board. The group has provided significant assistance in securing local funds for school construction as well as resolving numerous other school issues. The Advisory Council was still active in 1990. Few other school districts have such an organization to advise the school board.

229

THE DEPRESSION YEARS

The district's assessed valuation, never high during the first half of the century, plummeted 15 percent in a single year during the Depression. This reduced valuation resulted in a "drastic reduction" in school revenue, and teacher pay was reduced by five percent. Teachers were asked to teach ten months instead of the nine and one-half months called for in the contract at the same pay.

The district's problems did not end with the reduced revenue. In early 1933 the Washington State Education Department found the program at Foster High School lacking in a number of areas. School district officials met "informally" with L. M. Dimmitt, representing the State Superintendent of Public Instruction, to discuss means of correcting the situation. The minutes for the meeting conclude: "[Dimmitt] stated there would be no saving in closing the High School and transporting the children elsewhere. A general understanding satisfactory to all was arrived at."

THE WORLD WAR II YEARS

By the early 1940s, the area was changing rapidly. Jobs created by the regional defense industries, particularly Boeing and the Seattle shipyards, were pulling families into the Seattle area. For example, the new Boeing plant in Renton employed 500 in November of 1941 was expected to have a work force of 5,000 by 1943.

The year 1942 was a watershed for the Foster area and its schools. The land was still largely rural, but it was becoming more suburban and industrial. The *Growler* published the following thoughts in the school district's 50th anniversary commemoration issue, February 26, 1942:

> As a group of us stood on top of a high hill overlooking the beautiful Duwamish valley....we soliloquized on this point and wondered if ever our red-skinned brother had stood at that place and thought in his own way that the green valleys, the winding Duwamish, and wooded hills would ever change....

HERMAN ANDERSON

Among the many capable, dedicated school board members who have served the Foster/South Central district, one man stands out—Herman C. Anderson. Anderson served on the school board from 1928 to 1943 and played a central role in helping the district weather the financial disaster of the Great Depression, state pressure to consolidate Foster with a larger neighboring district, and the consolidation of the district's elementary school program from four small schools into Showalter. He helped organize the King County School Directors Association, was chairman of the state school reorganization committee, and was president of the Washington State School Directors Association in 1940.

Herman and Grace Anderson. Courtesy Wynn and Maxine Anderson.

Born June 28, 1891, in Kansas of Swedish immigrant parents, he moved to Skagit County as a child and graduated from LaConner High School in 1910. He graduated from the University of Washington in 1915, where he majored in political science and played football under Gil Dobie. He attended the United States Naval Academy and served as an ensign in the Navy during World War I. In 1922 he became principal of Renton High School and evolved the Golden Arrow Dairy business from a small start as Hermway Auto Station and Creamery. He operated the Golden Arrow Dairy until his retirement in 1952. He and his wife, Grace, moved to Conway, Skagit County, where he resided until his death Sept. 28, 1971. The Andersons' children are Wayne, Wynn and Jeanne.

THE SOUTH CENTRAL SCHOOL DISTRICT

Other substantive changes were underway as well. The county school superintendent had ruled in 1940 that the Foster School District was a consolidated school district (Foster and Black River) and, as such, required a five-member school board representing five director districts. In 1942, the county Committee for School District Reorganization ordered the consolidation of Foster and Duwamish, along with small portions of Highline, Renton and Seattle. The consolidated districts' name, South Central, was probably derived from the school district's location south of Seattle and between the larger Highline and Renton districts. Also in 1942, plans for a new high school were being discussed with Mallis and Fox, who built the original high school.

School Safety Patrol members on duty at the northeast corner of Pacific Highway and S. 144th in the 1940s. In the foreground is Dave Huson. Courtesy Wayne Weber.

The war years were a traumatic and uncertain time for the community and especially for high school students. Classmates left to join the military service, some even before they graduated. Several never returned. The 1943 *Klahowyah* shows a senior class with 20 girls and only six boys. The Showalter PTA hosted a dance for servicemen stationed at the Quarry Hill defense installation.

Two Japanese-American Foster students, Fusako Nobuyama and Hatsuji Hanada, both born and raised in the valley, went through an early graduation ceremony on May 7, 1942, before they were sent off to internment camps, as were thousands of others of Japanese ancestry on the Pacific Coast. The affection and concern of their fellow students, many of whom were heartbroken to see them go, is expressed by the *Growler* report on the graduation ceremony:

> We won't forget them. This graduation was perhaps more outstanding because of the sentiment behind it. Sympathy and understanding were apparent by all the students. To show our appreciation for all that these people have done for Foster, we the student body wish to express our deepest regret and hope that when the war is over we again can meet.

FOSTER HIGH SCHOOL TRADITIONS

Many of Foster High School's traditions were established between 1920 and 1940. Foster adopted the English bulldog as the school mascot in about 1926, but was using the colors purple and white much earlier. The school song "Loyal and True" was written by band director R. Paul Cronenberg in 1939. The school slogan "Let's Foster Courtesy," which graced a banner and later a sign in the school gym, was authored by Foster teacher, coach and principal Donovan Decker in 1947. The beautiful and unique "Alma Mater" was written by band director Robert Brown and was first performed by the graduating class of 1953.

NEW SCHOOLS, NEW SITES

Following the consolidation of the Duwamish and Foster districts in 1942, the new South Central School District

Teacher Josephine Waldo and high school students in the Foster High School library in the 1940s. Courtesy South Central School District.

was faced with updating or replacing the aging Duwamish Grade School and the crowded Foster High School, which had expanded into portables. But because of the district's low assessed property valuation, the effort to raise the money to secure new school sites and build new schools took several years. The estimated cost to build an elementary and a high school was $1.6 million, but the district expected state and federal help because of defense industry impacts. Using the approach of a series of levies rather than a single bond issue, school levies were approved in 1946, 1947 and 1948. A $125,000 bond issue, included on the 1948 ballot, brought the total building fund to $325,000.

The plan to build a new school at the Duwamish site was dropped when the district received word that the state board of education would not accept—and therefore would not fund—the Duwamish-Allentown site because it was in the path of the proposed Port of Seattle plan to construct the upper Duwamish River Waterway. The state board would not approve a site that it felt was destined to be hemmed in by industry. After consideration of other sites, the school board decided to build at Riverton on the site of the original Riverton School. The name Southgate was selected in a "name the school" contest, and Southgate Elementary School opened in 1950. However, because of the postwar "baby boom," Southgate augmented rather than replaced the Duwamish School.

School district officials had intended to rebuild Foster High School on the same site, but the state board of education informed the district that the central site was too small for a new high school. The new site selected was at the northeast corner of 42 Ave. S. and S. 144 St. Early on, the school district considered adding the Gaskill property, later the site of St. Thomas Catholic Church. As originally designed by architect Ralph Burkhard, the new school was to have included classrooms, a cafeteria, health rooms, kitchen, meeting room with a fireplace, public library, an 800-seat auditorium and a 1,500-seat gymnasium. The facility was to serve as a community center as well as a school.

STILL POOR, STILL IMPROVING

Plans for the new high school had to be modified when the voters of the district turned down one final building fund levy in November of 1950. The school was redesigned to fit the new budget, the auditorium was dropped and elimination of the gym was seriously considered. The school board decided to build as much school as the money would allow, hoping that federal money could be obtained. Eventually, the district obtained $538,780 in Federal Impact Funds and $330,269 in state funds to match the $104,142 in local funds on the $973,191 construction contract with Brazier Construction. A groundbreaking ceremony was held at the new site on February 4, 1952, with long-term teacher Josephine Waldo turning the first shovel of dirt. In an advisory ballot measure on naming the new high school that fall, the historic name Foster won narrowly over South Central. The school was completed in 1953.

THE SOUTH CENTRAL SCHOOL DISTRICT

Drum majorette, drill team and band leading the student body to the newly completed Foster High School on S. 144th St. on Jan. 5, 1953. Courtesy South Central School District.

Construction was completed by the first week in January, and it was with a mixture of excitement and sadness that the high school students gathered in the old school gymnasium at 8:45 the morning of January 5, 1953. Once assembled, they formed a parade led by the high school band, drill team and majorette, down 51 Ave. S. and up Brummer's Hill to the new school. Many community people joined in the parade. A brief ceremony was held at the new Foster School and then the pupils ventured out into the new building to find their lockers and classrooms.

At the dedication ceremony for the new school January 15, State Superintendent of Public Instruction Pearl Wanamaker told a *Growler* reporter, "I think your new school is very beautiful, functional, and economically constructed."

The building's design won for Burkhard the American Association of School Administrators first place award in the School Executives 1952 Competition for Better School Design. But there was also dissatisfaction with its design and construction. Indeed, ruptured heating pipes in the floors, a leaking roof, and its inexpensive construction led to its eventual replacement.

Foster High soon received a number of additions, including two classroom wings, 1956; the little gym, 1957; tennis courts and the stadium, 1964; power mechanics shop, 1970; and expansion of the library and locker rooms, 1979.

The old high school building at 51 Ave. S. and S. 139 St. did not stand vacant long after the high school students marched out to the new school. In the autumn of 1953 it was being used for kindergarten classes, and in 1954 it opened as Central Elementary School. It remained an elementary school until the completion of the new Tukwila Elementary in 1963. In 1967, it became home to the state's first occupational skills center, a vocational training program sponsored by South Central, Highline and

233

Federal Way school districts. When the skills center moved to its new home near Seattle-Tacoma International Airport in 1972, the old brick-façade building closed for the last time. It was demolished by a private contractor in the winter of 1973-74, and the site became Foster Park.

All of this school expansion and construction was in response to the postwar baby boom, the largest single demographic feature of the United States in the twentieth century. Enrollment grew from 1,414 in 1949 to 2,778 in 1961 without a break. Between 1956 and 1957 the district grew from 2,076 to 2,427.

Planning for growth in enrollment became one of the primary tasks of school officials, who had to provide new and enlarged buildings and hire new teachers to provide for the influx. Between 1949 and 1969, South Central built five new schools: Southgate, 1950, Cascade View, 1957, Tukwila, 1963, and Thorndyke, 1969, and Foster High, 1953. A new administration building was added in 1957. Showalter was enlarged with the addition of a new gymnasium complex in 1964 and began the move toward becoming first a junior high and then a middle school. The school district also was instrumental in providing for a new Foster public library in 1966 and a new county swimming pool in 1973 on land owned by the district.

New teachers were recruited from colleges throughout the Northwest in the postwar years, as South Central competed with other districts for candidates. Frank Horsfall, a former Foster teacher and district business manager under Superintendent Myron Colburn, described how he went to a convention of school administrators in Spokane in 1948 to find a teaching job. "I don't know what the school administrators did, but it was the hiring hall for prospective teachers. Every college placement bureau set up an office in the hotel, all the candidates were available for interviews, and appointments were set up. There was still a shortage of teachers, so candidates were often offered contracts on the spot."

Remarkably, most of the improvements at this time were accomplished with a tax base that was the lowest of any school district in King County. Often, the district simply had to "make do" with existing programs and facilities. For example, before the administrative building was built, the district administrative office was first a room in the high school building and then moved to an old house north of Foster High. Because of the impact of defense-related employment in the general area, in the period after World War II the district received considerable federal aid for construction and operations.

Freeway Construction Claims Homes and Families

Construction of the I-5 freeway through the area in the early 1960s had a large impact on South Central schools, particularly in terms of enrollment. According to Horsfall, as freeway construction claimed homes, families moved away and the schools lost enrollment, causing financial impacts that could not be predicted. From an all-time high of 2,778 in 1961, before freeway construction began, enrollment plummeted to 2,464 in 1963 and 2,350 in 1964. The debate over the route of the freeway took place in the early 1950s. The freeway route through the South Central area was always favored, but alternative routes were proposed that would have put the freeway through the Highline area or along the Northern Pacific railroad tracks. Lloyd Anderson of King County Planning Commission favored a Highline route, but State Highway Director William Bugge favored the South Central route. Freeway construction essentially cut the school district in two. The original state plan did not include any overpasses between the Tukwila Interchange and Interurban Ave. The school board pressed for and won the vital overpass at S. 144th St.

The South Central School District

An aerial view of Foster High School and environs in 1965, looking northeast. Note the construction of the Interstate 5 freeway in the background. Courtesy South Central School District.

School District Boundaries Change

The single event that abruptly changed the district's financial condition was the opening of Southcenter regional shopping center in 1968. Construction of attractive department stores and specialty shops with a high assessed value, on land that had been open pasture and marsh with a low assessed value, increased the tax base for local taxing districts, including the school district.

Much of the area where Southcenter stands was not within the South Central School District until a fortunate boundary change in 1961. Frank Horsfall, South Central business manager at the time, recalls that Renton School District was not interested in providing bus transportation to a family living near the Green River south of 160 St., the school district boundary at the time. The family petitioned to have the area transferred to South Central, which had agreed to provide transportation. Adjustment of the boundary was approved in May 1961 with barely a ripple of interest in either school district.

Revenue generated by Southcenter did not begin to affect the school district until the 1970s, and then it was only a short time until the state levy lid law went into effect, limiting the amount of money the district could seek in a maintenance and operation tax levy. The levy lid law, in conjunction with the state basic education act, was intended to avoid having "rich" and "poor" school districts, providing unequal educational prospects for students living in different locations.

Other boundary changes took place during the boom era as well. Through an agreement with Highline School District, the western boundary was moved west from 32 Ave. to Military Road, at the same time Cascade View Elementary was opened in 1957. While it was under construction, the new elementary was technically outside the South Central School District. In 1956, a planning consultant to the county School Reorganization Committee recommended that the boundaries of South Central be expanded south to Bow Lake and Seattle-Tacoma International Airport. Interest in joining the South Central district was also expressed by some McMicken Heights residents. In contrast, some members of the School Reorganization Committee favored merging the entire South Central School District with Highline. However, the majority of the committee "recognized that there are strong loyalties in

235

WERNER NEUDORF

Werner Neudorf was introduced to Foster High football when the Dayton High School team he was coaching defeated Foster for the unofficial state Class B championship in 1951. The next year, he was the Foster coach. A former Navy drill instructor, he proved a strict but caring disciplinarian. His no-nonsense approach produced two league titles and the best win-loss record in the school's history (51-44-4). In successive years, his teams beat (20-7 in 1956) and tied neighboring rival Renton, which at the time had more than double the enrollment of Foster. From such feats, he earned a reputation as a "giant killer." He coached an underdog West team to an upset victory in an East-West all-star game.

Through Neudorf's efforts, a booster club was formed and a years-long campaign to build a football stadium was won. He also coached track, winning the third-place trophy at the state Class A meet in 1966. On his retirement in 1976, the school football stadium was named Werner Neudorf Field after him, and later he was enshrined in the State Football Hall of Fame (1987).

In addition to being a first-class coach, Neudorf (affectionately known as Neudy) also was a dedicated teacher and community leader. His history, health and physical education classes were always well-prepared. His remedial physical education program was a model. The local Kiwanis Club and American Legion post benefitted from his active involvement. Throughout his teaching career and through volunteer tutoring after his retirement, he demonstrated his care for the young people of the community.

Werner Neudorf, with assistant coaches Floyd Robbins and Duane Magee, at football practice in the the late 1950s on the Foster High School field, later named for Neudorf. Robbins later served as principal, and the school gymnasium was named after him. Magee was a highly successful boys' basketball coach. Courtesy South Central School District.

South Central District," as one member of the committee told the *Growler*.

Those strong loyalties were much in evidence during school levy elections, when students, teachers, and public-spirited community members turned out to campaign for money to operate the existing schools or to build new schools. One year in the late 1940s, students drove around the district in a flatbed truck ringing the old school bell to draw community attention to the school's needs. Later, a sound truck served the same purpose. Teachers helped distribute fliers door to door. "I remember struggling through darkness to deliver reminders to vote next Tuesday," long-term Foster journalism teacher Grace Gylling recalls. The Advisory Council managed the levy campaigns, and the Foster Booster Club, formed in 1955 to support high school activities, played an important part in the bond issue for the stadium.

Teachers, parents and community members also sponsored school fund-raiser talent shows,

THE SOUTH CENTRAL SCHOOL DISTRICT

spaghetti dinners and carnivals, such as the Showalter Fun-nik and the Duwamish Carnival.

BABY BUST, BABY BOOMLET— THE 1970S AND 1980S

Encroachment of industry and apartments on what had been single-family neighborhoods hastened the enrollment decline in South Central after 1970. Birth rates and changing demographics had just as much impact on South Central schools in the 1970s and 1980s as they had in the postwar years, but in reverse. From 2,611 students in 1969, South Central's enrollment fell constantly through the 1970s and into the 1980s, hitting bottom in 1986 at 1,373. In response to the declining enrollment, South Central closed three of five elementary schools between 1971 and 1981—Duwamish (1973), Southgate (1978) and Cascade View (1981). Southgate became the City of Tukwila Community Center. In 1983-84, Cascade View was reopened to house the South Central Children's Center, a school district preschool and day care program begun under Superintendent John Fotheringham, and under Superintendent Michael Silver it was cited by Bank Street School of Wellesley College as one of 12 exemplary public school early childhood programs in the nation.

Enrollments reversed in 1987, and the enrollment climbed to 1,730 in 1989 and 1,800 in 1990. The enrollment increase is particularly evident in the lower grades. In 1990, the kindergarten class was twice as large as the graduating class. With the enrollment boom at the lower grade levels, the district placed one or two regular school classes per year at Cascade View until the school was a full elementary school once again in 1988. However, the elementary enrollment increase filled Cascade View and the other two elementary schools, leaving the district with the problem of how to accommodate the growing number of elementary students. Other facilities needs faced the district, too. Showalter needed modernization, and Foster High had outlived its useful life. As early

THE ROCK

A rock coated with countless layers of paint stands in a place of honor in front of Foster High School. Generations of Foster students have painted their class numerals and other visual statements on it.

According to accounts of a number of longtime area residents, the rock was unearthed during the grading of Brummer's Hill in the mid-1930s. It was placed at the southeast corner of 144 St. and Macadam Road, near the northwest corner of the Foster Community Hall. For a time it was known as Welch's rock, for one of the men who moved it. Many remember winter bonfires in front of the rock during sledding parties. It was originally painted "county yellow" with the name "FOSTER" in neat black letters on the flat face toward Macadam Road, probably by the county road crew that put it there.

Dr. Gordon Newton, son of former South Central school board member Lois Newton, recalls: "When I was in my early teens, I used to hang out at this same intersection. One evening, probably in 1941, I was looking at the large yellow rock and I got the idea to change the name. A couple of nights later, I put yellow paint over the word 'FOSTER' and under it painted the word 'TUKWILA' in black paint. Then I painted a black arrow around the side of the rock to point toward Tukwila." A short time later, 'TUKWILA' was painted over and replaced with the word 'FOSTER.' Over the years, the town rivalry was supplanted by rivalry between high school graduating classes. Young people began caring deeply about the hunk of geology.

Foster students could not bear the thought of The Rock being plowed under with the Interstate 5 freeway construction. In 1963 a group that included Tom Kilburg and Gary Sherbon loaded the rock into the back of Sherbon's pickup truck and hauled it to the new high school campus. In 1979 The Rock was briefly kidnapped and held for ransom.

When the high school building was demolished in 1990 to make way for the new school, one of the greatest concerns of students was "Will The Rock be saved?" It was.

237

TUKWILA—COMMUNITY AT THE CROSSROADS

> **FOSTER HIGH ACTIVITIES**
>
> School dances, such as the Junior-Senior Ball and Tolo, hold memories for many Fosterites. Many of those who went to Foster dances in the 1930s and 1940s recall the music of Foster grad Ky Fox and his orchestra. The first Homecoming dance was held at the Foster Community Club in 1948 with Queen Gerry Thompson reigning.
>
> In 1923-24 Foster High had a top debate squad which won the King County championship with a record of 11-1 on the question "Resolved: that the U.S. shall join the World Court." A national school assembly program in the 1930s brought many notable speakers to Foster High, including Olympic athletes Jesse Owens and Jim Thorpe.
>
> From 1940 to 1960 Foster High School bands earned high marks in competition and praise in concerts under a succession of talented directors. Leon Metcalf, who published a number of his own compositions, led the band in the 1940s. Robert Brown, who wrote the Alma Mater, continued the tradition in the early 1950s. The bands of Roland Schanzenbach brought statewide acclaim to Foster in the 1950s and 1960s.

as 1969, heating pipes in the concrete foundation had ruptured, flooding classrooms and leaving them without heat until emergency repairs were made.

100 YEARS LATER, A NEW FOSTER

In May 1988 voters turned down a $32 million bond issue that was intended to fund replacing Foster, modernizing Showalter, and expanding the elementary schools. The following November, they approved a $16 million bond issue for the new high school, as well as for computers and other high technology equipment, a measure endorsed by Governor Booth Gardner on a visit to the school shortly before the election.

After a farewell party called the Foster Final Fling, attended by several thousand alumni in May 1990, the 37-year-old Foster High School building was demolished, and construction of the new high school began on the same site.

The planned opening and dedication are scheduled for almost 100 years to the day from the founding of the original Foster School District.

THE CHANGING FACE OF CHILDREN, THE CHANGING NEEDS OF SCHOOLS

s public education in the Tukwila area begins its second century, it is faced with the daunting challenge of improving and fundamentally changing to prepare its diverse student population for success in a world far different from the one of only a generation ago.

Demographics of the community do not paint an encouraging picture. Like school districts across the nation, South Central has increasing signs of poverty, neglect and abuse among its students. In 1989, more than one third of South Central students were participating in the free and reduced price lunch program. Fewer students come from traditional two-parent homes. An alarming number of abuse and neglect cases are reported each year, and doubtless many more go unreported.

At the same time, the student population is more diverse. The minority enrollment climbed from under 10 percent in 1970 to more than 25 percent by 1990, giving South Central a minority enrollment percentage second only to Seattle in King County. The district also has a large number of children whose native language is not English. More than a dozen languages were represented in 1990. Although children benefit from the greater diversity through multicultural education and understanding, teaching English as a second language is a major task of the district.

In spite of these factors South Central School District has cause for optimism because of its manageable size, the commitment of the community, and the cooperation of state and local agencies, particularly the City of Tukwila, in recognizing that schools alone cannot address the grim realities that often result in students doing poorly in school.

THE SOUTH CENTRAL SCHOOL DISTRICT

FOSTER HIGH SPORTS

Foster High School's relatively small size has allowed a large percentage of the student body—especially those of modest talent—to participate in school sports. Despite its size, however, Foster has managed to offer a fairly wide range of sports, and Foster teams have often shown prowess.

Foster boys' and girls' basketball teams were playing against other high school teams on an irregular basis as early as 1917. Foster teams gained experience and met with increasing success. The 1923 football team compiled a 4-1 record, winning by scores of 52-0 against Issaquah and 62-0 against Vashon, losing only to Enumclaw 14-13. After the season, the newly organized Girls Club put on a banquet for the team at the home of coach Ralph Reed.

The 1923-24 basketball team took the South King County championship and went on to play in the second annual state tournament at the University of Washington. Foster returned to the state basketball tournament in 1929 and 1930 under Coach Tommy Smith.

Foster's strong tradition in basketball continued in the 1950s and 1960s with the boys' teams going to the state Class A tournament five times under coach Duane Magee. Foster football teams coached by Werner Neudorf in the 1950s and 1960s were always respected. The girls' basketball teams coached by Tim Parker won state championships in 1986 and 1987 and went to the state tournament 10 times.

The 1924 Foster High School football team which won four of five games. Coach Ralph Reed is at the left end of the back row. Oscar Wood, who also excelled at basketball and baseball, is sixth from the left in the back row. Wood, who later played professional baseball with the Seattle Indians, once struck out 24 batters in a Foster baseball game against Renton. Courtesy Oscar and Alice Wood.

In recent years, Foster also has found success in golf and tennis. Coached by Gary Luft, the boys' golf team won the state A/B championship three times and the girls' golf team won twice through 1991. The boys' tennis team under Steve Escame won the state A/B title in 1989.

Boys who did not make the varsity team could play intramural sports. In the 1930s and 1940s, the lunchtime intramural basketball league was called the Do-Nut League. Boys could also participate in the smoker boxing, and sometimes wrestling, matches in 1930s, 1940s, and 1950s. The smokers were usually sponsored by Hi-Y, a club that promoted citizenship and religious faith.

The district has not focused solely on the immediate problems, however. It is innovative in its academic program—for example, through its use of technology as an educational tool, its emphasis on students' ability to reason and solve problems, and its commitment to early childhood education with child care, preschool and intervention programs.

Such an educational program is, of necessity, far different from the one taught in Joseph Foster's living room a hundred years ago. But Foster no doubt would approve of the effort to provide children—the future of the community—with the best public education possible.

The history of the South Central School District is far more detailed than this brief chapter can convey. Names of teachers and students, recollections of fond memories, facts and figures—only a few could be included. A more complete account is yet to be told. Certainly within the next 100 years it will be.

CHAPTER 15
DISTRICTS AND NEIGHBORHOODS—
RENTON JUNCTION, RIVERTON HEIGHTS
AND MCMICKEN HEIGHTS

Renton Junction station, ca. 1915. Located one quarter of a mile west of historic Mox la Push (Black River Junction), in 1990 the station site is where Interurban Ave. crosses the Green River, south of the junction of Interurban Ave. and Southcenter Blvd. The tracks were raised on trestles to avoid the natural marsh. Courtesy Warren Wing.

RENTON JUNCTION

Of all the communities that grew up around the Interurban stations, the most important to the train service was Renton Junction. A country station, it was the interchange for trains to Renton, Kent, Tacoma and Seattle. In the 1910s and 1920s Renton Junction hummed with activity. The station was on the east side of the river across the tracks from both the Interurban and vehicle and pedestrian bridges. The station was manned 24 hours a day. The Chicago, Milwaukee and St. Paul, Great Northern and Northern Pacific tracks ran close by the Interurban tracks.

Orillia, in the Green (White) River Valley, was the closest community to Renton Junction and the two communities composed a single voting precinct which reported a total population of 243 in 1900, 440 in 1910, 544 in 1920, and 1026 in 1930. In 1990 terms Orillia was located near Tukwila's southern city limits in the vicinity of the Southcenter industrial park. Only vestiges remain of Orillia and the townsite has been annexed to Kent. Founded in the 1870s, Orillia was a thriving service and social center and was "town" for the people living in the south end of the Duwamish Valley.

In the 1909 *Polk's Directory*, Orillia is described as "one of the important minor towns of King County," having two general stores, two blacksmiths, a tinsmith, a shoemaker, a butcher, an Interurban station and a Northern Pacific siding. The community's institutions serving the valley included the White River Grange Hall, built around 1906, a neat frame church shared by the Lutherans and the Episcopalians, and the Orillia school, where two teachers taught grades 1 through 10.

The Orillia Post Office served the Renton Junction community and in the days before rural delivery most people made regular trips to town to check for mail. Helen Nelsen remembers that after rural delivery began, the mail came out of Kent and was delivered to farm families on the hills and down in the valley by the mailman who "drove a little red, white and blue boxy wagon drawn by a horse."

Several hundred people traveled through the Renton Junction crossroads each week. Around 1910 it seemed that almost everyone who lived close by was a Danish immigrant or was named Nelsen. A remarkable number of the locals were both. The 1911-12 *Polk's Directory* gives the population of Renton Junction as 45.

James and Mary Nelsen's home was within view of Renton station. At the crossroads lived

240

DISTRICTS AND NEIGHBORHOODS—RENTON JUNCTION, RIVERTON HEIGHTS AND MCMICKEN HEIGHTS

Chris and Amanda Jorgensen Hansen operated the Renton Junction Grocery Store in the 1910s and 1920s. Located close to the Interurban station, the store enjoyed brisk trade from travelers, who often had time to shop between trains at the country interchange. Courtesy Alma Nelsen Taylor.

Hardly a day passed when a hobo did not appear at the farmhouse back door asking for food. Dora Nelsen would never turn a hungry person away, but her husband liked to get the men to do a few chores such as splitting wood, helping move equipment or pitching hay for their home-cooked meal.

The children living at Renton Junction caught the Interurban to the Orillia School and later to high school in Renton or Kent. Alma Nelsen Taylor remembers how the Interurban motorman would watch for them. Occasionally, the train had already left the station when the Nelsens—there were always at least five of school age—"would come running underneath the tracks." Alma recalls, "He'd back the old Interurban up to wait for us. He didn't do that very often. He didn't like it, but he did it." Naturally,

the Fred Nelsens, their dairy milkers—a couple who lived in a small house Nelsen provided for them—and Dora's sister Amanda and her husband Chris Hansen. Fred and Dora Jorgensen Nelsen's home and dairy farm buildings were about a five-minute walk from the station. Chris and Amanda Jorgensen Hansen operated the Renton Junction Grocery and lived above the store.

In addition to the Danish immigrants there were several Japanese immigrant families just south, toward Orillia. Matsusuke and Tamayo Mikami settled in the Southcenter district and developed a prosperous garden market farm. The Mikamis' eight children were born on the farm, with Matsu serving as "midwife." Mikami had worked in the sugar-cane fields of Hawaii and the logging camps of Washington before settling down to farming.

There was a siding for the heavy rail at Renton Junction and close by a hobo colony, where men took a break from "riding the rails."

Fred and Dora Nelsen relax in their parlor. Daughters Alma and Eleanor recall that their home lay so close to the Northern Pacific railroad tracks that every time the train went through they had to straighten the pictures hanging on the parlor walls. Courtesy Eleanor Nelsen Robinson.

241

TUKWILA—COMMUNITY AT THE CROSSROADS

Sunday baseball game at Maple Grove Park, 1912. Fred Nelsen's barn is on the left and the house is behind the trees. Courtesy Alma Nelsen Taylor.

the motormen and conductors became friends with the Nelsen children, and occasionally a motorman would let one of them go up front in the car and run it, pulling the controller back and forth to stop and start the car.

Alma has memories of a very happy childhood filled with "regular work and chores every day and lots of fun." Like other children living in the valley, the Renton Junction young people focused on the river for their summer activities. When the children were going to spend the afternoon playing on the river, Dora Nelsen would take a blanket, a sun umbrella and the *Ladies Home Journal,* and spend the time relaxing on the bank and watching her brood. Hours were spent fishing, making sand castles and picking fragrant pink wild roses. Many a tasty fish fry was enjoyed after such a day. Besides the river there were other diversions including riding the horses bareback or hitching up the old buggy and driving down the dusty valley road. After supper in the summer the family would play baseball in the front yard. Dora Nelsen was an avid baseball player and fan.

When Alma or one of her sisters had a birthday party, the guests would come out after school on the Interurban—which was the only way to get around—all dressed up in frilly dresses, black patent leather shoes and big hair bows. The girls would inevitably end up in the barn climbing, jumping and rolling in the haymow. In the spring the children would cross the Renton Junction drawbridge and go up Tukwila Hill to walk in the hazel grove that was alive with pristine white trilliums by the thousands. They would return in the autumn to gather gunnysacks full of hazelnuts.

Maple Grove Park

Fred Nelsen was a very enterprising person, and in 1908 he developed a pretty piece of bottomland on the bank of the river into a public picnic grounds. Named Maple Grove Park for the trees that grew there, it was located south and west of the railroad tracks, where highway I-405 was later built.

The wonderful country setting and the short five-minute walk from the Renton Junction station made Maple Grove Park a very popular place with organizations from Renton, Kent, Seattle, and the Duwamish and Green River valley communities, which rented it for gatherings of all kinds, from family reunions to rallies and conventions. For example, the King County Pioneer Association held its annual summer picnic there, as did numerous local

DISTRICTS AND NEIGHBORHOODS—RENTON JUNCTION, RIVERTON HEIGHTS AND MCMICKEN HEIGHTS

lodges including the Woodmen and Woodwomen of the World, the Pythians, and the Odd Fellows. The Italians from Renton would reserve the park for huge Sunday gatherings with concertina and mandolin music and dancing. The Danes, Swedes and Norwegians would stage their Midsommar Fest at the park.

Soon after opening the park, Nelsen added a bowling alley and a dance pavilion to the basic picnic tables, fireplaces and rain shelters. For the simple small-ball bowling alley Nelsen hollowed out cedar trunks to serve as the ballreturn trough, and the Nelsen girls worked as pin setters for the players. On summer weekends Fred Nelsen was always on hand at the park overseeing everything, with three or four of the children helping out. Alma recalls the Nelsen children "did have a lot of fun over there at the park because [when big groups came in for the day] we kids would go over and [join their] foot races and always win" the prizes. Nelsen did not mind if the children joined in on visitors' activities—except the dances. His pretty daughters were forbidden to attend the dances held by the many ethnic communities that frequently came to the park.

THE DANCE PAVILION BY THE RIVER

Nelsen's natural wood dance pavilion had large windows all along the walls, with heavy hinged wooden shutters that were tied open, letting in cool breezes from the river. The pavilion was undoubtedly the most attractive feature, drawing people to the park in that ballroom dance-loving era. A typical dance event of this period was the Midsummer party put on by the Rainier Social Club of Seattle on Sunday, June 23, 1912. Beginning at noon, for the ten cents admission, one could enter the grounds and dance all day to the union orchestra composed of violins, an accordion and horns that played waltzes, schottisches, mazurkas, polkas and ragtime numbers. The pavilion was fragrant with garlands of fresh greens and flowers in celebration of Midsummer. Ice cream, popcorn and other food was for sale on the grounds, but most people brought their own picnic baskets.

The valley was given something to talk about for the rest of the year when, in 1923, the Washington Ku Klux Klan held its first state convention at Maple Grove Park. Nelsen was dismayed. There had been no mention of the KKK by the pair of conventional-looking men in dark suits who had come out to the farm to make the arrangements months earlier.

King County Sheriff Matt Starwich took a great personal interest in the Klan's meeting at Renton Junction. The KKK gathering at Maple Grove Park took on something of a "media event" quality when the Klan's Grand Kleagle, L. I. Powell, and Sheriff Starwich clashed over the Klan's announced intention to hold a rally with Klansmen in full regalia, including masks. The local newspapers whipped up countywide interest in the Renton Junction convention with daily reports of the impending trouble that the gathering would bring. When the day arrived, Saturday, July 14, Starwich arrived at the park in person at noon to confirm that the law forbidding the wearing of masks in public was upheld. The sheriff looked over the quiet gathering of farmers and their families in normal attire, and commented, according to the *Seattle Star:* "This doesn't look like a disorderly gathering. As long as they don't try to wear masks in violation of the law, they will not be arrested."

After the Interurban shut down in 1928 the crossroads energy left Renton Junction and it became a quiet place. With the hard times of the Depression keeping people home, Maple Grove Park closed, and the days of throngs of happy women in white gauze summer dresses and country-dapper men sporting straw boaters spilling off the Interurban lugging bulging picnic baskets were only a memory. Nelsen sold the park to a labor group that renamed it People's Park and it continued to be used for picnics through the 1930s. In 1937-39 a roller skating rink operated at the park. It closed permanently around World War II.

RIVERTON HEIGHTS

No one thought at the time that the hills would be cleared and cultivated. The hill country was so heavily timbered and the soil gravelly. It was good land with plenty of spring water, but very hard to clear.

Jane Fenton Kelly,
The Duwamish Valley in 1864

Almost a century was to pass before the hills above the Duwamish River would be regarded as a desirable place to live. The hills to the west of Riverton came to be known as Riverton Heights. The hills farther south above Southcenter became known as McMicken Heights. The hillside neighborhoods and communities annexed in 1989 each bring their own history. As the population in the valley grew, the hills became the site of first an isolated house here and there, and then more methodically laid-out neighborhoods. Just as the building boom accompanying the startup of the Interurban quickly built up neighborhoods in the valley in the 1910s and 1920s, the post-World War II boom established new suburban residential neighborhoods on the hills.

Riverton Heights is a large area that includes the Thorndyke district and Cascade View, dating from 1960. The political boundaries of the Cascade View annexation include parts of the old Thorndyke district. Community institutions are discussed here in the context of the neighborhood where they originated, rather than more recent political boundary designations.

THE BEGINNINGS OF THE THORNDYKE DISTRICT

Thorndyke had its beginning in the first decades of the twentieth century and was the name the area was known by for the first decades of the century. Around mid-century the name Riverton Heights became the more commonly used term. While the area is more of a residential neighborhood in 1990 than a community, it has pride and traditions. Several of the early families, including the Thorndikes and Hansons, still make their homes there. In the past the Thorndyke district has had a school, an active community club and the Church by the Side of the Road. The church and school continue to serve the community.

Around 1905 George L. Thorndike and Bessie Brown Thorndike bought six acres of land up on the hill above the Duwamish River and built a home for their family of seven children. Although originally from Nebraska, George Thorndike was not a farmer, and commuted on the Interurban to his job at a Seattle lumber mill. As a child Bessie Brown came to Puget Sound with her family in a wagon train around 1875. They traveled on fairly good roads and in many areas there were established farms that made the first three rows of crops by the road available to the migrants. It was a big improvement over the Oregon Trail that Joseph and Stephen Foster had walked in 1852.

At first the Thorndikes were the only people living in the area, which was covered with large trees and thick brush. Son Willard recalls, "Where they cut the trees great big stumps were left and we kids would get on top of them and jump into the hollows down below and make houses in them. The trees were very big in those days." There was a skid road in the vicinity of S. 154 St. where logs were skidded to a mill located in the area. In 1908 George Thorndike sold one acre to the Foster School District 144 and the school was named for the family—with a change in the spelling of the name to "Thorndyke."

Raising most of their own food, the Thorndikes cared for a very large vegetable and flower garden and kept chickens, pigs, cows and goats. The children did a substantial amount of the work caring for the garden and animals. They were not paid for their work at home, naturally, but did get paid when helping neighbors, which they did with diligence. In this way they managed to buy a crystal set (an early radio) and a bicycle. Like many others in the

DISTRICTS AND NEIGHBORHOODS—RENTON JUNCTION, RIVERTON HEIGHTS AND MCMICKEN HEIGHTS

George Lorenzo and Bessie Brown Thorndike moved to Thorndyke in 1916 and established the first home in this area of Riverton Heights. The district is named for them. Courtesy Sophia Thorndike Storey and Willard Thorndike.

valley, the family did their shopping in Riverton, travelling on the Interurban.

After World War I ended a few more people moved into the area, but homes were still far apart. Among the new families were the Yorks, an older couple. Mrs. York was a real asset for Thorndyke and nearby communities as well, since she was a licensed practical nurse and a midwife. She had received her training at the time of the Spanish-American War and met her husband in the war zone when he was injured. Mrs. York delivered most of the district's babies for many years.

O. I. HANSON'S GROCERY AND GAS STATION

In 1922 Hanna and Oscar Hanson moved to the Thorndyke district where Hanna's sister lived. In addition to establishing their home, the Hansons opened a grocery store in a rented building at S. 150 and Military Road. A few years later they built a new store at S. 148 St. and Military Road. In 1928 the business was relocated onto U.S. 99.

Oscar and Hanna Hanson were active members of the Riverton Heights Improvement Club and later the Thorndyke Improvement Club, and helped secure a public water system for the district. In addition, Oscar worked closely with the county commissioners in getting roads built into the community. After Oscar died suddenly in 1936, Hanna stayed in business with the help of the children. Daughter Alice recalls that the children missed out on extra activities at school because they had to come right home to deliver the grocery orders that had been phoned in during the day. On Saturday mornings Margaret, age 12, would walk around the neighborhood to take orders from people who did not have telephones or cars, and then Alice, Herta, and Hanna would put up the orders. Alice remembers making the deliveries with the family car at age 14.

Most customers charged their groceries and paid at the end of the month—if they had the money. In the early days the Hansons accepted payment in barter, particularly fresh produce, e.g., eggs, apples, vegetables that they could sell. Since they were the only store around, they maintained a "pharmacy shelf" and also carried merchandise like hosiery and jewelry which people would buy at Christmas or for special occasions. The Hanson Grocery Store and Gas Station played an important role in the community for decades since it was the only community business in the immediate area.

In 1940 the store-gas station was sold, and under Hanna Hanson's initiative the Riverton Heights Post Office was established. In addition

The new O. I. Hanson Grocery Store and Gas Station, Highway 99 and S. 150 St., had its grand opening the day the new Pacific Highway opened, October 28, 1928. The Hansons added living quarters to their building, and for many years the family worked together running the enterprise. In the left corner is Margaret, Hanna center, and Alice right. Courtesy Alice Hanson Gustafson.

to running the office, she served as the postmaster and delivered the mail under the rural delivery system. As the population grew it was determined that the rural delivery system was no longer appropriate, and Mrs. Hanson's post office was converted to the Riverton Heights Branch of the Seattle Post Office. Mrs. Hanson served as the branch supervisor until her retirement in 1950.

THORNDYKE SCHOOL

For 71 years, a structure now called "the old Thorndyke building" has stood on the northwest corner of 42 Ave. S. and S. 150 St. Originally the Thorndyke School, it has also served as a community center and meeting hall. The original structure was built in 1908 for $625 by F. Frost as a one-room schoolhouse, where grades 1 to 4 were taught. Some students traveled a fair distance to come to school, taking the Interurban to Riverton and then walking the one and a half miles up the hill to school in the Heights.

In the first ten years various improvements were made including clearing the grounds and adding fences. Cut timber was split and used as fuel for the stove. A second room was added, drinking fountains were installed, and an improved heating system installed in 1913. Up to this time the school had been heated with a single potbellied stove. In 1921 a heating plant was put in, as well as sanitary toilets. In 1921 the school district and the PTA together built a playshed. In the 1920s grades 1-3 were taught by Miss Francel Herstrom and in the "big room," as the students always called it, Mrs. Irene Anderson taught grades 4-6.

The Thorndyke School was small and personal. At recess the boys played marbles and jacks while the girls jumped rope and played hopscotch, and all took turns with the three swings and teeter-totter. Alice Hanson Gustafson recalls: "Thorndyke School had a good baseball team, uniforms and rooters. May Day or Field Day was special, with a May Pole, gunny-sack races and three-legged races, with winners receiving blue, red and white ribbons to

DISTRICTS AND NEIGHBORHOODS—RENTON JUNCTION, RIVERTON HEIGHTS AND MCMICKEN HEIGHTS

> ### HANNA JOHNSON HANSON GORANSON RIVERTON HEIGHTS COMMUNITY BUILDER—1922-1950
>
> Hanna A. Johnson was born in 1894 at Umea, Sweden, the daughter of farmers. At 18 she traveled alone to Seattle to join her sister and brother. While getting established she worked as a nursemaid and attended Broadway Technical High School, where she studied English and millinery. Completing her training, she worked as a milliner for the Frederick & Nelson Department Store. In 1915 Hanna married Oscar I. Hanson and eventually they established their home and business, Hanson's Grocery Store and Gas Station, in the Thorndyke district of Riverton Heights. The couple were mainstays of the new community, providing leadership in many areas, including founding the community church, serving on the school board and the Riverton Heights and Thorndyke community clubs, and encouraging road construction.
>
> After Oscar's death in 1936, Hanna continued to build the community, with her two most significant accomplishments being singlehandedly establishing the Riverton Heights Post Office and building up the community's church, the Church by the Side of the Road.
>
> The Hansons had four children: Margaret (Angle), Herta (Rogne), Alice (Gustafson) and Oscar. Alice and her husband Stan Gustafson, who grew up in Tukwila, continue to make their home in Thorndyke, where Alice carries on in her mother's tradition of community service. Margaret Hanson is married to Jim Angle and they live in Foster. Third-generation Hansons make their home in the community. Hanna Hanson married Joseph Goranson in 1950. She died in Thorndyke in 1982 at age 88.

cherish." Kitty Endert remembers the excitement students felt when they walked up the board sidewalk to the Foster High School to see a movie, which cost 10 cents. Another exciting outing was the entire school walking to the Foster High School to see the annual all-school play.

Many of the families that lived on the hill in the Thorndyke district were of modest means and the Great Depression caused real hardship. One man recalls: "We were so poor....When I went to school I'd have bread with just a little butter or maybe just a little mayonnaise and it was wrapped in a newspaper. I'd try to get other kids to trade sandwiches with me. One kid did one time, but when he unwrapped that newspaper and found this skimpy sandwich, he didn't want to trade anymore."

In 1938 the old Thorndyke School was closed as part of the consolidation of the area's students to the new school, Showalter Elementary. As a major residential neighborhood, the Riverton Heights area developed rapidly in the 1960s, and in 1969 a new Thorndyke School was built.

THORNDYKE COMMUNITY CLUB

The Thorndyke Improvement Club was founded on November 3, 1938, with its first officers being William Glithero, president; A. D. Taylor, vice president and A. J. Wellander, secretary/treasurer. Meetings were held the first Tuesday of each month and dues were 50 cents a year. The club's name was soon changed to the Thorndyke Community Club to avoid confusion with neighboring clubs.

The club immediately attracted a large and active membership and served as a focal point for people in the area who had concerns about local events and the well-being of the community. A number of committees were established focusing on community improvement and social enjoyment, including finance, building, roads, zoning, courtesy, health, publicity, membership, hospitality and maintenance. Without the benefit of a municipal government, the club provided the initiative and leadership necessary to bring about major improvements. For example, in April 1939 the club sent the following three resolutions to the King County Commission requesting road improvements: a) grade and drain the hill on S. 150 St. between 46 Ave. S. and 50 Ave. S.; b) grade 42 Ave. S. from 139 to 164; and 3) oil Military Road from Three Tree Point Road to S. 164 St., 42 Ave. S. from 139 to 164, and 150 from Pacific Highway to 50 Ave. S.

Thorndyke School class with teacher Elizabeth Rider Montgomery, the author of the much-used "Dick and Jane" children's readers, 1922. Courtesy Alice Hanson Gustafson.

ELIZABETH RIDER MONTGOMERY

Sally said, "Look, Spot.
Here is my new toy."

Those simple words, which helped a generation learn to decipher the English language in the Scott, Foresman reader *Fun with Dick and Jane,* were penned by former Thorndyke Elementary School teacher Elizabeth Rider Montgomery. Montgomery, born in Peru of missionary parents, wrote or co-authored eight of the stories in the "Dick and Jane" books used in first-grade classrooms across the country in the 1940s and 1950s. She was also the author of 16 textbooks, 12 works of juvenile fiction, 34 juvenile nonfiction books, three plays and one adult fiction title.

As Elizabeth Rider, she taught from 1921 to 1924 in the two-room Thorndyke School. She left Thorndyke to obtain a master's degree in 1925 at Washington State Normal School (Western Washington University) and then taught in Aberdeen and Los Angeles, California. From 1938 to 1963, she worked as a staff writer for Scott, Foresman. Returning to Seattle in 1963, she lived out her retirement years in West Seattle. In addition to being a writer she was an artist.

From the beginning the club was the center of social and cultural community activities. For many years the monthly meetings included a delicious communal potluck dinner. A youth softball team was started on April 5, 1939, and was active for many years. Community social activities included dances, card parties, raffles, picnics, showers for prospective brides and new mothers, and traditional holiday parties. The club members called on and often looked after people in the community who were ill or shut-in. The community club hall was also the meeting place for a variety of community organizations including the Garden Club, Cub Scouts, Boy Scouts, bazaars, baton-twirling classes, and the American Legion. The hall was also available to the public to rent for special occasions, such as wedding receptions and anniversary or birthday parties.

With energy and commitment the Thorndyke Community Club turned a condemned school into a community asset. The women of the Community Club worked very hard and deserve much credit for its continued success over the years. After a temporary setback during World War II, when attendance dropped and the treasury became very low, the club rallied after the war. Membership grew and dances were held—admission was 35 cents per person. Annual picnics attracted many members.

In April 1942 the Thorndyke Club invited the older Riverton Heights Improvement Club to use its hall for their meetings, since the Heights Club building at S. 138 St. and Military Road was being used by the government for wartime needs. In June 1942 the Thorndyke Club clarified its boundaries, and members of the Riverton Heights Improvement Club who desired and qualified merged with the Thorndyke club. However, the loss of the club's records prevents the telling of a detailed history after 1942. The Thorndyke Community Club continued to be active over the years until building maintenance and insurance became too expensive. The building was returned to the school district and sold in 1978. In 1990 it had been moved slightly from its original site and was in need of repair.

Church by the Side of the Road

In 1924 a small group from a Riverton Heights Sunday school received the baptism in the Holy Spirit, during a series of tent meetings conducted by Dr. Price. After the revival, the group continued meeting and held Sunday School in the Thorndyke School praying for a meeting place of their own and a spiritual leader to guide them. Church members Hanna and Oscar Hanson owned a thickly wooded lot in the Thorndyke district and donated it for the church site. The Hansons negotiated with the county commissioners to get a new road built connecting Pacific Highway (US-99) to Military Road. The little white church was built fronting on this road, S. 148 St., and in June 1933 was dedicated as the Little Church by the Side of the Road.

As the congregation grew, more room was needed. Between 1954 and 1962 a new education building and a new church were built. At this time "Little" was dropped from the name, and the church became known simply as the Church by the Side of the Road. Founder Hanna Hanson was an active leader in the church throughout her life, as her children who live in the area have continued to be.

Through the years of its growth and development, the Church by the Side of the Road has maintained a consistent commitment to the autonomy of the local church. As a result, the church has remained an independent, non-denominational body, cooperating in the spirit of inter-church fellowship with independent churches of the Fellowship of Christian Assemblies. The church has maintained a mission in Brazil since 1939 and another in Liberia, West Africa, since the 1970s. The church was included in the 1990 Cascade View annexation area.

Riverton Heights Grows

Just as the Depression hit the country, an enterprising man named Paul Koch opened Koch's Gilmore Service Station on Highway 99. Koch, the son of German immigrants, had come to the area in 1906 from New York. Business was slow the first years on the corner and Koch took up woodcarving to pass the time. Working mainly with a penknife, in the coming years the self-taught artist created dozens of intricate and beautiful wood carvings. His subjects ranged from the Gilmore lions to the Last Supper, which may be seen at the Foster-Tukwila Presbyterian Church. Daughter Evelyn Koch Santora recalls that he displayed many of his carvings at the station and people came from all over the Northwest to see them. Eventually, the remarkable woodcarvings by the Riverton service station owner made their way into churches, banks, clubs and homes.

As the Depression tapered off, businesses were established in Riverton Heights, which was attracting homeowners because of the reasonably priced lots and beautiful hillside location. Ludwig and Johanna Mayer emigrated from Germany in the mid-1920s. They made their

Paul Koch's Gilmore Station in Riverton Heights provided quality service to community and highway travelers alike for 36 years. Pacific Highway, a simple two-lane road, was not paved at the location for many years. Koch's station was at S. 154 St. and 99—a corner known in the Heights as "death corner" because of the high number of traffic accidents and fatalities. Finally, a 4-way stop signal light was installed in the 1950s. Courtesy Evelyn Koch Santora.

way to Riverton Heights and purchased one acre for $7,000. At that time there were only a few other houses in the immediate area. The Mayers cleared the land of 60 large tree stumps and built the Riverton Heights Cabinet Shop in 1937.

When Johanna learned that there was not a medical doctor in the immediate area, she and Ludwig helped bring Dr. Eugene Hunt to the community, where he established his practice in an empty building at the southeast intersection of 152 St. S. and Pacific Highway. Dr. Hunt eventually located his practice in a building south of the Riverton Heights Ice Creamery, which he shared with dentist Dr. Gordon Newton.

In 1934 George Helgeson assisted his sister in setting up the Central Trailer Exchange. The business manufactured and sold house trailers near the corner of S. 144 St. and Pacific Highway S. and in Seattle. George's sons John, Paul and Robert worked in the family-owned business, which at first produced 22- and 30-foot house trailers. In the 1950s the business started manufacturing recreational vehicles. In 1990 the firm was called Helgeson Trailer Exchange and had moved to south of the airport on Pacific Highway. In 1989 the company was the second-oldest family-owned travel trailer business in the nation.

Bernardo "Bernie" Salle, owner of Bernie and Boys, was born and raised in the Duwamish area and has spent at least 54 years at his present location on Pacific Highway. His father, Nunzio De Pasquale Salle, originally leased land from Elmer Robbins in the Cascade View area, operating a truck garden raising corn, peas, onions and cabbage, and running a fruit stand in the valley. His father built the grocery store known as Salle's Market in 1937, which Bernie and his sons operate in 1990. Salle's is widely known by travelers on the highway for its sign, "Live Butcher!" which has caused drivers to smile for decades. Nearby businesses have followed suit to Salle's. For example, in the 1980s the Derby Tavern proclaimed "Live Bartender!"

Trudy's Tavern, named after the locally known banjo entertainer Trudy Hawley, was owned and operated by Trudy from 1939 to 1958. The tavern served as a landmark since it was the only business along the highway between Seattle and Tacoma that left its sign on day and night. When you saw Trudy's sign you knew you were almost home.

Bill and Edna Norton began Norton's Pacific Grocery near the corner of S. 144 St. and Pacific Highway in October 1954. Marshall and Audrey McKinney purchased the store in 1960, changing the name to McKinney's Pacific Thriftway. Their son Larry McKinney worked in the store. Larry then started Larry's Market on the same corner in 1974. He has since developed a chain of grocery stores in the Seattle area.

POST-WORLD WAR II EXPLOSION

fter World War II the population exploded. New homes, motels, apartments, condominiums and businesses sprang up. The Boeing Airplane Co., new industries in the valley, and SeaTac Airport brought many new residents to the area. Some servicemen who were stationed in the Northwest liked it and returned with their families after the war.

Gradually businesses sprang up all over the Riverton Heights district, including Richfield and Cooper's gas stations, Cotton's Feed Store, Jack's Store, Smith's Pharmacy, Hi Line Lumber, Carlson's Grocery, and Karl Karlson's Grocery and Lockers. In addition, taverns, barber shops, real estate offices, restaurants, a hamburger drive-in, used car dealers, antique shops, a five and dime, and others opened. A number of these businesses are still in operation in 1990.

In 1946 Bob and Luella Carson began operating Hometown Hardware next to Lee's Riverton Market in Riverton. In 1960 the hardware store was moved to Riverton Heights, where it continues business as True Value Hometown Hardware. The Carsons sold the store in 1972.

Larry and Ida Runge purchased property on the west side of Pacific Highway at S. 141 St. in 1956. Ida remembers the property being surrounded by cow pasture at the time. The Runges built and operated the Puget Sound Auction, where Mr. Runge auctioned off furniture. In addition, they operated a car wash and the 21 Club restaurant. The restaurant was temporarily converted to a dormitory for visiting musicians during the Seattle World's Fair.

Don's Barber Shop at S. 144 St. and Pacific Highway has been owned and operated by Don DeMulling since 1957. He remembers his predecessor, Willis Hales, a barber and local Justice of Peace who served the community for 18 years. Hales had a chapel on the premises and the groom always got a haircut before the wedding ceremony.

CASCADE VIEW

he Cascade View section of old Riverton Heights acquired its name in the 1950s. Lying in the Susannah and Milton Robbins pioneer land-grant claim, Cascade View has much deeper roots and a longer history than the recent plat date suggests. The Cascade View annexation includes parts of the old Thorndyke district. The City of Tukwila has been greatly enriched by the annexation of Cascade View for the district brings with it important community institutions and services that are an integral part of a balanced modern city. These include a hospital, cemetery, two churches, and a school. The Cascade View School is discussed in Chapter 14.

TUKWILA—COMMUNITY AT THE CROSSROADS

RIVERTON PARK UNITED METHODIST CHURCH

The Riverton Park United Methodist Church is the result of the merger of three early congregations. The oldest of these congregations is the Wesley Methodist Episcopal Church founded in 1891-92 by Rev. E. S. Stockwell. He also founded the Shaw Memorial Methodist Episcopal Church as well as the South Seattle and West Seattle churches. In 1962 the Wesley congregation merged with the Riverton Methodist Church that had moved from its original 1909 location at S. 131 St. and 40 Ave. S. to property on Military Road and S. 140 St. in 1967. A new church had been built there in 1966 under the guidance of Rev. George Poor. The old church building was sold. In 1971 the South Park Methodist Church, originally the Shaw Memorial Methodist Episcopal, merged with the Riverton Methodist Church. The united church congregations formed the Riverton Park United Methodist Church. In 1989 the present pastor, Rev. David Hullin, was appointed.

The goal of the congregation for the 1990s is to realize the dream of the three churches when they first came together—continued growth and construction of a new worship center. As part of their outreach the congregation provides space for a day care program called "Learning Way," a pre-teen bridge tutorial program in conjunction with the Atlantic Street Center. The local Girl and Boy Scout troops and community Alcoholics Anonymous also meet at the church.

RIVERTON HEIGHTS LUTHERAN CHURCH

The Riverton Heights Lutheran Church was organized as a mission of the American Lutheran Church on October 2, 1945. Church services and Sunday School classes were conducted in the basement of the parsonage until the chapel was completed in 1947. The parsonage continued to be used for Sunday School for several more years. A building program in 1950 added the Parish Hall wing to the chapel. Further growth of the congregation led to the construction of a new church at S. 144 St. and 35 Ave. S. The building was completed and dedicated on April 25, 1960. On June 8, 1975, a new sanctuary was dedicated. Rev. Philip Rohrbacher was the congregation's first pastor, serving from 1945 to 1948. Other pastors have been Ernest Phillippi, Erich Knorr, Vernon Kraxberger, and Leonard Kutz. Richard Bersie, the pastor in 1990, has been serving the congregation since December 1968. At the 40th anniversary held in 1985, Kitty Endert, Arle Groven, Ella Johnson, Garda Mitchell, Ruby Armstrong and Clifford Wollum were five charter members of the church who were still active members.

FELLOWSHIP BIBLE CHURCH

The Fellowship Bible Church (formerly Riverton Heights Presbyterian Church) is located at the corner of S. 160 St. and Military Road S. It was organized in 1930 and the original building constructed in 1931. Two additional buildings and the pastor's home have been constructed since then. Dr. Ezra Giboney was the first pastor. He was also pastor of of the Foster-Tukwila Presbyterian Church at the same time, and held a service in the morning at one church and one in the evening at the other. Through the years, the Fellowship Bible Church has been an important part of the community and the lives of the people.

SOKA GAKKAI INTERNATIONAL

Reflecting the diversity of the area, the Soka Gakkai International, a world-based Buddhist organization, is building its Seattle Territory Cultural Center at 3505 S. 146 St. The center, expected to be completed in

Riverton Tuberculosis Sanitarium in Riverton Heights, opened around 1922, offered a restful haven for recuperating from the disease. The Riverton Hospital occupies the site of the earlier sanitarium and some of the original buildings are incorporated into the new buildings. Courtesy Riverton Hospital.

August 1991, will serve as a meeting place for members from Bellingham to Portland, Oregon.

THE RIVERTON SANITARIUM

Early in the twentieth century there was a chronic shortage of space in the public tuberculosis (TB) treatment centers in King County. Moreover, many people desired more extensive facilities than the county could offer, and private sanitariums were opened. The Riverton Sanitarium was among the most attractive of these places.

Built in 1928 on a 43-acre tract of high ground above the Duwamish River in Riverton Heights, the Riverton Sanitarium, also known as the Riverton Pulmonary Hospital, was beautifully situated in the midst of an extensive wood. The hilltop location guaranteed "pure and fresh air, with full exposure to sunshine." In the absence of other effective medical treatment, TB treatment was based on much bed rest, wholesome food, moderate exercise, sunshine, and what was called "a regulated mode of life," i.e., living in a relaxed environment. The objective was to save the sufferer's energy and make it possible for the body to combat the disease with all of its power.

The Riverton Sanitarium grounds were well laid out with buildings, walkways and drives winding around the grounds that were maintained as a lovely park. Providing a healthy environment for the characteristically long TB recuperation period, the sanitarium grounds held a collection of buildings, including a laboratory where regular medical examinations took place and treatments were administered, and the infirmary, where patients suffering with fever or needing special care would receive hospital-quality care from attending nurses. Most of the patients lived in residential cottages large enough for one to five people. A large house called the Ward had 20 beds in four separated large sleeping rooms. All of the residences had bathrooms and dressing rooms. The sanitarium had electrical power and steam heat in the main buildings.

Compared to the main buildings, the cottages, heated with open fireplaces, were cold and damp in the winter. However, it was firmly believed that sleeping in a well-aired room was a good preventative and treatment for TB. (Many progressive people of the day, like the Fred Nelsen family of Renton Junction, slept in open air "sleeping porches" year around.)

The Riverton Sanitarium buildings were built in the Swiss chalet style featuring very wide bracketed eaves, casement windows and second-floor balconies. In keeping with the philosophy of pursuing a wholesome life, most of the institution's food was raised on the grounds. The sanitarium maintained its own water supply fed by local springs. Large vegetable and flower gardens were maintained and residents were invited to work in the gardens as a form of mild

253

exercise and diversion. In addition to housing and treatment buildings, there were barns, chicken houses, a dairy and the typical outbuildings of a farm. A surviving original building, probably a barn, can be seen in the field across from the modern Riverton Hospital.

Many of the Riverton Sanitarium workers lived in Riverton, including several physicians, nurses and support staff. Each week Tom and Ted Scibor, Riverton lads, dropped by the sanitarium kitchen delivering the *Union Record*, the regional labor union weekly newspaper, to Mrs. Stephenson, the cook. Tom recalls that the sanitarium was a nice place with very pretty, well-kept-up grounds. The cook was always busy preparing good-smelling meals for a big crowd.

THE RIVERTON HOSPITAL

As tuberculosis was effectively treated and then controlled in the years following World War II, the need for the Riverton TB Sanitarium diminished and the hospital began to accept and treat a broad range of patients. The hospital was bought by West Seattle Hospital and for several years served as a branch of that hospital.

In 1961 the hospital was purchased by the Steward Foundation, a small not-for-profit chain, which also owned the Auburn Hospital and Centralia General. With more professional management and more capital the hospital changed quickly. The cabins were demolished immediately, and two of the larger buildings and the water tower were taken down during the next four years. A number of the buildings making up the contemporary Riverton Hospital incorporate buildings from the old Pulmonary Hospital. In 1969 a new wing was constructed including a new operating room, laboratory, emergency room, pharmacy, delivery room, nursery, medical floor and surgical floor. In 1978 a second wing was built that included a cardiac care/intensive care unit, an emergency room, pharmacy and doctor's lounge. A third wing,

constructed in 1981, included central supply, medical records, nursing office, personnel and a warehouse.

In 1982 the Riverton Hospital was purchased by Universal Health Systems. The corporation built a new medical office building adjacent to the hospital in 1987. In August 1989 Highline Community Hospital acquired the hospital and immediately began introducing new programs, beginning with the Transitions Geriopsychiatric Program in December and the Synergos Head Injury Program in March 1990. The presence of a full-service hospital in the City of Tukwila is an important asset for the community, and the city is proud of the fine quality of the Riverton Hospital's health care.

STAYING IN RIVERTON FOREVER

Susannah and Milton Robbins built their homestead on the hillside overlooking the Duwamish Valley. Above their house, at the very crest of the hill that marks the top of the valley wall, the family established its burial ground. Milton was buried here in 1899 and Susannah in 1916. There was no graveyard in the south end of the Duwamish Valley. Soon neighbors and friends around the valley were asking permission to bury their dead at the top of the hill in the Robbins family's graveyard, and the place became a community cemetery.

Many of the early graves were marked with wooden markers that have long since disappeared, thus it is not possible to identify many pioneer graves. It is likely that Susannah's parents, Joseph and Jean Campbell Steele, are buried here, as well as other pioneers. However, this has not been verified. As it became easier to travel, some valley residents chose for burial Mount Olivet in Renton or the Washington Memorial Cemetery on Pacific Highway.

In 1948 the Robbins family sold the cemetery to Helen and Elmer Sears, who named it Riverton Crest for its hilltop location. The Searses already owned Forest Lawn Cemetery in

West Seattle, which had been in Helen's family since 1903. In 1987 Uniserve Corp. of Portland bought both of the Searses' cemeteries and currently manages the Riverton Crest Cemetery.

McMicken Heights District

I can remember going wild blackberry picking with the kids and hiking up to lower McMicken Heights and spending the whole day gathering berries. Now it is all houses and it's hard to envision what it was like.

Anna May Charnell Gott

McMicken Heights is named for Maurice McMicken, land developer. Born on October 12, 1860, in Dodge County, Minnesota, to General William and Rowena J. Ostrander McMicken, Maurice McMicken moved with his parents to the Northwest when he was 13. As a graduate lawyer, McMicken was a well known and respected partner in several Seattle law firms. In 1890 he assisted with the incorporation of the First Ave. and Madison Street Cable companies, and became interested in the north and south Seattle street railway lines. As a result of McMicken's capable management these companies survived the Panic of 1893 and later were sold to the Seattle Electric Co. Reflecting his position at the center of business during this Seattle boom period, Maurice McMicken served as secretary of the South Seattle Land Co. started by C. D. Stimson in 1890. A real estate development venture, the corporation bought land throughout King County for investment and McMicken's name was given to the tract it owned south of Riverton Heights. The area did not develop for almost 50 years after the corporation owned it; however, Maurice McMicken's name continued to identify the area.

Only a portion of the larger McMicken Heights district was annexed to Tukwila. McMicken Heights is a residential neighborhood that has developed largely since the 1960s.

LaRee McKay, who moved to the district in April 1960 with her husband, was one of the area's earliest residents. Mrs. McKay recalls the area was all woods, with only two neighbors living in small white houses down the road. In 1966 a cul-de-sac was put in and several new homes were built. In the 1960s the beautiful woods were cut and new streets laid out and blacktopped. There were still only a few homes scattered along the streets. There was no effort to push development, and the lots sold slowly throughout the 1960s and 1970s. The only neighborhood business was a little grocery store at 42 Ave. S. operated by Jean and Betty Shimstock, since deceased. A Safeway store was built on the site of the old Water Department office. McMicken residents agree that since its annexation to Tukwila, there has been a big improvement in the streets and better police service.

CHAPTER 16

NEIGHBORING COMMUNITIES JOIN THE CITY AT THE CROSSROADS

Present-day Tukwila City Hall, symbol of the united communities of the upper Duwamish and lower Green River valley. Courtesy Patrick Brodin.

At times it is good to turn a page from the past so that we may better understand the future.
    Mayor Charles Baker
    Farewell Address, April 2, 1962

While this book was being written, Tukwila underwent a historic transformation, with far-reaching effect—the annexation of five surrounding, historically connected, communities and neighborhoods: Duwamish-Allentown-Quarry, Riverton, Foster, Thorndyke-Riverton Heights and Cascade View. Combined with the earlier McMicken Heights annexation, the addition of these districts more than doubled the City's area and more than tripled its population. In the first section of this chapter, community leaders from Tukwila and the annexed communities give first-hand accounts of the reasoning and events that led to the annexations. The chapter also looks at a number of enduring organizations that make up the community of "greater Tukwila" in 1991. It ends with a message from Mayor Gary VanDusen that puts the events, organizations and people of 1991 Tukwila in historical perspective.

PRELUDE TO THE ANNEXATIONS
Joan Hernandez, Chair
Tukwila City Council, 1989-1990

Between 1987 and 1990, the City of Tukwila accepted five major annexations, increasing the population from 4,780 to 14,800 citizens and its geographical size from 2,880 acres to 4,143 acres. The old communities of Duwamish-Allentown-North Riverton, Foster, Thorndyke, Riverton and a part of McMicken joined the City of Tukwila in 1989. In May of 1990 over 2,000 residents of the Cascade View (Riverton Heights) area voted to annex to the City of Tukwila. The Duwamish-Allentown annexation brought the Museum of Flight and part of Boeing Plant II and Boeing Field into the City of Tukwila. With the completion of the Cascade View annexation, the boundaries of the entire South Central School District were encompassed within the city limits of Tukwila.

What factors led to these major annexations that nearly tripled our population in just two years? In 1986, the Tukwila City Council had adopted a very pro-annexation policy. Resolution No. 992 states that "The City of Tukwila strongly encourages annexations within its planning area and contiguous to the city boundaries." This open-arms policy paved the way for citizens, groups interested in annexation to the city.

The flurry of annexations of 1989-90 was remarkable in that entire established communities petitioned to join the city. This unprecedented action was precipitated by the incorporation of the new municipality of Sea-Tac in 1988. Early in 1988 a group of citizens living in unincorporated King County on Tukwila's western border asked to be annexed to the city. However, the Tukwila City Council was reluctant to annex territory beyond the city planning area at that time. Unwilling to divide their community in half, the Sea-Tac group incorporated as an independent municipality and began to establish their boundaries on their own terms. The prospect of finding themselves in the City of Sea-Tac, when they really identified with the City of Tukwila, prompted citizen activists in Riverton, Foster, Thorndyke and Cascade to begin circulating petitions for annexation to the City of Tukwila.

It was an extremely busy time for the Tukwila City Council members as we carefully studied all drafts of the Environmental Impact Statement (EIS) for each proposed annexation area. Citizens advisory groups from each area made recommendations to the Tukwila City Council that guided the process of developing a comprehensive land use plan and zoning codes for each annexation area. In between regular weekly City Council meetings and Committee-of-the-Whole meetings, our evenings were filled with workshops, tours and public hearings, as we worked our way through each of the five annexation districts.

The Duwamish Valley "annexation movement" of 1989-90 was also influenced by the King County Council's directive encouraging unincorporated areas to either incorporate or annex to the nearest city or town that could provide them with the local services they needed. The major problem accompanying the process concerned boundaries. The City of Tukwila compromised and accepted the boundaries as defined by the county.

Land use, zoning codes, local police and fire protection all seemed to be strong motivating factors addressed by pro-annexation advocates. Many of the residential communities felt that the City of Tukwila would provide better police protection than they were receiving from King County. Some citizens felt threatened by the encroachment of multi-family housing upon single-family neighborhoods and were unhappy with the liberal King County zoning codes that allowed greater density than Tukwila codes. Tukwila's elected officials recognized that they were faced with the impacts of undesirable land use and high density at the city's borders. By annexing the petitioning areas, the City would gain some control over the land and zoning, and have legal authority in managing the problems.

A financial consideration lay in the county's revenue formula, by which Tukwila is assessed for regional services based on its high assessed valuation but receives regional revenue allotments based on the city's low population figures. Increasing the population base was looked upon as one way of attempting to achieve more equity in this distribution formula.

In summary, it was a combination of factors that evolved into a very conscientious decision by the entire Tukwila City Council to accept the petitions for annexation that were presented from the citizens of Duwamish-Allentown, Foster, Riverton, Thorndyke, Cascade View, and McMicken Heights. It was the very sincere appeals made by citizens living in those areas, who expressed their desire to become part of the city they identified with for library services, shopping, parks and schools, that persuaded me personally and many others on the council to proceed with the annexations.

The legacy of the annexations is a wider diversity of neighborhoods, an even stronger tax

TUKWILA—COMMUNITY AT THE CROSSROADS

View of the confluence of the Duwamish and Green rivers in the 1960s—the historic Mox la Push district. The Black River flowed into the Duwamish from the east until 1917. Courtesy Marvin Boys.

base, more registered voters, and eligibility for a larger proportion of regional revenue sharing. We have successfully entered into joint partnerships with the South Central School District and look forward to mutually beneficial relationships that will help produce the future leaders of the City of Tukwila for generations to come.

McMicken Heights Annexations
Dennis Robertson

The first annexation of a section of the McMicken Heights area to Tukwila occurred midnight, July 9, 1960, and set the stage for the many land use battles that would follow. The great freeway intersection of I-518 and I-5 had not been started nor had the Southcenter mall been built. The City of Tukwila was seeking a commercial tax base. Thus, when the property owners at what was to become the southwest corner of the Tukwila Interchange requested to annex, under the condition that they be zoned RMH, the highest density multi-family zoning available, Tukwila agreed and the annexation was completed in January 1961.

Ironically, the second annexation attempt in 1980 was precipitated by a land use battle over a large piece of the land zoned RMH in the first annexation, which was proposed for a 12-acre plot of apartments. The battle was fought first in the Planning Commission hearings and the developer won. The citizens opposing it were from both Tukwila and King County, since the development was on the border. The group formed the Tukwila-McMicken Action Committee (TMAC), Dennis Robertson, president. TMAC appealed and the battle was taken to the Tukwila City Council. On January 5, 1977, the City Council voted to deny the application because of the environmental sensitivity of the area. Several months later, the city bought the 12 acres for use as a park. Impressed with the openness of the small town form of government, the citizen group decided to look into annexing the entire neighborhood to Tukwila. TMAC sent out several questionnaires to see if the neighborhood was interested and found essentially an even split. Another unsuccessful effort was made to annex to Tukwila in 1980.

For several years all was quiet and TMAC and its leaders went into semi-retirement. Then, in 1984 Puget Western, a subsidiary of Puget Power, having recently won a court battle with Tukwila, applied to build a 108-unit apartment complex. TMAC awoke from retirement and led the battle to stop the last apartments. This battle still goes on in 1991 in the courts with Puget Western suing the city for denying the building permit because of hillside instability.

Brought together again by the land use battle, TMAC's leaders decided to try to annex their neighborhood into Tukwila again. This time they defined the neighborhood several blocks smaller, and called it the Crestview Annexation in an effort to avoid identifying with the much larger McMicken area. They also decided to avoid publicity and work quietly door to door to convince their neighbors of the advantages of annexation. On February 5, 1985, they were finally successful, with the ayes— 144—carrying the day to 73 nays.

RIVERTON, FOSTER, AND THORNDYKE ANNEXATIONS
Allan Ekberg and Ron Lamb

Throughout unincorporated King County, 1989 was a year of open rebellion against years of county indifference. The political landscape changed overnight with the annexations of Riverton, Foster, and Thorndyke to Tukwila, and the formation of the new cities of Federal Way and SeaTac in March of 1989. Woodinville voters narrowly defeated cityhood in the same election. Duwamish-Allentown annexed to Tukwila a month earlier, and Cascade View was moving toward annexation.

To the people who worked for the annexations, the campaigns forged lasting friendships, produced new community leaders, helped rekindle community spirit and gave neighborhoods with a formidable civic weapon—local control.

Talk of annexation—to either Seattle or Tukwila—began in the early 1960s, but it was not until the 1970s that annexation appeared on any ballot. Although the first attempts failed, they set the stage for 1989. Riverton's annexation effort grew out of a proposed 1987 county land use change that would have further industrialized the Riverton area at the expense of single-family residential neighborhoods. Residents organized to oppose the change. Led by the Stetsons, Schefflers, Ekbergs and others, the group agreed to seek annexation by Tukwila to gain local control over land use regulation. Calling themselves the Riverton Annexation Proposal (RAP) group, they filed an annexation petition with the city in February of 1988, setting as boundaries Pacific Highway on the west, Duwamish-Allentown on the north, the Tukwila city limits on the east, and S. 139 St. on the south.

That same month, Sea-Tac filed for incorporation. The incorporation included most of Riverton and all of Foster, Thorndyke and Cascade View. These communities did not want to be included in Sea-Tac incorporation, viewing Tukwila as better able to provide services and as a more natural affiliation. Within a month, a group from the Foster area led by Ron Lamb, Pam Carter, Rena Shawver, Diane Myers, Karen Leighton and Mary Zion filed a petition for annexation of the Foster area—S. 139 St. to S. 144 St. between Pacific Highway and the Tukwila city limits. The number of signatures represented 52 percent of Foster's turnout in the last general election. A group from Thorndyke led by the Meryhews, Lees, Lawrences, and others quickly followed with an annexation petition that gathered 137 signatures in four days. The Thorndyke boundary extended from S. 144 St. to S. 160 St. between Pacific Highway and the Tukwila city limits. These petitions set up a "showdown" with the Sea-Tac incorporation plan. In August the King County Council

TUKWILA—COMMUNITY AT THE CROSSROADS

sent the matter to the state Boundary Review Board (BRB), commenting that crime-ridden Pacific Highway should not be split between two jurisdictions.

Annexation proponents wanted to see all of the South Central School District in Tukwila, but they realized that Cascade View might end up in Sea-Tac if they did not take the initiative. They contacted Cascade View residents Richard and Dolores Simpson, who agreed to head a Cascade View annexation. Turning down a last-minute proposal from Sea-Tac supporters to establish a 42 Ave. S. boundary, annexation forces entered the BRB hearing with overwhelming numbers of supporters, sporting "Yes ANNEX" buttons and a well-researched, logical position: The primary statutory responsibility of the BRB is to keep communities together, and the South Central School District represents one community. Cascade View was to remain an unincorporated "island" for a future annexation vote, an arrangement the BRB had never before approved. Yet, in a December ruling, the BRB agreed with annexation proponents, reducing the Sea-Tac incorporation boundaries to Military Road, excluding not only the three annexation areas east of Pacific Highway but Cascade View as well.

The county council decided that the annexation and incorporation votes should be by mail, not at the polls. Ballots were sent out in the last week of February. Annexation proponents held community meetings and circulated leaflets, making one final round through the Riverton neighborhood as a freak March snowstorm blanketed the region. The pro-annexation ballot count was Riverton 64 percent, Foster 60 percent, Thorndyke 57 percent and Sea-Tac 51 percent.

THE ANNEXATION OF DUWAMISH-ALLENTOWN AND FOSTER POINT
George Gomez

In January 1967 the communities of Duwamish-Allentown and Foster Point first began serious talk of annexation to a nearby municipality. Over the next 22 years a spirited discussion continued as Seattle, Tukwila, the residents and the local businesses debated whether and to whom they should annex. Those residents who expressed an interest in annexing preferred the idea of joining Tukwila rather than Seattle; however, the majority preferred to remain unincorporated.

The Duwamish Improvement Club (DIC) began to study the many factors affecting future community development, including the advantages and pitfalls of self-government. At this time it was clear that Seattle was expanding its boundaries. Seattle had already annexed part of South Park, and in February 1970, when Seattle Mayor Wes Uhlman publicly announced that Seattle intended to annex areas immediately south of its city limits, DIC became alarmed.

In 1970 DIC formed a committee to study the annexation issues. Recognizing the importance of the Improvement Club's Annexation Study Committee, representatives from local industries, businesses and public utilities regularly attended meetings. Mayor Uhlman met with the committee chairman and president of DIC on October 13, 1970, to discuss Seattle's annexation plans. Seattle's intentions were not merely to annex South Park but to extend its boundaries from Tukwila to Puget Sound and as far south as S. 145 St., the northern extremity of the Sea-Tac Airport extension, excluding Burien.

From 1973 to 1979 the Duwamish Improvement Club temporarily discontinued discussion of initiating annexation for the community because the group was divided as to what action the community should take. In July 1979 a meeting was held at the Duwamish Fire Station regarding Seattle's efforts to annex the remainder of South Park and the area of Boeing Plant II, basically the old Meadows district. If Seattle had annexed the area, Duwamish-Allentown would have lost both its fire department and $16,000,000 in tax income. In spite of energetic efforts by DIC members assisting South Park residents fighting against the annexation, it carried and the Seattle city limits crept closer to the community.

NEIGHBORING COMMUNITIES JOIN THE CITY AT THE CROSSROADS

In 1973, Tukwila accepted a petition for annexation from Duwamish-Allentown. After some delays the petition was approved by Tukwila, with Mayor Todd casting the tie-breaking vote. The County Boundary Review Board vote ended in a tie, which according to the rules constitutes approval of incorporation.

Objecting to this outcome, King County Fire District No. 1, Duwamish, filed appeals to the Board decision with the Boundary Review Board and in King County Superior Court. A court order was released in October 1982 for an EIS, which Tukwila proceeded to compile. On September 20, 1983, the election results show the annexation attempt was defeated—91 against and 56 for.

After a lull, in 1987 an annexation task force was formed consisting of representatives from leading local industrial interests Boeing, Paccar, Rhone Poulec (formerly Monsanto), Jorgenson Steel, Metro, and the Duwamish-Allentown and Foster Point communities. Once again weekly meetings were held with coverage including comprehensive planning, zoning, water/sewer services, septic tanks, regulations/codes, transportation, capital improvements, taxes/fees and political representation. Two comprehensive EISs were compiled.

On February 7, 1989, King County Fire District No. 1, including registered voters in Duwamish-Allentown and Foster Point, voted on annexation. When the last returned ballots were counted, it was clear that after all the years of ambivalence the community favored joining Tukwila. The vote returns showed 573 deliverable ballots: Proposition #1, for annexation 233, against annexation 166; Proposition #2, for indebtedness assumption, 205 against, 183 for. The Tukwila City Council ratified the annexation on February 21, 1989, and the official "takeover" of Fire District No. 1 was accomplished on March 31, 1989, ending the final chapter of the 22-year annexation story.

CASCADE VIEW ANNEXATION
Mary Bosshart

n the eve of the King County Boundary Review Board deliberations regarding the Cascade View area in the spring of 1990, Richard Simpson, representing a group of citizens in the northern portion of the Cascade View area, turned in a citizens' petition with 212 signatures requesting that Cascade View be annexed to the City of Tukwila. This was after it became known that the City of Sea-Tac had included the area in its incorporation plans. Among the reasons listed on the petition were law enforcement problems along both sides of Pacific Highway, known as "the strip", boundary alignment with South Central School District, and the higher density codes for Cascade View proposed by King County. In contrast, Tukwila offered both single family zoning and safeguarded the area from becoming an isolated unincorporated area in King County.

The Cascade View voters already had a positive feeling about the City of Tukwila as a result of their fast action in supporting nearby areas annexed in 1989. For example, in March 1989, Foster, Riverton and Thorndyke were annexed into Tukwila, and on June 1, 1989, police began patrolling the annexed communities. The demonstration of Tukwila's efficiency and concern for the newly acquired communities had a positive effect on the Cascade View residents, since one of Tukwila's promises was "to clean up the strip."

The Cascade View area encompasses approximately 580 acres of land. Its boundaries are Military Road on the west, Highway 99 and Tukwila city limits on the east, S. 116 St. to the north and S. 152 St. on the south. The area has 3,100 residents. Ballots were mailed to 955 registered voters and the affirmative vote took place May 22, 1990. In September 1990 Cascade View annexed to the City of Tukwila, adding to the city two important institutions, Riverton Hospital and Riverton Crest Cemetery, two churches, the Cascade View School and a mix

261

TUKWILA—COMMUNITY AT THE CROSSROADS

> ### TUKWILA HISTORICAL SOCIETY
>
> The Tukwila Historical Society was founded on June 25, 1975, to preserve the rich heritage of the Green River basin in the environs of Tukwila, Renton Junction, Foster, Riverton and Duwamish-Allentown. The Society maintains a historical archive, preserves artifacts, collects oral histories and arranges educational programs for residents of the area. Together with the Washington Centennial Committee, the Society asked for and received Tukwila City Council approval to fund the writing of this community history book. Many society members actively participated in the history book project. Founding officers of the Society were Rudolf Regel, president, Joanne Davis, vice president, Louise Strander, secretary, Marie Gardner, treasurer, and Helen Nelsen, financial secretary.
>
> Recent preservation work includes accepting the deed to the Mess Family Pioneer Cemetery, located at the south border of the city, and placing historic markers at the sites of nineteenth-century riverboat landings on the lower Green and Duwamish rivers. Future plans of the Society include installing district historical markers, establishing a local history museum, and restoring the Mess Cemetery. The Tukwila Historical Society is a member of the Association of King County Historical Societies (AKCHO).

of commercial activities and an attractive single family residential neighborhood.

ORGANIZATIONS AND INSTITUTIONS IN TUKWILA IN 1990

Tukwila's City Parks

The tradition of community parks in Tukwila began in 1909, when the Ladies Improvement Club established a public park around the Interurban Station on the flats. The development of Tukwila Park on 65 Ave. S. in the early 1930s with a WPA grant-in-aid resulted in the construction of several buildings at Tukwila Park and trails being laid out through the woods. Some of these trails are still in use today, while others are not maintained.

In 1976 Bicentennial Park, with a log cabin as its centerpiece, was developed as a tribute to the nation's pioneer roots. Community volunteers built the 20-by-24 foot log cabin, complete with a fireplace made of rock hauled up from the banks of the Duwamish River. On October 8, 1990, the cabin was burned by vandals. However, the cabin was rebuilt in 1991.

The city's first section of the Christensen Greenbelt Park, a part of the longer Duwamish-Green River Trail system, was built in 1978 with a grant from the state. Local businesses donated $2,500 for trees. In 1990 there were 3.2 miles of trail with three additional miles planned for 1992, which will extend the trail from Kent to Seattle through Tukwila. During construction of the Christensen Trail, 10 additional foot trails were built in the community connecting neighborhoods and community institutions, such as schools or parks. More such trails are planned for the future.

Joseph Foster Memorial Park, established in 1982, is located on the former site of the Foster School. A historical monument placed in the park commemorates the Honorable Joseph Foster's donation of the land for the first community school in 1893. The steps from the upper school building area to the lower playfield have been preserved as a memory of the old school days. The land is leased from the school district. Duwamish Park, in Duwamish-Allentown, is located on a Duwamish School site.

Crystal Springs Park protects and preserves a beautiful pure spring used by the pioneers and named Crystal Springs by them. James Nelsen tapped this spring for many years when he operated the Independent Water Company. The clear springs still flow today; however, the water is no longer used by valley residents as it was years ago. Work developing the 11-acre park was begun in 1984 and will be completed in the 1990s.

Hazelnut Park, next to the Old Tukwila City Hall, currently the Tukwila Library, was

262

Neighboring Communities Join the City at the Crossroads

dedicated on December 17, 1983. New City Hall has Ikawa Park, which was built with design guidance and living gifts of plants from Tukwila's Japanese Sister City, Ikawa. The small, beautiful Japanese-style park is graced with traditional Japanese garden lanterns, a small stream, and a pond with koi fish. The fish and lanterns were gifts from Ikawa. It was dedicated November 12, 1987, during a visit of citizens from Ikawa.

The annexations of 1990 brought four parks into the city: Southgate Park, Pea Patch Park, Crestview Park and Fort Dent Park. The 12-acre Pea Patch site, attractively situated on the banks of the Duwamish River, is under consideration for development into a major city park in the years to come. Southgate Park is located in old Riverton. Crestview Park is a large tract leased from the Highline School District in Riverton Heights. The 40-year lease includes over half of the Crestview Elementary School site. Fort Dent Park, developed by the King County Parks Division, is located in the vicinity of Mox la Push, the historic confluence of the Black, White and Duwamish rivers. This large park has athletic fields and areas for field and track sports. Beautifully situated on the banks of the Duwamish, it is the largest park in Tukwila and is used for festivals as well as picnicking and playing. The park remains under the jurisdiction of the county at the time of writing.

Foster Golf Links began operation in the late 1940s under private ownership and became a municipal park in May, 1978. The 71-acre site provides 18 holes of golf, and in 1990 had just over 85,000 rounds of golf played.

Tukwila Southgate Community Center

In 1978 the City of Tukwila purchased the Southgate schoolhouse in Riverton, built in 1950 and closed in the 1970s because of low enrollments. The Southgate Community Center, under the direction of the Tukwila Parks and Recreation Department, was established in the building and grew rapidly in the 1980s with a full schedule of senior adult, athletic and youth activities offered throughout all seasons of the year. The community center offers a variety of arts and crafts classes, exercise and athletic programs, and serves senior lunches three days a week. In addition, rooms can be rented by community groups and by private parties for wedding receptions or church activities.

By 1991 the Parks and Recreation Department was serving over 65,000 people a year. The determination and dedication of the department staff is evident by the growth pattern since 1974, when the department was first created. The motto of the department is "We may not be one of the biggest departments in Washington, but we strive to be one of the best!"

Tukwila Library

The Tukwila Library opened on December 26, 1959. In its first 18 months the Tukwila Library served 1,082 adults and children who checked out over 27,000 books, magazines, records and cassettes. In 1990 the annual circulation had grown to 76,578 volumes.

The Tukwila Library sponsors monthly special programs, often featuring speakers or films that are well attended. Library patrons have access to the King County Branch Library System. The library is located in the Old Tukwila Grade School on 59 Ave. S. which is on the National Register of Historic Sites of Community Interest. The Friends of the Library received a grant to refurbish and restore the building in 1990. Additional grant revenues helped build Hazelnut Park on the grounds, and the Tukwila Arts Commission donated funds for a bronze sculpture of a cougar that rests on a native boulder in the park. The Library has a conveniently central location; a 1990 survey revealed that 75 percent of the patrons walked to the library.

Val Vue Sewer District

The Val Vue Sewer District is one of the oldest sewer districts in the State of Washington. It was formed in 1941 with general obligation bonds and served a large housing development and businesses along Pacific Highway. In

View of I-5 freeway interchange and the Southcenter district, historically a place where the confluence of several rivers created a dynamic crossroads for river travel. By the end of the twentieth century the Black and White rivers no longer flowed through the valley and the Green and Duwamish rivers were noted only by the bridge crossings. The new crossroads are rivers of asphalt. Courtesy Marvin Boys.

1990 the district boundaries reached from the north side of Pacific Highway to the Seattle city limits and Sea-Tac Airport on the south side of the highway. Riverton Heights is included on the west, and the eastern boundary includes Riverton, McMicken Heights, and Old Tukwila to I-5.

Val Vue's system has changed radically over the years, reflecting increased environmental sensitivity. The original part of the district system was built in 1946 and consisted of two miles of six-inch and eight-inch pipe and a spirogester-type treatment facility which discharged its effluent into the Duwamish River. In 1956 a new primary treatment plant replaced the old one and expanded the capacity. This plant operated until 1966, when the State Highway Department condemned the treatment plant to make way for SR-599. Since 1966 the district has contracted with Metro for treatment of its sewage.

Since 1969 the district has tripled the area served. Connections have increased from 900 to 3,600. In 1990 the district serviced 3,600 accounts within an area of 1,800 acres. The goal of protecting the environment and maintaining the health and safety of those living and working in the district is one to which the Board of Commissioners and the employees of the Val Vue Sewer District are totally committed.

Southcenter Community Baptist Church

The Tukwila Baptist Church began in 1959 as a missionary effort of the Bible Baptist Church of Burien with meetings held in an old bakery in Tukwila. Under Pastor Lawrence Pollock, in 1962 the church moved to its present location at 14742 S. Macadam Road. A machine shop on the two-acre site was converted into a chapel and the house became the parsonage.

Under the leadership of Pastor John H. Ruhlman, Sr., between 1968 and 1978 the congregation grew in terms of closer fellowship among the members and outreach to the community. Church facilities were also much improved by adding three portable classrooms, remodeling the parsonage and building a wing on the chapel.

In 1981 a new main sanctuary and classroom were added, with church members donating time and labor and assisting in constructing the building. In 1984 the congregation changed its name to Southcenter Community Baptist Church (SCBC). Gerald Cudney served as pastor in 1984, followed by David J. Lunsford in 1986. Adhering to the principle of congregational government, church business is conducted by a quorum of the church's active members.

SCBC has been in fellowship with the General Association of Regular Baptist Churches (GARBC) and elects representatives to serve on the planning and the administrative advisory councils of the GARBC. SCBC supports missionaries in Alaska, Japan, the Philippines, Bangladesh, Spain and Paraguay. SCBC participates in a local fellowship of GARBC churches which owns and operates Glendawn Baptist Bible Camp in Federal Way. Since 1984 the church has sponsored a chapter of Approved Workmen Are Not Ashamed (AWANA).

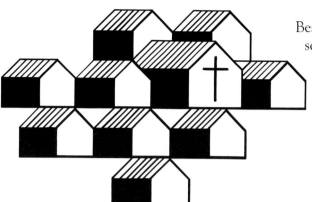
Southcenter Community Baptist Church logo.

Besides two worship services on Sunday and Sunday School, the church meets on Wednesday nights for a prayer meeting and Bible study.

The Southcenter Rotary Club

On August 28, 1968, the Rotary Club of Southcenter District was chartered with 23 members. Officers were Fred Suhler, president, Jack Weigand, vice president, William Bauman, secretary, and Don Pollock, treasurer. With 57 members in 1980, the club changed its name to Southcenter Rotary Club of Tukwila. The club's luncheon meetings are held at restaurants in the community.

Over the years the club has participated in community activities including providing food baskets and gifts to needy families at Thanksgiving and Christmas; funding the purchase of mirrors for the Senior Citizen Hall; contributing money and services to Operation First Harvest; and annually awarding two $1,000 scholarships to deserving Foster High School students. The group also participates in the Rotary International Exchange Student Program, which sends a local student to a foreign country for a school year in exchange for a foreign student living in the Tukwila Community.

Southgate Garden Club

Dorothy Haney and Loretta Moen founded the Southgate Garden Club in 1951 with 12 members. At the monthly meetings held at various times at the Cascade View Library, members' homes and the old Riverton Methodist Church, members enjoy learning about horticulture through lectures and demonstrations by members and guests.

When the new Cascade View School opened, the garden club beautified the grounds with trees, shrubs and flowers and maintained the area for many years. Riverton Park Methodist Church and a boulevard near Southgate School have been similarly beautified by the members' landscaping skills. Members of the Garden Club planted 400 trees on the west side of Highway 99, close to Cascade View. The club was also instrumental in the construction of neighborhood sidewalks and curbs. The club has put on flower shows at the Foster Library, Seattle Trust & Savings Bank and Cascade View School. Members regularly win ribbons and plaques in competition at regional flower shows.

Tukwila Little League

"Play ball" sounded for the first time in the Tukwila area in a Little League game in 1955 because of the efforts of Lee Phillips, Tukwila Police Court Judge from 1956 to 1964, and friends Al Merkle and Willy Bower. Practices were held at South Central Park, the old Foster High School property. In 1962 General Electric invited the League to use property behind its building in Andover Park. Games were played there until 1982, when GE sold the property.

In 1990 Tukwila Little League games were being played at the Cascade View School field. In 1990 about 130 8-to-10-year-old boys played in four major and four minor league teams. Youths 13 to 15 play in the South King County Babe Ruth League, and the District 7 American Legion League serves high-school-age boys. Team members and coaches come from all of the valley communities. Players beginning in Little League have gone on to play high school, college and even professional baseball.

Tukwila Chapter of the Independent Order of Foresters

The Tukwila Chapter of the Independent Order of Foresters (I.O.F.) is part of an international organization dating back to the fourteenth century which was formed to care for the sick. Its motto "Liberty, Benevolence and Concord" stands for "Liberty—respecting the rights of others; Benevolence—performing acts of kindness and help to those less fortunate; and Concord—working together in a common course."

Members benefit from insurance plans covering areas such as life and death, orphans, TB, cancer, infectious diseases and natural disasters. Foresters support a variety of community activities including donating to blood banks, food banks and Second Harvest; Special Olympics; purchasing vans for the transportation of the handicapped; awarding scholarships; and providing free coffee for travelers' highway rest stops. Its members regularly serve as volunteers with youth groups and many other worthwhile charitable endeavors, and enjoy campouts together. A monthly newspaper and a bimonthly magazine keep members informed of the activities and workings of the 20 Washington chapters. The Foresters have met at the Masonic Hall and at community schools.

Tukwila International Training in Communications

The goal of the Tukwila International Training in Communications (ITC) is to assist members in self-improvement through study and practice in speech, conversation, group leadership and analytic listening. Formerly known as the International Toastmistress Club, in the mid-1980s the international organization elected to change the name to ITC to encourage both male and female membership. The group meets twice a month with members alternating in giving speeches and critiquing others to assist them in learning. The ITC has been an important means for personal growth for many members.

Tukwila Chamber of Commerce

The Tukwila Chamber of Commerce was founded in 1963 by a group of businessmen led by Lawrence (Bill) Crostick of Southcenter Oil in Tukwila for the purpose of dealing with local development issues. Under the leadership of President Crostick, the Chamber drew its membership from Tukwila, Riverton, Riverton Heights, McMicken Heights, Andover Industrial Center and Southcenter. Among the early activities was sponsoring a Seafair Queen candidate from Tukwila each year. In its early years the Chamber met at 14060 Interurban

Ave. S. In the next years presidents included Tom Forsythe, who later became a King County councilman, and Frank Todd. In 1974 the group disbanded.

In 1979 the Chamber was reorganized by Randy Coplen, who was also elected president. The organizers felt that the community's business people needed a representative at City Hall to represent their point of view. Zoning proposals in the late 1970s were seen as very unfavorable by many business owners. Since reorganizing, the Chamber has been very active. The Chamber of Commerce offices have been located at Andover Park, Southcenter Blvd., and Tukwila Parkway. The Chamber was known as the Tukwila/Sea-Tac Chamber until January 1, 1989, when it consolidated with the Burien-Highline Chamber under the name Southwest King County Chamber of Commerce.

AFTERWORD
Gary VanDusen, Mayor, 1991

Any written history is but a brief slice of collective memory of events, places and people. While individual memory is colored by personal perception, a collective memory provides a much better view of what probably happened to make up who and what we are. Nonetheless, much is lost, particularly of attitudes and subtle, quiet factors that precipitate a destiny such as ours. Time and remembrance are often not good partners.

The City of Tukwila is a living thing—living because of the citizens that created it, nurtured it and guided it. The pages of this history book abound with the names of the notables among those citizens. Yet there were many quiet, hard-working, dedicated people whose names do not appear, but who indeed made a difference. A city is dependent upon each of its citizens. Unless it has the continuous interest, support and involvement of citizens, it will begin to deteriorate. The City of Tukwila is here today because of a history of active citizen participation. The earlier residents of this area had a vision of what could be and never lost faith in the future. Those citizens have left a legacy of hard work, planning and sacrifice that present and future citizens must duplicate to meet the challenges of the modern era with vitality and optimism.

Early visionaries who saw the strategic aspects of the Tukwila location and its potential future were Joseph Foster and municipal founder Joel Shomaker. Yet the community was a quiet place for many years, at least until the explosive growth of the Puget Sound area began to be widely felt in the 1950s. Fortunately, at that point, strong dedicated leadership was present for the city in the man Charles O. Baker. As mayor, Baker saw the transition ahead and knew the city needed a better balance between residential community and the strong business tax base essential to meet the challenges of growth. He and the City Council formed a planning commission to develop a comprehensive plan, to assure that the Tukwila of this modern era would emerge as a beautiful, useful and economically functional city.

We can only imagine the long hours of meetings, the many presentations, the input from citizens and developers. One of the significant controversies in those days was the long struggle to prevent the Port of Seattle from making the whole area into an industrial complex which, undoubtedly, would have led to the ultimate demise of Old Tukwila and the other valley communities. They would have been lost like many crossroads areas and places chronicled in this history book, for which nothing remains but a memory or a note on an old map. Fortunately, this did not happen because an aroused citizenry fought and defeated the Port's program. After this long struggle with regional power players, Mayor Baker created one of the first regional planning groups, called the Valley Regional Planning Commission.

Through the years of Mayor Baker's leadership, the assessed valuation of the City increased. Over the last three decades the City has been able to respond to changing social, cultural and environmental challenges with a treasury envied by many other communities whose early leadership did not have the vision, acute planning, and facilitative skills of Shomaker and Baker. Tukwila, with its substantial tax base, is burdened with little debt and has funded police and fire protection, built new public works, developed parks and nature trails, and erected municipal buildings for the growing city. With careful stewardship, the City has become unique among Washington cities. We have been able to offer better services than nearby cities, including Seattle; and surrounding communities have eventually annexed to Tukwila to ensure their survival as viable residential communities.

Joel Shomaker declared perfect harmony in 1908. No one would be so bold as to declare that today. As part of the urbanization of the region, Tukwila has gained what Shomaker called "paupers, criminals, idle, vicious and gambling population." But in this period the city has also gained new citizen input, new political leaders and new ideas for the challenges it faces. Charles Baker called the Port of Seattle development program a "tiger on our back," and maybe the tiger has returned in the form of social and environmental living issues.

The city has passed through a pioneer stage, an agricultural time and 30 years of development and transition. We can read only a few lines in this unique, latest chapter of Tukwila's history. We must wait and see what the future holds, praying that the City of Tukwila will have the committed citizenry and visionary leaders that will keep it a prosperous, livable community for future generations.

Appendix A

Tukwila City Government and its Leaders

Dreamer, visionary and promoter Joel B. Shomaker was the founder and first mayor of Tukwila, Washington. Born at Butler, Pendleton County, Kentucky, October 2, 1862, the son of Newton Shomaker and Melissa Taylor Shomaker, the niece of President Zachary Taylor, Joel Shomaker was thus President Taylor's great nephew. Shomaker had the advantage of a good education and cultured home life.

While still a young man, Shomaker became a minister in the Campbellite Christian Church and worked as a circuit rider riding horseback over the hills of Kentucky. He became disillusioned with religion when his fiancée Magnolia died of smallpox, and he left the ministry. Of a somewhat restless but highly creative temperament, Shomaker enjoyed variety. Throughout his life he was a man of many trades, but mainly he was a journalist.

He joined the U. S. Army and was stationed at Fort Douglas, Utah, in 1884, during which time he was sent out on skirmishes with the Indians. After finishing his military service Shomaker taught school the length and breadth of Utah. At this time he met and married Luella Billings, his second cousin from Manti, Utah, a schoolteacher and a Mormon. The Shomakers eventually moved to Yakima, where Joel worked as a newsman. Always interested in politics, Shomaker was soon engrossed in the Columbia Basin Reclamation Project and was appointed Chairman of the Washington Conservation Commission by President Theodore Roosevelt. He campaigned for Roosevelt's Bull Moose Party and was a strong Grange organizer. During this period the couple had Blaine, Nancy, and Winfield and several other children who died in infancy. A fourth child, Laura, was born in Tukwila in 1909.

FOUNDER OF
THE MUNICIPALITY OF TUKWILA
JOEL BUEL SHOMAKER
1862-1937

Coming to the Pacific Northwest in 1898, Shomaker first settled in Tacoma, where he published the *Washington Farmer and Dairyman*. In 1904 he moved to Seattle and became the farm editor for the *Seattle Post-Intelligencer*. His years in Tukwila were short, 1906 to 1909. After founding the municipality he left Tukwila in the autumn of 1909 and moved to Hood Canal. There he bought 160 acres and developed the Olympic Nature Nursery, where he processed rhododendron buds and shipped them to Seattle hotels to be used in floral arrangements. The business was unsuccessful, and eventually Shomaker returned to Seattle and worked for the Madison Street Cable Car Company.

Throughout his life Shomaker was involved with causes. For example, in 1931 he successfully lobbied in Washington, D. C., for government pensions for Indian War veterans. His last campaign, which he undertook in old age, was on the behalf of old-age pensioners. He headed a legal battle seeking to compel the State of Washington to pay $30 a month pension to elderly people.

Shomaker was a highly imaginative, creative, energetic person who wrote poetry and songs. He played several musical instruments and loved to dance. Regarded by some as an eccentric, as he got older, he never lost his zest for life and was found to be congenial by most who knew him. He was a man of strong character and high principles, dedicated to community service.

Shomaker died in 1937 at age 75 and is buried in the Veterans' Section of Washelli Cemetery, Seattle. Luella Billings Shomaker died in 1957 at the age of 93 and is buried at Forest Lawn, West Seattle. The Shomakers' youngest daughter, Laura Shomaker Bateham, was living in 1991.

TUKWILA—COMMUNITY AT THE CROSSROADS

TUKWILA'S MAYORS 1908-1990

Joel Shomaker	1908-1909
Ernest W. Engel	1910-1911
Jacob Guntert	1912-1913
John M. Hall	1913-1914
S. H. Stevens	1915-1918
E. G. Green	1919-1924
G. C. Bergquist	1925-1927
John R. Walkup	1928-1932
John P. Walkup	1933-1947
Charles O. Baker	1947-1962
John B. Strander	1962-1967
Stanley Minkler	1968-1971
Frank Todd	1972-1975
Edgar Bauch	1976-1979
Frank Todd	1980-1982
Gary VanDusen	1982-1991

DEDICATED CITY COUNCIL MEMBERS, 1908-1990

The following public-spirited citizens are commended for their long years of public service.

Edgar D. Bauch*
L. C. Bohrer
Richard Bowen
Joe Duffie
D. S. Duggan
Dwight Gardner
E. F. Greene
Mabel J. Harris, Treasurer
George D. Hill
A. E. Hull
Eugene W. Ives
Joseph R. Johanson
F. J. Klein
Stan Minkler*
Clarence Moriwaki
S. R. Naylor
A. G. Radford
Rudolph W. Regal
Daniel J. Saul
J. S. Storey
A. W. Thies
E. Thompson
Dwayne Traynor
Gary L. VanDusen*
J. C. Wickman
*also served as mayor

ERNEST W. ENGEL
MAYOR, 1910-1911

Ernest Engel was born in Germany in 1861 and emigrated to the United States in 1881 at age 20. Trained as a baker, in 1892 he made his way to the new state of Washington with his wife Anna. The Engels were among the most prosperous residents of Tukwila, where they operated a poultry-breeding farm, and Engel lent private funds to support the struggling town several years after he was mayor.

JOHN M. HALL
MAYOR, 1913-1914

John Hall was born in Maine in 1861, the son of Canadian immigrants. He moved to Washington State in 1892 and worked at logging, lumber milling, and land brokering, which was his livelihood during his term as mayor. Hall was a People's Party candidate (Populist), which was strong in King County in this period. He resigned before the end of his term for unknown reasons.

JOHN R. WALKUP
MAYOR, 1928-1932

John R. Walkup was born in upstate New York in 1855, and worked as a typographer, labor organizer, and newspaper publisher. In 1913 he bought a farm in Tukwila where he raised chickens and sold eggs. He served as a city councilman and became mayor in 1927, at age 72, and later city clerk upon retiring. He successfully shepherded the struggling town through a crucial period marked by a series of citizens' attempts to disincorporate the town.

JACOB GUNTERT
MAYOR, 1912

Jacob Guntert was a Swiss immigrant who was born in 1878 and came to the United States in 1901 at age 23. He was a trained machinist, which was his occupation while mayor. He came to Washington in 1903 with his bride Marie, also Swiss. After some time working in the Puget Sound area, Guntert bought a place in Tukwila. Guntert resigned while in office for unknown reasons.

S. H. STEVENS
MAYOR, 1915-1918

E. G. GREEN
MAYOR, 1919-1924

GEORGE CHRISTIAN BERGQUIST
MAYOR, 1924-1927

George C. Bergquist was born in Minneapolis, Minnesota, in 1888, the son of Swedish and Norwegian immigrants. He came to Puget Sound in 1904 at age 16, and later worked the gold fields of Alaska. He moved to Tukwila in 1917 after being transferred to Seattle by his employer, the Prudential Insurance Company. He laid the groundwork for the community's public water system. In addition to serving as mayor, he was also municipal treasurer.

APPENDIX A

JOHN POWELL WALKUP
MAYOR, 1933-1946

John P. Walkup was born in Anaconda, Montana, in 1891 and came to Tukwila in 1921. He was a founder of the Washington State Parks Association and worked for the Boeing Co. As Mayor of Tukwila he was very active in the regional Green River Flood Control Committee and also served as a county commissioner. Distinguished as the mayor with the longest tenure in office and as a capable administrator, J. P. Walkup was a significant force in stabilizing the city government during the Depression and World War II years.

JOHN B. STRANDER
MAYOR, 1962-1967

John B. Strander was born in Seattle in 1924. He studied landscape architecture at Cornell University and later ran his own award-winning landscaping firm, Strander Nursery. As the mayor, he implemented Tukwila's first residential sewers, water system upgrades and basic industrial infrastructure. Strander played a key role in the successful overthrow of the Port of Seattle's plan to industrialize the upper Duwamish Valley. Strander Blvd. is named for Mayor Strander.

STAN MINKLER
MAYOR, 1968-1971

Stan Minkler was born in Tukwila and attended Foster High School. He served many years on the Tukwila City Council and became involved in the planning processes necessary for the development of industrial sites. Minkler became mayor at the end of a period of intense industrial planning and on the eve of the launching of the Southcenter development.

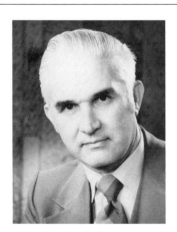

EDGAR D. BAUCH
MAYOR, 1976-1980

Edgar Bauch was born in Akron, Ohio, and moved to Tukwila in 1961 with his family to work for the Boeing Company. He was appointed to the Board of Adjustment in 1974 and served until he was elected mayor in 1975. As mayor he was responsible for the construction of the neighborhood trail system, the acquisition of Joseph Foster Park, the construction of the new City Hall, and the establishment of a Sister City program with the City of Ikawa in Japan.

FRANK TODD
MAYOR, 1972-1974; 1980-1982

Frank Todd moved to Tukwila in 1956 with his family. He worked as a flight engineer and later as a contractor, working on the first apartment complexes to be built in Tukwila. During his term as mayor he donated the flowering cherry trees along 59 Ave. S.

GARY L. VANDUSEN
MAYOR, 1982-1991

Gary L. VanDusen was born in South Dakota in 1941. He and his family moved to Tukwila in 1971. Before becoming mayor he taught high school and became involved in city committee issues, serving on the Tukwila City Council for seven years before becoming mayor in 1982. His accomplishments as mayor include developing a new Comprehensive Land Use Plan, new zoning ordinances, and encouraging a good commercial atmosphere for business.

Charles Otis Baker, tenth Mayor of the City of Tukwila, was born on February 14, 1908, in Kershaw County, South Carolina. His father, William E. Baker, and his mother, Molly V. Neal, both came from South Carolina pioneer families. Charles was the oldest of eight children. He attended the Cedar Swamp School, traveling in a two-horse wagon accompanied by brothers and sisters and neighbor children. The Baker family regularly attended the Cedar Grove Baptist Church.

CHARLES OTIS BAKER
MAYOR 1947-1962

Charles's mother enjoyed telling the story about the time she sent Charlie to get a haircut. He told Jud, the barber, to give him a "baldheaded" cut, as he was tired of coming to the barber shop, and that is what he got.

Graduating from the local high school in 1926, Baker enlisted in the Marines and served in Peking, China, for six years. He was welterweight champ of the American Colony in Peking. In January 1932 he was transferred to Bremerton, Washington. Through mutual friends Charlie met Ruth V. Bishop, who was born in Gloucester, Massachusetts. They were married June 7, 1932, in Bremerton. He left military service in 1934. During the Depression Charlie and Ruth moved to Seattle, where their children Charles O. Baker, Jr., Mary and Daniel W. were born. In the next years Baker was employed by H. R. L. Motors, a ship repair company; by Seattle Box Company as a fireman and engineer; and finally, in 1935, by Pacific Iron & Metal Company, where he remained for many years.

Tukwila owes a great deal to Mr. Jules Glant of Pacific Iron & Metal Co. for cooperating with the demands on Baker's time required during the period when he was Mayor of Tukwila. The family moved to Tukwila in 1940. Later they built a new home on 57 Ave. S. In 1947, "with a great amount of civic pride and love of community," Baker was elected Mayor of Tukwila. When he took over the leadership of the town the assessed valuation was several thousand dollars less than it was on the date of incorporation 40 years earlier.

In the 15 years he served the municipality of Tukwila it changed radically. Tukwila graduated from town status to a third-class city. The population increased to 2,251, and the land area had more than doubled. A comprehensive plan was adopted, a plan for streets and arterials was approved, the State Highway's I-5 and I-405 crossing through the City was approved, the first phase of the proposed water and sewer system was completed, a program for the undergrounding of utilities was initiated, and many other programs for the advancement of the City were undertaken by the Tukwila City Council.

For a decade Baker dedicated many nights a week to city business. He was a leader in organizing the Valley Cities, a closely knit association of Duwamish and Green River Valley communities. In addition, he became the permanent Chairman of the Architectural Control Commission for the Andover Industrial Park.

Charles Baker's love and devotion to Tukwila is simply stated in his farewell address given on April 2, 1962: "This is our City, forever keep it thus." His vision for his city, coupled with his intelligence, political acumen and administrative abilities, were crucial to the emergence of the modern City of Tukwila. Baker retired in 1970. He died on May 8, 1980. Both he and Ruth are buried at Washington Memorial Park Cemetery.

City of Tukwila Municipal Chronology, 1947-1990

January 1947
- Charles Otis Baker begins term as Mayor.

August 1948
- Golden Arrow Farms Dairy, 65th and S. 154th, annexed; first annexation on record.

1950-1959
- 1950 budget set at $18,979.
- Darwin A. Dibble appointed Police Judge, paid $50/year.
- Tukwila municipal employees become participants in the Social Security system.
- 12-member City Planning Commission created.
- Annexation of following properties: Southcenter/Andover Park (S. 154 to 180 and 51 Ave. to Green River); Codiga/Banchero (42 Ave. S. and Interurban); Segale (180 to S. 188); Nelsen, Kettering properties; S. 133/Interurban area.
- Zoning ordinances established.
- 50-year franchise granted to Seattle City Light.

1960-1969
- 1960 budget set at $156,635.42.
- Local Improvement Districts #2 and #3 created for improving Andover Park/Southcenter district.
- Residential water rate set at $3.25/700 c.f.
- Civil Service Commission created to select and appoint police department workers.
- Municipal Court established and first judge, Frank W. Payne, appointed.
- January 1962, John B. Strander begins term as mayor.
- Tukwila becomes third-class city with Resolution #150.
- Mabel J. (Thompson) Harris appointed City Treasurer by Mayor Strander.
- Local Improvement District #5 established for the purpose of providing sanitary sewers to the residential area.
- Curfew hours set for minors.
- Local Improvement District #11 established to construct Strander Blvd.
- Policy set for undergrounding electrical and communication facilities.
- Tukwila enters into Health Services agreement with King County.
- Interstate 405 opened through city.
- Green River Flood Control District approved by Council.
- Contracted with METRO for sewage disposal.
- Granted Puget Sound Power and Light 50-year franchise.
- Salary for Mayor set at $400/month and city council members at $20/meeting.
- Fees for volunteer firemen set at $5 per meeting and $5 per call.
- I-5 opens from Midway to Dearborn.
- January 1968, Stan D. Minkler begins term as mayor.
- Utility local improvement districts continue to form.
- Southcenter Retail Mall opens.
- City receives Forward Thrust funds.
- Office of Fire Chief created; Vic Bollinger hired as first chief.
- Portion of S. 154 St. renamed Southcenter Boulevard.
- Policies set for Civil Defense.

1970-1979
- 1970 budget set at $1,573,069.
- City fire station and maintenance building burned.
- Sales or use tax imposed of one half of one percent on retail sales.
- Orillia Bridge at S. 180 replaced and renamed the Frank W. Zepp Bridge for long-term city employee who originally looked after the municipality's streets, parks and other physical structures.
- New City Hall site purchased on Southcenter Boulevard for $162,000.
- Plans and construction begun on S. 144 St. project.
- January 1972, Frank Todd begins term as mayor.
- Plans made to build a new city maintenance facility.
- Receipt of first Federal Shared Revenue to be used for street improvements.
- Property purchased on Andover Park East for new fire station.
- City purchases first accounting machine.
- Planning Commission members reduced from 12 to 9.
- Five-member Board of Adjustment formed.
- Completion of Joseph Foster Memorial Park on original Foster High School site.
- Salary for mayor set at $750/month and council members at $200/month.
- January 1976, Edgar D. Bauch begins term as mayor.
- Height limitation for buildings established at 75 feet.
- City adopts classification of non-charter code city under the mayor-council form of government.
- Sidewalk plan adopted.

- New City Hall cornerstone laid by the Masons, with Delta Lodge No. 172 of Riverton in attendance, April 1978.
- City staff moves into City Hall, September 1978.
- Foster Golf Course purchased.
- Southgate Elementary School purchased to be used as community center.
- City Council adopts ordinance regulating the consumption of intoxicating beverages, disorderly conduct, indecent exposure and lewd conduct in public.
- Noise Control Ordinance adopted.
- Citizens of Tukwila entertain guests from Sister City of Ikawa, Japan.

1980-1989

- 1980 budget set at $8,800,702.
- January 1980, Frank Todd begins term as mayor.
- Library and Historical Society placed in old City Hall, originally the Tukwila Elementary School House.
- Council adopts ordinance reducing water and sewer rates for senior citizens.
- Council adopts handicapped parking regulations.
- Washington Natural Gas granted franchise for 25 years.
- Tukwila citizens visit Sister City of Ikawa, Japan.
- Flood Plain Management procedures established.
- Frank Todd resigns as mayor. Gary L. VanDusen selected by council to fill vacancy.
- Council adopts ordinance allowing planned residential development.
- City Administrator office created.
- Council adopts long-range Park and Open Space Plan.
- Automatic fire detectors required in all new and existing buildings.
- Property purchased for new water reservoir on 57 Ave. S.
- Section of McMicken Heights annexed.
- Salary for council members set at $400/month.
- Metro Park and Ride lot at 52 Ave. S. annexed.
- Speed limit of 35 mph set for Interurban Ave.
- Library Advisory Board created by council.
- Zoning regulations and maps adopted for Fire District No. 1, Duwamish-Allentown, Riverton, Foster, and Thorndyke annexations.
- Abatement requirements strengthened for abandoned and junked parked vehicles.
- Fire District No. 1 (Duwamish-Allentown) area annexed to City.
- Riverton, Foster, Thorndyke, Cascade View areas annexed to City.
- Council adopts legislation regarding prostitution.
- Council adopts ordinance making crime of leaving minor children in unattended vehicle.
- Zoning regulations and map adopted for Cascade View annexations.
- Council establishes moratorium on development of certain properties.
- Construction of two-million-gallon water reservoir begun.
- 1990 budget set at $47,777,013.

Population Growth of the City of Tukwila, 1940-1990

Year	Population
1940	521
1950	860
1960	1,804
1970	3,509
1980	3,578
1990	14,631

Tukwila's Parks

	Year Facility Established
Tukwila Park	1934
Bicentennial Park	1976
Duwamish Park	1976
Fort Dent, a King County Park	1977
Christensen Greenbelt Park	1978
Community Center Park (Riverton)	1978
Foot Trails (12)	1978
Foster Golf Links	1978
Joseph Foster Memorial Park–Lower	1982
Hazelnut Park	1983
Joseph Foster Memorial Park–Upper	1982
Crystal Springs Park (McMicken)	1986
Ikawa Park	1987
Crestview Park (Cascade View)	1990
Pea Patch Park (Allentown)	1990
Southgate Park (Riverton)	1990

APPENDIX B
HISTORIC HOUSES 1990

Many of the homes found in greater Tukwila were constructed between 1900 and 1939. A significant number of these are still standing and are listed here. While every effort has been made to identify all of the older homes, some may have been unintentionally overlooked by the field survey volunteer team. None of the houses listed have been officially designated as historic landmarks at the time of writing.

DUWAMISH-ALLENTOWN-QUARRY HISTORIC HOUSES

1900-1919

1906	11854 42 Ave. S.
1907	11850 42 Ave. S.
1908	11646 42 Ave. S.
1917	11830 42 Ave. S.
1918	13039 41 Ave. S.
1918	13751 41 Ave. S.
1918	12054 42 Ave. S.

1920-1939

1920	11818 42 Ave. S.
1920	13739 41 Ave. S.
1922	11620 42 Ave. S.
1929	12244 42 Ave. S.
1929	11616 42 Ave. S.
1931	12048 42 Ave. S.

FOSTER HISTORIC HOUSES

1900-1919

1904	4617 S. 144 St.
1904	4803 S. 144 St.
1906	4226 S. 139 St.
1910	16643 56 Ave. S.
1910	5131 S. 151 St.
1910	5668 S. 149 St.
1915	6427 S. 143 St.
1915	4820 S. 150 St.

1920-1939

1920	4823 S. 138 St.
1921	16205 51 Ave. S.
1921	4629 S. 144 St.
1922	4439 S. 160 St.
1925	4250 S. 164 St.
1926	4238 S. 164 St.
1928	4402 S. 164 St.
1929	5608 47 Ave. S.
1930	4256 S. 164 St.
1930	13940 51 Ave. S.
1931	16210 51 Ave. S.
1931	4251 S. 139 St.
1932	4440 S. 160 St.
1936	4321 S. 140 St.
1938	4712 S. 144 St.
1938	4029 S. 144 St.

RIVERTON HISTORIC HOUSES

1900-1919

1902	12816 S. 126
1907	13015 38 Ave. S.
1908	3521 S. 130
1908	13001 41 Ave. S.
1909	13007 37 Ave. S.
1910	13031 37 Ave. S.
1910	4417 S. 136
1910	3517 S. 130
1911	4033 S. 128
1912	4026 S. 130
1912	4623 S. 138
1912	4623 S. 138
1912	4631 S. 138
1913	12527 35 Ave. S.
1913	4106 S. 130
1913	4128 S. 130
1913	4136 S. 130
1914	13025 41 Ave. S.
1914	4049 S. 128
1915	3436 S. 130
1918	3832 S. 130
1918	4961 S. 128
1918	3809 S. 130
1919	3705 S. 130

1920-1939

1920	4044 S. 128
1920	3716 S. 126
1920	4503 S. 136
1921	3703 S. 126
1921	3836 S. 130
1922	15223 40 Ave. S.
1922	3709 S. 126
1922	3810 S. 130
1923	4126 S. 131
1926	4511 S. 136
1928	3513 S. 128
1928	4517 S. 137
1932	13029 41 Ave. S.
1930s	12816 35 Ave. S.
1937	13422 40 Ave.

TUKWILA HISTORIC HOUSES

1900-1919

1900	14206 56 Ave. S.
1900	14455 58 Ave. S.
1900	14431 58 Ave. S.
1900	14490 57 Ave. S.
1900	5630 S. 147 St.
1900	14951 57 Ave. S.
1900	5630 S. 147 St.
1901	14250 58 Ave. S.
1904	14433 59 Ave. S.
1904	14406 59 Ave. S.
1905	14419 59 Ave. S.
1907	14414 59 Ave. S.
1908	14219 57 Ave. S.
1908	14216 58 Ave. S.
1908	14711 57 Ave. S.
1908	14234 58 Ave. S.
1908	14488 58 Ave. S.
1908	14221 58 Ave. S.
1908	14246 57 Ave. S.
1908	14477 58 Ave. S.
1908	14444 56 Ave. S.
1908	14240 58 Ave. S.
1910	14201 56 Ave. S.
1910	14217 58 Ave. S.
1910	14210 58 Ave. S.
1910	14209 58 Ave. S.
1910	14215 57 Ave. S.
1913	5506 S. 144 St.
1913	14950 57 Ave. S.
1913	14921 57 Ave. S.
1913	14243 57 Ave. S.
1915	14243 58 Ave. S.
1915	14233 57 Ave. S.
1916	14915 62 Ave. S.
1918	14222 58 Ave. S.
1918	14462 58 Ave. S.
1918	14231 56 Ave. S.

1920-1939

1920	5702 S. 144 St.
1920	14402 56 Ave. S.
1920	14442 58 Ave. S.
1920	14471 58 Ave. S.
1928	14451 59 Ave. S.
1929	14235 58 Ave. S.
1936	5534 S. 144 St.
1937	14234 57 Ave. S.
1937	14228 59 Ave. S.

REFERENCES

PUBLISHED SOURCES

Bagley, Clarence. *History of Seattle, King County*. 3 Vols. Chicago, IL: S. Clarke Pub. Co., 1916, 1929.

Beaver, Lowell. *Memories from Historic Markers & Plaques*. Puyallup, WA: Privately printed, 1963.

"Big Sunday Picnic at Renton Junction." *Duwamish Valley News*, June 14, 1912.

"Bridge Truss Types: A Guide to Dating and Identifying." Technical Leaflet 95. *Historic News*. Vol. 32, No. 5. May 1977.

Buerge, David M. "Requiem for a River." *The Weekly*, Oct. 16-22, 1985.

"Busiest Man Runs Tukwila in Spare Time." *Seattle Times*, Jan. 26, 1944.

"The Case of C.D. Hillman." *Seattle Mail & Herald*, Nov. 19, 1912.

Cavanaugh, Mary Ann Maple. "Story of Pioneer Party in King County Forty Years [Ago]." *Seattle Post-Intelligencer*, Jan. 21, 1906.

"Chinook: Land Where the Hazelnuts Grow." *Renton Chronicle*, March 15, 1968.

Church by the Side of the Road. *Church by the Side of the Road Golden Jubilee, 1933-1983*. Seattle, WA: Privately printed, 1983.

"Clarence Hillman Trial." *Seattle Post-Intelligencer*, Sept. 3, 1910, March 4, 1911, March 5, 1911, March 11, 1911.

Clark, Thomas N. Obituary. *Seattle Times*, June 28, 1959.

Cleveland High School Laboratory Writing Students. *Duwamish Diary, 1849-1949*. Seattle, WA: Cleveland High School, Seattle Public Schools, 1949.

Conover, Charles Tolmange. "'Just Cogitating': Uncle Joe Foster Had a Long and Active Career." *Seattle Times*, June 17, 1948.

Cumming, William. *Sketchbook, A Memoir of the 1930s and the Northwest School*. Seattle, WA: University of Washington Press, 1984.

"Denied Ramble in the Country." *Seattle Post-Intelligencer*, Feb. 26, 1911.

Denny, Arthur A. *Pioneer Days on Puget Sound*, Fairfield, WA: Ye Galleon Press, 1888; rpt. 1965.

"Dredging the Duwamish." *Duwamish Valley News*, Oct. 17, 1913.

"Duwamish River." *Seattle Post-Intelligencer*, Sept. 4, 1909.

Duwamish Valley News, May 10, 16, 1912.

Edson, Lelah Jackson. "Northern Raiders & Col. Isaac N. Ebey." Bellingham, WA: The Fourth Corner.

"The Election." *Seattle Gazette*, Dec. 10, 1863.

Emmons Vine, Josephine. *Auburn: A Look Down Mainstreet*. Auburn, WA: City of Auburn, 1990.

Federal Writer's Project, WPA. *The New Washington, A Guide to the Evergreen State*. Portland, OR: Binfords & Mort, 1941.

Fish, Byron. "Slides Made from Family Album Mark Surprise Party for Tukwila Woman." *Seattle Times*, Feb. 21, 1961.

Fish, Laurie. "The Duwamish." *Seattle Times*, Aug. 23, 1959.

Fleming, Elaine. "Founder of Tukwila Colorful Southern Type Gentleman." *Renton Record-Chronicle*, April 27, 1969.

"Flower Show at Riverton." *Duwamish Valley News*, July 12, 1912.

"Former Tukwila Mayor Dies." Obituary. *Renton Chronicle*, Dec. 19, 1973.

"Foster Library celebrates '40 Years of Reading Pleasure.'" *Highline Times-Des Moines News*, Jan. 30, 1985.

Fun with Dick and Jane. 1946-47 Edition. New York, NY: Scott, Foresman and Company, 1946.

Grant, Fredric James. *History of Seattle*. New York, NY: American Publishing and Engraving, 1891.

Growler, Foster High School student newspaper, 1930-1990.

"Here's More About Tukwila." *Seattle Post-Intelligencer*, May 25, 1924.

Highline Times, Mar. 18, 1984.

Hoyt, Harold "Jiggs." *King County Fire Districts History*. Seattle, WA: Privately Printed, 1990.

Immigrant Handbook, Washington Territory. St. Paul, MN: Northern Pacific Railway, 1886, 1887.

"James Nelsen Funeral Thursday." Obituary. *Seattle Times*, 1952.

"Joseph Allen Dies at Minor Hospital." *Seattle Post-Intelligencer*, March 13, 1909.

Kennedy, Richard T., Ed. and Gretchen F. Schmidt, Assoc. Ed.. *One Hundred Years of the "Waterland" Community: A History of Des Moines, Washington*. Des Moines, WA: City of Des Moines, 1989.

King County Commissioners. *Beginnings, Progress and Achievement of King County*. Seattle, WA: King County Commissioners, 1931.

King County Executives. *50 Years, Boeing Field/King County International Airport, 1928-1978*. Privately printed, 1978.

"King County Fair Opens at the Meadows Next Monday." *Duwamish Valley News*, Sept. 6, 1912.

King County Road Engineer. *Third Annual Report*. Seattle, WA, 1937.

King County Road Engineer. *Fifth Annual Report*. Seattle, WA, 1939.

"King County, Washington." *Wilhelm's Magazine, The Coast*. June, 1909.

Klahowyah, Foster High School student yearbook. Seattle, WA: Foster High School, 1919-1990.

Luzier, J.E.. *Geology and Groundwater Resources of Southwestern King County, Washington*. Olympia, WA: State of Washington, 1969.

McAlester, Lee and Virginia McAlester. *A Field Guide to American Houses*. New York, NY: Alfred A. Knopf, 1984.

"Meadows Will be Re-opened as Permanent Sporting Resort." *Duwamish Valley News*, June 7, 1902.

Meeker, Ezra. "Pioneer Reminiscences of Puget Sound." Seattle, WA: 1905; rpt. 1980.

"Must Show Cause Why Brick Not Used." *Seattle Post-Intelligencer*, April 1, 1916.

Nelsen, John W. "Ku Klux Meet Minus Masks." *Seattle Star*, July 7-14, 1923.

"News of the Northwest." *Seattle Post-Intelligencer*, Aug. 17, 1902.

Norwood, Gus. *Washington Granges Celebrate a Century*. Seattle, WA: Washington State Grange, 1988.

Olympian. Oct. 3, 1857.

Oregon Spectator. Oregon City, Oregon. Oct. 17, 1850.

Polk's Directory of the City of Seattle, Seattle, WA: Polk, Inc., 1878.

Polk's King County Directory, 1911-1912. Seattle, WA: Polk, Inc., 1911.

"Purchasing Waterway Right of Way." *Duwamish Valley News*, May 10, 1912.

Price, Lyle. "A Lot of History Has Gone Under Green River's Bridges." *Valley Daily News*, July 5, 1988.

"Quarry Plant Improvement." *Duwamish Valley News*, June 14, 1912.

Reinartz, Kay F. *"Passport to Ballard."* Seattle, WA: *Ballard News-Tribune*, 1988.

Rinehart, Elsie. "Tukwila Pioneers Moved Here Half-Century Ago." *Renton Chronicle*, Aug. 8, 1962.

"Riverboats." *Valley Daily News*, June 10, 1988.

Riverton on the Duwamish: Seattle's Most Picturesque Suburb. Seattle, WA: Privately printed, n.d., ca. 1908.

"Riverton Memories Linger Amid Progress." *Seattle Times*, Nov. 8, 1963.

"Riverton Notices." *Duwamish Valley News*, Nov. 15, 1912.

"Road Specialists Examine Sample." *Seattle Post-Intelligencer*, July 8, 1906.

Ruthron, Alice. "Hop-Growing Farms in the Puyallup and White River Valleys of Washington State in 1884." *Pacific Northwest*. Heritage Quest Issue No. 29, July-August, 1971.

Seattle Chamber of Commerce. *Seattle Chamber of Commerce Report for 1884*. Seattle, WA: Privately printed, 1884.

Seattle-King County Department of Health. "*The Road to Health. A Short History of the Seattle-King County Department of Health.*" Seattle, WA: King County Department of Health, 1954.

Seattle Post-Intelligencer. July 5, 1908, July 18, 1906, Aug. 10, 1902, Jan. 17, 1911.

Seattle Post-Intellegencer, Northwest Magazine. April 27, 1980.

"September 12 will be Duwamish Valley Day." *Duwamish Valley News*, July 25, 1912; July 26, 1912; Aug. 2, 1912.

"70-Foot Concrete Tower Blasted at Riverton Quarry." *Seattle Times*, March 16, 1963.

Shomaker, Joel B. Obituary. *Seattle Post-Intelligencer*, Dec. 17, 1937.

Slauson, Morda C.. *Renton—From Coal to Jets: Renton Diamond Jubilee, 1901-1976*. Renton, WA: Sunset Press, 1976.

South Central School District Newsletter, Mar. 1970.

Strachan, Margaret Pitcairn. "Early Day Mansions." *Seattle Daily Times*, Dec., Jan., Feb., 1945.

This Man Robert Bridges. Pamphlet. Seattle, WA: Privately printed, 1906.

Toellner, Judge August. "Honest John, Race Horse." *Duwamish Valley News*, Dec. 1932.

____. "June 21, 1851 set as Date of First Settlers in Seattle (King County)." *Duwamish Valley News*, May 18, 1934; July 2, 1937.

____. "Pioneers Fete 89th Year of Landing on Duwamish." *Seattle Times*, June 21, 1940.

"Tukwila Aroused at Plot to Wipe It Out as Town." Seattle *Post-Intelligencer*, March 2, 1927.

"Tukwila Populists Oust Administration." *The Patriarch*, Dec. 18, 1922.

"Tukwila Topics." *Renton Chronicle*, October 16, 1910.

"Tukwila's Mayor." *Glendale-Highline Gazette*, March 20, 1947.

"The Union Resolution." *Seattle Gazette*, July 10, 1863.

Washington Department of Agriculture. *Washington's Centennial Farms, Yesterday and Today*. Olympia, WA: Washington Department of Agriculture, 1989.

Welch, Douglas. "Tukwila's 30-Foot Shelf Dusted Off for Duty." *Seattle Post-Intelligencer*, May 17, 1938.

Who's Who in the United States. Entry on Elizabeth Ryder Montgomery.

"Will Race Every Saturday." *Seattle Times*, Jun. 8, 1902.

Unpublished Sources

Anderson, Herman. Letter to the Foster School Board, May 24, 1933.

Cady, Donald I. Annual Report to the Board of Education. July 10, 1942.

Campbell, Sarah J.. "The Duwamish No. 1 Site—A Lower Puget Sound Shell Midden." Office of Public Archaeology Research Report, University of Washington, 1981.

Colburn, Myron. Superintendent's Annual Report to the Board of Directors, June 30, 1964.

Donation Claim Record. King County Recorder's Office, Seattle, WA.

Duwamish PTA. "*Duwamish School Days.*" Duwamish PTA Commemorative Booklet. June 6, 1973.

Duwamish Precinct Voter Registration Records, 1921, 1922, 1923.

"Foster Bridge Dedication and Time Capsule Ceremony," City of Tukwila Ceremony Program, 1985.

Foster, Flora Fleming. "The Honorable Joseph Foster, Life Sketch." ca. 1930. (Typewritten.)

Foster Precinct Voter Registration Records, 1921, 1922, 1923.

Foster School Board. Financial Statement of the Foster School District. March 31, 1917.

Foster and South Central School Board Minutes and Clerk's Records, 1905-1990.

Graves, James P. "A History of the Foster # 1 Coal Mine in Tukwila." May, 1990. (Typewritten.)

Hanford, Abbie Holgate. "Narrative of the Indian Uprising, 1855-1856."

Hart Crowser, Inc. "Abandoned Underground Coal Mine Hazard Assessment for Tukwila, Washington." May 3, 1990. (Typewritten.)

Hill, Ada S. "A History of the Snoqualmie Valley." Snoqualmie, WA. Snoqualmie Valley Historical Society, 1970. (Typewritten.)

Hillman, Clarence Day and Bessie Olive Hillman. Articles of Incorporation, 1901.

Isaac, Gary W., Ecological Analyst, Glen D. Farris, Senior Water Quality Analyst, Charles V. Gibbs, Chief, Water Quality Control Division. "Special Duwamish River Studies." Water Quality Series No. 1, Municipality of Metropolitan Seattle, Seattle, WA: 1964.

Kelly, Jane Fenton. "Tales of a Pioneer Family." Reprinted in its entirety in Esther Balzarini, *Our Burien*. Seattle, WA: Highline Business and Professional Women's Club, privately printed, 1968.

King County Assessor's Office, Plat Records, King County, Washington.

King County Census, Washington Territory, 1860, 1870, 1880, 1883, 1885, 1888.

King County Commissioner Records. Vols. 1-18, 1853-1914.

King County Commissioners, *Journal of Proceedings*. Vol. 29. Franchise No. 72, November 19, 1928.

King County Dept. of Planning & Community Development. King County Historic Sites Survey. "James Nelsen House," "Interurban Bridge," "Albert Tutt Property," "The Ray-Carrossino House," "Tom & Nell Clark Home," "Archie Codiga Farm." Seattle, WA, 1976-1979.

King County Library System Director's Report, January 1985. (Typewritten.)

King County Schools. "Outline of Course of Study," ca. 1890.

King County Superintendent of Schools Daily Record, Vol. 3-A, 1877-92.

Koch, Joe. White River Steam Boat Tabulation. (Typewritten.)

McCartney, Frank N. Chair, Washington State Grange Historical Committee, Letter, June 15, 1990.

"Matt Starwich Scrapbook." University of Washington, Microfilm Library.

Mitchell, Marian B. "Newspapers Published in Washington." Unpublished master's thesis, University of Washington, 1964.

Morton, Anne, Archivist, Hudson's Bay Company Archives. Letter, April 12, 1990.

Museum of Flight. Press Release. December, 1990.

North Riverton Precinct Voter Registration Records, 1924.

"On the Occasion of Ceremonies Marking the Closing of the Orillia School." Prepared by the Orillia P. T. A., Pauline Haug, President, January 21, 1958. (Typewritten manuscript.)

Patrons of Husbandry, Articles of Incorporation, Duwamish Grange; White River Grange, 1878.

Petition to create a King County flood control district in accordance with 1935 law. State of Washington, 1935.

Plat Records, King County Assessor's Records, King County, Washington.

Prosch, Thomas W. *"Chronological History of Seattle from 1850-1857."* (Typewritten manuscript.)

Rinehart, Elsie. "This Is Your Life, Tessie Kline Henke, of Tukwila, Washington." February 18, 1961. (Typewritten.)

Rinehart, Elsie. "Ellen and Fred Nord– This Is Your Life." (Typewritten.)

Riverton Precinct Voter Registration Records, 1921, 1922, 1923.

Shomaker, Joel. Manuscript Collection, Suzzallo Library, University of Washington.

South Seattle Land Company, Articles of Incorporation, 1890.

Spitzer, Paul. "Between Blue Ruin and Blue Laws: A History of Horserace Gambling." Seattle, Washington. (Typewritten manuscript.)

Steele-Shaw, Joseph Lee. "'Lest We Forget . . .' Summary of the Memoirs of Steele-Foster Family of Joseph Foster," University of Washington, 1948. (Typewritten manuscript.)

Swenson, L.O., High School Supervisor, Washington State Department of Education. Letter to Herman Anderson, May 10, 1933.

Thomas, Bertram P., Consulting Engineer, Walter F. Winters, County Engineer. "King County Comprehensive Plan for Flood Control." Unpublished report, Aug. 1964.

Tukwila City Council Minutes, 1908-1990.

Tukwila Precinct Voter Registration, 1910. Washington State Archives, King County Regional Branch.

U.S. Post Office Dept. Records: Duwamish, Black River, 1870, 1873, 1874, 1880; King County, Washington, 1938, 1947; Foster, Garden Station, Riverton, Riverton Heights, Tukwila.

U.S. Bureau of the Census. King County, Census, Washington State. Washington, DC: Government Publishing Office, 1880.

U.S. Bureau of the Census. Tenth Census of the United States, 1880. Thirteenth Census of the United States. Tukwila, 1910. Washington DC: Government Printing Office, 1910.

Wing, Warren. "The Interurban, A Brief History of the Puget Sound Electric Railway, 1902-1928." June 8, 1990. (Typewritten manuscript.)

Wolfstine, Manfred R. Blockhouse of Company B, 9th Regiment United States Infantry at Black River Junction, Washington Territory. "Fort Dent." Seattle, Washington, May 18, 1977. (Typewritten.)

COMMUNITY HISTORY SOURCES PREPARED BY COMMUNITY MEMBERS

Ben Aliment, "Foster Golf Links."

Eileen Avery, "History of Tukwila International Training in Communications."

Mary Bosshart, "Annexation History, Cascade View;" "The Cascade View Area," :Riverton Heights Neighborhood History."

Margaret Chumlea, "Foster Study Club."

Darlene Crostick, "History of the Tukwila Community Club," "History of the Thorndyke Community Club," "The Tukwila Chamber of Commerce."

Lynn DeVore, "Tukwila Southgate Community Center."

Delta Masonic Temple, "History of Delta Lodge No. 172, F & AM."

Duwamish Community Presbyterian Church.

Eastern Star Delta Chapter No. 109.

Allen Ekberg and Ron Lamb, "Foster, Riverton, Thorndyke Annexation."

Dick Fain, "History of Southcenter Rotary Club."

Foster Community Library, "The History of the Foster Library."

George Gomez, "Annexation History, Duwamish-Allentown."

Alice Hanson Gustafson, "History of the Thorndyke Community Club," "History of the Thorndyke-Riverton Heights Neighborhood."

Mabel Gylden and Elvira Gyselinck, "A Fraternal Insurance Society."

REFERENCES

Dorothy Haney, "Southgate Garden Club."

B.P. Hartl, "Primera Iglesia Bautista."

Debbie Hatton, "Christian Science Church."

Joan Hernandez, "Prelude to the Annexations of 1989-1990."

Jean Howat, "International Order of Job's Daugthers."

Donald Leahy, "Tukwila Volunteer Fire Department."

Freda Leahy, "Tukwila Quilting Club."

Karen Livermore, "Cascade View Neighborhood History."

Margaret Eileen McCulloch, "Royal Neighbors of America."

McCurdy, James, "The Riverton Quarry."

Wendy Morgan, "Tukwila Historical Society," "Foster Study Club."

Margaret Nesheim, "St. Thomas Church," "Central School District Minutes, 1930-1990."

Harry Peterson, "Duwamish Improvement Club."

Judy Peterson, "Riverton Hospital."

Lee R. Phillips, "Little League."

Marcela Revel, "The Sunshine Grandmothers Club," "Foster Friendly Garden Club."

Riverton Park United Methodist Church, "Historical Sketch of Riverton Park United Methodist Church."

Dennis Robertson, "History of the Annexation of McMicken."

Southwest King County Chamber of Commerce, "The Chamber."

John Strander Jr., "Southcenter Community Baptist Church."

Gary Tate, "Foster-Tukwila Presbyterian Church."

Mary Ellen Anderson Whitehead, "Foster Community Club."

Donald Williams, "History of Tukwila's Parks."

Warren Wing, "Duwamish Improvement Club."

Mary B. Zion, "The Foster Community Gets a Library," "Foster Friendly Garden Club."

MEMOIRS

Rev. Robert Abbot

Roger Baker

Viola Merkle Baker

Sue Boullard

Gus Charleson

Cecile Chelette, "A Tribute to Julia Nelson."

Jackie Doyle Coolidge

Darlene Crostick

Lawrence Crostick

Frank Cummings

Barbara Davidson, "The P.O.W. Camp on Quarry Hill."

Carol DeRose

Kitty Endert

Allen L. Erickson

Bill Fouty

Doris Manington George

Mary Raines Giboney

Anna May Charnell Gott

Mr. and Mrs. Forrest Gott, submitted by their children.

Alice Hanson Gustafson

Carl Stanley Gustafson

Mabel Gylden, "Doty Hall."

Grace Gylling

Jerry Hamilton

Doris Heppenstall Hanset

Ruth Gustafson Hawley, "I Grew Up in Tukwila."

Roy Henderson

Joan Hernandez

Pat Walkup Hopper, "Memories of Tukwila, Late 20s to Early 40s," "John Walkup."

Frank Horsfall

Olive Thompson Hozack

Gene Ives

Walter W. Kassner

Hazel Ketchersid

Don Leahy

Freda Leahy

Carl Lee

Donna and Merle Lee

Larry Linnell, "Growing Up in Riverton."

Frances LaFranchi Menalia

Susanne Minkler McVeigh, interview with the Clifford Minkler Family.

Ada Heppenstall Miller

William Morgan

Gladys and Grace Myers, "Family of Hamlin M. Myers."

Mabel Nelson

Werner Neudorf

Jerry Newton

Fred Nichols

Frances Codiga North

James M. North

Nora Nunan, "The Way I Remember It."

Jim O'Sullivan

Don Paulson

Phyllis D. Pesicka

Harry Peterson

Doris Phelps

Helen Ponchel

A.G. Radford

Vic Raffanelli

Elsie Anderson Rinehart, "A Child's Memory of Old Tukwila"; "A Most Unforgettable Person," Memoir of Tessie Henke.

Evelyn Robbins, "Robbins Family Tree."

Catherine Cerini Rooney

Barney Schwartz

Thomas Scibor

Leonard Snowden

Lorene Spencer

Sophia Thorndike Storey

Helen Stougard

Clarence Stutz

Henning Sundby

Curtis Sweeney

Lona Schwartz Sweeney

Alma Nelsen Taylor

Willard Thorndike

Dwayne Traynor

Harriett Bergquist Tombs, "Mayor Bergquist and Remarks on the Bergquist House and Garden," "My Memories of Tukwila."

Reverend James L. and Lenore M. Unger, "The Duwamish Years."

Josephine Waldo

Wayne Weber

Mary Ellen Anderson Whitehead

Charlotte Dobbs Widrig

Harold Wilson

Warren Wing

Alice Jorgenson Wood

Oscar Wood

Gerry Brooker Young

Kathy Zepp

Mary B. Zion

ORAL HISTORY SOURCES

George "Bearcat" Baker. Interviewer, Warren Wing, November 29, 1990.

Roger Baker. Interviewer, Dr. Kay Reinartz, April 17, 1990.

Viola Merkle Baker. Interviewer, Roger Baker, May 10, 1990.

Laura Shomaker Bateham. Interviewer, Maxine Anderson, February 28, 1990.

Carrol A. Bigelow. Interviewer, Maxine Anderson, January 30, 1990.

Leland Chumlea. Interviewer, Maxine Anderson, May 1990.

Thomas Clark. Interviewer, Wayne Weber, 1955.

Dewey Duggan. Interviewer, Jerry Hamilton, December 2, 1989.

Alice Hanson Gustafson. Interviewer, Maxine Anderson, November 17, 1990.

Anna Josie. Interviewer, Warren Wing, April 17, 1990.

John Needham. Interviewer, Warren Wing, November 21, 1989.

Helen B. Nelson. Interviewer, Maxine Anderson, March 1, 1990.

Fred Nichols. Interviewer, Warren Wing, November 9, 1989.

Kay Nielsen. Interviewer, Maxine Anderson, August 7, 1990.

Frances Codiga North. Interviewer, Maxine Anderson, May 17, 1990.

James M. North. Interviewer, Maxine Anderson, May 17, 1990.

Herman Schoenbachler. Interviewer, Maxine Anderson, June 21, 1990.

Akiko Mikami Shimatsu. Interviewer, Joan Hernandez, December 9, 1989.

Irene Prandi Siccardi. Interviewer, Joan Hernandez, June 23, 1990.

Henning Sundby. Interviewer, Warren Wing, January 17, 1990.

Lona Schwartz Sweeney. Interviewer, Warren Wing, November 2, 1989.

Alma Nelsen Taylor. Interviewer, Warren Wing, October 30, 1989.

Helen Walkup. Interviewer, Maxine Anderson, October 1990.

Mary Ellen Anderson Whitehead. Interviewer, Dr. Kay Reinartz, April 25, 1990.

Mike Yellem. Interviewer, Warren Wing, May 1990.

INTERVIEWS

Marvin Boys. Interviewer, Dr. Kay Reinartz, December 10, 1989.

Ronald Cameron, City Engineer, City of Tukwila. Interviewer, Dr. Kay Reinartz, January 19, 1990.

Cy Cysaski. Interviewer, Dr. Kay Reinartz, April 20, 1990.

Ross Earnst, Dir. Public Works, City of Tukwila. Interviewer, Dr. Kay Reinartz, February 10, 1990.

Phillip Frazer, Engineer, City of Tukwila. Interviewer, Dr. Kay Reinartz, March 1990

Al Harris. Interviewer, Dr. Kay Reinartz, April 12, 1990.

Harold & Irv Iverson. Interviewer, Dr. Kay Reinartz, October 12, 1989.

Rinehart, Elsie. Interviews conducted with the following community members: James and Nellie Blair; Ellen and Fred Nord; Carl Lee; Dorothy Lambert Lindberg; Jem Locke; Susanne Minkler McVeigh; Hamlin M. Myers family; Gus Charleson; Grace Myers Garbrich; Gladys Myers Omana; Ben and Corinne Gustman; James L. Durbin; Manington George; Hazel and Harold Serson.

Gary VanDusen. Interviewer, Maxine Anderson, May 1990.

PRELUDE—D. BUERGE

Adamson, Thelma. *Folk Tales of the Coast: Salish.* New York, NY: American Folklore Society, 1934.

Denny, Arthur A. *Pioneer Days on Puget Sound.* Fairfield, WA: Ye Galleon Press, 1888; rpt. 1965.

Ernst, Charles F., Ed. *Occurrences at Nisqually House: Told by the Pioneers.* Vol. 1. Seattle, WA: Washington Pioneer Project, 1937.

Gunther, Erna. *Klallam Ethnography.* Seattle, WA: University of Washington Press, 1927.

Hanford, Cornelius H., Ed. *Seattle and Its Environs.* Chicago and Seattle: Pioneer Historical Publishing Co., 1924.

Harrington, John Peabody. *The Papers of John Peabody Harrington in the Smithsonian Institution, 1907-1957.* Millwood, NY, Kraus Microfilm, 1981.

Kelly, Elizabeth Jane Fenton. "The Trail of a Pioneer Family To Washington." *Duwamish Valley News,* 1934.

Tolmie, William Fraser. *The Journals of Wm. Fraser Tolmie, Physician and Fur Trader.* Vancouver, B.C.: Mitchell Press Limited, 1963.

Waterman, Thomas Talbot. *Puget Sound Geography.* Washington, D.C.: Smithsonian Office of Anthropology, Bureau of American Ethnology Manuscript Collection, ca. 1920. Ms. 1864.

Waterman, Thomas Talbot. "The Geographical Names Used by the Indians of the Pacific Coast." *The Geographical Review.* Vol. 12, Pt. 2, 1922.

UNPUBLISHED SOURCES

Ballard, Arthur. "Puget Sound Mythology." *University of Washington Publications in Anthropology.* Vol 3. Seattle, WA, 1929. Unpublished manuscript.

Buerge, David M. "Before Seattle." 1980. Unpublished manuscript.

Griffen, Arthur H. "Ah Mo." Seattle, WA. (Typewritten.)

INDEX

Abbott, Edith Gjersee, 146
Abbott, Rev. Frank C., 146
About Half-Way Up (scow), 11-12
Adams, Ava Sophia, 227
Adams, Beulah, 227
Adams, Henry, xix, 19, 20, 22, 29, 33, 53, 62, 72
Adams, Lester M., 150
Addie (steamboat), 55
Adelphia, Del, 183, 184, 185
Alaska gold rush, 65, 77, 111, 112, 113
Alaska-Yukon Exposition, 75, 186
Algona land venture, 183
Alien Land Law, 221
Aliment, Hazel, 211
Aliment, Joe, 207, 211
Alki, 24, 25
Alki Beach, 140-141
Alki Point, 7, 8, 10
Allen, Flora Moore, 114, 155, 156
Allen, Florence, 156
Allen, H.M., 156
Allen, Joseph, 114, 155, 156, 215
Allen, Robert D., 156
Allen, Rosetta, 156
Allentown, xi, 95, 99, 114, 155, 156
 see also Duwamish-Allentown
Allentown Station, 155
Allied Stores, 210, 213
Allison, Rex, 213
Alvord's Landing, 48
Andersen, Margaret, *see* Nelsen, Margaret Andersen
Andersen, Neils, 72
Anderson, Ben, 195
Anderson, Gota, 195
Anderson, Grace, 216, 230
Anderson, Herman, 210, 216, 230
Anderson, Irene, 246
Anderson, Jeanne, 230
Anderson, John, 97, 114, 116
Anderson, Lloyd, 234
Anderson, Mary Ellen, *see* Toon, Mary Ellen Anderson
Anderson, Wayne, 230
Anderson, Wynn, 216, 230
Andover, Inc., 210, 211, 216
Andover Industrial Park, 212, 213, 216
Angeline (daughter of Chief Seattle), 26
Angle, Jim, 125, 247
Angle, Margaret Hanson, 245, 246, 247
Angle Lake, 140, 202
annexation, 108, 210, 211, 256-261
Anti-Tuberculosis League, 86
Arbogast, M.S., 145
Arcade Rest Home, 112
Armstrong, Ruby, 252
artists, 126, 205
Association of Washington Cities, 201
Astor, John Jacob, 3
automobiles, 80-81, 95-96, 139-140, 216
Avery, Eveline M., *see* Grow, Eveline Avery
Avery, John, 25

Back, Michael, 214
Bacon, Lula, 148
Badgeo, W., 97
Badten, Mark, 214
Bagley, Clarence, 8-9, 18, 36
Bagley, Daniel, 9, 32
Bagnariol, John, 165
Baker, Adolph, 110
Baker, Charles O., 207, 210, 211, 212, 213, 214, 256, 267, 268, 272
Baker, Charles O. Jr., 272
Baker, Daniel, 272
Baker, Ernie, 169
Baker, Frank, 93
Baker, George "Bearcat," 178
Baker, Mary, 110, 272
Baker, Molly Neal, 272
Baker, Roger, 169, 173
Baker, Ruth Bishop, 272
Baker, Viola Merkle, 166
Baker, William E., 272
Baker chicken farm, 195
Ballard, *see* Lake Washington Ship Canal
Banta, Robey G., 190
Barker, Rev. Everett, 147
Barrett, Sam, 71
Bartholme, Fr., 123
Bateham, Laura Shomaker, 269
Bates, Gil, 173
Bates, Mrs., 200
Bauch, Edgar D., 151, 271
"Beach Road," 33
Belaire, Victoria O., *see* Nichols, Victoria Belaire
Bell & Scott (contractors), 174, 175
Bell, William N., 19, 21
Benedict, Edwin H., 150
Bennett, Constance, *see* Fouty, Constance Bennett
Berberich, Fr., 123
Berg, Cherie, 164
Bergquist, George C., 196, 270
Bergsma, Frank, 218
Bergsma, George, 218
Bergsma, Joe, 218
Bergsma, Josephine, 218
Bergsma, Rudy, 217, 218
Bersie, Rev. Richard, 252
Beth Ha Shofar, 147
Bicentennial Park, 262
Bigelow, Dr. M., 30, 189
Bigelow, Frank, 176
Bigelow, Lewis, 176
Bigelow, Mabel, 162
Bigelow, Neil, 165, 171
Bigelow, Ransome, 158
Bigelow, Walter, 165
Bigelow Shingle Mill, 176
Biglow, Vira, 162
Billings, Luella, *see* Shomaker, Luella Billings
Bishop, Ruth V., *see* Baker, Ruth Bishop
Bissel, G.P., 20
Bitzig, Chris, 145
Bitzig, Terry, 145
Black Diamond (riverboat), 37

281

Black River, xiii, 19-20, 24, 97, 103, 104, 106, 108
    ceases to exist, 107
    coal discovered near, 30, 189
    and Native Americans, xix, 4, 181
Black River Bridge, 33, 34, 35, 52, 98, 114
Black River Junction, 36, 69, 73, 98
Black River Post Office, 33, 60
Black River School, 48-49, 54, 55
Black River School District No. 6, 224, 225, 231
Blaine, Catherine, 26
Blaine, Rev. David, 13, 26
Blair, Gertrude, 149
Blair, James, 176
Blair, Nellie, 176
Blankenship, Hiram, 198
Blue Gallery, 126
Boeing, William, 87, 148
Boeing Company, 78, 87, 148, 205, 230, 251, 260
Boeing Field, 87, 88
Bonneville Power Administration, 209
Bookmyer, Mr., 170
Boren, Carson, 19
Borst, Diana, *see* Collins, Diana Borst
Borst, G.M. "Jerry," 11
Bow, J., 97
Bow, Joe, 93
Bowen, Richard, 213
Bower, Willy, 266
boxing, 140, 178
Boys, Marvin, 213
Brandon, Ragnar, 162
Brazier Construction Co., 232
Brewer, Ura, 200
bridges, 34-35, 98-102
    Black River Bridge, 33, 34, 35, 52, 98, 224
    Codiga Bridge, 99
    corduroy, 35
    covered, 99
    Duwamish-Allentown Bridge, 101
    Duwamish footbridge, 100
    Foster footbridge, 99
    Interurban, 93, 101, 220
    list of, 100
    Pratt Truss design, 100-102
    Riverton drawspan, 98, 114, 133, 155, 157, 169
    U.S. 99, 101, 102
Broomall, J.J., 110
Broomall, Margaret, 110
Brother Horn, 176
Brown, Bessie, *see* Thorndike, Bessie Brown
Brown, Robert, 231, 238
Brown and Mann chicken farm, 118
Brownell, Charles, 19, 20, 22, 29
Brownell, Sarah Meader, 22, 29
Brummer, Henry, 116, 117, 119
Brummer, Maria, 116, 117
Brummer's Hill, xiii, 109, 112, 114, 116
Brummer's Store, 116-117, 125
Bryant, Abraham F., 16, 20, 24
Buck, Catherine, 137
Buckley, Eva Burger, 10, 15, 22, 23
Buckley, John, 10, 12, 15, 19, 22
Bugge, William, 211, 234

Bull, Harlan, 211
Bull, Ruby, 211
Burdick's feed store, 139
Burger, Eva, *see* Buckley, Eva Burger
Burke, G.M., 97
Burkhard, Ralph, 232, 233
Burlington Northern Railway, 169
Burton, Ella Fenton, 41, 48, 49, 54, 63
buses, 95

Caffrey, J.H., 170
California gold rush, 5-6, 12, 14
Cameron, James, 63
Cameron, R.J., 97
Campbell, D., 97
Canada, *see* Fraser River gold rush
Carey, Fr. William, 123
Carib (brig), 15
Carr, Edmund, 32
Carr, William, 19
Carrossino, Bruno, 219
Carrossino, Joseph, 154
Carrossino, Rinaldo, 219, 220
Carrossino, Teresa, 144, 154, 219
cars, *see* automobiles
Carson, Bob, 138, 251
Carson, Luella (Lou), 138, 251
Carstenson store, 195
Carter, Pam, 259
Carter, Roy, 173
Cartner, Bessie, 121
Cascade View, xi, 244, 250, 251, 260, 261-262
Cascade View School, 234, 235, 237, 261
Catholics, 47-48, 60, 123-124
Cavanaugh, Martin, 38, 39-40, 48, 51
Cavanaugh, Mary Ann Maple, 38, 39, 50, 51
Cavanaugh, Tabitha, 38
Cedar River, xiii, 15, 103, 107, 108, 198
celebrations
    Christmas, 74, 168
    Fourth of July, 25, 51, 191
    Maple party, 50, 51
    Thanksgiving Day (1860), 31
    Tukwila incorporation, 185
    weddings, 25, 26, 39
    see also social activities
Central Elementary School, 171, 233
Cerini, Peter, 69, 86, 166
Cerini Station, 166
Chamber of Commerce, 266-267
Champion, Maxine Henderson, 167
Chandler, George, 122
Chandler, Grace, 227
Chapman, Anna, 121
Chapman store, 117
"Charles River," 4
Charnell, Anna May, *see* Gott, Anna May Charnell
Charnell, Mrs., 200
Chief Seattle, xvii-xviii, 26, 39, 50, 59
Chinook Wind (myth), xvii
Chinook winds, 102, 103
Chittenden, H.M., 104, 106
Christensen Greenbelt Park, 262

Christensen Road, 214
Christian Science Church, 147, 192
Christianson, Martin, 150
Christmas, 74, 168
Church by the Side of the Road, 244, 247, 249
Church Society, 26
churches, 26, 47-48
    community church on Duwamish River, 162-164
    Danish Lutheran Church, 71, 75
    in Duwamish-Allentown, 162-164
    in Foster, 122-124
    Foster-Tukwila Presbyterian Church, 121, 122-123, 126, 249, 252
    in Riverton, 145-147, 252-253
    Southcenter Community Baptist Church, 265
    St. Thomas Catholic Church, 123-124, 232
    in Tukwila, 192, 265
Citizens of the Flat District of Tukwila, 193
City of Sea-Tac, xi, 257, 259, 260, 261
City of Tukwila, see Tukwila
Civil War, 40
Clark, James, 97, 225
Clark, John, 162
Clark, Nellie Starr, 112, 113, 147, 192, 225
Clark, Ralph, 162
Clark, Thomas N. (Tom), ix, 36, 97, 109, 110, 111, 112, 113, 116, 119, 120, 225
Cleasby, Harold, 165, 173
Cleasby, Muriel, 165
Clifton, Richard, 227
climate, 31-32, 56, 103
    see also floods
coal, 189
    carried by Interurban, 94, 189
    discovery of, 30, 55, 189
    geologic formation, xii
Codiga, Anna Hadeen, 159, 161, 170, 211
Codiga, Archie, 69, 99, 159, 211, 216
Codiga, Emma, 93
Codiga, Frances, see North, Frances Codiga
Codiga, James, 159, 216
Codiga Bridge, 99
Colburn, Myron, 234
Collins, Diana Borst, 5, 7, 9, 10, 11, 15, 22, 23, 24, 26, 29, 60
Collins, Lucinda, see Fares, Lucinda Collins
Collins, Luther M., 5-7, 8, 9-10, 11-12, 15, 18, 19, 20, 22, 24, 26, 27, 28-29, 30, 60, 189
Collins, Stephen, 5, 8, 9, 11, 25, 27, 57, 66
Collins party, 5-7, 8, 30
    vs. Denny party, 7-8, 9
    Duwamish exploration and settlement of, 9-10
    and scow, 9-10
Columbia Rediviva, 3
Columbia River, 3, 14
"Columbia" territory, 19
Comet (riverboat), 37
Commencement Bay, 55
Commercial Waterway District No. 1, 87, 106
communicable diseases, 58, 59, 60, 85
    see also health care; tuberculosis
Communicator, 228

community halls
    Delta Masonic Lodge No. 172, 149, 150-151
    Doty Hall, 118-119, 227
    Foster Hall, 119, 120, 227
    Fredricks' Hall, 158
    Hull's Hall, 184, 185
    Ladies Improvement Club Hall, 194, 204
    McCoy Hall, 135, 145, 149, 150
    Petersen Hall, 166
    Plummer's Hall, 28
    Robbins Hall, 123, 131, 134, 146, 148, 149, 150
    Thompson's Hall, 140, 149
community organizations, 57-58
    Delta Masonic Lodge No. 172, 113, 131, 135, 149, 150-151, 164
    in Duwamish-Allentown, 164-166
    Duwamish Improvement Club, 160-161, 164, 165-166, 260
    in Foster, 119-125
    Foster Community Club, 119-121
    in Riverton, 149-151
    Riverton Heights Improvement Club, 245, 249
    Riverton Improvement Club, 149
    Southgate Community Center, 263
    Thorndyke Improvement Club, 245
    in Tukwila, 189-190, 194, 203-204, 206, 263, 265-267
    Tukwila Community Club, 203-204, 205, 206
    Tukwila Ladies Improvement Club, 188, 189-190, 194, 203, 206
Conover, C.T., ix
Constitution (steamship), 58
Cook, Mr., 148
cooperatives, 73
Coplen, Randy, 267
Corrigan, Dorothy, see Wiese, Dorothy Corrigan
Costello, J.F., 97
Cox, Doris, 214
Crawford and Conover (realtors), 129
Crestview Annexation, 259
Crestview Park, 263
Cronenberg, R. Paul, 231
crops, see farming
Crostick, Lawrence (Bill), 213, 266
Crowley, Hubert, 214
Crystal Springs Park, 262
Cudney, Rev. Gerald, 265
Cumming, Helen, 202
Cumming, James, 228
Cumming, William (Bill), 202, 205
Cunningham, Edward, 229
Curtis, Asahel, 98
Curtiss, Emma, 117

dairy farms, 215-218
    Archie Codiga, 159, 216
    Fred Nelsen, 73
    Golden Arrow Dairy, 210, 216, 230
    Herman Nelsen, 72
    James Nelsen, 70
    Joe LaFranchi, 215-216
    Robbins family, 46
    and typhoid fever, 60
Danish Brotherhood and Sisterhood, 71, 75
Danish Lutheran Church, 71, 75
Davis, Bessie, 86

Davis, C.C., 78
Davis, Ed, 125
Davis, H.A., 78
Davis, Joanne, 262
Dawson, Ted, 173
Day, Neal, 120
Dayton, Frank, 150
Decker, Donovan, 231
Delta Chapter No. 109, Eastern Star, 113, 137, 149, 150, 151
Delta Masonic Lodge No. 172, 113, 131, 135, 149, 150-151, 164
DeMulling, Don, 251
Dennis, Gertie, 138
Dennis, Gladys, 138
Dennis, Jack, 138
Dennis, Johnny, 136, 138
Denny, Arthur A., 5, 7, 8, 9, 10, 18, 19, 30, 32
Denny, David, 5, 8, 10, 11
Denny Hill, 77
Denny party, 5
    arrives to settle Alki Point, 10
    vs. Collins party, 7-8, 9
Dent, Frederick, 30
Depression, 120, 144, 146, 199-200, 201, 230
Desimone, Giuseppe (Joe), 87, 221
Dick and Jane, 248
Dimmitt, Charlotte, 226
Dimmitt, Ellsworth, 226
Dimmitt, Emma, 226
Dimmitt, Helen, 226
Dimmitt, Lorris Myrvin, 187, 226, 227, 230
Dimmitt, Myrvin, 226
Dimmitt, Vannetta, 226
diphtheria, viii, 59, 85
diseases, 58-60, 85
    see also health care; tuberculosis
Ditlivesen, Fred, 69
Ditlivesen, Sophia Nelsen, 69
Dobbs, Charlotte, *see* Widrig, Charlotte Dobbs
Dobbs, Mr., 160
Dobie, Gil, 230
Dobler, Mary, *see* Nelsen, Mary Dobler
Donation Land Act of 1850, 15
donation land grants, 15-17, 23-24, 53
Doty, Edwin, 117, 118, 188
Doty, Emma, 118
Doty, Jennie LaVera, 118, 119
Doty Hall, 118-119, 227
Douglas, Dorothy, 139-140
Douglas, Gladys, 139
Douglas, Mabel, 139
Douglas, Margaret, 139
Douglas, Maud, 139
Douglas, W.R., 139
Douglas's Garage, 136, 139-140
Drake, Sir Francis, 2
Drew, George, 171
Dunbar, Andrew, 117
Dunlap, Rev. A. Taylor, 122
Durbin, Judge Joseph L., 191
Duwamish, meaning of name, xiii, 2
Duwamish-Allentown, 93, 153-174
    annexed to Tukwila, 157, 174, 260-261
    businesses in, 157-159, 162

    community organizations in, 164-166
    fire department, 125, 165, 166, 167, 172-174, 206, 261
    first residents of, 153
    historic houses in, 275
    map of, 179
    move to incorporate, 160-161
    naming of, 154
    population of, 156, 161-162
    and quarry blasting, 175-176
    social activities in, 158-159
Duwamish Bulletin, 166, 171
Duwamish Chapel, 164
Duwamish Commercial Club, 83, 84, 86
Duwamish Community Club, 172
Duwamish Community Presbyterian Church, 164
Duwamish Day, King County Fair, 83-84
Duwamish District, 155, 161
    see also Duwamish-Allentown
Duwamish et al. v. the United States, xix
Duwamish Gardens, 219, 220
Duwamish Grange No. 11, 57
Duwamish Improvement Club, 160-161, 164, 165-166, 260
Duwamish Industrial District, 209
Duwamish Junction, 166
Duwamish Library, 171
Duwamish Park, 172, 262
Duwamish people, *see* Native Americans
Duwamish precinct, 33, 60
Duwamish River, xiii, xviii, 3
    bridges across, 34-35, 98-102
    explored by Collins party, 7
    ferries on, 12, 35-36, 37
    flooding of, 46-47, 102-104, 116, 196
    original crossing point, 99
    oxbow, 52, 78, 88, 159-160
    plan for further straightening, 208, 209
    playing in, 169-170
    straightening of, 78, 85, 87, 89, 104-106, 185
Duwamish River Road, 20, 21, 30, 33, 35, 98, 109, 110
Duwamish Road (Beacon Avenue), 90
Duwamish School, 8, 60, 86, 94, 100, 159, 170-171, 172, 177, 225-226, 232, 237
Duwamish School District No. 175, 170, 226, 231
Duwamish Singing Society, 51
Duwamish Station, 155
Duwamish Valley, xi, 3
    in the 1910s and 1920s, 166-170
    annexation movement, 256-258
    early exploration of, 3-5
    farming in, 11, 24, 47, 53-54, 62, 68-69, 195-196, 215-223
    first settlers in, 2, 5-10
    formation of communities in, 90, 91
    geology of, xii-xiii
    Native American sites in, xvi-xvii
    natural abundance of, 13, 53, 215
    roads in, 33-35, 96-98, 108
    subdivision in, 78, 90-91, 110, 114, 128-130, 155, 175, 182-183
Duwamish Valley Tribune, 185
Duwamish Waterway, 78, 85, 87, 89, 106

East Marginal Way, 135, 136, 142
Eastern Star, *see* Delta Chapter No. 109, Eastern Star
Ebey, Col. Isaac Neff, 4-5, 28

INDEX

Eder, Frances, 164
Edwards, Beulah, 117
Edwards, Mel, 117
Edwards' Garage and Gas Station, 125
Eider, Francis, 165
Eliza Anderson, 20-21, 24, 44
Elliott Bay, 2, 5, 8, 24, 37-38
Endert, Kitty, 247, 252
Engel, Ernest W., 184, 185, 188, 270
Engel, Ernest W. Jr., 190
Engle, Gertrude, 191
epidemics, 59-60, 85
Erickson, Allen, 195
Erickson, Augusta, 195
Erickson, Charles J., 126
Erickson, John, 195
Escame, Steve, 239
Eshelman, J.F., 182
Exact (schooner), 10
explorers, 2-3

Fander, Bud, 169
Fares, John, 11
Fares, Lucinda Collins, 5, 8, 9, 11, 25, 27, 66
farming, 47, 53-54, 62, 215
    Collins family, 11, 24
    and Great Migration, 68-69
    hops, 62-64
    market-garden, 68, 215
    Nelsen family, 68-75
    nurseries, 222-223
    poultry, 118, 195-196
    in Riverton, 133
    transporting goods, 20, 46, 91, 94
    in Tukwila, 195
    vegetables, 219-221
    see also dairy farms
Fellowship Bible Church, 252
Fenton, Ella, *see* Burton, Ella Fenton
Fenton, James, 41
Fenton, Jane, *see* Kelly, Jane Fenton
Ferrelo, Bartolome, 2
ferries, 12, 35-36, 37, 153-154, 177
    see also Lewis/Steele landing
Fidlier and Walters (builders), 145
Finucan, Delia Agnes, *see* Merkle, Delia Agnes Finucan
fire departments, 199
    Duwamish, 125, 165, 166, 167, 172-174, 261
    Foster, 116, 120, 125-126
    Tukwila, 204, 206-207
    White Center Fire District No. 11, 126
First People, xiii-xix
    see also Native Americans
Fish, Byron, 136
Fleming, Flora, *see* Foster, Flora Fleming (daughter-in-law)
Flesch, A.W., 135
Fletcher, Dr., 157
floods, 102-103, 116, 196
    controlling, 103-104
    first, 46-47
Foreman, Bert, 193, 195
Foreman, Eileen, 193
Foreman's Store, 193, 203

Forrest, Aileen, 162
Forrest, Evelyn Jarvis, 162
Forsythe, Tom, 213, 267
Fort Dent, 16, 29
Fort Dent Park, xiv, 26, 263
Fort Duwamish, xviii, 29
Fort Vancouver, 13
Foster, xi, 77, 91, 93, 95, 109-127
    annexed to Tukwila, 126, 259-260
    businesses in, 110-112
    churches in, 122-124
    community organizations in, 119-125
    first post office in, 110
    historic houses in, 275
    and I-5, 121
    Lower Foster vs. Upper Foster, 116-117
    map of, 127
    naming of, 155
    population of, 110, 114
Foster, Charles (brother), 109, 110, 112
Foster, Charles (son), viii, 45, 59
Foster, Emily (daughter), viii, 45, 59
Foster, Flora Fleming (daughter-in-law), viii, 13, 14, 45
Foster, Hillory Adams (son), ix, viii, 111, 224
Foster, Jack (Indian), xix
Foster, Joseph, vii-ix, 267
    book dedication, vii-ix
    as businessman, viii, 24, 45, 47, 110
    death of, ix
    death of children, viii, 59
    and Delta Masonic Lodge No. 172, 150
    and Foster community, ix, 109, 224-225
    friendships of, 26, 113
    and gold rushes, 12, 30
    homestead of, 15, 16, 44, 45-46
    and hops, 62
    and Indian hostilities, 27, 28, 29
    and Interurban, 110
    journey to Duwamish Valley, 13-15
    as King County leader, 18, 19, 20, 21, 33, 48, 97
    land grant claim at Mox la Push, viii, 15, 16
    marriage of, 25, 44-45
    stance on Civil War, 40
    subdivides land, 90, 110
    in Territorial Legislature, 32, 44, 60-61
    vocations of, 22, 24, 25
Foster, Joseph Thomas (son), ix, viii, 97, 111, 224
Foster, Leo (brother), 109, 110, 112
Foster, Martha Steele (wife), ix, viii, 12, 25, 35, 36, 42, 44, 45, 46, 50, 59, 109
Foster, Rosetta (daughter), viii, 45, 59
Foster, Rosetta Laska (mother), vii
Foster, Stephen (brother), viii, 12, 13-15, 19, 22, 24, 27, 30, 44, 222
Foster, Thomas (father), vii
Foster Auditorium, 119
Foster Bridge, 97, 99, 101
Foster Coal Company, 189
Foster Community Club, 116, 119-121, 126, 238
Foster Community Hall, 119, 120, 227
Foster Friendly Garden Club, 121-122
Foster General Mercantile, 110-111
Foster Golf Course, 202, 263

Foster High School, ix, 117, 120, 121, 137, 148, 204, 227-229, 230, 232-234, 235, 236, 237-238, 239, 247
Foster Improvement Club, 119
Foster Ladies' Improvement Club, 119, 120, 121
Foster Library, 121, 234
Foster Memorial Park, 225, 234, 262
Foster No. 1 Coal Mine, 189
Foster Point, 15, 36, 42, 44, 99, 114-116, 260-261
Foster Presbyterian Church, *see* Foster-Tukwila Presbyterian Church
Foster School, 55, 113, 116, 118, 119, 148, 151, 170, 177, 225, 226-227, 229, 262
Foster School District No. 104, ix, 225, 238
Foster School District No. 144, 119, 126, 147, 170, 186-187, 192, 201, 225, 226, 231
Foster Station, 110, 114
Foster Study Club, 113, 124-125, 126
Foster-Tukwila Presbyterian Church, 116, 121, 122-123, 126, 192, 249, 252
Foster Volunteer Fire District No. 18, 116, 120, 125-126
Fotheringham, John, 237
Fourth of July, 25, 51, 191
Fouty, Almond, 181
Fouty, Constance Bennett, 181
Fouty, F.B. (Ben), 181
Fouty, Joseph, 181
Fouty, William J., 181, 190, 191
Fox, Fred, 137, 150, 228, 231
Fox, Ky, 137, 151, 238
Frame, Elmer, 229
Fraser River gold rush, 30, 31
Fred Nelsen Junion High School, 73, 75
Fredricks, Oscar, 158, 161
Fredricks' Hall, 158
Fredrickson, Mr. (councilman), 201
Friberg, Mrs., 192
Front Street, 157-159
Frost, Etta, 190
Frost, F., 246
Fuller, Bob, 137
Fullerton, Charley, 158
Fun with Dick and Jane, 248
Furth, Jacob, 70

Gallacher, Win, 125
Garden Station, 180, 181, 182, 183, 191
Garden Station Post Office, 180, 184
Gardner, Dwight, 213
Gardner, Gov. Booth, 238
Gardner, Marie, 262
Gaskill, A., 97
Gaskill, J.A., 225
Gatzert, Bailey, 50, 70
Gaviglio, Albert, 165, 219, 221
Gaviglio, Giovanni, 221
Gaviglio, Mary, 162
Gelino, Mr., 138
Gem (riverboat), 37, 48
geology, xii-xiii
George, Mary Henderson, 167
George, Mrs. (teacher), 170
Georgetown, 10, 77, 87, 92, 93, 134, 157, 161, 184
Georgetown drawbridge, 98

Giblin, Charles, 224
Giblin, John, 224
Giboney, Dr. Ezra, 122, 252
Giboney, Edgar, 118
Giboney, Mary Rains, 118
Gilbert, Eugene, 229
Gilbert, Rev. Cyrus L., 146
Gilbert, Richard, 202
Gilliam, Mary Jane Russell, 25, 59
Gilliam, William H., 16-17, 19, 22, 24, 25, 28, 29, 33, 45, 48, 53, 58, 59
Gilliland, J.R., 188
Gilman hotel, 157
Gjersee, Edith, *see* Abbott, Edith Gjersee
Glithero, William, 247
Glithero store, 117
Godfry, Charley, 125
Goff, Samuel D., 133, 134, 150
Goff Store, 133-134
gold
    Alaska gold rush, 65, 77, 111, 112, 113
    California gold rush, 5-6, 12, 14
    discovery in Northwest, 27, 30
Golden Arrow Dairy, 210, 216, 230
Goldsmith, Bill, 159, 172, 173
Gomez, George, 171
Good Roads Association, 97, 98
Goodale, Frank, 160, 165
Goodale, Violet, 160
Goranson, Hanna Johnson Hanson, 245, 246, 247, 249
Goranson, Joseph, 247
Gott, Anna May Charnell, 255
Gott, Emeline, 199, 200, 203
Gott, Forrest, 144, 203
Gott children, 144
Graham, David, 153
Graham, F.H., 182
Graham, R.J., 182
Graham, Susannah Mercer, 153
Graham's Point, 15
Grange, the, 57-58, 71, 72, 73, 83, 240
Grant, Ulysses S., 30
Graves, Harley, 139
Gray, Robert, 3
Great Depression, 120, 144, 146, 199-200, 201, 230
Great Migration, 67, 68, 131
Great Panic of 1893, 65, 77
Great Western Circus, 51
Green, E.G., 184, 191, 196
Green River
    geology of, xii
    Howard Hanson Dam on, 103, 107, 108, 207, 209
    vs. White River, xi, 104, 108
Greene, Robert, 120
Greyhound Bus Co., 95
Grezech, Mr., 170
Grooms, Mrs. (midwife), 181, 192
Groven, Arle, 252
Grow, Dr. Samuel L., 15, 20, 22, 25, 29
Grow, Elizabeth Johns, 22, 25, 26, 30, 46, 90, 153
Grow, Eveline Avery, 25
Grow, Louis Kossuth, 25, 30
Grow, Timothy, 15, 19, 22, 25, 29, 30, 46, 90, 153

INDEX

Grylden, Mabel, 214
Gunsul, Dr. Alan L.W., 117
Guntert, Jacob, 188, 270
Gus's Shoe Repair, 134, 136
Gustafson, Agnes, 192
Gustafson, Alice Hanson, 245, 246, 247
Gustafson, Carl, 192
Gustafson, Stanley, 202, 247
Gustavson, Algot "Gus," 134
Gylling, Grace, 228, 236

Hadeen, Anna, *see* Codiga, Anna Hadeen
Hale, Mrs. E.M., 157
Hales, Willis, 251
Hall, Agnes M., 189
Hall, John M., 184, 185, 186, 187, 189, 190, 270
Hall family, 176
halls, *see* community halls
Hamilton, Charles K., 84
Hammer, Bill, 118
Hampson, Floyd, 229
Hanada, Hatsuji, 205, 231
Hanford, Abbie Holgate, 5
Hanford, Cornelius, xviii
Hanford, Edward, 5
Hansen, Amanda Jorgensen, 241
Hansen, Chris, 241
Hanson, Alice, *see* Gustafson, Alice Hanson
Hanson, Col. Howard A., 107
Hanson, Hanna Johnson, *see* Goranson, Hanna Johnson Hanson
Hanson, Herta, *see* Rogne, Herta Hanson
Hanson, Margaret, *see* Angle, Margaret Hanson
Hanson, Oscar I., 245-246, 247, 249
Hanson, Oscar (son), 247
Hanson Grocery Store and Gas Station, 245-246, 247
Harmon, Hill, 6
Harms family, 211
Harrington, John Peabody, xvii
Harris, E.M., 160
Harris, Mabel (Mae), 208
Hartsock, Chet, 171
Hasper, Herman, 134
Hawley, Trudy, 251
Hazelnut Park, 262-263
health care, 58-60, 85-87, 141-144, 157
Heath, R.H., 184
Heceta, Bruno, 2
Heemink, Al, 195
Heinz straberry farm, 195, 201
Held, Adam, 110
Helgeson, George, 250
Helgeson, John, 250
Helgeson, Paul, 250
Helgeson, Robert, 250
Henderson, Alethea, 167
Henderson, Coral Hoskin, 167
Henderson, Mary, *see* George, Mary Henderson
Henderson, Maxine, *see* Champion, Maxine Henderson
Henderson, Roy J., 92, 93, 135-136, 164, 167, 169, 173
Henderson's Hardware Store, 136
Heneghan, Fr. Jarlath, 123
Henke, Franz, 191, 194
Henke, Tessie Kline, 119, 190, 191, 194, 203, 206

Heppenstall, Edward, 111, 112
Heppenstall, Mildred, 123
Heppenstall's Grocery, 111-112
Herd Law, 156, 168
Hermway Dairy, 216, 230
Herstrom, Francel, 246
Hewitt, C.C., 28
highways, *see* Interstate 5; Pacific Highway
Hill, Chet, 173, 174
Hill, George, 214
Hill, Sam, 97
Hillman, Bessie Olive, 155, 183
Hillman, Clarence D., 155, 183
Hillman City land venture, 183
historic houses, 70, 71, 154-155, 275
historic study area, xi
History of King County, 8-9
Hoffner, Ben, 173
Hograve, August, 22, 27
Holgate, Abby, *see* Hanford, Abby Holgate
Holgate, John, 5, 19, 30, 33
Holgate, Lemuel, 33
Holly Day, 186
Holmquist, Mr., 159
Holmquist, Olga, 162
Holt, George, 19, 21, 27, 48
homes
    building, 129-131, 145
    historic, list of, 275
    original Foster homestead, 15, 16
    see also land, subdivision of
Homestead Act of 1862, 39
Hometown Hardware, 138, 251
Hopkins, J.G., 185
hops, 46, 62-64
Hore, Bob, 173
Horn, Brother, 176
horse racing, 78, 79-83, 139
Horsfall, Frank, 234, 235
Horton, Dexter, 47
Horton, George, 77
Horton, Julius, 57, 77
Horton, Mrs. A.E., 57
Hoskin, Coral, *see* Henderson, Coral Hoskin
Houge, Lucille, 211
Houge, Shannon, 211
Howard Hanson Dam, 89, 103, 107, 108, 207, 209, 211
Howe Truss bridge design, 99
Howlet, Gene, 173
Hudson's Bay Company, xviii, 3
Huff, Emma, 55
Hullin, Rev. David, 252
Hull's Hall, 184, 185
Hull's Store, 180, 182, 193, 195
Hultz, Vera, 227
Hultz store, 137
Hunt, Dr. Eugene, 250
Huson, Dave, 231

Ice Age, xii-xiii
Ikawa Park, 263
immigrants, 67, 68-69, 131
    among early settlers, 22, 67

287

Italians, 154, 220
Japanese, 205, 221, 223, 241
Scandinavians, 68
Independent Order of Foresters, 266
Independent Water Company, 71
Indian War, 28, 40
Indians, *see* Native Americans
"inside people," xiii, 2
International Training in Communications, 266
Interstate 5 (I-5), 108, 121, 122, 123, 151, 212, 213, 222, 234, 235
Interstate 405 (I-405), 108, 213, 214
Interurban Avenue, 93, 98, 111, 191
    see also Pacific Highway
Interurban electric rail service, 90-95, 96, 140
    Allentown Station, 155
    beginning of, 77
    bridges for, 93, 101, 220
    Cerini Station, 166
    and development, 77, 90-91, 151
    Duwamish Station, 155
    fares on, 94-95
    Foster Station, 110
    freight on, 91, 94
    Garden Station, 180, 181, 182, 183, 191
    Mortimer Station, 110, 123, 192
    Renton Junction Station, 240
    Riverton Station, 128, 129, 133, 134
    route of, 92-93
    third rail, 91-92
    Tukwila Station, 180, 184, 188
Ives, Gene, 120, 213

Jack, Ann, xvii
Jackson, Capt. Sam, 38
Jackson, Dorothy, 162
Jacobus, B.W., 97
Jake's Antiques, 136
James, Ada, 218
James, Dr. Jim, 63
James, John, 218
James, Sybil Bergsma, 218
James Clark Road, 98
Japanese-Americans, 205, 221, 223, 241
Jay Cook & Co., 55
jitneys, 95
Johanson store, 117
Johns, Bennett, 19, 20, 22, 26, 29, 35, 153, 155
Johns, Elizabeth, *see* Grow, Elizabeth Johns
Johnson, Ella, 252
Johnson, Frank W., 185, 188
Johnson, Henry, 117
Jones, Hillman F., 8
Jones Saloon, 157-158
Jonientz, Meta, *see* Nelsen, Meta Jonientz
Jorgensen, Alice, *see* Wood, Alice Jorgensen
Jorgensen, Amanda, *see* Hansen, Amanda Jorgensen
Jorgensen, Anna, 117
Jorgensen, Chris, 69, 73, 97
Jorgensen, Dora, *see* Nelsen, Dora Jorgensen
Jorgensen, Walter, 117
Jose, Anna, 219
Judaism, Messianic, 147

Jungle Dance, 158
Juno, Larry, 125

Kaiser, Ben, 145, 160
Kassner, Arthur, 125, 181
Kassner, Ben, 190, 191
Kassner, Bernard, 181
Kassner, Mary, 181, 182
Kassner, Sarah, 194
Kassner, Walter, 125, 181-182, 190, 191
Kato, Hisako, 195, 205
Kato, Michio, 195, 205
Kelly, Jane Fenton, 36, 41, 42, 43, 45, 48, 49-50, 50, 61, 162
Kelly, Michael, 43, 61, 149
Kelly, Nora, 170
Kerr store, 139
Kettering, Sidonia Nelsen, 70, 71
Kilburg, Tom, 237
Kilburg store, 117
King, Rufus, 18
King County, xi, 18
    conflicts between Indians and settlers in, xviii-xix, 27-30, 52
    Duwamish Valley settlers as leaders in, 18-19, 33
    first settlers in, 2, 5-10
    formation of, 18
    population of, 22, 31, 52, 66-67, 77
    roads in, 21-22, 33-35, 96-98
    voting precincts in, 19-20, 32-33, 60, 109
King County Agricultural Society, 47
King County Airport, 78, *see also* Boeing Field
    see also Meadows, the
King County Dairymen's Association, 71
King County Drainage District No. 1, 104
King County Fair, 47, 79, 83-84
King County Farm, 59-60
King County Fire District No. 1, Duwamish, 125, 166, 167, 172-174, 261
King County Fire District No. 18, Foster, 116, 120, 125-126
King County Hospital, 60
King County Library system, 121, 124-125, 171
King County Pioneer Association, 71, 242
King County Planning Commission, 209, 211, 234
King County Rifles, 40
King County Tuberculosis Hospital, 87
Klahowyah (yearbook), 228, 229, 231
Klein, Alpha, 200
Klein, Barbara, 200
Klein, Leonard, 200
Kline, Frank, 182, 192-193, 194, 206
Kline, John, 194
Kline, Mary, 182, 190, 191, 193, 206
Kline, Tessie, *see* Henke, Tessie Kline
Knapp, Harley, 136, 140
Knapp, Miss, 149
Knapp's Garage, 140
Knorr, Rev. Erich, 252
Knudsen, Mrs., 200
Knudson, Jan, 200
Koch, Evelyn, *see* Santora, Evelyn Koch
Koch, Paul, 249, 250
Koenig, Joe, 123
Koenig, Rev., 195, 202
Kozlinsky, George, 173

INDEX

Krantz, Rev. Nick, 122
Kraxberger, Rev. Vernon, 252
Krueger, Otto "Skeets," 140
Ku Klux Klan, 243
Kutz, Rev. Leonard, 252
Kyle, Miss (teacher), 161

Lacava, Mr., 138
Ladd, Elizabeth, 110
Ladd, W.N., 110
Ladies Improvement Club Hall, 194, 204
LaFranchi, Joe, 69, 215, 216
Laird, Frank, 228
Lake Duwamish, see Lake Washington
Lake Geneva, 4
Lake Washington, xii, xiii, 4, 15, 20, 103, 107, 181
Lake Washington Ship Canal, 77, 89, 102, 104, 106-107, 108
Lakin, Charlie, 140
Lamb, Mrs. (teacher), 187
Lamb, Ron, 259
land
    claims of first settlers, 10, 15
    clearing title to, 15-17, 23-24, 53, 54, 70
    subdivision of, 78, 90-91, 110, 114, 128-130, 155, 175, 182-183
Landon, Miss, 148
Landstrom, Anna, 195
Lang, Rev. Harold, 122
Larson, Bernice, 194
Larson, Bud, 173
Larson, Mr., 134, 136
Lassen, Valdemar, 145, 150
Lassen, Walter, 145
Latimer, Marjorie, 121
Latimer, Roy, 120
Lawrence, Mabel, 170
Lee, E.E., 97
Lee, Jason, 3
Lee's Market, 138, 251
Leighton, Karen, 259
Lewis, Caroline, 26
Lewis, Cyrus C., 12, 16, 19, 20, 21, 22, 25, 26, 29, 33, 35, 45, 109, 153
Lewis, Ira, 26
Lewis, Joseph, 26
Lewis, Mr., 160
Lewis, Polly, 26, 29, 153
Lewis and Clark Expedition, 3
Lewis/Steele landing, 20, 35, 36, 42, 99, 109, 114
libraries, 48
    Duwamish Library, 171
    Foster Library, 121, 234
    Tukwila Library, 194, 199, 204, 262, 263
    Tukwila Schoolhouse, 124-125
Lily (riverboat), 37
Lincoln, Abraham, 40
Lincoln, Charles, 128, 150
Lincoln, Maude E., 128
Lincoln Park, 141
Lindgard, Elmer, 137
Linnell, Frances, 136, 137
Linnell, Janice, 137
Linnell, Larry, 135, 137, 138, 139, 146, 176
Linnell, Villard, 136, 137

Linnell store, 137, 138
Linset, Arthur, 112
Linset, Ethel, 112
Linset, Herman, 112
Linset Mansion, 112
Liston family, 211
Litle Church by the Side of the Road, 244, 247, 249
Little League, 266
Locke, Jim, 195
Locke, Lilly, 195
lodges, 149
    see also Delta Masonic Lodge No. 172
logging, 15, 24, 110, 176
Longacres Racetrack, 139
longhouses, xiii-xiv
Loomis, G.W., 26
Lovejoy, Emma Engle, 191
Lovejoy, Frank, 191
Low, John, 5, 8, 10, 18, 19, 24
Lowrey, Pat, 214
Ludington, Rabbi Roger A., 147
Luft, Gary, 239
Lunsford, Rev. David J., 265
Lute family, 176
Lutz, Eugene, 188
Lutz, Minnie, 117, 180
Lynch, Archie, 92
Lynch, Fr. Ibar, 123

Macadam Road, 97, 116, 117, 130, 134, 136, 148
macadam roads, 97-98
Maddock, M.B., 50
Magee, Duane, 239
Mahill, Mac, 158, 161
Mahill's Grocery, 158
mail, see postal service
Mallis, William, 228, 231
Malloy, Capt. (Indian War), 28
Malmo Nurseries, 134
Mann, Belva, 146
Mann, Miss (teacher), 161
Manson Construction Company, 99
Maple, Catherine, see Van Asselt, Catherine Maple
Maple, Cora Ellen, 58
Maple, Dora Helen, 58
Maple, Eli, 7, 8, 9, 10-11, 39, 50
Maple, Mrs. Eli, 57
Maple, Eliza Jane Snyder, 38, 58
Maple, Jacob, 5, 6, 7, 8, 9, 10, 19, 22, 26, 38, 39, 40, 47, 50, 51, 66
Maple, John Wesley, 38, 50, 58
Maple, Lucinda, see Schneider, Lucinda Maple
Maple, Mary Ann, see Cavanaugh, Mary Ann Maple
Maple, Robert, 50
Maple, Samuel, 5, 6, 7, 8, 10, 15, 27, 39, 47, 50, 57, 66, 83
Maple family, 12, 22, 27, 28, 29, 38-40, 52
Maple Grove Park, 242-243
Maple School, 54-55, 60
Maple Town, 155
maps
    Duwamish-Allentown, 179
    Foster, 127
    Old Tukwila, 197

Quarry, 179
river channels (1899 and 1989), 105
Riverton, 152
Markland, Leonard (Lee), 136, 138
Marshall, Mrs., 149
Martin, Gov. Clarence D., 229
Masons, see Delta Masonic Lodge No. 172
Mathews, C., 97
Mathiesen, Martin, 195
Matthews, Dr. Mark A., 122
Mauret, David, 19
Maxwell, Earl, 229
Mayer, Johanna, 249-250
Mayer, Ludwig, 249-250
Maynard, David "Doc," 11, 16, 19, 24, 33
McAdam, John Loudon, 97
McBreen service station, 139
McConahan, George N., 19
McCoy, Charles K., 130, 135, 145, 148, 150
McCoy Hall, 135, 145, 149, 150
McDonald, Mr., 201-202
McElroy, Jas. F., 97
McGee family, 176
McGill, Henry M., 31
McGloughlin, Glen, 225
McGloughlin, Roy, 225
McIntyre, Arthur B., 188
McIntyre, Benjamin N., 188
McIntyre, George E., 188
McIntyre, William A., 188
McKay, LaRee, 255
McKee, W.E., 161
McKinney, Audrey, 251
McKinney, Larry, 251
McKinney, Marshall, 251
McLaughlin, May, 139
McMicken, Gen. William, 255
McMicken, Maurice, 182, 255
McMicken, Rowena Ostrander, 255
McMicken Heights, xi, 235, 244, 255, 258-259
McMillan, James, 3
McNatt, Ann Kelly, 47, 57
McNatt, Francis, 19, 47, 57, 62, 78
McVeigh, Susanne Minkler, 193
Meader, Henry, 22, 29, 70
Meader, Sarah, see Brownell, Sarah Meader
Meadows, the, 7, 8, 9, 36, 78-88, 260
    and anti-racing movement, 82-83
    and first King County Fair, 83-84
    and Museum of Flight, 88
    opening season of racetrack, 79-81
    as sporting resort, 84-85
    today, 78-79, 88
Meadows Tuberculosis Sanitarium, 78, 85, 87
Meeker, Ezra, 39, 157
Menalia, Hazel, 165
Mercer, Don, 173
Mercer, Susannah, see Graham, Susannah Mercer
Mercer, Thomas, 12, 39, 153
Merkle, Al, 266
Merkle, Amy, 162
Merkle, Catherine, 162
Merkle, Delia Agnes Finucan, 156, 157, 170, 176

Merkle, Ernest, 156
Merkle, Lydia, 171
Merkle, Nora, 162
Merkle, Viola, 162
Mess, Fred, 97
Mess Cemetery, 262
Messianic Judaism, 147
Metcalf, Leon, 238
Mikami, Akiko, 221
Mikami, Haruko, 221
Mikami, Imio Sasumara, 241
Mikami, Kiyoto, 221
Mikami, Masao, 221
Mikami, Matsusuke, 205, 207, 221, 241
Mikami, Matt, 221
Mikami, Takumi, 221
Mikami, Tamayo, 221
Mikami, Yaeko, 221
Military Road, 21, 32, 33, 34, 35, 96, 98, 109, 235, 260
Miller, Don, 139
Miller, Henry, 62, 97
Miller, Mr. (councilman), 188
Miller Feeds, 138-139
Miller's Beach, 141
Minkler, Clifford, 194
Minkler, Ramona Scott, 194
Minkler, Stan, 213, 271
Minkler, Susanne, see McVeigh, Susanne Minkler
Mitchell, Garda, 252
Miyao, Bill, 223
Miyao, Jerry, 223
Miyao, Kaijiro, 223
Miyao, Sharon, 223
Miyao, Ume, 223
Monroe, Bertha, 162
Monroe, James, 150
Monroe, Paul, 158, 162
Montgomery, Elizabeth Rider, 248
Monticello, 19, 24, 30
Moore, Flora, see Allen, Flora Moore
Morrison, D.A., 130, 145, 160
Morrison, Dr. Jack R., 117
Morrison, Kenneth, 120
Mortimer Station, 110, 123, 192
Moses, Chief Joe, 181
Moss, John, 19
motor vehicles, 95-96
    see also automobiles
Mount Rainier, xiii
Mountain Beaver Woman, xvii
Mountain View, 155
Mox la Push, 15, 16, 19-20, 29, 32-33, 60, 109, 263
Moxlie, Robert, 24
Murphy, Charles S., 59
Murphy, Mary Jane Russell, see Gilliam, Mary Jane Russell
Murray, Silas, 165, 173
Museum of Flight, 78, 88
Musselman, Clara, 136, 137, 146, 149
Musselman's Dry Goods, 136, 137
Myers, Agnes, 182
Myers, Diana, 259
Myers, Hamlin, 195
Myers, Miss (teacher), 148

Myers, Samuel, 182
Myers' General Store, 182

Native Americans, xiii-xix
    on Black River, xix, 4, 181
    as hop pickers, 63-64
    and Hudson's Bay Company, xviii
    life of, xiii-xvi
    location of main village, xiii
    longhouses of, xiii-xiv
    mythic sites of, xvi-xvii
    name children after white men, 26
    relationship with settlers, xviii-xix, 11, 26-30, 39, 50, 52, 181-182
    sighted by Dr. Tolmie, 4
    and treaty aftermath, xix
    tribal identity of, xix
Naylor, Kate, 121
Naylor, Stuart, 137
Naylor's Bakery, 136, 137
Neal, Molly V., *see* Baker, Molly Neal
Needham, John, 116, 167
Neil, Bess, 200
Nelsen, Alma, *see* Taylor, Alma Nelsen
Nelsen, Charlie, 217
Nelsen, Dora Jorgensen, 73-75, 241
Nelsen, Dorothy, 73
Nelsen, Eleanor, 73, 241
Nelsen, Elsie, 73
Nelsen, Evan, 73, 217
Nelsen, Frank, 70, 71
Nelsen, Fred, 68, 69, 73-75, 93, 97, 217, 218, 241, 242, 243
Nelsen, Harry, 70, 71
Nelsen, Helen, 70, 71, 116, 211, 240, 262
Nelsen, Herman, 68, 69, 72, 97
Nelsen, Hilda, 73
Nelsen, James, 36, 68, 69-72, 96, 97, 216, 240
Nelsen, Marcus, 72
Nelsen, Margaret Andersen, 72
Nelsen, Martin, 69
Nelsen, Mary Dobler, 70, 240
Nelsen, Meta Jonientz, 75
Nelsen, Ole, 69, 70, 72
Nelsen, Peter, 97
Nelsen, Rose, 73
Nelsen, Sidonia, *see* Kettering, Sidonia Nelsen
Nelsen, Sophia, *see* Ditlivesen, Sophia Nelsen
Nelson, Frank, 158, 168, 169
Nelson, Hans, 97
Nelson, Mabel, 156, 158, 159, 162, 166, 168, 169, 170
Nelson, Nellie, 162
Nelson, O.F., 161
Nelson, Peter, 97
Neudorf, Werner, 236, 239
New York Markook House, 24
Newton, Dr. Gordon, 237, 250
Newton, Florence, 203
Newton, Lois, 203, 237
Nichols, Bonnie, 141
Nichols, Dr. Frederick G., 141-144, 157, 176, 178
Nichols, Ella Wadell, 141, 142, 143
Nichols, Fred (son), 141, 142, 143-144
Nichols, George H., 128, 140, 150

Nichols, Hattie, 128, 150
Nichols, James, 141
Nichols, Victoria Belaire, 139, 143-144
Nichols, Winnie, 141
Nielsen, Jacob, 69, 218
Nielsen, Ray, 217, 218
Nisqually River, 5, 7, 11
Nobuyama, Fusako, 205, 231
Nolan, Bruce, 140
Nolan, Vern, 140
Nootka Harbor, 2-3
Nord, Ellen, 186, 194
Nord, Fred, 186, 194
Normandy Park, 141
North, Frances Codiga, 93, 94, 159, 216
North, Jim, 159, 193
North, Vic, 206
North Riverton, 174, 175
North Wind (myth), xvii
Northern Pacific Railroad, 38, 55, 67, 89
Northrup, Mr. (councilman), 188
Northwest Coast Indians, *see* Native Americans
Northwest gold rushes, 27, 30
Northwest Speedway Company, 84
Norton, Bill, 251
Norton, Edna, 251
Nugent, Lieut. (Indian War), 28
Nunan, Nora, 207

O'Connell, Fr. John C., 123
Odle, M.F., 227
Oien, Mary, *see* Sundby, Mary Oien
Old Tukwila, xi, 126, 183-185
    incorporation of, 183-184
    map of, 197
    see also Tukwila
Oldfield, Barney, 157
Olmstead, Dr. W.E., 161
Olsen, Maren, 69
Olsen, Mr. (carpenter), 70
Olsen, Nels, 69
Olson, Nettie, 119
Ord, J.F., 129
Order of Eastern Star, *see* Delta Chapter No. 109, Eastern Star
Oregon Country, 3
Oregon Spectator, 4
Oregon Territorial Legislature, 3, 18-19
Oregon Territory, 4, 5, 9, 10, 11, 13-14, 15, 18
Oregon Trail, 3, 4, 5, 6, 39, 43
organizations, *see* community oganizations
Orillia, 36, 53, 63-64, 69, 89, 240
Orillia Post Office, 240
Orillia School, 54, 55, 240, 241
Orillia Water Supply Co., 72
Osceola Mudflow, xiii
Ostrander, Rowena J., *see* McMicken, Rowena Ostrander
O'Sullivan, Jim, 117, 119
Ouvrie, Jean Baptiste, xviii, 4
"Ouvrie's River," xviii, 4
Oxbow, 98, 155, 209
oxbow, Duwamish River, 52, 78, 85, 88
Oyen, J.H., 161

Pacific City land venture, 183
Pacific Highway, 98, 157, 190-192, 196
    see also Interurban Avenue; U.S. 99 (highway)
Pacific Mail Company, 68
Pacific Northwest Aviation Historical Foundation, 88
Palmasani, Fr. Anthony, 123
Panic of 1893, 65, 77
Parker, Tim, 239
Parrott, Rev. Charles, 164
Patrons of Husbandry, 57
Patten, William P., 114
Paulson, Don, 205
Pea Patch Park, 263
Pearce brothers, 26-27
Peoples Bank, 71
People's Park, 243
Peppar, Tom, 27
Perez, Juan, 2
Personnetta, Annette, 162
Peters, Ernest, 166
Petersen, Harry, 165, 166, 171
Petersen Hall, 166
Peterson, Anna, 148
Peterson, Eric, 189
Peterson, J.C., 97
Phelps, Doris, 214
Phelps, Ken, 173
Phillippi, Rev. Ernest, 252
Phillips, Lee, 266
Pigeon Point, 4, 8
Pike Place Market, 221
pioneers, see settlers
Pioneers of Washington, 71
Pioneers on Puget Sound, 8
Plummer's Hall, 28
Point Grenville, 2
Pollock, Rev. Lawrence, 265
Pomona Grange, 83
Poor, Rev. George, 252
population
    18th century, xiii
    1850, 18
    1853, 22
    1860, 31
    1870, 52
    1880s, 66-67
    1890-1920, xix, 77, 161-162
    Foster, 110, 114
    King County, 22, 31, 52, 66-67, 77
    Native Americans, xiii, xix
    Renton Junction, 240
    Riverton, 129-130, 131-132, 133
    and schools, 234, 237-238
    Tukwila, 187-188, 256, 274
Port of Seattle, 106, 208-212, 232
Portland, Oregon, 14, 68, 141
Portland (steamship), 65
postal service, 23, 24, 33
    Black River Post Office, 33, 60
    Garden Station Post Office, 180, 184
    Orillia Post Office, 240
    to Poverty Hill, 162
    Riverton Post Office, 134

potlatches, xv
Poverty Hill, xvii, 87, 158, 162
Powell, L.I., 243
Prandi, Irene, see Siccardi, Irene Prandi
Prandi, John, 221
Prather, Tom, 30
Pratt Truss bridge design, 100-102
Pre-Emption Land Act of 1841, 15
Prefontaine, Fr., 47
prices
    ferry crossings, 36
    food/supplies (1857), 25
    at Foster Mercantile, 111
    homes and lots (1900s), 129, 130
    Interurban trips, 94-95
    learning materials, 55
    rail trips, 67
    steamboat travel, 21
Primera Iglesia Bautista, 147
Profanity Hill, 183
Prosch, Charles, 24
public health, 59-60, 85-87
    see also health care
public water systems
    Foster, 196
    lack of, 157, 168
    Tukwila, 126, 198-199
public works, 77, 89, 108, see also WPA
Puget Sound Bridge and Dredging Company, 174
Puget Sound Electric Railway Co., 91, 92, 94, 95, 110, 134
    see also Interurban electric rail service
Puget Sound Traction, Light and Power Company, 190
Puget Western, Inc., 213, 259
Putnam, O.H., 160, 161

quarries
    and blasting, 175-176
    Riverton Quarry, 102, 174-175, 177-178
    Tukwila Quarry, 102, 189
Quarry District, 95, 100, 102, 175-178, 179, 275
Quarry Hill, xvii, 87-88, 174, 177, 178, 205, 231
Quealey, Bill, 139
Quilting Club, 200
Quivist, Mr., 190

racetracks, 78, 79-83, 139
Radford, Arlie, 213
Radnich, Virginia, 123
railroads, 38, 55-56, 66, 67-68, 77
    see also Interurban electric rail service
Rains, David, 118
Rains, Dorothy, see Robbins, Dorothy Rains
Rains, Dr. Jesse L., 118
Rains, Lewis, 118
Rains, Mary, see Giboney, Mary Rains
Ramage, Jack, 137, 151
Randall, D.W., 97
Ray, Thomas, 153-155
Ray-Carrossino house, 154
Rector, Roy, 195, 203
Reddin, John J., 98
Reed, Rev., 192
Regel, Rudy, 213, 262

Reid, Milton, 229
Reliable Ladder Works, 145
religion, *see* churches
rendering works, 114, 115-116
Renton Citizens Bank, 71
Renton Coal Co., 55
Renton Formation, xii
Renton Junction, 69, 71, 73, 95, 217, 222, 223, 240-242, 243
Renton Junction drawbridge, 98, 99
Renton Junction Station, 92, 93, 240
Renton-Kent National Farm Loan Association, 72
Rhinehart, Rev., 146
Ridder, Robert C., 121
Rider, Elizabeth, *see* Montgomery, Elizabeth Rider
Ringdorfs' land, 70
Rininger, Dr. E.M., 94, 134
riverboats, 20-21, 35-36, 37-38
rivers
    bottom land, 20, 70, 215
    crossing, 12, 34-36, 37, 98-102, 153-154, 177
    flooding, 46-47, 102-104, 116
    map of channels, 105
    used for travel, 20-21, 35-38
Riverside Quarry, 174-175
Riverside Street, *see* Front Street
Riverton, xi, 93, 94, 98, 114, 125, 128-152, 263
    annexed to Tukwila, 259-260
    automobiles in, 139-140
    businesses in, 133-138
    community organizations in, 149-151
    and Delta Masonic Lodge No. 172, 150-151
    growth of, 129-138, 145
    historic houses in, 275
    map of, 152
    naming of, 128-129
    population of, 129-130, 131-132, 133
    social activities in, 140-141
    see also North Riverton
Riverton Crest Cemetery, 254-255, 261
Riverton drawspan, 98, 114, 133, 155, 157, 169
Riverton Heights, 62, 98, 120, 132, 133, 145, 146-147, 244-255, 263
Riverton Heights Improvement Club, 245, 249
Riverton Heights Lutheran Church, 252
Riverton Heights Post Office, 245-246
Riverton Heights Presbyterian Church, 122, 252
Riverton Heights School, 134, 145
Riverton Hospital, 139, 142-144, 254, 261
Riverton Improvement Club, 149
Riverton Machinery Works, 139
Riverton Methodist Church, 145-147, 192, 252
Riverton Park United Methodist Church, 147, 252
Riverton Post Office, 134
Riverton Pulmonary Hospital, 132, 141, 253-254
Riverton Quarry, 102, 174-175, 177-178
Riverton Realty and Building Company, 130, 145
Riverton Road, 97
Riverton School, 123, 132, 147-148, 149, 177, 225, 226, 228, 229, 232
Riverton Station, 128, 129, 133, 134
Riverton Water Company, Inc., 131
Riverton Women's Civic Club, 149
Riverview Farms, 218

roads, 21-22, 33-35, 96-98
    see also Interstate 5; Pacific Highway
Robbins, Agnes, 131
Robbins, Bill (Nevelle), 131, 134, 140
Robbins, Chester, 225
Robbins, Clement, 46
Robbins, Edith, 46
Robbins, Elmer, 250
Robbins, Emmett L., 46, 131, 134, 146, 148, 150, 225
Robbins, Evelyn, 46
Robbins, Ida, 46
Robbins, Leigh, 225
Robbins, Mae, 149
Robbins, Margaret, 134
Robbins, Marvin, 118, 131
Robbins, Milton, 42, 43, 45-46, 57, 62, 128, 131, 251, 254
Robbins, Nevelle (Bill), 131, 134, 140
Robbins, Susannah Steele, 41, 42, 45-46, 57, 128, 149, 251, 254
Robbins family, 42-46, 128-129
Robbins Hall, 123, 131, 134, 146, 148, 149, 150
Robbins' Hill, 110, 138
Robbins Water Works, 131
Robertson, Dennis, 258
Robertson, Ernie, 125
Rogne, Herta Hanson, 245, 247
Rohrbacher, Rev. Philip, 252
Romano, Mr., 174
Roosevelt, Franklin, 102
Roosevelt, Theodore, 269
Rose, D.B., 97
Roseberg, Neva, 162
Roseburg, O.G., 161, 170
Roseburg, Russell, 162
Rosenberg, Clara, 134
Rosenberg, Henry, 134
Ruffino, Tony, 125
Ruhlman, Kathryn, 214
Ruhlman, Rev. John H., 265
Rumery, Horace, 93
Runge, Ida, 251
Runge, Larry, 251
Russell, Mary Ann, *see* Thomas, Mary Ann Russell
Russell, Mary Jane, *see* Gilliam, Mary Jane Russell
Russell, Samuel, 59
Ryan, Fr. Robert, 123

St. George's Catholic School, 93
St. Joseph Mission, 123, 192
St. Thomas Catholic Church, 123-124, 232
Sakuman family, 176
Salem, Oregon, 18, 19
Salish, 2, 181
Salle, Bernardo (Bernie), 250, 251
Salle, Nunzio De Pasquale, 250-251
Salmon Bay, 58, 106
salmon packing, 54
Sandahl, Eugene, 150, 188
Santora, Evelyn Koch, 249
Sarver, Lois, 229
sawmills, 15, 24, 176
scarlet fever, 60
Schanzenbach, Roland, 238
Schefflers, 259

Scherrer, Bill, 166
Schley, Melvin, 171
Schmidt, Florence, 227
Schneider, Daniel, 40
Schneider, Lucinda Maple, 38, 40, 50
Schoenbachler, Herman, 217
School Directors Association, 230
schools, ix, 224-239
    consolidation of districts, 225, 231-232
    early, 26, 48-49, 54-55, 224-225
    effect of Interstate 5 on, 234-235
    and population, 234, 237-238
Schuenemann, Mr., 161
Schuer, Mr., 186
Schwartz, Barney, 139
Schwartz, Ben, 137, 166
Schwartz, Glen, 140, 166, 178
Schwartz, Lona, *see* Sweeney, Lona Schwartz
Schwindt, Maggie, 214
Scibor, Rozalia Wolotzyn, 132, 133
Scibor, Ted, 254
Scibor, Thomas, 132, 133
Scibor, Thomas Jr., 133, 140, 254
Scoones, Bernice, 121
Scott, Mae, 194
Scott, P., 145
Scott, Ramona, *see* Minkler, Ramona Scott
Sea-Tac, City of, xi, 257, 259, 260, 261
Sea-Tac Airport, 251
Sealth, Chief Noah, *see* Chief Seattle
Sears, Elmer, 254, 255
Sears, Helen, 254, 255
Seattle, xi, 1, 12, 20, 33, 35, 38, 55, 77, 104, 259, 260
    see also Chief Seattle; Port of Seattle
Seattle Brick Company, 98
Seattle Electric Company, 91, 94, 189
Seattle Gazette, 33, 40
Seattle Intelligencer, 48
Seattle Library Association, 48
Seattle Milk Shippers Association, 72
Seattle Planning Commission, 209
Seattle Rendering Company, 115
Seattle Rifle Team, 58
Seattle-Tacoma Interurban Railway, 91
Seattle-Walla Walla Railroad, 38, 56, 89
Seattle Water District No. 35, 157
Selah, Mary, *see* Solomon, Mary Selah
Semple, Gov. Eugene, 61
settlers
    in 1852, 12-13
    arrival by rail, 67-68
    backgrounds of, 22-23
    and Chief Seattle, 26, 39, 50, 59
    children among, 25-26
    chronology of events, 30
    Collins party, 5-12
    conflicts with Native Americans, xviii-xix, 27-30, 52
    description of, 22-23
    farming, 11, 24, 47, 53-54, 62, 68-69
    financial difficulties of, 64-65
    first, 2, 5-10, 12, 22
    Foster family, vii-ix, 13-15
    health of, 58-60, 85-86
    land-claim process, 15-17, 23-24, 53, 54, 70
    life of, 18-30
    livelihoods of, 23-25
    Maple family, 38-40
    relationship with Native Americans, xviii-xix, 11, 26-30, 39, 50, 181-182
    religion among, 26, 47-48
    Robbins family, 42-46, 128-129
    schooling of children, 26, 48-49, 54-55, 224-225
    social activities of, 25, 49-51, 140-141, 158-159
    Steele family, 41-44, 62, 109
    weddings of, 25, 26, 39
    women among, 23, 53, 61, 84
Shaw, John, 123
Shaw, William, 123
Shawver, Rena, 259
Sheperd, Katherine, 183
Sherbon, Gary, 237
Shimstock, Betty, 255
Shimstock, Jean, 255
Shinn brothers, 62
Shomaker, Blaine, 184, 269
Shomaker, Joel B., 183-185, 202, 214, 267, 268, 269
Shomaker, Laura, 184, *see* Bateham, Laura Shomaker
Shomaker, Luella Billings, 184, 269
Shomaker, Melissa Taylor, 269
Shomaker, Nancy, 184, 269
Shomaker, Newton, 269
Shomaker, Winfield, 184, 269
Shorey and Russell (contractors), 35
Showalter, Noah D., 226, 229
Showalter School, 125, 229, 234, 237, 238, 247
Shults, Mabel, 214
Shulz, Charles, 173
Siccardi, Irene Prandi, 220, 221
Silver, Michael, 237
Simmons, Michael T., 4
Simpson, John, 19
Skeel, John, 171
Slaughter, Lieut. (Indian War), 28
smallpox, 59, 60
Smith, Agnes, 162
Smith, Charles, 120
Smith, Dr. Henry A., 58
Smith, F.H., 173
Smith, Florence, 162
Smith, George, 170, 173
Smith, Hobart, 162, 173
Smith, J.A., 182
Smith, Lucille, 162
Smith, O.P., 228
Smithers, E.M., 55, 189
Smithers family, 49
Smith's Cove, 58
Smith's General Store, 48
Smoyver, Harry, 173
Sneva, Byron, 214
Snoqualmie Valley, 11
Snyder, John, 50
social activities, 49-51, 140-141, 158-159
    see also celebrations; community organizations
Soka Gakkai International, 252-253
Solomon, Ben, xix

INDEX

Sorensen, Martin, 134
South Central School District, ix, 126, 171, 231-232, 234, 235-239, 258, 260
South End News, 190
South Park, 155, 260
South Seattle Land Company, 182
Southcenter, 210, 212, 213, 216, 235
Southcenter Community Baptist Church, 265
Southcenter Rotary Club, 265
Southgate Community Center, 263
Southgate Garden Club, 265-266
Southgate Park, 263
Southgate School, 148, 163, 232, 234, 237
Spaulding, Rev. D.L., 26
Spencer, Lorene, 126
Spencer, Ralph, 126
Spencer Pottery, 126
Spirit Canoe, xvi
Spleen, Nellie, 170
Sprague, J.M., 110
Sprague precinct, 110
Springer, Don, 140
Springer, Ozzie, 134
Squamish, 26
"squatters' rights," 15
Squires, Shirley, 130
Squires, Watson, 130, 174, 175
Squires Investment Company, 174
SR-509 (highway), 108
SR-599 (highway), 151
Standard (territorial newspaper), 40
Stanford, Dorothy Sweeney, 158
Stanford, Elmer, 158, 173
Stanley family, 177
Starbard, Fred, 122
Starr, Nellie, *see* Clark, Nellie Starr
Starwich, Matt, 139, 196, 243
steamboats, 20-21, 37-38, 68
Steele, Emily, 35, 42
Steele, Hugh, 42, 44
Steele, James, 35, 36, 42, 46, 49, 109, 110
Steele, Jean Campbell, 41, 109
Steele, John, 35, 36, 42, 49, 109
Steele, Joseph, 20, 35, 41, 42, 109
Steele, Joseph William (son), 42
Steele, Martha Jane, *see* Foster, Martha Steele
Steele, Mary Ann, 42
Steele, Susannah C., *see* Robbins, Susannah Steele
Steele family, 41-44, 62, 109
Steele Hill Bridge, 99
Steinbrueck, Victor, 154, 162
Stephenson, Mrs., 254
Stevens, Lelah, 200
Stevens, S.H., 160, 190, 191
Stevens, Mrs. S.H., 200
Stimson, C.D., 182, 255
Stimson, Thomas, 182
Stockwell, Rev. E.S., 252
Stone and Webster firm, 91
Stougard, Helen, 141
Strander, John, 69, 208, 210, 211, 213, 222, 271
Strander, Louise, 211, 222, 262
Strobel, John, 19

Struve, H.G., 182
Stuck River, 104
Stutz, Charles, 136, 137
Stutz, E.J., 97
Stutz, Marie, 137
Stutz's Mercantile, 136
Sundby, Barnhard, 176-177
Sundby, Henning, 176, 178
Sundby, Mary Oien, 176
Sunnydale Methodist Church, 146
Sunshine Grandmothers Club, 122
Suquamish, xix, xvii
Sutter family, 14
Swanson, Alice, 227
Swanson, Fred, 111
Swanson, Lena, 111
Swanson, Mr. (inventor), 148
Swanson's Bakery and Confectionery, 111
Swarthouse, W.D., 173
Swartout, Bill, 165
Swedish Tabernacle Church, 192
Sweeney, Clarence, 158, 165, 170, 173
Sweeney, Curt Jr., 169, 173
Sweeney, Curtis, 173, 174
Sweeney, Dorothy, *see* Stanford, Dorothy Sweeney
Sweeney, Leo, 173
Sweeney, Lily, 158, 165
Sweeney, Lona Schwartz, 162, 166, 169
Swenson, Marie, 227

Tacoma, 55, 92, 93
Taylor, A.D., 247
Taylor, Alma Nelsen, 73, 74, 217, 241-242, 243
Taylor, Melissa, *see* Shomaker, Melissa Taylor
Technocracy movement, 146
telegraph, 33
Terrence, Frank, 97
Terry, Charles, 8, 10, 15, 19, 24, 59, 78
Terry, Lee, 5
Thanksgiving Day (1860), 31
Thies, councilman, 201
Thomas, Jay, 173
Thomas, John, 20, 25, 53
Thomas, Mary Ann Russell, 25, 59
Thompson, David, 3
Thompson, Dr. Nile, 180-181
Thompson, Ellen, 134
Thompson, Gerry, 238
Thompson, John, 59
Thompson, Naomi, 227
Thompson, O.C., 94, 134, 135, 136, 145
Thompson, Rivera, 94
Thompson's Hall, 140, 149
Thorndike, Bessie Brown, 244, 245
Thorndike, George L., 244, 245
Thorndike, Willard, 244
Thorndyke Community Club, 121, 244, 247-249
Thorndyke District, xi, 125, 199, 244-245, 259-260
Thorndyke Improvement Club, 245, 247
Thorndyke School, 226, 229, 234, 244, 246-247, 248, 249
Thornton, Jesse Quinn, 2
Thornton, John, 7
Thrall, Roger, 171

Thurber, E.J., 161
Timber Culture Act, 52-53
Titus family, 62
Tobin, Charlie, 49
Tobin's sawmill, 24
Todd, Frank, 261, 271
Toellner, August, 8, 83
Tolmie, Dr. William F., 4
Tombs, Harriet Bergquist, 194
Toon, Bill, 114
Toon, Mary Ellen Anderson, 114
Torres, Mr., 154, 162
Torres-Siccardi house, 154-155
Trabert, Fr., 123
trains, see Interurban electric rail service; railroads
transportation, 20-22, 56, 89, 108
    automobiles, 95-96, 139-140, 216
    bridges, 34-35, 98-102
    buses, 95
    ferries, 12, 35-36, 37, 153-154, 177
    Interurban, 90-95, 96, 140
    jitneys, 95
    macadam roads, 97-98
    railroads, 38, 55-56, 66, 67-68, 77
    riverboats, 35-36, 37-38
    roads, 21-22, 33-35, 96-98
    Tukwila as crossroads, 213-214
    see also Interstate 5; Pacific Highway
Traveler (steamboat), 28
Treadwell, Mr., 211
Trepanier, Ralph, 214
True, Capt. C.G., 38
tuberculosis (TB), 58, 86-87, 253-254
Tukwila, xi
    in the 1920s, 196
    in the 1930s, 201
    1957 to 1990, 212-213
    and annexation, 108, 210, 211, 256-258
    annexes Cascade View, 251, 261-262
    annexes Duwamish-Allentown, 174, 260-261
    annexes Foster, 126, 259-260
    annexes Foster Point, 260-261
    annexes part of McMicken Heights, 255, 258-259
    annexes Riverton, 259-260
    annexes Thorndyke, 259-260
    artists in, 205
    boundaries of, xi
    businesses in, 182
    chronology of, 273-274
    community organizations in, 189-190, 194, 203-204, 206, 263, 265-267
    as crossroads, 108, 213-214
    establishes professional fire department, 207
    farming in, 195
    fights Port of Seattle, 208-212
    first families in, 181-182
    geology of, xii
    growing up in, 201-202
    and historic communities, xi, 77
    historic houses in, 275
    hospital in, 254
    improvements to, 185-186, 189-190, 192-194
    incorporation of, 183-185, 194

    and Interurban, 93, 95
    list of City Council members, 270
    map of, 197
    map of (1904-1930), 197
    mayors of, 214, 269-272
    movement to disincorporate, 196, 198
    naming of, 180-181, 183-184
    Native American sites in, xvi-xvii
    original town of, xi, 126, 183-185, 197, 203, 205
    parks in, 262-263, 274
    population of, 187-188, 256, 274
    post-war, 207
    viaduct, 190, 201
    during World War II, 205
    and WPA, 202-203
Tukwila Baptist Church, 265
Tukwila Chamber of Commerce, 266-267
Tukwila City Council, x, 211, 257, 258, 270
Tukwila City Hall, 151
Tukwila Community Center, 148, 263
Tukwila Community Club, 203-204, 205, 206
Tukwila Elementary School, 233, 234
Tukwila Formation, xii
Tukwila Grocery, 195
Tukwila Hazelnut, 185
Tukwila Hill, xiii, 181, 182-183, 195
Tukwila Historical Society, x, 262
Tukwila Improvement Assocation, 186, 189
Tukwila Interchange, 108, 258, 264
Tukwila Ladies Improvement Club, 188, 189-190, 194, 203, 206
Tukwila Library, 194, 199, 204, 262, 263
Tukwila Park, 74, 190, 201, 204, 262
Tukwila Planning Commission, 210, 211, 213
Tukwila Post Office, 182, 195, 203
Tukwila Quarry, 102, 189
Tukwila Quilting Club, 200
Tukwila School, 122, 184, 186-187, 192, 201, 206, 225, 226, 228, 229
Tukwila Station, 180, 184, 188
Tukwila Volunteer Fire Department, 204, 206-207
typhoid fever, 60

Uhlman, Wes, 260
Unger, Rev. James L., 164
Union Pacific Railroad, 51, 99
Union Trust Co., 130, 174
University of Washington, viii, 32
Uno, T.S., 182
Upper Foster, 116-117, 125
U.S. 99 (highway), 98, 101, 102, 157, 165
Uttendorfer, Mrs., 119

Vails, Carrie E., 90
Vails, I.H., 90
Val Vue Sewer District, 263-264
Valley Highway, 135, 138-139
Valley Industrial Planning Council, 211
Van Asselt, Catherine Maple, 25, 26, 38, 39, 50
Van Asselt, Henry, 5, 6, 7, 8, 9, 10, 12, 15, 19, 21, 22, 25, 26, 27, 28, 39, 40, 47, 48, 50, 52, 58, 66, 78, 83
Van Asselt school, 30, 54
Van Asselton, 155

INDEX

Van de Water, Daniel, 139
Van deVanter, E., 97
Vancouver Island, 2-3
VanDusen, Gary, x, 214, 267-268, 271
Verhoef brothers, 139
viaduct, 190, 201
Victoria, B.C., 42, 44
Voss, Mr., 144
voting precincts, 19-20, 32-33, 60, 109

Wadell, Ella, *see* Nichols, Ella Wadell
Waldo, Josephine, 232
Walkup, Emma, 200
Walkup, Helen, 203
Walkup, John P., 195, 196, 198, 201, 207, 229, 271
Walkup, John R., 120, 196, 198, 201, 270
Wallenberg, Alva, 182, 229
Walsh, Fr., 123
Walters, Marion, 225
Walters, Wiley, 225
Waltz, Mr., 182
Wanamaker, Pearl, 233
Ward, John, 166
Ware, Madge, 227
Warren, Ray, 139
Washington, Alex, 160, 161
Washington, Henry, 173
Washington State Supreme Court, 212
Washington Territorial Legislature, 30, 40, 44
    Joseph Foster in, vii, viii, 32
    and Woman Suffrage, viii, 60-61
Washington Territorial University, *see* University of Washington
Washington Territory, 22, 24
    establishment of, 19, 30
    Foster offered governorship of, 61
Washington Territory Pioneers Association, 58
water supply, 71, 72, 131
    see also public water systems
Watson family, 88
weather, 31-32, 56, 103
    see also floods
Weatherbee store, 117
Weber, Mr., 158
Webster, John, 32
Webster, W.H., 189
weddings, 25, 26, 39
Wellander, A.J., 247
Welsh, Wesley, 120
Wessman, Peter, 222
Weston, Howard, 49
Whitcomb, C.L., 130, 145, 150
White Center Fire District No. 11, 126
White Lake, xiv, 32
White River
    bottom land, 70
    changes course, 104
    and First People, xiii
    flooding of, 46-47, 102-104
    geology of, xiii
    vs. Green River, xi, 104, 108
    see also Green River

White River Grange, 57, 71, 72, 73, 240
White River precinct, 60
Whitehead, Mary Ellen Anderson, 113
Whitehead, Stanley, 171
Whitman, Marcus and Narcissa, 5
Widrig, Charlotte Dobbs, 102, 153, 176
Wiederman strawberry farm, 201
Wiese, Bill, 116
Wiese, Dorothy Corrigan, 116
Wieser, Beatrice, 211
Wieser, Paul, 211
Wildenthaler, May, *see* Rains, May Wildenthaler
Williams, Chief Mike, 156
Williams, D.A., 188
Williams, Don, 214
Wilson, Annie, 112, 119
Wilson, George, 117
Wilson, Harvold, 112
Wilson, James, 112
Wilson, J., 184, 185, 188
Winette (riverboat), 37
Wing, Warren, 89, 91, 92, 158, 165, 171
Witherbee, C.G., 171
Wolbert, Kenneth, 162
Wolbert, May, 162
Wolbert, Ray, 162
Wold, John O., 184, 188
Wolfe, Rev., 146
Wollum, Clifford, 252
Wolotzyn, Rozalia, *see* Scibor, Rozalia Wolotzyn
Woman Suffrage, viii, 60-61
women pioneers, 23, 53, 61, 84
Wood, Alice Jorgensen, 117, 228
Work, John, 3
World War II, 120, 205, 230-231
    and Boeing Field, 87
    prisoner of war camp, 87-88
WPA (Works Progress Administration), 102, 202-203, 204
Wright, Bertha, 162
Wright, Nomi, 162
Wyckoff, Louis V., 19, 20, 22, 24, 25, 32, 33

Yeast, Carl, 120
Yellam, Mike, 138, 171
Yesler, Henry, 11, 15, 19, 24, 30, 50, 55
Yoder, Mr., 204
York, Mrs. (midwife), 245
Young, Gerry Brooker, 113

Zion, Mary, 259

297